Christianity in Suriname
An Overview of its History, Theologians and Sources

Franklin Steven Jabini

ACADEMIC

© 2012 by Franklin Steven Jabini

Published 2012 by Langham Academic (Previously Langham Monographs)
An imprint of Langham Publishing
www.langhampublishing.org

Langham Publishing and its imprints are a ministry of Langham Partnership

Langham Partnership
PO Box 296, Carlisle, Cumbria CA3 9WZ
www.langham.org

ISBNs:
978-1-907713-43-9 Print
978-1-907713-44-6 ePub
978-1-783680-14-6 PDF

Franklin Steven Jabini has asserted his right under the Copyright, Designs and Patents Act, 1988 to be identified as the Author of this work.

All rights reserved. No part of this publication may be reproduced, stored in a retrieval system or transmitted, in any form or by any means, electronic, mechanical, photocopying, recording or otherwise, without the prior written permission of the publisher or the Copyright Licensing Agency.

Requests to reuse content from Langham are processed through PLSclear. Please visit www.plsclear.com to complete your request.

All Scripture quotations, unless otherwise indicated, are from the New English Translation (NET). NET Bible® copyright ©1996-2006 by Biblical Studies Press, L.L.C. www.bible.org. Used by permission. All rights reserved worldwide.

British Library Cataloguing in Publication Data
Jabini, Frank Steven.
  Christianity in Suriname : an overview of its history,
  theologians and sources.
  1. Christianity--Suriname. 2. Theology, Doctrinal--
  Suriname. 3. Christianity--Suriname--Sources.
  4. Christianity--Suriname--Bibliography.
  I. Title
  278.8'3-dc23

ISBN-13: 9781907713439

Cover & Book Design: projectluz.com
Maps: Franklin Steven Jabini, Jr.

Langham Partnership actively supports theological dialogue and a scholars right to publish but does not necessarily endorse the views and opinions set forth within this publication or guarantee its technical and grammatical correctness. Langham Partnership does not accept any responsibility or liability to persons or property as a consequence of the reading, use or interpretation of its published content.

Considering that two-thirds of world Christianity is now in Asia, Africa, Latin America and Oceania, local and regional histories of churches and missions are increasingly significant and urgently needed. Dr Frank Jabini offers the world church an invaluable contribution with this history of church, mission and theologians of Suriname. Dr Jabini's impressive primary documentation and encyclopaedic treatment seeks to set the record straight concerning Christianity in Suriname. This work is a precious gift that fills a serious gap in the history of the church in the Americas. Here, Dr Jabini gives us a marvellously detailed, very readable, highly informative, wonderfully inspiring, and masterfully told narrative of the work of the Holy Spirit in the birth and life of the Christian church in Suriname.

Dr Charles E van Engen
Arthur F Glasser Professor of Biblical Theology of Mission,
Fuller Seminary's School of World Mission

For the first time in Suriname's history someone has undertaken the task to document a chronological account of the history of Christianity in Suriname. This fact alone makes this book a unique reading. However, putting this against the backdrop of secular contemporaneous history provides an even clearer perspective of the accounts described. Aware of the laborious investment in research which Prof Dr Franklin S Jabini has put into this book, I can confidently label it the prime source of information on Christianity in Suriname for anyone who endeavours to gain insights in its Christian heritage. What has been preserved in numerous writings, documents, letters and few books has been skilfully brought together with academic integrity in this one volume you now hold in your hand. I happily and highly recommend this handbook on 'Christianity in Suriname' for your perusal or study.

Rev Erle S Deira
Executive Director Eradicating Bible Poverty – American Bible Society
Founder and President of Paraklesis Ministries International – Suriname

Church history has two sides, a divine and a human. On God's part, it is his revelation. Someone said church history is HIS story. In our Surinamese church history we see this part as well. On the other hand church history reveals the part of man. Man with his ups and downs, his highs and lows. In my opinion the first part is absolute, the second full of relativity. The positive side is that we can always learn from mistakes and victories presented to us in church history.

I truly applaud this initiative and I am very content that this time it is a native Surinamer who did the research and wrote this book. Franklin Jabini is one of our theologians who is a good example of someone who invested years of hard work into Bible translation and serving the church in Suriname as a whole. He therefore can be seen as one who understands God's and man's part in the developments in the history of the church in general and in Suriname as well. An in-depth study like this will profit us all. It will contribute to not only a greater knowledge of Surinamese church history, but will develop a better insight in the 'why's' sometimes people are struggling with. It was Martin Luther, the great reformer, who cried out: 'History is the mother of truth'. This is one of the reasons why we need to study history, so that we can become better skilled to answer questions in general or questions we ourselves are wrestling with.

CARL BREEVELD
Member of the National Assembly of the Republic of Suriname

Dr Franklin Jabini can be called one of the leading theologians of his country, and certainly one of the fittest authors to write such a wonderful and detailed church history of Suriname. No country can afford to forget its history, and a largely Christian country cannot afford to ignore its church history and theology history. A plant cannot be understood without its roots. It was therefore appropriate that someone would undertake to write Suriname's Christian story, and no one could be better equipped than this son of Suriname's own soil, Dr Jabini. He did a marvellous job at that. For a Dutchman, the story is particularly touching because slavery played such an important role in it. Also the role of the Jews is of great interest, because Jews constituted such a large part of the White population and because they were slave drivers too (being themselves at the same time persecuted in Europe). All in all, I highly recommend this scholarly work, which for a long time will be the source of reference for the Christian history of Suriname.

PROF DR WILLEM J OUWENEEL
Evangelical Theological Faculty, Leuven (Belgium)

Contents

Foreword xv

Preface xvii

Acknowledgments xix

Abstract xxi

Chapter 1 1
Introduction
    1.1. Surinamese Christianity in academic sources 1
        1.1.1. Evangelical Dictionary of World Missions 2
        1.1.2. The New International Dictionary of Pentecostal and Charismatic Movements 2
        1.1.3. Religions of the World 3
        1.1.4. Encyclopedia of Protestantism 5
        1.1.5. Worldmark Encyclopedia of Religious Practices 6
        1.1.6. The Encyclopedia of Christianity 6
    1.2. Problem 7
    1.3. Purpose 7
    1.4. Structure and method 7

PART I. HISTORY

Chapter 2 11
Background to Surinamese Christianity
    2.1. Suriname: its location 11
    2.2. Early colonisation efforts 11
    2.3. The people 12
        2.3.1. The Natives 13
        2.3.2. The Europeans 13
        2.3.3. The Africans 14
        2.3.4. The Asians 14
        2.3.5. Others 15
        2.3.6. Population statistics 15
    2.4. Dividing the history of Christianity in Suriname 16
    2.5. Approach and overview 18

Chapter 3 21
The Beginning of the Church of England in Suriname
- 3.1. Introduction 21
- 3.2. Background 21
  - 3.2.1. Government and the people..21
  - 3.2.2. The Church of England and its different factions..............23
- 3.3. Christianity in Suriname in the seventeenth century 24
  - 3.3.1. The Church of England in Suriname 24
  - 3.3.2. Christianity, the Natives and the Quakers.......................30
  - 3.3.3. The Puritans 32
  - 3.3.4. Justinianus Ernst Von Weltz...34
- 3.4. Conclusion 36

Chapter 4 37
The Beginning of Reformed Christianity
- 4.1. Introduction: The era of Zeeland (1667-1683).........................37
  - 4.1.1. The colony...37
  - 4.1.2. Reformed Christianity in Suriname (1667-1683) 39
  - 4.1.3. The colony under new management 43
- 4.2. The era of Van Aerssen van Sommelsdijck: 1683-1688............44
  - 4.2.1. Cornelis van Aerssen van Sommelsdijck.........................44
  - 4.2.2. Christianity 45
- 4.3. Towards a Christian colony: 1688-1734 50
  - 4.3.1. People and economy..50
  - 4.3.2. Christianity 51
  - 4.3.3. Joannes Guiljelmus Kals 55
- 4.4. Conclusion 56

Chapter 5 59
Surinamese Protestantism in the Eighteenth Century
- 5.1. Introduction 59
  - 5.1.1. Peace treaties and economy..59
  - 5.1.2. Population 60
- 5.2. Lutheran Church in Suriname 61
- 5.3. The Protestants in the colony 62
- 5.4. The Moravian missions 64
  - 5.4.1. Introduction 64
  - 5.4.2. Missions among the Natives 65
  - 5.4.3. Missions among the Saramaccans 71
  - 5.4.4. Missions among the slaves 76
- 5.5. Conclusion 78

Chapter 6 79
The Roman Catholic Church and the Beginning of the Nineteenth Century
- 6.1. Introduction 79
- 6.2. The Roman Catholic Church in Suriname 80
- 6.3. Roman Catholics and Protestants 84
- 6.4. At the beginning of the nineteenth century 85
  - 6.4.1. Under British rule 86
  - 6.4.2. The population 86
  - 6.4.3. Freedom of religion and new regulations 87

Chapter 7 89
Christianity and Slavery in Suriname
- 7.1. Introduction 89
- 7.2. Slavery in Suriname 89
- 7.3. Christianity in Suriname 91
  - 7.3.1. Christianity and slavery 91
  - 7.3.2. The relation between Afro-Surinamese people and Whites... 95
- 7.4. Biblical and theological motives used in support of slavery 96
- 7.5. Conclusion 99

Chapter 8 103
The Era of Growth: 1830-1863
- 8.1. Introduction 103
- 8.2. The Growth of Christianity 105
  - 8.2.1. Growth of the Lutheran Church 106
  - 8.2.2. Growth of the Reformed Church 107
  - 8.2.3. Growth of the Roman Catholic Church 108
  - 8.2.4. Growth of the Moravian Church 109
- 8.3. Conclusion 112

Chapter 9 113
The Church in Paramaribo after the Abolition of Slavery
- 9.1. Introduction 113
- 9.2. The Creole Church 114
  - 9.2.1. The Moravian Church 115
  - 9.2.2. The Roman Catholic Church 117
- 9.3. Beginning of the Baptist, Adventist and Methodist Churches 119
  - 9.3.1. The Vrije Evangelisatie 120
  - 9.3.2. The Surinaamse Baptistenkerk 121
  - 9.3.3. The Seventh-day Adventists 122

  9.3.4. The African Methodist Episcopal Church 122
  9.3.5. The Salvation Army 123
 9.4. Conclusion 123
 Appendix to chapter 9: Jehovah's Witnesses...124

Chapter 10 125
Missions to the Ethnic Groups
 10.1. Introduction 125
 10.2. The Indians..126
  10.2.1. The Moravians...127
  10.2.2. The Roman Catholics 128
  10.2.3. Other Churches..129
  10.2.4. Conclusion 129
 10.3. The Javanese..130
  10.3.1. The Moravians...131
  10.3.2. The Roman Catholics 132
  10.3.3. Other Churches..132
  10.3.4. Conclusion 132
 10.4. Maroons 133
  10.4.1. Matawai, Kwinti and Paramaccan 133
  10.4.2. Saramaccans...135
  10.4.3. Ndyuka 138
  10.4.4. Conclusion 141

Chapter 11 143
Christendom in the Autonomous Suriname
 11.1. Introduction: Nationalism 143
  11.1.1. Killinger, Doedel and De Kom 143
  11.1.2. Rier, Comvalius, Rijts and the Nimrod beweging 144
 11.2. Autonomy..147
 11.3. The Committee of Christian Churches 148
 11.4. Developments within the Moravian Church 149
 11.5. Developments within the Roman Catholic Church 150
 11.6. Conclusion 152

Chapter 12 155
The Beginning of Pentecostal Churches
 12.1. Introduction 155
 12.2. Full Gospel Church in Suriname...155
  12.2.1. Introduction 155
  12.2.2. Assemblies of God 156
  12.2.3. The Movement Stromen van Kracht 158

  12.2.4. Evangelisch Centrum Suriname 163
  12.3. Conclusion 165

Chapter 13 167
Bible Translation Organisations
  13.1. Introduction 167
  13.2. The Bible distribution agencies 168
  13.3. Summer Institute of Linguistics 170
    13.3.1. Introduction 170
    13.3.2. Saramaccans 170
    13.3.3. Ndyuka 171
    13.3.4. Sarnami Hindostani 171
    13.3.5. Carib 171
    13.3.6. Sranantongo 172
    13.3.7. Surinamese Javanese 173
  13.4. Gijsbertus Roest and Eddy van der Hilst 173
  13.5. Robert Patton 174
  13.6. Conclusion 175

Chapter 14 177
Christianity, Autonomy and Revolution
  14.1. Introduction 177
  14.2. Independence 179
    14.2.1. Churches and Independence 179
    14.2.2. Population and religion 180
    14.2.3. Christian movements 182
    14.2.4. Towards Surinamese leadership in the churches 184
  14.3. Christianity during the era of the revolution 186
    14.3.1. Introduction 186
    14.3.2. Christianity and revolution 187
    14.3.3. Christianity and the civil war 192
  14.4. Conclusion 193
  Appendix to chapter 14: The Church of Jesus Christ of Latter-day Saints (Mormons) 194

PART II. THEOLOGIANS

Chapter 15 197
Survey of Surinamese Theological Scholarship
  15.1. Introduction 197
  15.2. Surinamese Moravian scholars 198
    15.2.1. Theodorus Alexander Darnoud 199
    15.2.2. Johan Frits Jones 201

  15.2.3. Ronald Ewald Berggraaf...213
  15.2.4. Karel August Zeefuik..217
  15.2.5. Johannes Rambaran..220
  15.2.6. Toekiman Remanuel Wongsodikromo.........................224
  15.2.7. Edgar Loswijk..226
  15.2.8. John Kent..235
  15.2.9. Hesdie Zamuel...245
  15.2.10. Frederik Muktisahai Rambaran....................................256
 15.3. Surinamese Roman Catholic theologians....................................264
  15.3.1. Aloysius Ferdinandus Zichem.......................................264
  15.3.2. Peter Sjak-Shie..264
  15.3.3. Karel Choennie...265
  15.3.4. Esteban Kross...275
  15.3.5. Kenneth Vigelandzoon...281
  15.3.6. Duncan R Wielzen...281
  15.3.7. Gerda Misidjang...282
 15.4. Others..285

PART III. SOURCES

Chapter 16..291
Sources for the Study of Surinamese Christianity

 16.1. Introduction...291
  16.1.1. Approaches to the study of theological sources.............291
  16.1.2. Approaches in this study...292
  16.1.3. Issues for further research...292
  16.1.4. Limitations..292
 16.2. Challenges..293
  16.2.1. Geographical barriers..293
  16.2.2. Denominational barriers...294
  16.2.3. Linguistic barriers...294
  16.2.4. Methodological challenges..296
 16.3. General sources...297
  16.3.1. Writings on the general history of Suriname.................298
  16.3.2. Church-related documents..299
  16.3.3. Church papers and magazines.......................................300
  16.3.4. Political documents...303
 16.4. Denominational sources..304
  16.4.1. Anglican Church...304
  16.4.2. Dutch Reformed Church..306
  16.4.3. Moravians...311

  16.4.4. Lutheran Church 320
  16.4.5. The Roman Catholic Church..321
  16.4.6. Baptist Churches 330
  16.4.7. Pentecostal Churches 331
  16.4.8. Other Churches..334
 16.5. New generation of theologians..336

Maps..339

Photos..342

Bibliography..353

Index..383

About the author..391
 Other works by the author on Christianity in Suriname 391

LIST OF TABLES

Table 1 Population of Suriname in 2004 15
Table 2 Religions in Suriname in 2004 15
Table 3 Branches of Christianity in Suriname and their arrival 17
Table 4 Ethnic missions emphasis 18
Table 5 Governors of Suriname 1651-1667 22
Table 6 Caretaker governors of Suriname 1672-1683 38
Table 7 Government and Administration of Justice in Suriname 43
Table 8 The Reformed Church membership in 1684 49
Table 9 Estimated population in 1688 49
Table 10 Suriname between 1710 and 1730 51
Table 11 The population in 1738 60
Table 12 The population in 1791 60
Table 13 Moravian attempts to establish itself in Suriname 65
Table 14 Overview of missionary stations among the Natives 70
Table 15 Overview of missionary stations among the Saramaccans 75
Table 16 Moravian Church membership in 1791 77
Table 17 Catholic attempts to establish itself in Suriname 82
Table 18 Statistics of the Catholic Church: 1817 and 1826 83
Table 19 Religious population of Suriname in 1862 106
Table 20 Membership of the Moravian Church 115
Table 21 Numerical growth of the Catholic Church between 1859 and 1964 151
Table 22 Pentecostal Churches in Suriname 165
Table 23 Bible Translations published in Surinamese languages after 1960 167
Table 24 Religions in Suriname 1964 180
Table 25 Churches not included on the 1964 census 181
Table 26 Religions in Suriname in 1972 181
Table 27 Christians in 1980 188

Table 28 Similarities between Rāma and Jesus 223
Table 29 Overview of exegetical interpretations of 2 Cor 5:3 279

LIST OF MAPS

Map 1 Western part of Suriname and Berbice 339
Map 2 Eastern part of Suriname 340
Map 3 Location of Suriname in South America 341

LIST OF PHOTOS

Picture 1 Interdenominational church service 342
Picture 2 Interdenominational church service 342
Picture 3 Students of the Evangelical School of Theology with visiting professor 343
Picture 4 Children's church outing 343
Picture 5 Interdenominational Saramaccan church service 343
Picture 6 Interdenominational celebration of Easter 344
Picture 7 Interdenominational Evangelistic crusade 344
Picture 8 Church and government leaders at the inauguration of a church building 344
Picture 9 Pentecostal Church building 345
Picture 10 Pentecostal Church building 345
Picture 11 Church outing Christian and Missionary Alliance 345
Picture 12 Church building in Coronie 346
Picture 13 Children's club among Natives in Bigi Poika 346
Picture 14 Christian men visiting the interior 347

Picture 15 Javanese traditional dance during evangelistic service 347

Picture 16 Day of prayer with President DD Bouterse 347

Picture 17 Newly baptised Indian Christians 348

Picture 18 Ndyuka traditional Gospel Music 348

Picture 19 Young men praying 349

Picture 20 Vacation Bible School 349

Picture 21 Interdenominational Indian church service 350

Picture 22 Boarding school Stoelmanseiland 350

Picture 23 Moravian theology graduate receives his certificate 350

Picture 24 Men at an interdenominational church service 351

Picture 25 Author's family with visiting Dutch professor Van Bruggen and wife 351

Picture 26 Former President Drs R R Venetiaan with church leaders at a national interdenominational leader's conference 352

Picture 27 Small group discussions at a national and interdenominational leader's conference 352

Foreword

Writing this foreword to Frank Jabini's book *Christianity in Suriname: An overview of its History, Theologians and Sources* is a real privilege and honour to me.

Somewhere in the nineteen nineties, I came in close contact with Frank, who was attending Hebrew and Greek classes at the Moravian Seminary in Paramaribo, as one of the first students from an independent church. After his Master's degree, he became a colleague at the seminary, and I have enjoyed the cooperation with him on several occasions, due to our collective preference for Bible translation.

Until now one, who wanted to study Surinamese church history, was dependent on historians from abroad who described the history of a specific denomination, e.g., Hermann Georg Steinberg (1932) and Jos Fontaine (1985) on the Moravian Church, and Joop Vernooij (1985) on the Roman Catholic Church. But in this book we find an all-inclusive overview of all the church denominations in Suriname, drawn up by a 'native son', descending from enslaved Africans, who in an early stage after their being transferred from Africa to the 'New World' escaped to the forests and established there, what is called, maroon societies.

Especially with this book, Frank Jabini is setting a trend, by giving the example how to contribute to the re-writing of our own history. Having come to the conclusion that our history needs to be re-written, he does not start reacting against historians of the past, but he looked for a passable way forward. Here, he only gives an overview, but there is a promise for a more profound and voluminous exercise which is in preparation.

It is the first time someone has tried to give an overview of the Surinamese churches and the theological achievements that have been achieved during the period of their existence in this country. To me this makes Frank Jabini one of the forerunners of the necessary reconstruction of our Surinamese history. The first step in that process is, according to David Ndegwah (2007), to collect the facts and then try to look at them in a fresh way without prejudices. And that is just what Frank is trying to do.

With pleasure I, therefore, heartily recommend this book as a reference work for Christianity in Suriname.

Rev Dr Hesdie Zamuel
Paramaribo, June 2012

Preface

Utrecht University is well-known in colonial and postcolonial Suriname. Since the arrival of the West Indian Company in Suriname (1667), Dutch ministers have served the Reformed Church in Suriname. Several ministers were alumni of Utrecht University. In the seventeenth century, Rev Antonius Ketelaer served in Suriname. He refused to accept the segregation between the Europeans and the Africans and for that reason, the authorities removed him from the capital Paramaribo to the remote Commewijne area. In the eighteenth century, Rev Jan W Kals, born in Germany and an alumnus of Utrecht University, argued even stronger than Ketelaer did. After he arrived in Paramaribo he protested against the flourishing slave trade and the expulsion of the Natives. According to him, Non-white Christians should be permitted to attend the church services of the Europeans. For that matter, the colonial authorities regarded him as an undesirable element in their community and sent him back to the Netherlands within two years after arrival. Jan M van der Linde honoured Kals by writing a monograph on his person and work: *Jan Willem Kals 1700-1781: Leraar der Hervormden, Advocaat van Indiaan en Neger* (1987).

My predecessor at Utrecht University is Jan M van der Linde. He was instrumental in creating Reformed and Moravian theological scholarship in Suriname. He engaged in the establishment of an own Suriname Theological School. Due to a serious illness of his wife, the family Van der Linde came back to the Netherlands earlier than expected. Seven Surinamese students followed him to the Netherlands and studied under his supervision in the Moravian community in Zeist and at Utrecht University. At this university Van der Linde defended his dissertation entitled: *Het visioen van Herrnhut en het apostolaat der Moravische broeders in Suriname, 1735-1863* (1956). Subsequently the university welcomed him as the professor of 'the history of the Unitas fratrum and the Caribbean region' (1958). In this new capacity Van der Linde supervised the dissertation of Karel A Zeefuik and the MTh thesis of Hesdie Zamuel and others.

The study of Franklin Jabini on Christianity in Suriname, with special reference to Surinamese theological scholarship, is much broader in scope than what Utrecht University in general and Van der Linde especially have contributed to Suriname in the past. First of all, it takes not only the Reformed and the Moravians into account, but all churches: Roman Catholics, Anglicans, Lutherans, Baptists, Pentecostals, and others. Secondly, it takes the socio-economic, political, and religious context of the nation very seriously. Today Suriname belongs to the most multicultural and multireligious, and multilingual societies of South America. Surinamese Christians and theologians function in this complex and challenging setting.

Franklin Jabini is the right man to describe and analyse the recent developments in Surinamese Christianity and in Surinamese theology. His survey is unique and contributes to their recognition in the independent nation Suriname, in South, Middle and North America, and in the global setting. I wholeheartedly congratulate him with the results of his hard work to collect the data, and to describe and analyse them properly. With great joy I recommend this new and innovative study to Surinamese citizens and to other people around the globe.

God bless the reading of this book!

Jan A B Jongeneel
Honorary Professor Emeritus Utrecht University
Bunnik, Ascension Day 2012

Acknowledgments

This research has taken more than twenty years to complete and many people have contributed to making it possible. It is not possible to name them all. However, I do want to express my appreciation to:

The Surinamese theologians and or their families who made their works available for review, *grantangi*; friends and colleagues who wrote a recommendation for the book and made pictures available;

The librarians and archivists who helped in finding resources: Rudi de Groot, University of Leuven (Belgium); Dr Ulrike Mühlschlegel, Ibero-American Institute – Prussian Cultural Heritage Foundation (Germany); Dr Paul Peucker, Unitätsarchiv Herrnhut (Germany); Carlos Hasselnook and Miss H Doelwijt, Archief der EBGS (Suriname); Paul Tjon Kiem Sang, Archief Rooms Katholieke Bisdom (Suriname); Jenny Sopawiro, Dienst voor Geloof, Cultuur en Communicatie (Suriname); Yvonne Tjin A Kiem - Palis (†) and Mina Gobiend, Surinaams Museum (Suriname); Ingrid A Roderick, British and Foreign Bible Society (UK); Stephen Tabor, Huntington Library (USA);

My friend Dr Kees van der Ziel MA for his helpful comments and recommendations on the entire manuscript;

Dr Robert Brodie for editing the entire manuscript;

Prof Jan Jongeneel and Dr Hesdie Zamuel for their willingness to write a foreword to the book.

I am grateful to my wife Irene and our three children Samuel, Franklin Jr. and Anna for allowing me to write this book and for their willingness to hear the stories over and over again.

I thank Franklin Jr. for drawing the maps.

I thank my brothers and sisters in Christ of the Brethren Assemblies in Suriname for their prayers and support and for allowing me to do research for the kingdom of God;

And last but not least, I thank God who gave me the strength and guided me throughout this long journey and as I continue to try "to comprehend with all the saints what is the breadth and length and height and depth, and thus to know the love of Christ that surpasses knowledge, so that [I] may be filled up to all the fullness of God. Now to him who by the power that is working within us is able to do far beyond all that we ask or think, to him be the glory in the church and in Christ Jesus to all generations, forever and ever. Amen" (Eph 3:18-21 NET).

Abstract

A survey of the articles that appeared in major theological works at the beginning of the twenty-first century revealed a lack of correct information about Christianity in Suriname (South America). This was possibly because the history was not available in English and the works of Surinamese theologians appeared to be unknown to the scholarly community. The purpose of this study therefore is to give a survey of the history, a summary of the works of theologians and a guide to sources about Christianity in Suriname.

The survey of the history (Part I) describes colonial Christianity in Suriname in a chronological way. Colonial Christianity as was represented by the Anglican, Reformed and Lutheran Churches, focused on the European colonists and generally ignored the African slaves and their descendants and the Natives. These Churches' raison d'être was confined to the needs of the 'whites' in the colony. On the other hand, the Moravian and Roman Catholic Churches focused their missions on the people who were ignored by the colonial churches. They provided not only the gospel in the language of the people, but also education and medical and social care. Both Churches faced a unique form of Christianity. Because of their own religious background and the pressure put upon them by laws that forced them to become Christians, the slaves and their descendants developed what was called the Creole Church. Migrant workers from Asia who came after the 1860's were taken care of in ethnically-established branches of these churches. From the 1960's onwards churches started their process of becoming independent, Surinamese churches. This struggle was well articulated by the academically-trained theologians who emerged in that period. Part II presents a summary of their works. Part III is an annotated guide to sources that were used in the historical section of the study and should serve as the starting point for the study of Christianity in Suriname and the works of the new generation of theologians.

The work follows a descriptive method. Sources were gathered from writers, libraries and archives. In the case of the Pentecostal churches, where literature was not readily available, some unstructured interviews were conducted.

This work is unique in a number of ways. It is the first of its kind and the first in English. It describes an ecumenical history of all the major denominations in Suriname covering a period of more than three centuries. A work of such a wide scope has its limitations. Firstly, it can only be a brief overview and not a detailed work. Secondly, it can only describe some issues about Christianity, leaving others untouched. Thirdly, I chose not to present a technical work with learned footnotes in which I enter into debates with others. That, I will take on in a Dutch publication, that is forthcoming. A work like the present one provides necessary information about the most important aspects of Christianity in a single volume. It is accessible to a broad reading public and can serve as a starting point for further research.

CHAPTER 1

Introduction

1.1. Surinamese Christianity in academic sources

The first decade of the twenty-first century saw the publication of some major Christian dictionaries and encyclopedias that presented global research on specific branches of Christianity. These include the *Evangelical Dictionary of World Mission* (Deiros 2000), *The New International Dictionary of Pentecostal and Charismatic Movements* (Norwood 2002), the *Religions of the World* (Melton and Baumann 2002), the *Encyclopedia of Protestantism* (Freston 2004), the *Encyclopedia of Protestantism* (Melton 2005), the *Worldmark Encyclopedia of Religious Practices* (Holland 2006) and *The Encyclopedia of Christianity* (Jap A Joe 2000-2008). They studied movements such as Protestantism, Pentecostalism and charismatics, evangelicals and religions of the world in general.

Most of these sources included references to Suriname. One article about Suriname was written by the Surinamese social scientist Harold Jap A Joe. It appeared in volume five of *The Encyclopedia of Christianity*. Scholars outside of Suriname wrote all the other articles in the above references. These included articles by Pablos Deiros on 'Evangelicals', Douglass Norwood Jr on 'Charismatic and Pentecostal Movements' and Clifton Holland on 'Religion in Suriname'. The articles on the 'Moravian Church in Suriname' and 'Suriname' in *Religions of the World* did not include the names of the

1

writers (see Melton & Baumann 2002).[1] The same was true for the article on 'South America' in the *Encyclopedia of Protestantism*.

Remarkably Surinamese Christianity was omitted in *A documentary source book on the history of Christianity in Asia, Africa, and Latin America, 1450-1990* (Koschorke et al. 2007). The bibliography of West Indian Church history compiled by Dayfoot and Pierson (2004) listed only a small number of resources on the history of the Surinamese church during the British period (1651-1667).

In this introduction I give a brief but critical review of the presentations about Suriname in these works. I will review them in chronological order of publication.

1.1.1. Evangelical Dictionary of World Missions

The well-respected Argentinian scholar, Dr Pablos A Deiros, wrote the article on 'evangelicals' in Suriname. The article is very short, one column. Consequently he did not have much space to write. The article therefore could not present a balanced background of Suriname or a clear view of evangelical Christianity in Suriname. The date of the successful colonisation of Suriname by the British was in 1651 and not in 1630. Most of the article was devoted to Justinianus von Weltz (1666-1668) and the work of the Moravians among the Saramaccans. The information presented was not up to date.

1.1.2. The New International Dictionary of Pentecostal and Charismatic Movements

Dr Douglass Norwood Jr, a former American Moravian pastor, wrote the article on Pentecostals and Charismatics in Suriname. He visited Suriname on a number of occasions and held meetings with church leaders. The article's general background of Suriname was not balanced and full of wrong conclusions. It claimed that Suriname remained one of the poorest countries in the western hemisphere; that in the mid-1990's rioting and civil disturbance were aimed at Hindu store owners. Furthermore, due to the increase of the Muslim population the government declared Suriname

---

1. The articles were probably written by Dr Clifton Holland.

Introduction 3

an Islamic republic in 1998. The source for his information on these matters was not given.

The article further claimed that Baptists and Lutherans came to Suriname in the middle of the twentieth century. The Baptists started in the 1880's and the Lutherans in the 1740's. It attributed the beginning of several 'small' Pentecostal fellowships in Suriname (e.g. *Pinksterzending* and *Evangelisch Centrum Suriname*) to the crusades held by Karel Hoekendijk in the 1960's. None of these two denominations was the result of the Hoekendijk crusade. Pinksterzending came out of a split within the Assemblies of God, the first Pentecostal Church in Suriname, which started in 1959. Evangelisch Centrum Suriname started in the late 1960's as a result of the ministry of the American missionary James Cooper and the Dutch missionary Jan Kool. The article has many factual errors. Its main point however was the reference to two Moravian pastors who held evangelistic rallies in Suriname in the mid 1980's. The author happened to be one of these two pastors. His ministry in Suriname seemed to have had much more results than that of those who were there before him. As a result of a two-day prayer conference which the writer led in the western part of the country, Christian churches were united.

> A stunning development in November 1994 has led to the possibility of more growth and charismatic/Pentecostal unity in Suriname ... More Hindus came to Christ in that one night than in the previous 140 years of mission work. Since that time, attendance in older churches in the region has swelled, and new churches have been established (p. 254).

Sadly, the writer seemed to ignore all the Surinamese charismatic and Pentecostal leaders, who laboured and are still labouring in Suriname.

1.1.3. Religions of the World

The writers of the articles in Melton and Baumann's the *Religions of the World* were not stated. The lemma on the 'Moravian Church in Suriname' started as follows:

> Moravians received an invitation to begin work in the Dutch territory of Suriname in 1836, and two years later missionaries arrived and settled on a plantation on the Berbice River. Their primary work was among the Africans on the plantation and nearby (p. 888).

The invitation to the Moravians came a few years earlier. The first team arrived in 1735 and settled in Suriname, not in Berbice. The article has a lot of factual errors. The Moravians did not translate 'a portion of the New Testament into the new language, Sranana Tongo, which the Africans had developed' (p. 889). First of all the whole New Testament and many books of the Old Testament were translated. Secondly, the language is 'Sranantongo', and thirdly, it was not developed by the slaves. It was a lingua franca, the language of communication between the colonists and the slaves. Too much credit was given to the missionaries, when the article suggested that 'King studied with the missionaries over the next four years and was ordained in 1861' (p. 889). It is a known fact that King spent a few months with the missionaries, after 1861. He studied mostly on his own and depended on the dreams and visions that he received. King did not 'spend the next thirty-five years taking Christianity to the residents of the interior' (p. 889). He was suspended by the Moravians for many years and could not minister.[2] When did the growth in the Moravian Church take place? According to the article 'some twenty-five thousand former slaves became Moravian in the decade during the transition to complete freedom (1863–1873)' (p. 889). The growth took place before the abolition of slavery and not afterwards. Actually the years after the abolition saw a decline, when many Moravians left to join the Roman Catholic Church. The article did not say anything about the church's mission to the other ethnic groups, e.g. Indians and Javanese.

The lemma on 'Suriname' in the encyclopaedia shared the same weaknesses as that on the Moravians, as can be seen in the following statements:

---

[2]. This could have been verified by using the Surinamese Dr Hesdie Zamuel's article on 'Johannes King' in Anderson (1999). Zamuel stated: 'Between 1870 and 1890 he made no missionary journeys' (p. 366).

'The Dutch introduced slavery into the colony' (p. 1233); 'Christianity was introduced to Suriname in 1683 with the arrival of several Catholic priests'; 'the Evangelical Lutheran Church ... and the Reformed churches ... established works in 1741 and 1750'; 'The Suriname Committee of Christian churches dates to 1960' (p. 1234).

The British introduced slavery in Suriname and not the Dutch. They also established the Anglican Church in 1651. Christianity was not introduced to Suriname in 1683. The Reformed Church started in 1668 and not 1750. The Committee of Christian Churches dates to the 1940's and not 1960's.

1.1.4. Encyclopedia of Protestantism

The absence of Surinamese Christianity in the *Encyclopedia of Protestantism* (Hillerbrand 2004) is remarkable. Protestant Christianity had a long standing in Suriname. It can be argued that Suriname was the first country of South America that had a permanent presence of Protestantism from 1651 onwards. According to the *Encyclopedia of Protestantism*, a permanent presence of Protestantism in Latin America 'was established only around or after independence in the early nineteenth century' (Freston 2004:1069). This conclusion was probably based on the notion that Suriname was not part of Latin America.[3]

In a second, one-volume *Encyclopedia of Protestantism* edited by J Gordon Melton, reference was made to Suriname. In two paragraphs the author stated the following about Protestantism in South America:

> Most of South America had become dominantly Roman Catholic by the time Protestants began to develop their missionary programs.[4] The exceptions were Guyana and Surinam [sic], which were under British and Dutch control, respectively (p. 505, 506).

---

3. Latin America is defined linguistically into those countries that speak languages that were derived from Latin, e.g. Spanish, French and Portuguese.
4. I have not attempted to convert quotations in Amerian English spelling to suit British English convention

The author indicated that the Reformed Church had a presence in Suriname since the seventeenth century but served the Dutch settlers. According to him, 'Moravians arrived in both Guyana and Surinam [sic] in 1738' (p. 506). This date, as indicated earlier, is incorrect.

1.1.5. Worldmark Encyclopedia of Religious Practices

The American scholar, Dr Clifton Holland, served first as a minister and later as a professor at the Evangelical University of the Americas (UNELA) in Costa Rica for many years. He taught in many Latin American countries as part of the extension programme of UNELA.

His article on Suriname was detailed. His presentation was not limited to Christianity, but included the other religions as well (so also Melton & Baumann 2002). He divided the Surinamese from African descent into Creoles and Maroons and made Indians the largest ethnic group in Suriname (see also Melton & Baumann 2002:1233). What was the major religion in Suriname? According to him, Hinduism was. He arrived at that conclusion, because he failed to differentiate the *Sanatan Dharm* Hindus from the *Arya Dewaker* Hindus. In the case of Christianity he divided them between Protestants and Roman Catholics. He dated the origin of Protestantism in Suriname to around 1735, even though he acknowledged the Reformed Church to be the oldest. However, he ignored the Anglican Church that came to Suriname in 1651. It was not clear how Holland defined major theologians when he argued that Suriname did not produce any major Protestant theologians.[5] All the writers in his bibliography were foreigners, none of whom was a theologian.

1.1.6. The Encyclopedia of Christianity

Besides articles on theological themes, the Encyclopedia of Christianity studied various branches of Christianity in different countries. Harold Jap A Joe's presentation was generally correct. However there are some details that need attention. The Baptists and the Adventists did not arrive in the first decades of the twentieth century, but in 1887 and 1894 respectively.

---

5. See the reviews in part II.

Pentecostalism was not introduced in the 1960's, but in 1959. The beginning of the Bible Society was not in 1963, but in 1966.

1.2. Problem

Engaging the articles raised some serious questions. Why were foreign scholars, and not Surinamese, asked to write the lemma? Why did the writers not interact with works written about Christianity in Suriname and with Surinamese scholars? It was clear that the work done by Surinamese theologians and on Christianity in Suriname did not receive enough international attention. Secondly, most if not all the works of Surinamese theologians were written in Dutch. Because of this, the access for the international community was difficult or impossible.

1.3. Purpose

This book intends to serve four purposes. First of all it presents an overview, be it brief, of the history of Christianity in Suriname (Part I). Secondly, it gives a summary of some of the most important works of Surinamese theologians and allows scholars to get acquainted with Surinamese scholarship (Part II). Thirdly, it gives the scholarly community the state of the art of research into Surinamese Christianity and fourthly it is a guide to documents for the study of Christianity in Suriname (Part III). Masters and doctoral candidates will find unexplored areas in this brief overview that require further research. Some unexplored fields are identified as such throughout the study.

1.4. Structure and method

The book consists of three parts. The first part presents an overview of the history of Christianity in Suriname. This part describes colonial Christianity. Churches from predominantly European background established Christianity in Suriname. The first recipients were the European colonists, followed by the descendants of Africans and Asians. This part of the work is descriptive and avoids technicalities or learned footnotes. References to resources that were used were kept to a minimum, except for direct quotations.

The second part is a study of Surinamese theologians. These Surinamese theologians, from the second half of the twentieth century onwards, engaged the West European form of Christianity that was brought to Suriname, and called for a Surinamese version. This section summarises the works of Moravian, Roman Catholic and Lutheran theologians.

The third part of the study, the sources for the study of Christianity in Suriname, includes an annotated bibliography and can be consulted for further details.

PART I. HISTORY

CHAPTER 2

Background to Surinamese Christianity

2.1. Suriname: its location

Suriname is located on the northern coast of South America between the Atlantic Ocean in the north, French Guyana in the east, Brazil in the south and Guyana in the west. It lies between 54° and 58° longitude west and 2° and 6° north latitude. Its surface area is 163,265 square kilometres. Many rivers cross the country. Suriname has a tropical climate, with temperatures between 23 and 32 degrees Celsius.

2.2. Early colonisation efforts

The arrival of Christopher Columbus in the New World in 1492 and the opening of a sea route to India by Vasco da Gama in 1497 were major turning points in the history of the world and of Christianity. These events opened new doors for the European nations that were cut off from the rest of the world, due to Islamic dominance. Europe used these open doors to colonise Africa, India and America. The reason for the colonisation was first and foremost economic. In order to maximise the economic benefits from the colonies, the colonisers made use of slaves. After a failed attempt in Latin America to use the Natives as slaves and following protests from Roman Catholic clergymen, such as Bartholome de Las Casas, the colonisers turned to Africa to find 'labourers'. This decision changed the world.

In 1593, Domingo de Vera conquered Suriname for the king of Spain. On board of the ships were Roman Catholic clergymen. The task of these clergymen was to give the Natives instruction in baptism, so that they may be converted to Christianity. The purpose of the colonisers was not only to bring the Natives to Christianity. They also took the land for the Catholic king of Spain. To do that, a big cross facing Jerusalem was raised on the soil. The cross faced Jerusalem, the place where the cross of Jesus Christ stood. After that ritual, the whole area was declared holy. De Vera and his men knelt down, prayed and sang a song. Then the rites of possession were performed. Suriname was taken over spiritually.

The Natives, who did not want their land to be taken, fought back. The Spanish had to leave the area. The Roman Catholics could not settle in Suriname at that time as they did in other parts of the New World.

Various Europeans tried to colonise Suriname after the Spanish left. In 1613, a group of Dutch people settled on the Corantine River and the Suriname River. The group consisted of approximately 50 couples. They grew tobacco and were involved in timber. They were probably visited by various clergymen, but did not establish a congregation. A new group of 60 British arrived in 1630 under the leadership of Captain Marshall. They settled at the Suriname River. Marshall founded Torarica, which served as the capital of Suriname. However, the British were expelled by the French in 1640.

The early colonisation attempts were carried out by Christians. These Christians were not successful in establishing Christianity in Suriname. This would only take place in 1651, when the British successfully colonised Suriname. In chapter 3 of this book I will start with the history of Christianity in Suriname from that time on.

2.3. *The people*

The population of Suriname is less than half a million. However, the people came from diverse backgrounds.

2.3.1. The Natives

The original inhabitants of Suriname and the Americas were the Natives or Indigenous[1], who were wrongly called 'Indians' by Columbus. The predominant group was the Arawak people. The Carib and the smaller groups Akuriyo, Trio and Wayana arrived at a later date. Sadly many of the Natives died due to slavery, the war against the colonisers and different kinds of diseases. The Natives in Suriname are currently divided into two major groups:

- The Natives of the interior: Trio, Akuriyo, Wayana and Warau.
- The Natives of the coastal area: Arawak and Carib.

2.3.2. The Europeans

In 1651, the British colonised Suriname successfully. They settled with their slaves of African descent in the colony, signed a peace treaty with the Natives and allowed Portuguese Jews, who had experience with plantations, to settle in the country. During the British period (1651-1667) about 1,500 plantation owners lived here, with about 3,000 Africans and 400 Natives. In 1666, the colony was attacked by an epidemic and many people died. In that same year, 200 Jewish refugees arrived from Brazil with their slaves and settled here.

In 1667, the British were conquered by the Dutch captain, Abraham Crijnssen, and Suriname became a Dutch colony.[2] The Dutch colonisers did not have it easy in the beginning. The Natives attacked the plantations and the British came again in 1668 and raided the most important plantations. In addition, most slaves used these attacks of the British to run away from the plantations into the jungle. Thereafter, most of the British colonisers (about 1,000) left Suriname, with their 2,000 African slaves.

---

1. The indigenous peoples of the Americas were wrongly called 'Indians' and 'Amerindians'. In this book they are referred to as 'Natives' or 'Indigenous'. The two names are used interchangeably throughout the book.

2. It should be said that the British successfully attacked Suriname a few times, in 1799 and in 1804, but the Dutch took over again. In 1815, the British gave Suriname to the Dutch, but the size of the country was reduced. Berbice, Demerara and Essequibo were given to Britain, and they jointly became British Guyana, the present-day Co-operative Republic of Guyana.

By 1715, Suriname was populated by Dutch, French, Portuguese Jews, Germans, Scandinavians and other European settlers.

2.3.3. The Africans

The majority of the Surinamese population however consisted of the descendants of Africans. They were brought from Africa to work as slaves on the plantations. Many of them however escaped slavery and became known as the Maroons. The Maroons lived in the interior for many centuries, while their fellow Africans remained on the plantations. The population of African descendants was divided into two major groups. This division was a heritage of the colonial era. It was based on the area where people lived and nothing else.[3]

- City Creoles, the descendants of Africans who remained in slavery.
- Bush Creoles or Maroons. These consisted of six tribes: Aluku, Ndyuka (Aukan), Kwinti, Matawai, Saramaccan and Paramaccan.

2.3.4. The Asians

In 1863, some 33,000 slaves in Suriname were emancipated. In order to keep the plantations going, it was necessary to find other people to do the work. Starting from 1853, immigrants were imported from Java and Madeira. In the ensuing years, more immigrants came from China (1858), Barbados (1863), India (1873) and Java (1890). The Surinamese of Asian descent were:

- Indians[4]
- Javanese
- Chinese

---

3. Descendants of the Africans are referred to as Afro-Surinamese in this book. When attention is given to a specific group, they are called Creoles or Maroons.

4. The Indians are also known as 'East Indians' to distinguish them from the so-called 'Red Indians', the Indigenous (Native) people of the Americas. In Suriname the Indians are known as Hindostanen (Hindostani). In this work we call them 'Indians'.

2.3.5. Others

Lebanese arrived in Suriname in the 1890's. Due to the problems after their independence in the 1960's, Guyanese relocated to Suriname. The 1980's saw a huge influx of Haitians, who came to work in the agriculture sector. The 1990's saw Brazilians coming in to work in the gold sector.

2.3.6. Population statistics

The total population of Suriname, according to the 2004 census, was 492,829.

Table 1 *Population of Suriname in 2004*

Ethnicity	Total	Percentage Christian
Afro-Surinamese[5]	159,755	68.95
Indian	135,117	6.48
Javanese	71,879	14.46
Mixed	61,524	69.76
Unknown	32,579	26.08
Native	18,037	82.38
Chinese	8,775	24.84
Caucasian	2,899	56.12
Others	2,264	60.42

Table 2 *Religions in Suriname in 2004*

Religion	Total	Percentage
Christianity	200,744	40.73
Hinduism	98,240	19.93
Islam	66,307	13.45

---

5. This group consisted of 87,202 City Creoles of which 76.77% professed to be Christians and 72,553 Maroons with 59.55% professing Christianity.

Traditional Religion	16,291	3.31
Others	12,258	2.49
None	21,785	4.42
Unknown	77,204	15.67

2.4. Dividing the history of Christianity in Suriname

The history of Christianity in Suriname can be divided in two parts. The first part is the history up to the abolition of slavery. The second part consists of Christianity after the era of slavery. This division can be applied for various reasons.

In the first place we have the division according to the arrival of the churches: the older churches and the new churches. The older churches (Anglican, Reformed, Moravian, Lutheran and Roman Catholic) settled in the Surinamese society during the era of slavery. This period roughly covered 1651-1863.

The second phase started after the abolition of slavery and the arrival of the new churches. The first Baptist Church was founded by a Surinamese around 1887. It was also the first church to go through a church split in 1898. Out of this separated group, another splintered group founded the first Plymouth Brethren assembly around 1907. The Baptists were followed by the Seventh-day Adventists (1894) and the Methodist Churches (African Methodist Episcopal Church 1912; Salvation Army 1924; Wesleyan Church 1945; Evangelical Methodist Church 1949).

A new group of churches in this phase consisted of different American Baptist Churches (e.g. Worldteam 1954), Pentecostal and Full Gospel Churches (Assemblies of God 1959; and many others starting from 1961) and other groups (e.g. Southern Baptists 1971; Christian and Missionary Alliance 1979). The phenomenon of church split that started with the Baptist Church was prevalent in this second phase of Surinamese church history.

Surinamese society changed drastically after the abolition of slavery. It was the time of emerging Surinamese nationalism, independence, military regime and a civil war. These changes have influenced the development of Christianity in Suriname. The process of contextualisation was started within the Surinamese church.

Table 3 *Branches of Christianity in Suriname and their arrival*

Phase 1: 1651-1863	Phase 2: 1863-present
Anglican 1651	Baptist 1887
Reformed Church 1667	Adventist 1894
Roman Catholic 1683-1686; 1786-1793; 1810-1816; 1818	African Methodist Episcopal Church 1912
Moravian 1735	Salvation Army 1924
Lutheran 1741	Wesleyan Church 1945
	Evangelical Methodist Church 1949
	Worldteam 1954
	Assemblies of God 1959
	Stromen van Kracht 1961
	Evangelisch Centrum 1969
	Southern Baptists 1971
	Christian and Missionary Alliance 1979
	Plymouth Brethren 1907-1935; 1983
	Nazarenes 1984

A second reason why the history of Christianity should be studied in two parts is because of the inhabitants of the country. Besides the Europeans, there were Natives and the descendants of the Africans (slaves, free and Maroons) in the country. The older churches worked among these ethnic groups.

After the abolition, the outlook of the population changed drastically. Instead of slaves coming from Africa, indentured labourers came from China, India and Java. These labourers, many of whom remained in Suriname after their contract expired, became an important part of the population. A second inflow of migrants came from Guyana, Haiti and Brazil. Their presence had an impact on the history of Christianity in Suriname. Both the older and newer churches had to respond to an ethnically and religiously diverse population.

Table 4 *Ethnic missions emphasis*

Phase 1: 1651-1863	Phase 2: 1863-present
Europeans (1651)	Chinese (1858)
Mixed	Indians (1873)
Natives (1730)	Javanese (1890)
Slaves (1749)	Lebanese (1890's)
Maroons (1765)	Guyanese (1960's)
	Haitians (1980's)
	Brazilians (1990's)

2.5. Approach and overview

It is not an easy task to write an ecumenical history of Christianity in Suriname. In the past, writings about church and missions paid more attention to the achievements of the Western Christians of their own denominations, with little or no attention being paid to those of the local Christians. Local Christians were not seen as colleagues of the foreign missionaries. They were known as 'black helpers', 'old Johannes' or 'people who went with the missionaries'. It became very difficult to know the role that local Christians played, especially in the early days. This one-sidedness has to be rectified, if we want to have a correct picture of the history of Christianity.

On the other hand, postcolonial writers started to react against the dominant Western historiography. The role of Western missionaries was therefore evaluated critically by writers in the 1960's. This method also had its own dangers. The role of the non-western missionaries was overemphasised at the expense of what Western missionaries did. It should be stated that with all their weaknesses, Western missionaries contributed a lot to Christianity in many of the countries in the global South. Western missionaries laid a foundation, sometimes at the expense of missions and evangelism in their own countries and at the cost of their own lives. Historiography therefore needed a balance. This study tried to find a balance. It was an ecumenical history of Christianity in Suriname, in which attention was given to roles that various people and institutions played. Organised Christianity in Suriname started in 1651, when the British settled in Suriname.

CHAPTER 3

The Beginning of the Church of England in Suriname

3.1. Introduction

This chapter presents a general background to Suriname during the British period, including government and the people (2.1), followed by the Church of England and its different factions (2.2).[1] The next section studies the colonial Church of England as a church of the Barbadian settlers (3.1), followed by missionary activities done by the Quakers (3.2) and, the Puritans (3.3). A separate section is devoted to Von Weltz (3.4), followed by some conclusions (4).

3.2. Background

3.2.1. Government and the people

3.2.1.1. Government

In 1651, Lord Francis Willoughby, Count of Parham, sent a ship with a hundred colonists under the leadership of Anthony Rowse, from Barbados to Suriname. They founded a few plantations and let their slaves, whom

---

[1]. This chapter is based on my article 'The beginning of the Church of England in Suriname' that first appeared in the *Academic Journal of Suriname* 2011. Volume 2:210-220. Used with permission.

they brought from Barbados and some Natives, work on them. The *Kalihna* or Carib Natives opposed the British settlement in their territory.

After the colony was founded, a battle started about its leadership. Willoughby, who spent a lot of money on this venture thought he had all rights to the colony. A Colonel John Scott, who supported the venture both financially and militarily, also claimed his rights to the colony. Rowse, who carried out the plan, saw himself as one of the leaders as well. Due to the political instability in Britain in those days, none of the gentlemen were able to receive ownership of the colony.

In 1657 William Byam was chosen as governor. He signed a peace treaty with the Kalihna Natives. They became his ally in the battle against the Maroons, the slaves who ran away from slavery.

In 1662, Suriname was finally officially given to Lord Francis Willoughby by the British king Charles II. All things pertaining to life in the colony were written in a charter. Willoughby died on 23 July 1666 in a hurricane on his way to Saint Kitts.

Table 5 *Governors of Suriname 1651-1667*

Richard Holdip	1652-1654
Planters	1654-1657
William Byam	1657-1667

3.2.1.2. *The people*

In 1664, in order to help the further development of the plantations, the leaders of Suriname allowed a group of Jews from Cayenne to settle in the country. Earlier in 1652, a group had already settled in Suriname. The Jews fled the Inquisition in Portugal and Spain to the Netherlands and the Dutch colonies. They had many years in the tropics and the sugar cane industry and were to play a significant role in the history of Suriname. Besides the British and the Jews, there were French and Dutch plantation owners in Suriname.

During the British period (1651-1667), the colony had 1,500 White colonists. They owned 40-50 profitmaking sugar cane plantations.

The majority of people in the colony, apart from the Natives, were the slaves who worked on both the Jewish and British plantations. Many slaves escaped slavery, by running away into the forest. There were approximately 3,000 slaves from African descent in the colony during the British period.

3.2.2. The Church of England and its different factions

The Church of England was one of the churches that broke away from the Roman Catholic Church. Different than in the other European countries, the church reformation in England was not based on doctrinal differences with the Church of Rome. The then English king Henry VIII (1509-1547) got into conflict with the Pope when the Pope refused to approve of his intended divorce of his wife Catherine of Aragon. In order to get done what he wanted Henry decided to break ties with Rome and the Church of England was established. The church took its own direction.

However, there were people within the church, who thought the reformation was not carried out properly. These people were known as Puritans. They insisted on a Presbyterian system of church governance and more room for preaching during the church service. The Church of England had maintained the episcopal system of Rome. The Puritans were able to make major changes in the church between 1640 and 1660. However, they were not united. Christianity in England then was divided into those who were loyal to the Catholic Church and the Conformists, who accepted the changes that were made in the church so far. Then there were the Puritans, who were calling for further reformation in the church. Out of the Puritans came another group, the Children of Light, later known as Quakers, under the leadership of George Fox. This divided and subdivided Christianity was exported to the New World.

With the arrival of the British in 1651, the Church of England came to Suriname. This was based on the principle of *cuius region eius religio*, 'whose region, his religion'. The parish was named 'Saint Bridget' after an Irish nun of the fifth century AD. It was founded on 23 July 1651.[2]

---

[2]. In some documents 'Saint Bridget' was also spelled as 'Santo Bridges' or 'Sinto Bridges'.

Which branch of the divided church came to Suriname? Based on the literature consulted, it appeared that Conformists, Nonconformists, Puritans and Quakers were all present in Suriname during the seventeenth century.

Since the colonists came from Barbados, the situation in Barbados was transplanted into Suriname.

3.3. Christianity in Suriname in the seventeenth century

3.3.1. The Church of England in Suriname

3.3.1.1. The Barbadian context

At the time of the colonisation there was a surplus of population in Barbados. According to one historian the number of Whites in 1650 was 50,000 (Oldmixon 1741:13). This number may have been exaggerated. According to another source, the number of Whites in 1646 was 20,000 (Cited in Schomburgk 1848:80). White colonists left Britain to find refuge in the West Indies. Some of them were soldiers whose lives were spared by the courts and were shipped to Barbados. They served as 'servants' (slaves) on the plantations and received the same treatment as the slaves from Africa. Because Barbados was overcrowded, colonists took the opportunity to settle in other parts of the West.

However, there was also another factor that led to the migration to Suriname. The leaders of Barbados at that time were royalists. They were devoted to the British king Charles II, who was in exile, and not the parliamentarians under the leadership of Oliver Cromwell. Lord Willoughby for example, initially was a parliamentarian and was not supportive of the royalists. However, he turned his back on the violence used by the parliamentarians and openly supported the exiled king, Charles II, in Barbados. In 1651, a ship was sent by the British parliamentarians to Barbados to diminish the influence of the royalists. After a few weeks of resistance, Willoughby appointed William Byam along with three other commissioners to negotiate surrender with the parliamentarians. When the parliamentarians came to power, they demanded that Willoughby, Byam and the leading royalists be banned from the colony. Suriname was the first choice of these exiles.

The royalists were Conformists in their Christian conviction, whereas the parliamentarians were Puritans. The two groups brought their religious difference with them to Barbados and exported it from there to Suriname. The colonisers of the West Indies were not the most devoted men and women. The Christian community in Suriname therefore was of mixed nature. Most of the writings that survived addressed the spirituality of the non-devoted Christian segment of the colony. It is also evident that the various branches of Christianity did not have a great view of each other's spirituality. On top of that, the colonisers in Barbados were as selfish as other colonisers of the New World. Their only purpose, apart from a few dissenting voices, was not to spread Christianity but to gain wealth.

3.3.1.2. *Organisation of the church in Suriname*

In Barbados, as was also the case in Suriname, the Church of England was an English church. It served the English colonists and their families. It was not a missionary church. In the seventeenth century, the established church was supported financially and materially by the state. With the problems in England the state did not support expansion to the New World. In Barbados an Act was passed in 1651 to appoint and regulate an appropriate salary for the clergymen. The Act was repealed the following year. The clergymen, as was the case in Barbados, were volunteers and were not appointed by the church in England. The governor established them in their ministry. They received their income from their plantations. In Suriname the proceeds of five plantations that Mr John Allen forfeited were used to support the church. It was not before 1675 that the Church of England had any say in the appointment of clergymen in the West. The various branches of the Church of England in the West had church councils, which consisted of members of the church, all of whom were plantation owners. More than the clergymen, the council influenced the spiritual life in the colony. Just like in Barbados, the leadership of the church in England did not provide theological or missiological guidance for the church of the settlers in Suriname.

The clergy served the colonists and their families and were concerned with their well-being. Services were held daily in a building in Torarica, a plantation along the Suriname River. Torarica was an important place at that time. Besides the government building and the church, there were about one hundred houses. The first clergyman of the church was the Rev George (Joris) Vernon. Apart from Vernon there were two planter clergymen, who had their plantations close to Torarica. One of them was the Rev John Overbridge.

3.3.1.3. *Spiritual life in the colony*

What do we know about the spiritual life of the people in the colony? The reports that we find in the early documents were not positive.

> If we consult the history of our colonies, it will generally be found that the first settlers were of that class of society in which morals and virtue are seldom to be met with. Ruthless and unprincipled, it was not amelioration of their Christian virtues which led them to distant climes, but the desire of enriching themselves by any means at their command (Schomburgk 1848:92).

In Barbados, the first clergyman Nicholas Leverton, who also served in Suriname, left the island because of the 'profligate conduct' of the colonists. During the time of Governor Philip Bell (1642-1650) in Barbados, he did much to improve the ministry of the church on the island. He passed an Act relating to public worship. The Act gave an indication of the attitude of the members of the different groups within the church towards the official church in Barbados at that time. These include: an absolute dislike of the Government of the Church of England, aversion and utter neglect or refusal of the prayers, sermons, and administration of the sacraments, and other rites and ordinances. People were holding conventicles in private houses and other places. They were scandalising ministers, endeavouring to seduce others and to alter the method of church government. The Act sought to address these issues and bring order and unity to the church.

It is hereby ordered, published, and declared, and all persons whatsoever inhabiting or resident, or which shall inhabit or reside in this Island, are, in his Majesty's name, hereby strictly charged and commanded, that they, and every one of them, from henceforth give due obedience, and conform themselves unto the Government and Discipline of the Church of England, as the same hath been established by several Acts of Parliament, and especially those which are at large expressed in the fronts of most English Bibles (Cited in Anderson II 1848:205).

This however was not successful. The colonists were not united in their understanding of the structure and government of the church. Just like the situation in England, there were different branches of the church in the West. Adherents were faithful to their own convictions. This led to religious persecution of the Nonconformists and Quakers both in Barbados and later on in Suriname. The different branches of the Church of England were present in the colonies to stay, each with its own approach to devotion to God. There are a few documents written in the 1660's that speak about the spirituality of the colonists in Suriname.

3.3.1.3.1. *Henry Adis*

Henry Adis, a Baptist, wrote a letter in which he spoke about his fellow countrymen, who called themselves Christians (Adis 1664). He accused them of 'debauched atheistical actions' which 'evidence themselves more brutish by far, than the very heathens themselves, to the shame and stink of Christianity among them'. He continued to describe what he saw as 'the rude rabble, drunkenness, and so much debauchery'. He heard to the great trouble of his soul 'so many bitter oaths, horrid execrations, and lascivious abominations'. Adis' judgment of the colony was correct. He was of the opinion that Willoughby himself had to be in the colony, to bring about a reformation in the colony. In his answer to Adis, Willoughby seems to agree with what Adis said. He wrote:

> I hope that in time God will work upon the hearts of the people to be more civil in life and conversation. All new colonies you know of what sort of people generally they are made up of; so that, what we in probability can expect from them, must be from length of time, and the good example of those who have been more civilly bred, and God hath wrought upon, and better principled, which I do with great expectation hope in time may produce good effects in that poor and sad colony of Syrranam: I do pray to God to strengthen you in those your resolutions for the good of the people of that poor place (Cited in Adis 1664:7).

Willoughby was of the opinion that a reformation would not suddenly take place among a group of people like those that Adis described. 'Endeavours are to be used by degrees to draw them to better carriages'. Adis spoke in his letter about another group of people from England who were willing to come to Suriname. It is not clear if that group ever came.[3] Adis' letter gave some indications of the spirituality of some of the colonists. It should be borne in mind that he was a Baptist, who did not necessarily agree with the other Christians in the colony. The question remained open whether what he described was the general situation in the colony or that of a segment of it.

3.3.1.3.2. John Allen

A year after Adis wrote his letter, William Byam wrote about an incident that happened with a member of the church (Byam 1665). John Allen (Allin) lived in Barbados a few years before he came to Suriname in April 1657. He owned five plantations. According to Byam, Allen was addicted to 'swearing, cursing and drunkenness'. In 1659 he was accused and tried for cursing the 'most blessed Redeemer of the world'. Allen denied the accusations. He expected Willoughby to grant him pardon. In 1664

---

3. One person who considered emigration to Suriname or Marryland at that time was the Rev John Wesley, the grandfather of the well-known John Wesley. Rev Wesley was a Nonconformist. He decided to remain in England and started to preach in private only (Calamy & Palmer 1775:485).

Willoughby came to the colony. He spoke with Allen, but did not grant him pardon. During an evening prayer meeting in an upper room at Willoughby's plantation in Parham, Allen attempted to kill Willoughby.[4]

The scripture reading that evening was remarkable. It was taken from 2 Sam 3:27, which reads as follow:

> And when Abner was returned to Hebron, Joab took him aside in the gate to speak with him quietly, and smote him there under the fifth rib....

The meeting was attended by Willoughby, Byam, the council, several gentlemen in the colony and domestic workers. Allen, who was not invited, came into the meeting with his cutlass. Fortunately, Byam and others who were there prevented Allen from doing what he intended to do. He cut off two fingers from Willoughby and wounded him on his forehead. Allen was apprehended and later committed suicide in prison. All his possessions were confiscated and given to the church. He did not voluntarily leave his estates as a gift to the church. Again this attitude of one colonist does not speak about all colonists. It may be possible that Henry Adis' letter was influenced by the previous incident with Allen.

3.3.1.3.3. Dutch testimonies

The comments on the low spirituality of British Christianity were not limited to the different groups within the church at that time. According to the Dutch governor Lichtenbergh, the majority of the British people were of low descent, a sentiment shared by Willoughby. They went round begging among the Natives to stay alive. This was possibly because some of the Britons who came may have been servants (slaves). The first Dutch clergyman, the Rev Johannes Basseliers, accused the British in a letter that he wrote in 1676, of excesses and extravagant godlessness. According to him they created Sodom and Gomorrah in Suriname. As such the Dutch testimony agrees with that of Adis and Byam.

---

4. Dentz (1916:2) said the event took place on a Sunday. Byam's report seems to indicate an evening during the week.

3.3.1.3.4. Conclusion

The sexual immorality of the colonists with their female slaves was well-known. The clergy were forced to remain silent, because the colonists threatened to withhold their remuneration. This of course had its impact on the way the clergy functioned. It was therefore obvious that they became planters, to be able to support themselves. It can be argued that even though the sugar business in Suriname was in its early days, sugar was dictating the way of life of the colony.

In Barbados there were rules which regulated the life of the church including a regular church service every Sunday. Some of them were also applied in Suriname. As can be seen in the letter from Byam, there was also a set time for prayers during the week.

3.3.2. Christianity, the Natives and the Quakers

The English church in Suriname was the church of the British colonists. When the colony was given to Willoughby in 1662, it was clearly stated that the colony should evangelise the Natives. The Natives had to be instructed so that as time passed they would behave in the right manner. And in the end, they would come to the knowledge of the true God and only Saviour of the world, Jesus Christ. The British were in a fortunate position to do that, because William Byam had signed a peace treaty with the Natives. But instead of evangelising them, the British used them to protect themselves against the slaves who fled from slavery.

3.3.2.1. John Bowron

The official Church did not evangelise the Natives. A few Quakers preached the gospel to them. One of them was John Bowron (1627-1704). He became a Christian at twenty-six through the preaching of George Fox and James Naylor in 1653. Not long after that, he started to preach the gospel in different places in England. Everywhere he went, he was opposed, because he was a Quaker. He therefore left England for Scotland. He experienced the same persecution there from the clergymen. In 1656, he left for Barbados. After he preached the gospel there for a while, he went to Suriname. Here he attended religious meetings of the Natives. At these meetings the Natives sang and made music on their drums. Through an interpreter that Bowron brought from Barbados, he was able to preach the gospel to them. He preached to various chiefs and in various villages. According to him, the Natives accepted him as a good man, who came to tell them about the God of the Whites. There is no evidence that any Native became a believer in Jesus Christ. As far as we could see he was the first one to preach the gospel to the Natives.

3.3.2.2. Henry Fell and four other Quakers

When Bowron left for Barbados, Henry Fell came to Suriname. Henry Fell (ca. 1630-1674) was a clerk of a judge, who felt the calling to make missionary journeys to preach the gospel. In September 1658, he went to Barbados. There he met Bowron. Bowron told him about the work that he did in Suriname. Fell also received a letter from someone who spoke about a big harvest in Suriname that needed labourers. He came to Suriname in 1658 with four other Quakers from Barbados. They worked among the Natives and British up to 1659. Fell wrote a detailed report about this mission in May 1659. As far as we can see, this is the first missionary report about missions in Suriname (see Carrol 1973). Fell and his team found it very difficult to communicate with the Natives, because of their language. According to him a few people in Suriname were convicted by the gospel message. They took the cross and became followers of Christ. He trusted that they would endure and that others would accept the gospel as well. The British in the colony were not a good example of what a Christian should be. They were a bad model for the Natives, who followed in their example. After ten weeks in Suriname the group experienced hostility from the governor and the other members of the governing council. The governor banished them to a desolate place across the Suriname River. Their books and other documents were burned and they were jailed for two weeks.

It is clear that the Quakers suffered persecution not only in Britain, but also in other parts of the world where they preached the gospel.

It is not clear if the Quakers preached to the slaves in Suriname as well. In Britain they opposed the notion of slavery strongly. The way Byam and the council treated the Quakers is an indication of the religious hostility between the different segments within the English church. It is not clear if there were other British in the colony who were Quakers. The report of the Quakers confirmed the low level of spirituality among the colonisers as well.

3.3.3. The Puritans

The Puritans were of the opinion that the gospel was also meant for the descendants of the Africans. Two of them, Nicholas Leverton and John Oxenbridge, ministered in Suriname.

3.3.3.1. Nicholas Leverton

Nicholas Leverton (1610-1660/1) was the first clergyman of the Church of England in Barbados. He arrived there in 1625. Due to problems with his congregation, he left for Tobago. When he left there, he served in Bermuda for a short while. At the invitation of Willoughby he came to Suriname, where he died shortly after arrival. Leverton started as a minister in the Church of England. Later on he became a Nonconformist. He served the Nonconformists in the colony. According to Dentz they had a chapel in Torarica, where the official Church was (Dentz 1916:2).

3.3.3.2. John Oxenbridge

John Oxenbridge (1609-1669) came to Suriname in 1662, due to the persecution of the Nonconformists. He arrived here after the death of his friend and fellow Nonconformist minister Nicholas Leverton. Oxenbridge stayed in Suriname up to 1667, when Zeeland took over the colony. He wrote a few things about the situation in Suriname in his journal that give us an indication of his personal life.

In 1666 he buried his wife and two children. She was probably his third wife, a widow whom he met in Barbados. On 19 November 1666 he wrote that that day was a dark day for him. He could not look up to God. This experience allowed him to understand what it means when God abandoned a soul. God did not allow his situation to continue because on the 20th and the 21st God filled his heart with consolation. His major grief however was not the passing away of his wife and children. It was the fact that his thoughts were not focused strongly on the Lord.

Oxenbridge published a brochure in 1661 before he came to Suriname, entitled *A double watch-word, or, The duty of watching and watching to duty*, both echoed. However one of his publications written in 1671, when he left Suriname, is better known, *A seasonable proposition of propagating the gospel by Christian colonies in the continent of Guaiana: being some gleanings of a larger discourse drawn, but not published*. In this work, he gave some suggestions on how to preach the gospel through Christian colonies in the continent of Guyana. He felt that that region was especially suitable for such an endeavour. In the first place Suriname was established by Willoughby at the request of the Natives. Willoughby paid a price for the colony that was agreed upon with the Natives. Secondly, Suriname was a place of relative peace. This is confirmed by the fact that a single family, the family of Jacob Enosh, lived there two years before the British arrived, without being hindered by the Natives. Furthermore, the Natives needed the protection of the British against their enemies. Thirdly, the passage from Britain to Suriname was shorter than to North America. Fourthly, the country was good. You do not need the kind of houses that are built in European countries where there is a severe winter. Therefore building a house in Suriname is much cheaper. The plants also grow much better. Cotton bears in nine month after planting. There is also a greater variety of food in Suriname than in Britain.

The people who should give heed to his call were to be real believers and practicers of the Christian religion. They should prize and love Christ's name and interest in such a way, that they are willing to go forth to the gentiles in His name. Oxenbridge was of the opinion that Christians should use colonies to propagate the gospel, because the promises of Christ were not fully fulfilled in the days of the apostles.

Just like Oxenbridge, many clergymen in England were without a job when they refused to sign the Act of Conformity. These colleagues could mean a lot for the gospel in a Christian colony. By saying this, he clearly disagreed with people of his time, who suggested that the great commission was only meant for the days of the apostles. He stated that the gospel came to England and other countries many years after the apostles died. If it came to those countries at a later stage, it could also go to other countries during his time. Oxenbridge contributed to the missiological thinking of his days with his booklet. He also wrote a pamphlet which he completed in 1670, entitled *Conversion of the Gentiles*. In that pamphlet he defended the conversion of the gentiles, arguing that the church should not despise or distrust converted Natives. This is against the Abrahamic convent of grace.

> And shall then any of the Jewish legal spirit conceited of their own (English or other) nation dare to build up a new partition wall between Gentile and Gentile and exclude and set at naught the poor … Natives as once the proud Jews did all Gentiles! Let such a one take heed lest he be accused of the Lord for building that which God will have utterly destroyed. . . the same blood runs in the veins of a Native as thine . . . God hath made of one blood all nations of men not the Natives of one blood and the English of another (Cited in Breen 2001:161).

It is not clear how he applied his principles in Suriname. Just like his contemporaries, he owned a plantation on which slaves had to work.

3.3.4. Justinianus Ernst Von Weltz

In this chapter on British Christianity in Suriname, attention should be given to another missionary. It was the Austrian Justinianus Ernst Baron Von Weltz (1621-1668).[5] After a dramatic conversion, he began to correspond with the theologians of his time. He reminded the church in papers that he wrote in 1664 of its missionary duties. He suggested that the Protestants should establish a Jesus Loving Society to promote Christianity and for missionary activities among the heathen, just as the Roman Catholics did. In another paper he called for pastors and academics to establish an institution to train missionaries. Von Weltz disagreed with Christians in his days, who kept the gospel for themselves. He asked three questions: Was it right for evangelical Christians to keep the gospel for themselves and not spread it? Why were theological students not taught to serve in the vineyard of Christ elsewhere? Is it right for Christians to spend a lot of money on

---

5. See Scherer 1969. Some documents spelt his name 'Von Welz'.

clothes, food, drink, and delicacies, without thinking about the spreading of the gospel?

At a meeting in Regenburg he was sharply criticised by the influential Lutheran theologian Johann Heinrich Ursinus. Ursinus regarded the heathens as dogs and a holy thing such as the gospel should not be given to them. The theological faculty of the University of Wittenberg had expressed a clear opinion with regard to the great commission in 1651. According to the university, the great commission was completed with the passing of the original apostles. Von Weltz's reply was very simple. The church recognised the command to baptise disciples in Matt 28 to be universal. If that is true than the command 'to go' and 'to teach' all nations and 'to repent' was also universal. He gave four reasons for preaching the gospel to the heathens. Firstly, it is God's will that all men should be saved (1Tim 2:4). Secondly, godly men down through Christian history suffered and died to bring God's Word to the heathen. Thirdly, the church's liturgy called for prayer for the conversion of those who are in spiritual darkness and error. Finally, the Roman Catholics were doing that. Von Weltz was supported in his views by the Rev Friedrich Breckling of Zwolle. Because the Lutheran Church did not want to accept its responsibility, Breckling ordained him as an apostle to the gentiles. Von Weltz went to Suriname personally as a missionary in 1666. In that year the colony was stricken by an epidemic, which caused many people to die. Approximately 200 colonists left the colony with their slaves, because of this.

It is not clear if the British and Jewish plantation owners in Suriname allowed Von Weltz to preach to their slaves. The situation in the country was such that the plantation owners had their attention on other things, that is, their possessions. There was also a language barrier for Von Weltz. Up to this moment records of his work in Suriname have not been found. Von Weltz died in his mission field in 1668. According to some he was torn apart by wild beasts, while others said he died from malaria. With his action he proved a critical point: the church had a responsibility for missions. Von Weltz became a model for many missionaries who would come to Suriname after him. The message of Jesus Christ was not only for the European, but also for the other nations.

3.4. Conclusion

What is the conclusion that can be drawn from this period? The church in Suriname was in a difficult position, since it was not officially established by the church in England. It was also plagued by the different factions among its members. The type of Christianity that the British brought from Barbados to Suriname was focused on the British colonists. It seems to have been a nominal Christianity, since most of the colonists did not practice what they believed. They communicated a wrong message through their behaviour.

The early pioneers of missionary activities and missiological thinking were the Puritans, the Quakers and Von Weltz. Their contribution to missiology seems to have been the argument that the great commission was not completed during the time of the apostles. Oxenbridge proposed a model in which a Christian colony could be used for propagation of the gospel. Suriname however was never a Christian colony. It was not the priority of the colonists at that stage to propagate Christianity on their plantations, let alone the whole country. Von Weltz went to the mission field personally to demonstrate how the church should carry out the missionary mandate.

The English church in Suriname started as a church for the English, a church for the elite. Throughout its history, it remained an English church. In its early days in Suriname, there was no clear evidence of true discipleship among the British. However, there is not enough evidence to make a clear judgement on the true character of its spirituality. Further research is necessary to establish this. The British however, gave Suriname a lingua franca Sranantongo that was used by other churches to spread the gospel to the slaves.

CHAPTER 4

The Beginning of Reformed Christianity

4.1. Introduction: The era of Zeeland (1667-1683)

This chapter presents a brief general background to Suriname during the beginning of Reformed Christianity in Suriname. It is divided into three periods. The first two are the foundational years of the church. These are the era of Zeeland, from 1667-1683 (4.1) and the era of Van Sommelsdijck from 1683-1688 (4.2). During the third period the church was established and it was working towards founding a Christian colony (4.3).

4.1.1. The colony

On 27 February 1667 the Zeelander, Admiral Abraham Crijnssen conquered the colony. Following this, Governor William Byam transferred the leadership of the colony to him on 6 March 1667. Suriname came into the hands of Zeeland (the Netherlands) and was officially assigned to the Netherlands at the peace treaty in Breda on 31 July 1667. Despite this treaty Henry Willoughby, the son of Francis Willoughby, came in 1668 and plundered the important plantations or burned them completely. Around 1,000 British colonists left with their 2,000 slaves. Many slaves used the situation to escape to the jungle where they joined other Maroons.

In the following years other colonisers sold their plantations and left Suriname. The Dutch were accused of not treating their British subjects fairly. They did not allow some of the British to take their possessions out of Suriname.

4.1.1.1. The colony and its rulers

The years following the settlement of the Zeelanders were very difficult. Many colonists had left. There were only 24 plantations remaining, with 69 Whites and 714 slaves. Suriname also suffered from disagreements between the General States of the Netherlands and Zeeland about its administration. The two could not agree on major issues, including who to appoint as the governor. When Philip Lichtenbergh returned to the Netherlands in 1671, caretaker governors had to lead the colony, except for Heinsius.

Table 6 *Caretaker governors of Suriname 1672-1683*

Pieter Versterre	April 1672-March 1677
Abel Thisso	April 1677-December 1677; March 1678-December 1678
Tobias Adriaensen	December 1677-March 1678
Heinsius	December 1678-1680
E van Hemert	April - September 1680
Laurens Verboom	September 1680-November 1683

4.1.1.2. The freedom fight of the Natives and Maroons

Besides the problems in the Netherlands, the Dutch faced another problem in the colony, for the Natives fought against them. The Natives helped the British in their fight against the Dutch and when the British left, they continued with their fight. The Dutch had taken some of them as slaves, to work on the plantations. Earlier the British exempted the Natives from slavery, as the Roman Catholics had done before in countries where they dominated.

During the time of these freedom fights there were small numbers of European soldiers in the country and a few hundred civilians. In 1678 various plantations were raided in Perica, Para and Commewijne. The raiders under the leadership of Kaaikusi encouraged slaves to escape from slavery. Ganimet was one of those slaves who escaped. Ganimet joined Kaaikusi and the two led the freedom fight and carried it to a more intensive level. It became a joint action of the Natives and the Maroons. Contrary to what happened in other countries, the war did not lead to a massive slave revolt.

4.1.1.3. *The colonists*

Another problem in the colony was the fact that the colonists were not united. Furthermore, many of them were people who did not have a future in their home country. They came to Suriname to try to rebuild their lives. Their lifestyle, which was evident in the structure of the city in those days, indicated that they were not successful. Suriname in those days, according to early sources, consisted of a few houses and many pubs.

4.1.2. Reformed Christianity in Suriname (1667-1683)

On board of the fleet of Abraham Crijnssen, who conquered Suriname from the British for the second time in 1668, was the Reverend Johannes Basseliers. He was the first clergyman of the Reformed Church who settled in Suriname.

4.1.2.1. *Johannes Basseliers in Suriname*

Johannes Basseliers married Sara van Scharphuizen, a sister of Joan van Scharphuizen. Joan later became a governor in Suriname. Their children Elisabeth and Nicolaes were in Suriname. Probably two other children died during a plague in 1675. Johannes wrote that six people died in his house, including two beloved children, an Afro-Surinamese, a Native and two others. Johannes probably died during another plague in 1689. Besides being a clergyman, Basseliers was a plantation owner. Around 1682 he had more than 50 slaves, who were working on his plantations. He was one of the six largest slave-owners from among 152 during his time in Suriname. Because of his education at the University of Utrecht, which possibly included classes with Gisbertus Voetius, Basseliers was theoretically well prepared for missions in a foreign nation.

4.1.2.2. *Ministry of Johannes Basseliers in Suriname (1668-1674)*

4.1.2.2.1. *Lifestyle of the congregants*

The ministry of Basseliers among the colonists was very difficult. His parishioners consisted of people whose lives were far from being Christian. The small group of British people who lived in Suriname at that time felt that the Dutch were not good as colonists, slave-masters and evangelists. This was remarkable because the Dutch accused the British of creating Sodom and Gomorrah in Suriname. Now, the British said the same thing about the Dutch. Rev Adrianus Backer, a contemporary of Basseliers, lamented the unrepentant attitude of most of the inhabitants of the colony. Due to the lifestyle of the colonists, Basseliers felt that it was important to work on their conversion, before he could focus on the slaves. Basseliers' view of focusing on the colonists was not shared by his later colleague Francois Chaillou. Chaillou was of the opinion that pastoral care towards the colonists did not exclude missions to the Natives.

His plantation did not keep Basseliers back from his work as the clergyman. He devoted his time well to the planting of the Reformed Church. The church music, the way the church was organised and how the services were conducted were carried over from the Netherlands. The church was therefore and is still known as *Bakra-kerki*, 'Church of the Whites'.

The colony knew different types of Christians. One of them was Julius Caesar Bovetius. Bovetius wanted to kill Governor Heinsius in 1669, because he did not give him a position that he had promised him. He also instructed his servant to steal chickens from Heinsius and to serve them at his meals. He was typical of a group of people who would continue to emerge in Suriname. They were people serving their own interest at the expense of others, even if sometimes they had to kill.

In 1669, the church appointed its first deacon Nicolaas Combé. Up to that time, all the church services in Paramaribo were held in Combé's home. He and Basseliers formed the first church council. This two-man council was understandable, because when Basseliers arrived there were only two or three Dutch families consisting of seven or eight people in the colony.

Another church member had a plantation in the Para district. He legislated that the poor people in that district should receive his possessions. This he did before the plantation was destroyed during the attack of the Natives. His example was followed by other colonists as well. They legislated that part of their possessions should be given to their slaves. Bovetius, Combé and the testator demonstrated the diversity that was in the church. This diversity continued throughout the history of the church.

4.1.2.2.2. Geographical distances between the congregants

The lifestyle of the congregants was not the only problem that Basseliers faced. Because of the big geographical distances between the plantations, Basseliers could not gather all congregants in one place. There were two meeting points in the colony at that time, both along the Suriname River: Torarica and Paramaribo. Due to the distances between the plantations, he also had to visit the congregants on their plantations. Apart from the geographical distances, congregants were also unwilling to attend church services on Sunday. They preferred to use Sundays for social visitations and celebrations.

4.1.2.2.3. Financial problems

Basseliers had financial problems. He did not receive a salary during the first six years of his ministry. The church was suffering from the differences of opinion between the General States and Zeeland. The British destroyed the plantations that were confiscated from Mr Allen and given to the church. Basseliers was able to support himself, because he had his own plantation. The fact that Basseliers needed to do something to earn additional income was in itself not against the general opinion of his time.

4.1.2.2.4. His colleague

Basseliers worked in the colony for six years as the only clergyman of the Reformed Church. In 1674 he received support from Rev Francois Chaillou. Chaillou, who first laboured in Trinidad from 1668-1671, had the intention to start missionary work among the Natives. However, due to the freedom struggle that was going on, he had to give up on his idea. Instead, he served the church in Paramaribo. Basseliers then focused on the church in Torarica.

Chaillou did not show the same godly attitude as his colleague. According to Governor Heinsius, Chaillou drove people out of the church due to his personality. He was a drunk and used to drink with the Natives and the slaves. Even his colleague was not pleased with him. Because of his ungodly lifestyle, he was suspended from the ministry. He died in 1681.

4.1.2.2.5. Church building

In a letter to the directors in Zeeland, Governor Heinsius spoke about the need for a new church building. The church met in a building of timber that was covered with leaves. During the rainy season, the church could not meet in the building, since the roof was leaking. The building was also very small and could only seat a hundred and fifteen people. Normally about a hundred people attended the church service. The governor therefore asked that a special collection should be held in the Netherlands for a new church building. Despite the freedom struggle or maybe due to this struggle the number of people attending the church service in Paramaribo grew significantly. It was remarkable that the members of the church did not contribute towards a new church building. Paramaribo expected the church overseas to pay for its new building. This attitude of expecting help from the outside continued to haunt the church in Suriname throughout its history.

4.1.2.3. Expansion of the church

Between 1668 and 1679, more Dutch colonists came to Suriname. Some settled in Paramaribo, but most settled in the north-eastern part of the country. Due to this growth, there was a need for a church in Commewijne. In 1679, Rev Adrianus Backer came to Suriname. Backer who was suspended in the Netherlands was allowed to come to Suriname, but he was not on the pay list of Zeeland. The church in Commewijne was willing to hire him and pay his salary. He received on top of a salary a plantation with slaves. Things however did not work out well for him. The Natives attacked his plantation and took four of his slaves away. It also appeared that the church could not pay his agreed annual salary. Backer was very disappointed with the state of the church in Suriname. In a letter that he wrote in 1681, he spoke about the 'sober state' of the colony. This according to him was due to the 'unreasonable unrepentant attitude' of most of the inhabitants. They were not willing to repent, even when the heathens attacked the colony. Backer saw the freedom fight of the Natives and Maroons as a judgment from God. In 1682, he was appointed as the clergyman for Paramaribo. Things were not different for him in that congregation. That church also did not pay his salary. Backer resigned and returned to the Netherlands in

1683. Basseliers was again the only clergyman of the Reformed Church in the colony.

4.1.3. The colony under new management

The joint Native and Maroon war and the attacks on the plantations became too much for Zeeland. It sold the colony on 6 June 1682 to the West Indian Company (WIC). Within a short time, it became clear that WIC was not able to take care of the colony due to the high expenses. It sold two-thirds of its possessions to the city of Amsterdam and Mr Cornelis van Aerssen van Sommelsdijck. In 1683, the three new owners founded the Geoctrooieerde Sociëteit van Suriname (Chartered Society of Suriname). The purpose of the society was to govern and protect the colony. This new partnership led to the beginning of a new era. One of the partners, Van Sommelsdijck was appointed as the governor.

Table 7 *Government and Administration of Justice in Suriname*

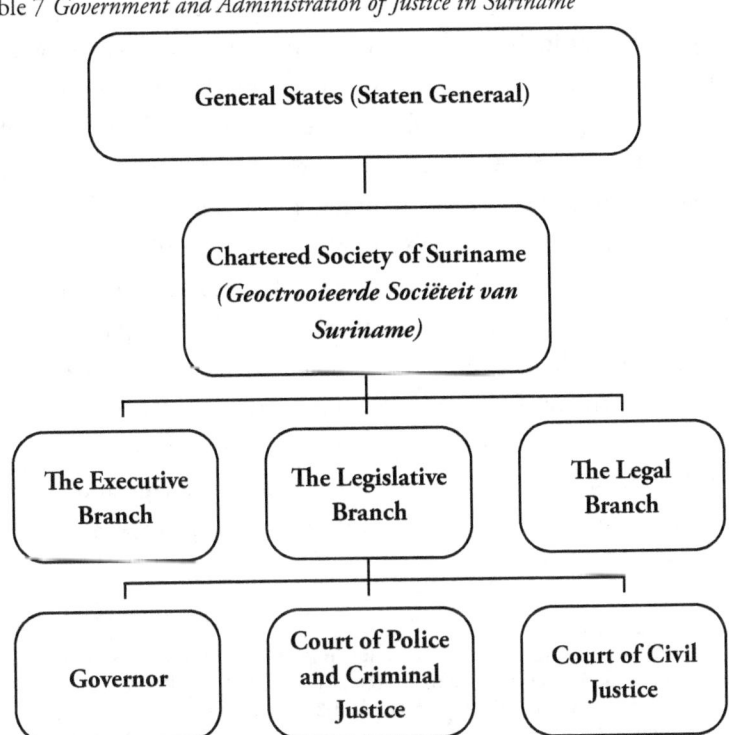

4.2. The era of Van Aerssen van Sommelsdijck: 1683-1688

4.2.1. Cornelis van Aerssen van Sommelsdijck

In 1683, Cornelis van Aerssen van Sommelsdijck came to Suriname as the new governor. He was hailed as a friend of God. He wanted to inspire others to follow in his footsteps through his own exemplary lifestyle. He was a devoted Calvinist, who kept the 'Christian Sabbath' (Sunday). Yet, he was open to people of other Judaeo-Christian persuasions. He allowed the Labadists and even the Roman Catholic Church to settle in the colony. He gave the Jews permission to let their slaves work on Sundays.

Van Sommelsdijck tried to address the many challenges that the colony faced. He signed a peace treaty with the Natives in 1684. To seal the treaty and keep the peace, he organised trips for Native children to the Netherlands. Besides arranging the trips, he took a Native woman as a concubine.[1] The Maroon group under leadership of Ganimet was successfully overpowered by the government in 1681. With a Maroon coalition or commonwealth, led by a Cormantine slave Jermes, along the Suriname-, Coppename- and Saramacca Rivers, Van Sommelsdijck signed a peace treaty around 1685. The peace treaties that were signed with the freedom fighters allowed Van Sommelsdijck to start the process of building the colony.

Under his leadership the number of plantations in Suriname grew from 50 to approximately 200. The Jews in the colony contributed a lot to its growth. In 1684, they consisted of a third of the White population. They built their own settlement along the Suriname River, called Jodensavanne (Jewish Savannah) in 1669. In 1685, they erected the *Berāchâ Vešālôm* (Blessing and Peace), their second synagogue in the country.

Van Sommelsdijck instituted a few changes in the regulations of the colony, which were not well accepted by the colonists, such as the protection

---

1. Van Sommelsdijck was married to Marguerite du Puys de St. André Montbrun. She never came to Suriname and died in Gravenhage in 1695 (Berg 1845:52; Wolbers 1861:65, footnote). This may explain Van Sommelsdijck's acceptance of the Native concubine.

of slaves. His work however was for a short while, because he was murdered by a group of rebellious military in 1688.

4.2.2. Christianity

Christianity started to diversify during the time of Van Sommelsdijck. He did not only support the Reformed Church, he allowed Roman Catholics, Labadists and Huguenots to settle in the colony.

4.2.2.1. Roman Catholics in Suriname

At the request of one Mr Philippus van Hulten, three Catholic clergymen came to Suriname on the same ship as Van Sommelsdijck. These clergymen were the Franciscan Fathers, Frederikus van der Hofstadt and Thomas Fuller and Frater Johannes Graefdorf. Later on Father Petrus Croll joined them. The Roman Catholic Mission to Suriname was founded on 22 September 1683 by a decree of the Sacred Congregation for the Propagation of the Faith (*Sacra Congregatio de Propaganda Fide*). The mission of the priests was to feed the European Catholics in the colony and the 'savages' (Natives) with the bread of the divine word. Every other week a priest travelled throughout the colony to serve the Catholics with the word. Even though many Roman Catholic colonists and military were in the colony, the church did not receive permission to start its own church. This first Catholic attempt to establish itself in the colony came to an end on 29 August 1686. There were a number of reasons for this. In the first place the clergymen died. Secondly, Europe decided to stop the mission. Finally, there was opposition from the Natives and the predominantly Calvinistic plantation owners. The Calvinistic rulers were not ready to accept Catholics. Zeeland on the other hand was not happy with the decision of Van Sommelsdijck to allow Roman Catholics into the colony. It therefore requested that the clergymen be deported. Van Sommelsdijck responded to this by exhuming the remains of the clergymen and sending them to Zeeland. Zeeland returned the remains, which were reburied in Suriname.

4.2.2.2. The Labadists

Things went differently with the Labadists.[2] In 1683 a group arrived with Governor Van Sommelsdijck. Their task was to explore the land. Some of these explorers brought a negative report back to the Netherlands. Another group was very positive. According to them, the Lord was going to build a 'Zoar' in Suriname, just as in the days of Lot.[3] Among the members of the church in Amsterdam, were Anna Maria van Schuurman and Lady Lucia van Sommelsdijck, a sister of Governor Van Sommelsdijck.

In 1684 a group of Labadists came to Suriname and settled on the plantation La Providence, in the neighbourhood of Berg en Dal, approximately 65 km away from Fort Zeelandia. They declined the offer of the governor to stay close to the fort. As children of God they wanted to live far from the sinful world and the gentiles. Even the offer of the governor to let a group of newly-arrived slaves work on their plantation was rejected. Later on they took slaves, but treated them with love.

Shortly after their arrival they were introduced to tropical Suriname with its blessings, but also with its insects and diseases. Many of them died. The leadership of the group was under the impression that the colonists who died were punished by God, because they disobeyed their leaders. They compared this to the biblical account in Num 16. The people who disobeyed their leader were just like Korah, Dathan and Abiram. They were punished because of their rebellion. Probably the leaders' ignorance of tropical diseases was the reason for such accusations.

The group decided to move to the eastern part of the country. In May 1686, a group travelled to Cottica and Coermotibo to find a good place to settle. The outcome of the journey was not clear. It was also not known if the group actually moved to the east.

---

2. See Knappert, 1926/27. The Movement of the Labadists was founded by Jean de Labadie. He was a student at the Jesuit school. In 1650 he left the Catholic Church and joined the Reformed Church in Montauban, Geneva. Years later Labadie went to the French-speaking, Walloon Church in Middelburg. He tried to bring this church back to biblical truth. However, his attempts failed. He started a new evangelical church, with about 300 people.

3. See Gen 19:21 ff. 'Zoar' probably means 'small place'.

The Labadists were very missions minded. Among them was a clergyman, Rev Johannes Wesener.[4] The Labadists wanted to reach slaves with the gospel of Jesus Christ. That was inevitable, because Anna Maria Schuurman was a pupil of the Dutch professor Gisbertus Voetius, who was very mission minded. In 1680 a dying member of the Labadists' Church in Wieuwerd said that she was going to pray to the Lord Jesus for the conversion of the 'poor' Natives, since she could not go to the mission field anymore, due to her old age and illness. The opportunity to serve in Suriname was an answer to this prayer.

Research so far did not reveal anything about their missions in Suriname. Were they a closed community that focused on its own people? In other words, were they only gathering with people who were 'separated' from the world? The Labadists were well known. This was gathered from the fact that people in the colony trusted them with the upbringing of their children. A Native boy who lived with them learned Dutch and could serve as an interpreter when they took the journey to Cottica. A detailed report was written about this journey. The writer of the report spoke with different people during the journey and made different observations about their spiritual life.

According to him the daughter of Rev Basseliers and some of her female friends wore worldly clothes. He was also not impressed with the worldly dress of another lady, a former Quaker. Even her behaviour was worldly. She even dared to marry on a Sunday, the day they considered to be the Lord's Sabbath!

He also met a certain person named Cyprianus, who left the world to serve the Lord. However, he was so engaged with the world, that he was not able to let go of it. The grace working in him was not powerful and triumphant enough. He also met people who really served the Lord.

Had he spoken to these people about the Lord? And what did he mean when he said that their clothes were worldly? Did he expect the people in a tropical country like Suriname to dress as they would normally do in a cold country like the Netherlands?

---

4. Wesener was clergyman in Britswerd and Wieuwerd. He was removed from the ministry in May 1679, because of his 'Labadist ideas'. He then joined the Labadists' house church in Wieuwerd. Wesener died in Suriname in 1687.

The mission of the Labadists in Suriname failed. In the first place, they chose a wrong place in which to settle. Secondly, they were attacked by the Maroons. Thirdly, there were misunderstandings among them. Fourthly, they were not prepared for life in the tropics. And finally, they were misunderstood by the slaves. The slaves did not understand them and their mission. They did not respond to the love shown to them. How was it possible that the Labadists (also White!) took them away from their cruel masters, showed them love and treated them humanely? Was there a hidden agenda? The slaves did not comprehend that. The settlement of the Labadists was closed in 1732.

In spite of this failure to establish a lasting missionary work among the Afro-Surinamese and Natives, Maria Sybilla Merian, a prominent Labadist, who lived in Suriname from 1699-1701, left us with an inheritance of lasting beauty that still 'speaks': a collection of great drawings of tropical plants and insects.[5]

4.2.2.3. *The Huguenots – The Walloon Church*

A third group that established itself in the colony during the era of Van Sommelsdijck was the French refugees, the Huguenots. This French-speaking Reformed Church was known as the Walloon Church. Contrary to the Labadists, the Huguenots became a branch of the Reformed Church. They remained a separate branch up to 1800. Huguenots were very influential in Surinamese society. Many plantations were named after them and these names are still known to the country.

4.2.2.4. *The Reformed Church*

In 1684, Rev Basseliers resigned. He gave the government about a year's notice. However, since there was no one to take over his place he continued to serve the church until he passed away at the age of 50 in 1689.

---

5. *Metamorphosis Insectorum Surinamensium* (Or, Transformations of Surinamese Insects) was published in 1705.

The Beginning of Reformed Christianity

Table 8 *The Reformed Church membership in 1684*

Paramaribo	81
Torarica	58
Commewijne	350
Children	90
Total	579

According to Backer the three churches had ninety members in 1681, of which thirty-six were in Commewijne. In 1684, the churches had 489 members above 12 years old and 90 children under 12.

In 1688 the population of Suriname consisted of 811 Europeans and 4,181 slaves. The population was further subdivided as follows: 579 'Christians' owning a total of 2,983 slaves, 232 Jews with a total of 1,198 slaves. Not included in these numbers were the Natives and the Maroons. It was customary in those days to label all non-Jewish Europeans as Christians.

Table 9 *Estimated population in 1688*

Christians	579
Jews	232
Slaves	4,181
Total	4,992

The growth of the church towards the end of the period of Van Sommelsdijck was due to his good policies. He attracted new colonists to the colony. This led to more members for the church. In 1687, churches were founded in Cottica and Perica, bringing the number of Reformed Churches in Suriname to six. Two churches were located in Paramaribo (Dutch and French), two in Commewijne (Upper and Lower divisions of Commewijne), one in Perica and one in Cottica.

4.3. Towards a Christian colony: 1688-1734

4.3.1. People and economy

During Van Sommelsdijck's term as governor the number of people in the colony grew. Besides the planters, he brought orphans from the Netherlands. His intention was to give these orphans a Christian upbringing.

In the Netherlands, there were people who recruited 'White servants' to serve in the colony. These 'servants' were thieves, convicted criminals who were deported out of the Dutch cities, wanderers, deserters, simple people or adventurers. Van Sommelsdijck called them 'drunkards, people who were good-for-nothing and liars'. They were used as soldiers and 'servants'.

In the eighteenth century many of the colonists' families needed help from the church's social welfare fund. It appeared that the men were using their income to satisfy their alcohol addiction. The church council had requested that the judiciary should pass a law that would allow for the attachment of part of their salary. If that happened the social welfare fund could be used in other ways. It was not clear if all these alcohol addicts were White slaves.

Many social events in those days had a religious character. Between 1687 and 1700 two hundred weddings were recorded in Paramaribo. The majority of the couples came from the Netherlands. But there were also people from France (31), Germany (26), Sweden, Denmark, Brazil and the Caribbean. In 1733, a new group of colonists arrived in the colony. They were Paltzers. In the following years, a few more family members joined them. In 1734, the Moravians received permission to establish themselves in Suriname. This international character was not only true for Paramaribo. Other parts of the colony had a similar international outlook. This explains why the communication language in the colony was Sranantongo, the communication language developed during the British colonisation period.

The majority of people in the colony however were slaves and the Natives. In 1710, there were 1,500 Whites and 10,000 slaves in the colony. This number grew to approximately 40,000 slaves and less than 2,000 Whites in 1730. Yet, the affairs of the colony centred on the needs and wants of the White minority.

Table 10 *Suriname between 1710 and 1730*

Year	1710	1730
Christians	1,500	2,000
Slaves	10,000	40,000
Plantations		400

In 1712, the colony suffered a major loss. The French admiral Jacques Cassard attacked and conquered it. He exacted a levy under threat of approximately one-third of the value of the colony. Many slaves used that opportunity to escape into the jungle. Some colonists hid their slaves in the jungle until Cassard left. These slaves never returned to the plantations.

Besides sugar, the colony exported letter wood. In the first half of the eighteenth century new products were added, such as coffee (1724), cocoa (1733) and cotton (1735). In 1688, there were twenty-three plantations in the colony. In 1730, the number of plantations grew to 400. The economic prospects of the colony were good. However, the focus was not on developing the colony itself. The colonists were interested in gaining as much riches as they could, so they could return to their home countries.

4.3.2. Christianity

There were Christians from different denominational backgrounds in Suriname. Besides the Reformed Christians there were Roman Catholics, Lutherans, Labadists and Anglicans. The Reformed Church was the official church.

Between 1668 and 1734, twenty Reformed clergymen served the church in Paramaribo. More than 60 per cent of them died, some in less than a year after their arrival. The situation in the Commewijne, Cottica and Perica was not much different. Suriname became the graveyard of many clergymen. These early pioneers were willing to accept this risk in order to serve the people of God in the colony. The next generation was better prepared to serve the church in this tropical colony. The early death of the clergymen made it very difficult to give the necessary on-going pastoral care and education to the colonists. In an era where the Bible was not readily available, the colonists were left on their own and they developed views that were not necessarily built on a serious study of Scripture.

The number of colonists who settled along the Suriname River declined. This had its impact on the membership of the church in Torarica. In 1700, the church decided to sell what was left of its buildings. Even the Jews left their Jewish Savannah in 1726 and built a synagogue in Paramaribo. The new colonists settled in Commewijne. This led to the growth of the church there.

Paramaribo was also doing well and took over the place of Torarica. The church of Paramaribo acquired a central function and kept the church register of all the churches and a general church register for the whole colony. In order to cater for the need of a church building, it was agreed in 1697 that the church and the council would use the same building. The church could conduct its meetings in the upper room and the council on the lower level.

One of the most important developments towards the end of the seventeenth century was the first general church council meeting. It took place in 1690 and was known as the Conventus Deputatorum. Representatives from all the churches in the colony and two members from the council of police attended the meeting. It was normal within the Reformed tradition to cluster churches in a particular area into a classis. A classis is a regional church meeting. This meeting could take decisions for a group of churches and was above the local church council. A group of classes formed a synod (provincial or nationwide). The Surinamese gathering however was not considered to be a classis, but a Conventus, a meeting.

The meeting of the Conventus took place once a year in the month of February. This initiative was a first step towards a Surinamese Reformed Church. However, the Conventus was not an independent church body. It made recommendations, which had to be sanctioned by the government of the colony and the classis of Amsterdam. The Surinamese church was considered to be part of the classis of Amsterdam. Amsterdam therefore was against a classis for Suriname. The churches in Suriname were allowed to meet, but should not become a cluster of churches on their own. They were to be part of the cluster of Amsterdam. They could not decide for themselves what was best for the churches in the colony. Amsterdam was responsible for the Surinamese church. It had to supply the clergymen, therefore it wanted to remain involved and guide the work in Suriname.

4.3.2.1. Church and the government

Besides the classis of Amsterdam, the church also had to submit to the local government. The government had to sanction all decisions taken by the church's general council. The government also dismissed clergymen with whom it was not happy. Despite this situation, the church and its leaders played an important role in the development of the colony.

After the military coup in 1688, which saw the death of Van Sommelsdijck, the Rev Antonius Ketelaer from Commewijne convinced the military to surrender. After their surrender and punishment, a day of prayer was observed in the country. The murder was seen as a disaster that happened through the hand of God. The nation was therefore called to pray to God, so that in the future he would not visit the colony in a similar way. The nation asked God to grant them a quiet life to glorify his holy name and to sing Psalms to him. It was also remarkable that the dying commander Laurens Verboom, who was killed with Van Sommelsdijck, wrote in his journal that he forgave all those who wounded him in such a way and that he had prepared himself to die as a Christian.

The government regularly proclaimed days of prayer and fasting at specific moments for special events. In 1698, it was decreed that the governor was responsible to make sure that the public servants lived a life that was consistent with the Christian faith. All meetings of the council of police were opened with the reading of a prayer. When weddings were conducted the groom and the bride had to make promises before God and the 'holy church' according to the gospel. The placards that were made by the government were based on the teachings of the Bible, particularly the Ten Commandments.

It was clear that the colony was governed in a theocratic way. Sadly, this theocracy was not successful in Suriname. The government was not able to establish a Christian colony simply by issuing Christian-based decrees. Without downplaying the importance of good laws, it can be argued that morality can never be legislated in the hearts of people. Much more was needed to establish a truly Christian society.

4.3.2.2. Lutherans and Catholics

In the colony there were many German colonists, who were Lutherans. The Lutherans and the Reformed had some theological differences. Therefore the Reformed Churches wanted all Lutherans to become Reformed in order to be part of the church. In 1696, Georgius Bruynenberg came to Suriname as a school teacher. He was requested to sign a form with regard to the teaching he had to give from the Heidelberg Catechism. Because he was Lutheran he did not sign it. The Conventus protested against this at the council of justice. The commissioner of political affairs insisted that the clergymen had to do everything in their power to bring Bruynenberg to a point where he would accept the Reformed confession. In order to keep his job Bruynenberg accepted the Reformed faith. The church started to face more of these problems.

What should happen if Lutheran or Catholic parents wanted to baptise their children? The Conventus decided that in cases where a Catholic father wanted to baptise his child, the church was not going to read three of the baptism questions. These questions had to do with the promise of being faithful to the Reformed religion. The government however, did not agree with this decision. Roman Catholics had to renounce the foundations of Roman Catholicism and accept the Reformed faith.

4.3.2.3. Christianity and the non-European

Towards the end of the seventeenth century, the Reformed Church baptised children who were born from White fathers and Native mothers. In 1698, the Conventus approved the decision to baptise children from Natives and slave mothers under two conditions. In the first place, the White father had to be present. He was required to promise in the presence of two Christian witnesses, that he would educate the child in the Reformed faith. Secondly, the owner of the plantation where the mother of the child lived had to give his permission. In 1699, it was further agreed that such a baptism was to take place at home.

It appeared that the fathers did not keep their promises. The children were not educated in the Christian faith. In 1720, young people in the colony between the ages of eighteen and twenty did not know the content of the catechism. For this reason, the church council approached the judiciary with the request that the foster parents be forced to send their children to the government school. However, this was not successful.

In 1721, the first slave (named Isabella) was accepted as a member of the church in Perica. Isabella's joy in the church was for a short while. According to her, she was despised and mocked by the Whites. Male members of the church wanted to force her into a life of illicit sexual relationships. Because she refused, she was called all sorts of names. At the end, Isabella decided to leave the church and to go back to her previous life. The White members were not impressed with this first-fruit from among the slaves. The fact that Isabella was backslidden was to them clear evidence that the gospel was not meant for the Afro-Surinamese people. It was not good to accept them into the church, since they could not let go of their heathenism. Many years later, the Rev Joannes Kals, a prophetic voice that God raised against the practices of the church, visited Isabella and listened to her side of the story.

4.3.3. Joannes Guiljelmus Kals

Joannes Guiljelmus Kals was an important voice in the history of Christianity. When he arrived in Suriname, he refused to accept slaves as workers on his plantation. He did not consider himself a 'sugar lord', but a clergyman. He was the first Reformed clergyman who clearly spoke out about the preaching of the gospel among the non-Europeans.

Kals came to Suriname in 1731. He completed his theological training in Utrecht, in the Netherlands. While he was on his way to Suriname, he shared his views with the people on board the ship. He spoke about the passage in Romans that says that the fullness of the gentiles will go into God's kingdom, before the whole of Israel will be saved. This clearly referred to the importance of reaching out to the gentiles. Kals also wanted to have an open school to educate Natives' and slaves' children. Upon arrival, the captain of the ship shared Kals' ideas with the governor. The governor was not enthusiastic. In a meeting with Kals, he made it very clear that Kals was not allowed to speak openly about his ideas and he was not even to bring accusations against cursing soldiers. Kals also thought of the relation between the government and the church to be that of Moses (government) and Aaron (church). But the governor did not appreciate that. He was the leader of the colony and he was the head of both the church and the government.

The colonists also had problems with Kals' ideas. In their view, slaves who became Christians might become a threat to the existence of the colony. The stereotypical views of the colonists misrepresented Christianity and were not based on a good knowledge of Scripture. Kals was not against slavery as such. In his view, the church should preach the gospel to the slaves. However, when they became Christians they should remain in their 'bodily bondage', but enjoy spiritual liberty.

In 1732, Kals came into conflict with the government and the church. The reason was the fact that Kals criticised the church for neglecting its calling to preach to the Natives and Afro-Surinamese. Since the church could not contradict this, it tried to find another reason for dismissing Kals. This it found in the relationship between Kals and his wife Anna Twisker. In the early years there was a lot of quarrelling between them, even in public. The church used this to recommend to the government that Kals be expelled from the colony. In 1733, he was defrocked and deported.

Kals was not able to do a lot in the colony because of his short term of service. However, his voice was heard. He made it clear that the gospel was not only for the Whites. The Natives and the Afro-Surinamese were also entitled to education, the gospel and reception into the church. Kals therefore was a good herald for the Moravians. He was a transitional figure and concluded an important era of Christianity in Suriname.

4.4. Conclusion

Due to the hard work of Reformed clergymen like Basseliers and others, the Reformed Church established itself in Suriname. The clergymen served the colonists and their families to the best of their abilities under challenging circumstances. Apart from a few clergymen, the church was not yet ready to proclaim the gospel of the Lord Jesus Christ among the Natives and Afro-Surinamese.

The colonial church had its own challenges to face. In the first place, it had to deal with members who were not devoted to the cause of the gospel and needed to be converted. Secondly, it had to follow the directions given to it by the local government. Its decisions were subjected to the approval of the political leaders, who wanted to establish a theocracy in the colony. This was not successful. Thirdly, it was seen as a branch of the classis of Amsterdam, which was 5,600 miles away. Attempts of the clergymen to establish a Surinamese classis were not successful. The established Reformed Church therefore remained a copy and an annexure of the Dutch Reformed Church in the Netherlands. Its agenda was to take care of the Dutch people in the colony.

CHAPTER 5

Surinamese Protestantism in the Eighteenth Century

5.1. Introduction

This chapter presents a general background to Suriname during the eighteenth century (5.1). It continues to focus on the Lutheran Church (5.2), followed by developments among the Lutheran and Reformed Churches (5.3) and the work of the Moravians (5.4).

5.1.1. Peace treaties and economy

The second half of the eighteenth century saw intensive attacks by the Maroons on the plantations. Governor Jan Jacob Mauricius (1742-1751) knew that fighting against the Maroons would not bring a solution. Therefore, he proposed a peace treaty with them in 1742. This did not come into effect until 1760 and 1762. After these treaties were signed, it looked initially as if the colony would experience some growth.

The economy was very promising. From 1751 onwards, thirty-six million guilders were given in credits to the colony. The credit-providers agreed that the repayment could start after twenty years. However, the colonists mismanaged the capital. Those who received the credits did not travel to the colony, but remained in the Netherlands and appointed others to look after their business. The executors of the plantations locally however did not use the money properly. Most of it was used for travelling and a life of luxury. Another part was invested in coffee plantations. These however did not provide the expected result. Because of this and a crisis at the stock exchange of Amsterdam in 1773, the colony suffered a major setback.

5.1.2. Population

The total population of Suriname, without the Natives and Maroons, in 1738 was estimated at 52,827, of which 1,828 were 'Whites' older than twelve, and 305 younger than twelve. There were 409 'Free Mulattos' older than twelve and 189 under the age of twelve years. The majority of people however were the slaves. There were 40,456 slaves above twelve years and 10,640 under the age of twelve.

Table 11 *The population in 1738*

White	2,133
Mulatto	598
Slaves	51,096
Total	53,827

The estimates of 1791, without the Natives and Maroons, were as follows. There were 2,030 'Christians', of whom 1,080 lived on the plantations and 950 in the city. There were 1,350 Jews in the colony, of whom 1,070 were in the city and 280 on the plantations. There were 58,000 slaves and 1,620 Free men and women.

Table 12 *The population in 1791*

Christians	2,030
Jews	1,350
Slaves	58,000
Free	1,680
Total	63,060

The estimates of 1791 did not indicate how many Free and slaves were Christians. Towards the end of the eighteenth century, the colonial government wanted the Free to play an active role in the upbuilding of the colony. It appeared that most of the plantation owners were not willing to live in Suriname. Therefore, if the colonists wanted to develop the colony, the Free people had to play a big role. The Whites however did not consider them to be on the same level as them. The Free people had to fight to earn that place.

A certain Elisabeth Samson, a Free black woman, had to fight in order to be allowed to marry a White person, Christoph Brabandt the organist of the Reformed Church. The committee for marriage affairs did not know what to do when the two registered to get married. The committee asked for advice from the Netherlands. After three years of waiting, the permission came in 1767. At that time, the bridegroom had already passed away. Samson now decided to marry another White person, Hermanus Daniel Zobre, who was much younger than she was.[1] Samson did not want to marry a White person out of love, but because of the status. Being a wealthy woman in the colony, she wanted to have the same status as the Whites. This however, she never attained. Other members of her family also married White men. These marriages were an exception and not a rule.

For a White person to marry a slave was more difficult. The Rev Paulus Snijderhans, a Reformed clergyman, married a slave named Constantia. Constantia grew up in a Moravian family. The wedding was not approved by the church's council. However, the authorities in the Netherlands approved of the wedding.

The eighteenth century saw the arrival of new Protestant churches in the colony. The Moravians made their first attempt in 1735, and in 1741, the Lutheran Church was officially launched.

5.2. Lutheran Church in Suriname

On 6 May 1740 a group of 71 people signed a petition requesting the court to allow the Lutheran Church to be established in Suriname. In 1741, permission was granted. 'The Church adhering to the unchanged Augsburg

---

1. Cynthia Macleod wrote a well-researched historical novel on the life of Elisabeth Samson, which was translated into English and published unter the title: *The Free Negress Elisabeth*. London: Arcadia Books (2008).

confession, in the colony Suriname, rivers and districts' as the Lutheran Church was known, was established in Suriname.

The first clergyman of the congregation, Johannes Pfaff arrived on 29 October 1742, under the following conditions. The church had to provide his housing. He was allowed to select two Afro-Surinamese men and two Afro-Surinamese women to serve him. Besides his salary, he would receive a freewill offering for other services, such as weddings, baptisms and sick visitations. Since the church did not have its own building it was allowed to use that of the Reformed Church for two years. Its services had to conclude before nine o'clock in the morning.

The new church soon faced problems. What started as a small misunderstanding between the clergyman and the church council grew into a major problem. This led to the closure of the church service. The clergyman, who remarried a rich Reformed widow after his wife died, neglected the church because of the problems and was dismissed in 1745.

A new clergyman, Joannes Henricus Mellinghuijs arrived and started his services on 5 June 1746. Even though his wife died within four months, he continued to serve the church faithfully. In April 1747, he inaugurated the first church building of the Lutheran Church. The church had also built a house for its clergyman and one for the elderly and the orphans. The Lutheran Church had officially established itself in Suriname. In reality however, the predominantly Reformed government only tolerated the Lutheran Church!

5.3. The Protestants in the colony

The relationship between the two churches was not good in the early years. One of the points of contestation was the issue of baptism. The Lutherans were of the opinion that they were allowed to baptise all children who were not yet baptised, if they were requested to do so. The Reformed Church did not accept this view. In their view, the Lutherans should not baptise children of whom one of the parents belonged to the Reformed Church. Furthermore the Lutherans had to announce the baptism ahead of the event.

In the last quarter of the eighteenth century the churches seemed to work better with each other. This was partly due to the efforts of the Governors Bernard Texier (1779-1783) and Jurriaan François de Frederici (1790-1802). In August 1779 for example, Texier made arrangement with the churches to have a day of prayer in both churches. He asked the Reformed Church to hold their Dutch service in the morning and French service in the evening. The Lutherans should have theirs in the afternoon. The governor attended all three meetings. In 1793, De Frederici made an appeal to the Lutherans to make their church building available to the Reformed Church. At that time the building of the Reformed Church needed some repairs. The governor offered to pay the expenses for the use of the Lutheran building from the government fund. One person wrote the following about the religious tolerance in those days:

> Possibly, one will not find a similar place in the whole world where tolerance is so widely accepted and strictly observed as in Suriname. One never hears about religious disputes, everyone worships God in his own way; everybody does what is the best to save his own soul.[2]

The last half of the eighteenth century brought many changes to the Reformed Church. In 1797, the churches in Commewijne and Cottica-Perica were joined with the church of Paramaribo. This was necessary because most of the members who lived in that area had moved to Paramaribo. The attacks of the Ndyuka Maroons were severe on the plantations in the eastern part of the country. At the beginning of the nineteenth century the Reformed Church had only one place of meeting, Paramaribo.

The membership of the church started to include people of colour as well. In 1747, the Afro-Surinamese slave Jan Jacob van Paramaribo was baptised. This opened the door for slaves to enter the Reformed Church. This door however did not appear to be fully open, because when Pieter

---

[2]. This was written by a group of learned Jewish men (Nassy 1791 II:20). They illustrated this with an example given by a Frenchman, who had dinner with a family consisting of Gentiles, Jews, Roman Catholics, Greek Orthodox and Calvinists. This freedom may have been due to the influence of the changes in Europe (see 6.1.).

Christoffel Johanson baptised two slaves in 1767, he was questioned about this move by the authorities. Around 1791, many Free Afro-Surinamese people became members of the church.

The Reformed Church was also the first to baptise a Maroon. On 9 December 1770 the first was baptised during the sermon in front of a full church. Earlier, on 3 December he had confessed his faith together with a Free Mulatto. He was given the name Jan Abini. Among his own people, he was known as Dyaku. He was the son of the Saramaccan paramount chief Abini, who signed the peace treaty with the colonial government.

Johan Hendrik Mellinghuijs served the Lutheran Church for almost twenty years, from 1746 to 1765. On March 4, 1762 he baptised the very first Afro-Surinamese man, who was given the name Christian Schöning. Ten days later he baptised the first Afro-Surinamese woman. She was named Wilhelmina Christina van Graafstad. However, these baptised Afro-Surinamese people did not become full members of the church. It took until 22 April 1800 for the first Afro-Surinamese to become a full member of the Lutheran Church. And yet, this event did not fully open the door of the Lutheran Church for the Afro-Surinamese people. In 1814, a deacon of the church resigned from his task when Johan Andrea Koops accepted a Mulatto girl as member of the church. The deacon felt that the girl was not educated properly in the Christian religion. Fortunately the other members of the church council disagreed with the deacon.

5.4. The Moravian missions

5.4.1. Introduction

On 20 December 1735 three young men from the Moravian Brothers, Georg Piesch, Georg Berwig and Heinrich Christof von Larisch, arrived in Suriname. Their mission was to see if, while doing their normal work, it was possible to win some 'Wilds' (Natives) and 'Moors' (Afro-Surinamese slaves) for the Lamb. This first attempt to establish the Moravian Church in Suriname was unsuccessful. After three unsuccessful efforts, the missionaries moved to Berbice. In Suriname the Moravian Church established itself successfully in 1765, after three more attempts.

Table 13 *Moravian attempts to establish itself in Suriname*[3]

	Mission leader	Beginning	End
First	Georg Berwig	1735	1736
Second	Georg Berwig	1736	1739
Third	Johann Reynier	1740	1741
Fourth	Wilhelm Zander	1742	1745
Fifth	Lodewijk Christoffel Dehne	1754	1764
Sixth	Christoph Kersten	1765	Permanent

The Moravians were the first Christian church to start missions among the non-Europeans. This section will study their missions among the Natives, Saramaccans and Slaves.

5.4.2. Missions among the Natives

5.4.2.1. Introduction

Early sources spoke of the Natives as a people without religion or a people with a vague knowledge of a Supreme Being. The Natives feared an evil spirit, the devil, who did them much harm. The worldview of the Native was different from that of the Europeans. Most of the descriptions given by Westerners of the Native religion and/or culture were based on an ethnocentric view of culture. Therefore it was difficult to have factual knowledge of the religion and the culture of these people in the earlier period.

5.4.2.2. Altona in Suriname

The missionaries started their work among the Natives in Suriname in 1743, in the north-eastern part of the country where they built their first mission station called Altona. The Natives who lived in or passed through that area

---

3. This list gives the name of one missionary. Often there were more.

were Caribs. This work remained unsuccessful for more than two years and was closed down after one missionary who joined the team, and also the missionary helper named Frans died. After its closure, it was decided that the missionaries should join the work at the station Pilgerhut which started in 1738 among the Arawaks.

5.4.2.3. *Pilgerhut in Berbice*

Pilgerhut was in Berbice, a part of what is now known as Guyana. At that time, it was a Dutch colony. The missionaries could move freely from one part of the colony to the other. We will therefore discuss this work as a part of the Moravian mission in Suriname.

The missionaries Lodewijk Christoffel Dehne and Johann Güttner started the work. They learned the language of the Arawaks and taught some of the Arawaks German. With the help of a twelve-year-old Arawak boy, whom they called Jantje, they started to gather a list of Arawak words.

When more missionaries joined the team in Pilgerhut, they expanded their visits to villages of other Native tribes such as the Warau, Akawaio and the Caribs. However, the work among the Arawaks was their primary concern. The first Native was baptised on 31 March 1748 and was renamed Hanna. Hanna was a respected mother to all in the Native community. The step that she took encouraged others to follow her. Within two months after her baptism, thirty-eight others were also baptised. This was an encouragement to the missionaries. However, the language barrier continued to be a problem for them and they could not communicate freely with the people. The missionaries used a half-Native boy to help them when they were writing their sermons. The need for more in-depth knowledge of the language became evident when a missionary visitor took the boy with him to America and afterwards to Europe. One of the early Arawak converts was Jephta, a converted leader of the traditional religion. He became an important helper for the missionaries and was a successful evangelist. The same was also true for Esther, who undertook many missionary trips.

In October 1748, Theophilus Salomo Schumann joined the group in Pilgerhut. He was a very gifted man and was able to preach his first trial sermon five months later in Arawak, without the help of a native speaker. With the help of Jephta and other Native workers, he worked on the translation of the Bible into the Arawak language. Schumann had the opportunity to baptise about four hundred converts in twelve years. He is therefore called the 'Apostle of the Arawaks'.[4]

The Arawaks who were baptised joined the missionaries at the mission station, and by the end of 1750, about 300 Arawaks were living there. In February 1753, during the Helferkonferenz (Helpers' conference) it was decided that Natives were allowed to lead church services and to undertake mission trips. The Natives who knew their own culture very well, were allowed to share in the mission work. This was a new direction in the work of the Moravians.

The fact that the Natives lived at the station also caused many problems. Sometimes the missionaries witnessed that baptised Arawaks were drunk or behaved in a way which was not appropriate for a Christian. These Christians were excluded from the fellowship. From outside, soldiers and slaves regularly attacked and destroyed the fields of the Arawaks who lived in Pilgerhut. When one Native spoke with the governor about what was happening, he and the other Natives were advised to leave the missionaries and the attacks would stop. Instead of listening to the governor, the Natives were more determined to stay with the missionaries and share in the missions work. Because the attacks continued, the Natives had to look for other places to grow their crops.

Starting from 1760-1762, the work in Berbice was under much pressure. Most of the Arawaks moved to the mission station at Saron, others died because of an epidemic and of a shortage of food. The 'Apostle of the Arawaks' died in 1760. During a revolt of the slaves in Berbice in 1762, Pilgerhut was destroyed.

---

4. Before Schumann came, the missionaries had gathered about 500 words, but a systematic study of the language was not done. Schumann was the first to start the work on a German-Arawak dictionary and a grammar in 1752. Both, however, were damaged in 1762 during a revolt of the Berbice slaves. It was, however, possible to publish them posthumously in 1892 in Paris.

5.4.2.4. Saron

In 1757, the mission started a new station called Saron in Suriname at the Saramacca River. In that same year, some people left Pilgerhut and came to live at Saron. In 1759, the Caribs started to visit the missionaries and Arawaks at Saron. Since some of the baptised Arawaks knew the Carib language, they were able to speak about the Saviour with the Caribs in their own language, with positive results. Caribs came to live closer to the station. In January 1761, however, Maroons attacked and destroyed the station. The missionaries left but by the end of January they returned and resumed their work. The mission station had to be closed down in September 1779, because of problems, quarrels among the Natives and attacks of the Maroons.

One of the reasons why the Maroons attacked the station was because of the following course of events. When the government signed the peace treaty with the Maroons in 1760 and 1762, it was agreed that the Maroons would no longer hide slaves who escaped from the plantations. However, a group of Maroons kept protecting slaves and the Dutch soldiers pursued them. One of the Natives, whose hammock was stolen by a Maroon, showed the soldiers the way to the camp of the Maroons and some were killed. The Maroons then wanted to take revenge on the Natives and attacked Saron.

5.4.2.5. Ephrem

In 1757, the mission from Pilgerhut started a new station at the Corantine River, which they called Ephrem. Many Arawaks lived in that area, but they were not open to the gospel. For almost two years, a missionary was the only one living in Ephrem. After some successful encounters with the missionary, some people came to live there. During the slave revolt of Berbice in 1762, this small group of people had to flee from Ephrem, just like the group of Pilgerhut.

5.4.2.6. Hoop

In 1764, a new group of missionaries visited Ephrem and decided to start a new station on the Corantine River. This station was called Hoop. By the end of 1768, there were seventy-five Arawaks living there with the missionaries. When the work at Saron was closed, Hoop was the only 'hope' of the missionaries to reach the Natives. The work grew and even Natives from other tribes joined them.

Johann Jakob Gottlieb Fischer started a school in Hoop just one month after his arrival in March 1789. He taught a few adults and thirty children how to read and write. Most of the children, twenty, were boys.

The Natives were impressed with this project. They decided to construct a larger building for the school. The school also started to teach the Natives other skills and crafts, including woodworking. The men prepared planks, balks and roof battens that were sold in Berbice and Paramaribo. The women and the girls prepared hammocks. Fischer made sure that all those who were involved received payment for their work. The schoolchildren received a stipend for taking care of the village square and the garden of the mission house. The mission station grew plantain, vegetables and cassava on a large scale. It also reared cows, sheep and chickens.

The activities at Hoop motivated Natives to come and stay there. Within a short period of time, there were 300 people living there. Fischer trained a personal assistant, who became involved in the school and Bible translation work. Unfortunately, this assistant, Bernhard, died very young. The time of Fischer was seen as a revival among the Natives.

In 1795, the first Warau Native was baptised. In 1796 and 1797 the work experienced a tremendous growth, with 427 Natives, of whom 171 were baptised, living in the areas surrounding the station.

From 1798 onwards, the mission's work among the Arawaks started to deteriorate. This happened after Fischer was put out of the country, because he had transported a few English-speaking people to Berbice. These men were British, who pretended to be Americans. Fischer's deed was seen as treason against the state since the Netherlands, of which Berbice was a colony, and Britain were officially at war. The leader of the Moravian mission at that time, Hans Wied, did not support Fischer's plea, since the relationship between Fischer and the other colleagues was not good. Fischer and his family left Suriname.

5.4.2.7. *Conclusion*

In May 1808, during the Helferkonferenz in Paramaribo, it was decided to stop the work among the Arawaks. Almost seventy years of missionary work among the Natives, at the cost of the lives of twenty-nine missionaries, came to an end. Although the Moravians stopped their work among the Natives after almost seven decades of missionary work, they tried to stay in touch with them.

Table 14 *Overview of missionary stations among the Natives*

Station	Beginning	Closing
Altona	1743	1745
Pilgerhut	1740	1762
Saron	1757	1779
Ephrem	1757	1762
Hoop	1764	1808

Were the Moravians successful in their work among the Natives? A few issues should be raised here before we attempt to answer this question. In the first place, the relation between gospel and culture should be addressed. Was it possible that the difference in culture between the Natives and the missionaries contributed to some of the problems that this mission faced? This issue was not a primary concern of early missionaries.

In the second place there was the issue of the relationship between Whites and the people of colour. The work of the early missionaries among the people of colour was ground-breaking. They introduced Christianity to the indigenous people. They also had to prove themselves to be different from their fellow Westerners, who failed to live according to Christian standards. Most writers have criticised the conduct of Westerners in Suriname. The missionaries, therefore, had to present biblical Christianity to the people in their preaching and correct the planters' wrong practice of Christianity. The missionaries were very often a thorn in the flesh of the planters.

A third problem was the relationship among the missionaries themselves. There were tensions among them. The Natives who lived there with them saw these as well. One missionary for example had an intimate relationship with a Native woman and was therefore excommunicated.

Fourthly, the Maroons and other Native tribes were a threat to the missions.

Despite these factors a few things referred to the positive effects of the gospel on the Natives.

In the first place, the fact that a nomadic tribe like the Arawaks lived for many years at one place with the missionaries and enjoyed the Lord's Supper can be seen as God's work. The appeal of the gospel was stronger than their nomadic drive.

In the second place, there was a numeric success. In 1756, 121 of the 367 baptised Natives were taking communion in Pilgerhut; 21 members from the congregation were 'Helpers'. During the seventy years in which missionary work was conducted in Pilgerhut (Berbice), Saron (Saramacca), Ephrem and Hoop (Corantine), 888 Natives were baptised.

Thirdly, the initiative of the Natives to take the gospel to their own tribes was an evidence of the fruits of the mission. The Moravians trained local workers, who played a critical role in the mission work. Although in those days this was not the general approach, the Moravians saw the importance of it.

5.4.3. Missions among the Saramaccans

5.4.3.1. Introduction

The Saramaccan Maroons were descended from African slaves who escaped slavery. Some of these slaves were able to escape from the plantations not long after their arrival in Suriname. They settled in the jungle of Suriname and became an enemy of the government in the city. The date when the first group escaped is not certain. One person identified them with a group of slaves that belonged to a British captain Marshall, who came to Suriname in 1630. Most scholars today consider the date of escape of the core group of Saramaccans to be 1690. In that year a group of slaves killed their Jewish master Immanuel Machado and escaped. A large group joined the Saramaccans in the forest during 1712, when the Frenchman

Cassard attacked Suriname. These slaves lived in the jungle and built settlements there.

Saramaccans spoke a Portuguese-based African Surinamese language. It differed from most of the other African Surinamese languages, such as Sranantongo and Ndyuka, which were English-based.

According to Saramaccan oral traditions the gods, whom they carried from Africa, helped them in the war against the 'White people'. Through divination, they were able to find out when the government army was going to attack them. The gods also prepared them ritually to be able to disappear from the sight of the enemy.

The Saramaccans are a strong-believing people. Their religion has its roots in Africa. Within the Saramaccan pantheon, an Upper Being and various others gods exist, such as bush and water gods. Some deceased ancestors are also considered gods, but in the sense of an avenging spirit, *kunu*. Other deceased ancestors are consulted as guides in every area of life. The deceased ancestors are still present among the living. The gods are everywhere and should be reverenced by the people by keeping their sabbaths, bringing offerings, and offering prayers. Some of the religious laws of the Saramaccans resemble the holiness laws in the Old Testament, such as the position of a woman during her period and after childbirth. These could have been taken from their Jewish masters, but possibly they have African roots. On the other hand, practices such as ancestor worship, for example, shaving of the head for a dead person, seem to reflect their African heritage. This African heritage is treasured by the Saramaccans and they will not let go of it.

Coincidence is non-existent in the Saramaccan worldview. The gods guide every aspect of their daily lives. Besides the gods, enemies can also cause bad things to happen to people. For example, recently a young nurse died of AIDS. His family felt that people who wanted to take his position worked witchcraft on him and killed him.

When the government realised that it was impossible to destroy the Maroons, it decided to sign peace treaties with them. In 1762, at the recommendation of the Ndyuka Maroons who had signed a treaty two years before, the Saramaccans signed a treaty with the government. This opened the door for missionaries to go and live among them.

5.4.3.2. Missions among the Saramaccans

In December 1765, three Moravian missionaries, Thomas Jones, Lodewijk Christoffel Dehne and Rudolf Stoll arrived in the territory of the Saramaccans. The mission's work started in the Saramaccan village Senthea Creek. Jones, however, died on February 7, 1766, as the first of many missionaries who would lay down their lives in the service of the Lamb among the Saramaccans. The two other brothers continued to study the language and the people. The paramount chief Abini was very helpful to the missionaries. In August 1766 a son-in-law of Abini brought his twelve-year old son Skipio to Stoll, so that he could teach him how to read and write. Soon after that Grego followed. Grego would prove to be a good student, who later became the writer of the community.

In 1768, the Saramaccans moved to a new village, which was called Kwama. On May 13, 1770, brother Stoll preached his first message in the Saramaccan language. The message was about God, who came as a man and died on the cross. This was difficult for the Saramaccans to accept. In their worldview, a person who was killed become an avenging spirit (kunu or god), just for the group that killed him. Since avenging spirits were difficult to appease, nobody would want to take up the service of such a spirit voluntarily. But Stoll continued to preach the message of the Lamb to them, and he won some for the Saviour. The first was Alabi, who was baptised as the first-fruit on 6 January 1771.[5] He took the Christian name Johannes. On the day of his baptism, he made the following confession before the assembled people:

> Jesus Christ can and wants only to help us. I believe in him, and I foreswear with all my heart the works and service of Satan, and wish until the end of my days only to be with Jesus.[6]

The case of Alabi was important. He put his gods to a test before he took such an important step. It appeared that the God of the Whites was the real God. In the judgment of Price, the decision of Alabi was based on a

---

5. He is sometimes called Arabi or Arrabini.
6. Cited in Price 1990:126.

disappointment. Just a few years earlier his father Abini was killed in a war against the Matawais. Madanfo one of the powerful gods, brought from Africa, did not prevent the Matawais from killing Abini. Although Alabi may have been disappointed in Madanfo, the power of the gospel cannot be resisted. God may have used these things to open the eyes of Alabi to the work that his Son did for him at the Cross. Alabi was especially touched by the Saviour, for what he had done for him on the Cross. Alabi became an important asset to the missionaries. He helped them to prepare dictionaries of the language and to translate books of the Bible and hymns.

In November 1773, the community moved to a new village, which was called Gwafu Bambai (Bambai I). The number of Saramaccans becoming Christians remained very low. Around twelve people were normally attending the church. The others remained hostile towards the religion of the Whites. Alabi's mother, who was the oldest woman in the village, had warned the women not to join the church. After Alabi and the missionary spoke with her, she changed her opinion and a few women started to attend the church. Due to a growing number of deaths in the village, the group moved to another place. The Saramaccans attributed the high number of deaths to the missionary, who cut down a tree that the people were venerating.

Life in the new village, Awana Bambai (Bambai II), was not better for the small Christian community. There was an on-going battle with the spiritual leaders from the traditional religion. At the end of the eighteenth century that religion saw a revival. Some of the Christians continued to participate in these practices. Their lifestyle was a thorn in the flesh of the missionaries.

There were also problems with the attitude of the missionaries. In 1791, it appeared that a missionary had sexual affairs with various Saramaccan women. Instead of being put under discipline in the Saramaccan Church, the leadership of the church decided to send him to Europe. Another missionary decided to accept the task of government representative. This brought the missionary and his work under suspicion and created tension in his relationship with the Saramaccans. In 1813, the last missionary left the Saramaccan community and the mission decided to close the work.

Johannes Alabi, the first-fruit, and Christiaan Grego, who knew how to read and write, became the leaders of the church. In 1818, the group of Christians left Awana Bambai and settled at Ginge Bambai (Bambai III), where Johannes Alabi died in 1821; his friend Christian Grego followed three years later. When these leaders died, the church became weak.

5.4.3.3. Conclusion

What was the result of almost sixty years of missionary work among the Saramaccans?

Table 15 *Overview of missionary stations among the Saramaccans*

Station	Beginning	Closing
Senthea Creek	1765	1768
Kwama	1768	1773
Gwafu Bambai (Bambai I)	1773	1785/86
Awana Bambai (Bambai II)	1786	1818
Ginge Bambai (Bambai III)	1818	1824

Up to 1813, when the last missionary left, eighty-three Saramaccans were baptised, twenty-three men, ten women, twenty-six boys and twenty-four girls.

In evaluating missions among the Saramaccans in this early period, it should be taken into consideration that there was a hostile situation between the Saramaccans and the Whites. Could these people, who called themselves missionaries, be trusted? Were they not a working arm of the colonial government? When the missionaries came to the Saramaccans, the peace treaty had just been signed. The efforts of the missionaries were therefore to be commended. The number of missionaries, who died among the Saramaccans before the missions were closed, testified of a great love for the cause of the Saviour. The number of people who were willing to accept the new faith of the missionaries was not great. But there were lasting fruits in people such as Alabi and Grego. They were able to lead the church when the leadership in the city no longer sent missionaries to them.

Despite these positive results, the approach of the missionaries among the Saramaccans should be questioned. Missionaries tried to isolate the believers from their fellow non-believers. This method was successful among the nomadic Arawaks. But among the Saramaccans it caused much tension and division. Saramaccans lived more like a community and people who left the community were seen as traitors. Also, taking away the believing Saramaccans from their original villages meant that those villages were left without a witness for Christ.

The church was seen as a family activity, since it worked among one of the twelve clans. Because Johannes Alabi was from the Awana-clan, the church was connected with this clan. Later on the Dombi-clan was added.

5.4.4. Missions among the slaves

Missions among the slaves received much attention from researchers in Suriname. The slaves were descendants of Africans, who remained on the plantations. At the abolition of slavery, most of them left the plantations and lived in Paramaribo, the 'City'. In Suriname, they were known as Stadsnegers, 'City Negroes' or 'Creoles'. There were other African Surinamese such as the Para and Coronie 'Negroes'.[7]

Missions conducted among the Afro-Surinamese slaves by White people could never have been easy. The slaves saw every White person as one who abused them. The missionaries had to prove that they were different. This could never be done in words only, but above all with deeds. The work of the Moravians among these people should be seen from this perspective. The missionaries saw the slaves not as 'goods' as was the common view in those days, but as valuable persons loved by the Saviour of the World.

Missions among the Afro-Surinamese people started successfully in 1765, by the missionaries Christoph Kersten, Christiaan Schmidt and Gottlieb Krohn. As was the case with the previous missionaries, these missionaries started their own trades in order to earn money and support the missions. One of the missionaries was a tailor. The quality of his work helped him to earn respect from the colonial government and most of the

---

7. As mentioned earlier, in this book, all of them will be referred to as 'Afro-Surinamese people'.

White colonists. This caused his business to grow and to become a well-established company in Suriname, known for its quality. The company, C Kersten & Co, used the proceeds to support the work of the church. It serves as a model for contemporary integration of business goals and the missionary calling of the church, known as 'business as missions'.

On July 21, 1767, the first Afro-Surinamese slave, a helper to the tailor, was baptised. He took the new name Christiaan Cupido. In that same year, eighteen other persons were baptised. That year, the first 'Afro-Surinamese church' was formed and met in the house of the missionaries. This work grew and in 1778 a building was erected.

The language that was used in the church service was Sranantongo, the lingua franca of the colony. Missionaries translated hymns and Scripture portions that were used in the church services. A complete manuscript of the whole New Testament was available in 1783. A harmony of the four Gospels was printed in 1816 by the Dutch Bible Society, followed by the whole New Testament in 1829, printed by the British and Foreign Bible Society.

With the small beginning in Paramaribo, the missionaries started to visit the plantations outside of the capital city. Slaves were baptised in various plantations. In 1791, the membership of the church in Paramaribo was 254 and in the surrounding plantations 100.

Table 16 *Moravian Church membership in 1791*

Paramaribo	254
Plantations: Sommelsdijck (Fairfield, Breukelward)	100
Bambai (Saramaccans)	25
Hoop (Natives)	174

It was difficult for the missionaries to maintain contact with the new Christians, due to lack of cooperation from the plantation owners. Many plantation owners still believed that slaves should remain in their sins and continue serving their masters. They were not allowed to share the honour of being their brothers and sisters in Christ. The resistance of the plantation owners, prevented missionaries from discipling the new converts properly.

Besides these problems, the missionaries suffered from various sicknesses, some even died. They were able to reach some of the slaves with the gospel of Jesus Christ, the Lamb of God.

The problems however were much more than the successes. Just like what was done before with the Native (1808) and Saramaccan (1813) missions, the Creole mission was also stopped at the plantations around Paramaribo. In 1818, the only mission station of the Moravians where missionaries were active in Suriname was Paramaribo.

The question of why slaves joined the church remains open. Was it because of the message that was preached? Or was it because membership of a church gave them certain privileges? The answer to this question is not simple. The preaching of the missionaries by word and deed was effective, because slaves came to know Christ as their *Helpiman* 'Helper, Redeemer'. The opportunity to express their faith and emotions in singing probably was a great attraction. The existence of Christian churches was an evidence of the reaction of the Afro-Surinamese people to the grace of Christ.

5.5. Conclusion

Towards the end of the eighteenth century, Christianity in Suriname was no longer the religion of the Whites. Natives and Afro-Surinamese people received the gospel. Christianity became the religion of some of these people as well. The Afro-Surinamese and Native churches were in their infancy and had to survive on their own, for various reasons. The seed planted started to grow, but it did not become a tree yet. The nineteenth century would bring better hope for the Moravian missionaries.

CHAPTER 6

The Roman Catholic Church and the Beginning of the Nineteenth Century

6.1. Introduction

The first attempt of the Roman Catholic Church to establish itself in Suriname in the seventeenth century failed. Even though there were many Catholics in the colony, the predominantly Reformed leadership of the colony did not allow them to start their own denomination. It was almost a hundred years after the first attempt that the church received permission again in 1785 to establish itself in Suriname. This change cannot be understood apart from the political and social situation in Europe at that time. The influence of the Enlightenment philosophy and afterwards the French Revolution, with its message of freedom, brotherhood and equality were also felt in the colony, because some prominent citizens spread these ideals through books and literary societies. Around the same time the freemasonry was introduced in Suriname. In 1775, the first theatre and in 1785, the first literary society were founded. A prominent Jew donated his large library to the literary society. The government realised that the colony could no longer be governed as a Calvinistic Christian colony. Many colonists were characterised by unbelief and religious indifference. This led to more tolerance of people of other religious persuasions.

This freedom however was not visible everywhere. Governor De Frederici passed a law in 1795 that forbade civilians from attending meetings in which human rights were discussed. He was afraid that the slaves would abuse the notion of freedom and organise an uprising of slaves against the White oppressors.

Suriname was governed by the British from 1651-1667. In 1667, it was taken over by the Dutch. After 1668, various European nations tried to conquer the colony. Whenever there was a war in Europe, the colonies in the New World were in danger. In 1793, France declared war on Britain. Two years later, the Dutch joined the French. This had consequences for Suriname. In 1793, slavery was abolished in the neighbouring French colony, French Guyana, due to the ideals of the French Revolution.[1] Now that the Netherlands had joined France, the same had to happen in its colonies. The colonists in Suriname however were not open to these French ideas, and certainly not the equality of all people, including the Afro-Surinamese.

Another consequence of the war between Britain and France was that the British could attack the French and Dutch colonies overseas. This happened in August 1799. Governor de Frederici handed over the colony to the British without resistance. With a short break between 1802 and 1804, Suriname was a British colony again up to 1816. In that year, Suriname was given back to the Netherlands. The Netherlands had to give away the present-day Guyana, which was their colony, to the British.[2]

At the beginning of the nineteenth century, the Netherlands became the 'Kingdom of the Netherlands' with a new constitution. The new constitution gave the king more authority, including the rule of the colonies. The colonies came under the direct rule of King Willem I. From that time on, up to 1848, the king had to appoint the governors personally.

6.2. *The Roman Catholic Church in Suriname*

The Catholics in Suriname were aware of the developments in Europe and saw opportunities for change. They therefore tried to get a priest to the colony. Joannes Gerardus Lemmers, who was born in Suriname, may have played a critical role in this new attempt. Lemmers was born of

---

[1]. Napoleon reintroduced slavery in 1802.
[2]. It consisted of the following places: Berbice, Essequibo and Demerara.

Protestant parents, but became a Catholic at a young age. After his training he was consecrated as a priest in 1761 at the age of twenty-six. In the Netherlands he approached the General States on behalf of the Catholic Church. Lemmers himself did not come to Suriname, instead in October 1786 Albertus van Doornik and Adrianus Kerstens arrived. The conditions under which the Catholic Church was allowed to establish itself were very strict. It was not allowed to have more than one church in Paramaribo. It should meet in an ordinary house, had to take care of its own poor and should not convert slaves. Processions were not allowed and priests should not walk in their robes on the street. If the priests refused to adhere to these conditions they were going to be expelled from the colony. On 1 April 1787, the church dedicated a house at the Wagenwegstraat in Paramaribo for its church services. The membership of the church consisted of 400 military personnel and 250 colonists.

As was the case with the Lutheran Church when it established itself in Suriname, the two priests and the church council had difficulties working together. Among the two priests there were also differences of approach. Kerstens left Suriname the same year and Van Doornik died. A new priest arrived in 1788. Contrary to his predecessors he was able to work very well with the council. He expanded the work of the church to Voorzorg in Saramacca where the church started a leprosarium. This second attempt to establish the church came to an end in March 1793, due to financial problems. The priest left and the members were without a priest again.

In 1810, the sixty-two-year-old priest Jacobus Schinck undertook a third attempt to establish the church in Suriname. Schinck had worked for thirty years in Curacao and knew the tropics very well. He started a school and received permission to print a catechism. In 1815, the membership of the church consisted of 340 colonists, 60 Coloureds and 30 Afro-Surinamese people. But this attempt was also not successful.

A fourth attempt was made in 1817 by Paulus Antonius Wennekers and Ludovicus van der Horst.

Table 17 *Catholic attempts to establish itself in Suriname*[3]

	Clergy	Beginning	End
First	Frederikus van der Hofstadt	1683	1686
Second	Albertus van Doornik	1786	1793
Third	Jacobus Schinck	1810	1816
Fourth	Paulus Antonius Wennekers	1817	Permanent

With their arrival the church established itself in the colony. In the Netherlands, the king had declared freedom of religion. This gave the Catholics a legal right to operate freely in the colony. Despite the religious freedom, some colonists did not allow the priests to work on their plantations. In 1819 the priests wrote a letter to all the Catholic plantation owners, in which they indicated their willingness to serve them. Wennekers also wrote a letter to the general public, in which he asked for a better lifestyle among Christians and the members of the Roman Catholic Church. A better lifestyle of the Christians would have a positive impact on the slaves. Mister E van den Berg was a devoted Roman Catholic and member of the church council. He was also a member of the court of police and the administrator of about 20 plantations. The owners of the plantations were in the Netherlands. Van den Berg did not allow the priests to visit the slaves on the plantations that he managed. This was true for other Catholic plantation owners and administrators as well.

In 1819, Father Wennekers requested permission from King Willem I for slaves to get married officially. Furthermore he requested that slave couples who were married in church should not be sold as individuals. Up to that time they were sold as individuals. The slaves had their own wedding traditions, but the government and the Christian churches did not recognise these.[4] Wennekers' request was not honoured. The government argued that slaves were not considered common citizens and could therefore not be joined in a civil wedding. They did not have the freedom to

---

3. This list gives the name of one person. Often there were more.

4. These marriage traditions are still found among the Maroons. It was normal for church leaders among the Saramaccans to marry the same wife three times: 1) according to the Saramaccan marital traditions; 2) in the church and 3) before a public officer.

make a contract. On top of that, they would live above their social position, would no longer accept the authority of their masters and would never reject the worship of idols. The reaction from the government was given at the recommendation of, among others, the Dutch Reformed minister, Hendrik Uden Masman.

The priests reorganised the school that Father Jacobus Schinck started by preparing regulations for it and teaching classes. They started missions work among the lepers in Voorzorg in Saramacca. In 1820 Wennekers baptised a few Native children at the request of a Native chief. This however did not lead to a systematic missions work among the Natives.

Wennekers learned the Sranantongo language and worked actively in Paramaribo, Coronie and Nickerie. Within five years he prepared a catechism in Sranantongo. His catechism, with some songs, was published in March 1822.[5] One of these songs was sung when Wennekers requested that a *kankantri* (cotton tree), which the slaves venerated, be cut down on the plantation La Resource in Saramacca. Wennekers died in 1823 and Van der Horst in 1825. They were able to establish the Roman Catholic Church in Suriname. They worked in Paramaribo and on plantations in other districts such as Saramacca and Coronie. The translation of the catechism into Sranantongo laid the foundation for work among the slaves. What is the result of the work done between 1817 and 1826?

Table 18 *Statistics of the Catholic Church: 1817 and 1826*

	Baptism	**Marriages**	**First Communion**
Paramaribo	1,182	74	64
Coronie	141	17	2
Voorzorg (Lepers)	96	12	
Total	1,419	103	66

---

5. The title translated is: Roman Catholic Cathecism or a short synopsis of the Christian teaching in Sranantongo for the Colony Suriname, with prayer for the lay baptism, the morning- and evening prayers, as they are prayed daily in the RCC of Paramaribo, with additional prayers, litanies and hymns.

The Propagande Fide of the Roman Catholic Church elevated the Surinamese work to an Apostolic Prefecture. The first apostolic prefect was Martinus van de Weyden. This was the first step towards independence in this mission's area.

6.3. Roman Catholics and Protestants

How were relations between the Roman Catholics and Protestants after the Catholics established themselves? In 1818, Uden Masman of the Reformed Church accused Father Wennekers of proselytism. According to him Wennekers tried to persuade a slave who did her confession in the Reformed Church to join the Catholic Church. In a letter to Wennekers, Uden Masman threatened to call upon the 'worldly powers' to address this deed. The priest replied by saying that the woman belonged to the Catholic Church and that he was not afraid of the intimidations of the pastor. It was not clear what happened afterwards.

Wennekers also wrote a letter to the Lutheran Church in response to an invitation. The Lutheran Church invited the Roman Catholic Church to attend the farewell sermon of Rev Johan Andrea Koop on 23 July 1820 and the inauguration sermon of Rev Arend Meyer on 30 July 1820. Pater Wennekers did not accept the invitation and the reason for that according to him was not because he had mass at the same time. He gave an open and honest reason for his refusal. According to him it was generally known that the Catholic Church would fellowship with people of other religious persuasion at a social level, but never at a religious level. This was not because they did not love others. It was because of the schism that had taken place.

> According to Christian love we must rightly regret your separation from our Church. We must not give you the impression that we approved of your separation. We do not want you to be of the view, by us having religious fellowship with you, that the old mother Church stopped to be a true

mother and no longer maintains its noble character towards an unlawful slave (Bossers 1884:139).

Father Wennekers and the Roman Catholic Church were not willing to have what he called 'only an outward and short fellowship'. They were longing for the 'general fellowship and unity, which the divine Bible described'.

Wennekers also wrote a letter to the Moravians. In April 1821, he wrote to missionary Thomas Langballe, who was about to leave Suriname for the United States of America. The approach in this letter was different than that to the Lutherans. He spoke about things that were missing in the Moravian Church. Wennekers spoke about the missions of the apostles. The apostles were sent by the Lord Jesus Christ himself. The Bible and the traditions did not speak about other people who were sent by him directly. The Moravians were therefore not sent directly by God. Their missions did not come through the apostolic line, which was kept in the Catholic Church. Therefore, the Moravians were not permitted to preach the word. In his letter, Wennekers referred to Rom 10:15, which read: 'And how are they to preach unless they are sent?' (NET).

He also spoke about the need of reunification. He recommended that the Protestants take the first step towards that. They were the ones who separated themselves from the church.

The reaction of the Protestants on this matter is not clear. History however made it clear that the 'great unification in Christ' did not come in Suriname. The ways of the Catholics and Protestants in Suriname were very far from each other.

6.4. At the beginning of the nineteenth century

The first half of the nineteenth century was remembered for the two fierce blazes that had broken out in Paramaribo. The first one was in 1821 and the second in 1832. The first fire destroyed many houses and buildings in Paramaribo, including the church buildings of the Reformed and the Roman Catholic Churches. The second fire destroyed the building of the

Lutheran Church. Miraculously, the building of the Moravian Church was spared.

6.4.1. Under British rule

The re-arrival of the British gave the Anglican Church in Suriname a renewed presence. In 1805, Governor Sir Charles Green requested that the Lutheran Church make its building available to the Anglican Church for worship on Sundays. The Anglicans were also allowed to make use of the building of the Roman Catholics at the expense of the government. During the term of office of Governor Pinson Bonham (1811-1816) the planter clergyman Rev Richard Austin was appointed as the official clergyman of the Anglican Church. Austin received the authority to baptise, marry and officiate at funeral ceremonies of the British in the colony.

One of the lasting benefits that Suriname received from this time of British rule was the result of the struggle of the abolitionists. The abolitionists fought against slavery and wanted to abolish it. Now that Suriname was a British colony, they called attention to the plight of the slaves. It was an open secret that slaves in the Dutch colonies were treated in a cruel way. On 1 January 1808, the transatlantic slave trade was abolished. This had consequences for the plantations and led to a shortage of slaves. Before, slaves were mistreated and if they died, the owner would buy another one. This was no longer possible and due to the shortage another abuse of the slaves became prevalent. They had to work much harder than before and this led to illness and the death of many. The colonists therefore went to the illegal slave market to purchase slaves. It was estimated that around 1,000 slaves were smuggled into the country annually.

6.4.2. The population

At the beginning of the nineteenth century Suriname was still suffering from the influence of absenteeism. Most of the plantation owners were living outside of the country. Their plantations were directed by people who wanted to become rich quickly and then leave the colony. This new group was not the same as the early settlers or those in America and South

Africa. The Europeans in those countries settled there. The new directors in Suriname were not willing to strive for the independence of the colony or for the formation of the nation. They were fortune seekers. The colony was just a raw-material producing area for the benefit of the colonisers abroad. This had its impact on the development of the colony.

The true Surinamese were people who were not considered to be important. They were the Natives, the Maroons, the slaves and the Coloureds. In the seventeenth and eighteenth centuries the Maroons and Natives fought for their freedom. They both signed peace treaties with the colonial government. These people however stayed inland.

In Paramaribo there was a group of people, who bought themselves free. And yet, even though they were no longer slaves, it was stipulated in 1743 that they had to show respect to the White people. This was because the White people gave them their freedom. Governor Jan Wichers (1784-1790) tried to develop them into a middle class. As such, they would be able to serve the colony and work towards its development and growth. This was not easy.

The majority of people in the colony remained the Afro-Surinamese slaves. They were the means through which the colonisers were trying to become rich.

6.4.3. Freedom of religion and new regulations

In the Netherlands, the idea of separation between government and church became prominent. The state would no longer cover the expenses of the Reformed Church. Every church had to exist through the funding of its members and not through government subsidy. All churches were considered equal in the Netherlands. The developments there led to the formation in 1797 of the *Nederlandsch Zendeling Genootschap* (Netherlands Missionary Society), to support the Protestants' mission work. This society sent one missionary to Suriname, in 1823.

In Suriname, the government continued to pay the salaries of the Reformed clergymen and from 1823 onwards, also that of the Lutheran clergymen. The Moravians received special privileges as well, which may among other reasons have contributed to their growth.

In 1815, all the religious groups that were in the colony received the freedom to practice their religion.[6] These good regulations were not adhered to in nineteenth-century Suriname. Yet, they opened some doors for the Roman Catholic Church especially, since the other Protestants were tolerated.[7] The animosity between these two branches of Christianity went on up to the end of the first half of the twentieth century. At that time, a council of churches was established. The nineteenth century saw the growth of Christianity in Suriname in a way that has never happened since then.

---

6. See 'Article 22' of the regulation of 1815. Article 26 indicated that people in the colony could join the police service, without discriminating against their Christian religious background. When the Jews protested against this, the words 'Christian religious background' in the article were changed into 'religious background' (*Gouvernementsblad*).

7. The freedom of religion did not apply to the Natives and Afro-Surinamese people. It was only for the Jews and the Christians. The religions of the other groups were not recognised by the government.

CHAPTER 7

Christianity and Slavery in Suriname

7.1. Introduction

The abolition of the slave trade in 1808 and the introduction of new laws and regulations in Suriname in 1828 had an impact on slavery in Suriname.[1] This chapter will look at slavery and Christianity. It will first look at slavery as an institution (7.2). Secondly, it will look at the role that Christianity played in Suriname during the era of slavery (7.3). Thirdly, it will interact with the biblical-theological motives that were used to justify slavery (7.4). Finally it will argue that greed was the main motive for slavery in Suriname (7.5).

7.2. Slavery in Suriname

Between 1650 and 1808, thousands of slaves were exported from West Africa to Suriname. The correct figure probably was between 215,000 and 350,000. It is not clear when the first African slaves arrived in Suriname. Europe knew slavery before Columbus visited the New World and slaves were known in Africa. According to Neill (1966:269) 'The white man did not introduce the slave-trade into Africa; he took over what he found and developed it with his own peculiar ruthlessness'. This 'peculiar

---

1. This chapter is based on my article 'Christianity and slavery in Suriname' that first appeared in the *Academic Journal of Suriname* 2010. Volume 1:104-112. Used with permission,

ruthlessness' gave slavery a different turn. The slave-trade became an international business between African leaders and European slave-traders. Merchants from Europe were able to purchase slaves from African slave-traders and recruiters. These slaves were then shipped to the New World under miserable conditions. About 13 per cent of them died during this transatlantic journey. Those who arrived alive were divided into city- and district-slaves. These two groups were further divided into plantation and household slaves.

In 1828 a new law was passed in the colony that declared that slaves were 'persons'. In the past slaves were seen as commodities or things. The law stated that the relationship between slaves and their owners was one of 'an infant and his guardian'. The law abolished 'the unjust principle' that slaves 'could only be treated as things juridically and not as persons'. The law also indicated that the government had to watch over the way in which slaves were treated.[2]

Slaves who arrived alive in the New World and did not escape from the plantations endured hardship. It was not easy to judge what happened in the past. Since the slaves did not write, there were little or no direct messages from them. In the oral tradition, these stories were not told, due to the shame and the honour culture of the Afro-Surinamese people. In this culture they will speak about the heroic deeds of their past leaders (honour) but not of the cruelties that happened to them (shame).

We find some references to the atrocities in the official documents of the colony and various writings on the history of Suriname. One thing was for sure, the descriptions of the treatment of slaves that we found in these documents were not the exception, but the rule. What was written was just the tip of the iceberg.[3]

---

2. Article 117, GB no. 3. Juli 1828. Besides the slaves, there were other Blacks in the colony. They enjoyed some privileges that the slaves did not enjoy. In 1760, for example, they were allowed to educate themselves. The classes however had to take place during the night, when the Whites were no longer there (see Gobardhan-Rambocus 2000:63).

3. One author described, based on official documents, events that took place between 1728 and 1750 (Wolbers 1861:133-136). These included:

In 1729 Kwaku resisted a White officer. He was whipped and one of his legs was cut off. Between 1730 and 1741 four more slaves lost their legs in the same manner. In 1728 three slaves were whipped and mutilated. Two of them had their ears cut off.

Very often slaves were sentenced to death, and the death penalty was executed in

Even though there was a court of justice in the country, many cruelties took place during the period of slavery. Most of the members of the court were slave-owners and respected Christian leaders. Slaves were not allowed to testify against their owners and could not take their issues to court, since they were not considered persons, but things.

7.3. Christianity in Suriname

As described earlier, the colonists, who came to Suriname, brought different branches of Christianity with them. These churches, with the exception of the Moravians and the Roman Catholics, were churches for the European plantation owners. Missions among the Afro-Surinamese people started with the arrival of the Moravians and Roman Catholic Church.

7.3.1. Christianity and slavery

When the British came to Suriname in the second half of the seventeenth century they brought their own slaves with them. In the seventeenth century, the clergymen of the Church of England, with a few exceptions, did not consider slavery to be against the teaching of the church. The bishops owned hundreds of slaves in the West Indies and the Anglican

---

different ways including: hanging, burning alive etc. Sometimes they drove an iron hook through their ribs and then hanged them on the gallows, where they remained until they died. Then they chopped off their head and hung it on a post.

Slaves suffered cruel treatment. However, the most important form of suffering was their dehumanising.

Slaves did not have free time. The normal work hours were from six in the morning to six in the evening. During harvest time, they had to work much longer. In 1769, a decree was issued that included a curfew for slaves. They were not allowed to leave their homes from eight in the night until the next morning. Because of this law, slaves could not have social activities.

They were also strictly forbidden to practice their own religion. During Sundays and holidays, slaves were not allowed to dance or play their drums without permission of the governor. Governors Temming (1721-1727) and Mauricius (1742-1751) allowed slaves to practice some of their traditional dances, the doe and the banja. Throughout the history of slavery and afterwards, they practiced their winti-religion in secret, because it was called idolatry by the predominantly Calvinistic government. Church leaders lamented the fact that even their members continued to practice the winti-religion.

Church there had its own slave plantation. The clergy in Suriname also adhered to this view, since they were slaveholders themselves.

The Reformed Church and its clergymen also kept slaves. The first Reformed clergyman, Rev Johannes Basseliers, had more than 50 slaves and was the sixth largest slaveholder out of 152 in the colony at that time. Rev Adrianus Backer, who arrived in Suriname in 1679, was given a plantation with slaves by the church. Up until 1768, Reformed pastors who came to Suriname were promised one or more slaves. The social services of the Reformed Church made use of slaves. The White members of the church in the colony had their own slaves to work in their homes, besides those on the plantations.

Some church leaders accused the government of the fact that the gospel was not preached to the slaves and that the slaves were treated barbarously. According to them, the government did everything to prevent the gospel from reaching the slaves. Even though this cannot be denied, the problem was not only with the government. The lives and attitudes of the Christian colonists and of some of their clergymen was a serious obstacle to the preaching of the gospel.

> The same man, who whipped the brother with his right hand until he bled, offered him the book of life with his left hand…
> This caused more damage to Christianity than what ten missionaries could repair in one year (Wolbers 1853:5).

The Rev Joannes Guiljelmus Kals was a different voice. After he was expelled from Suriname, he published a pamphlet in which he accused the Netherlands of neglecting the conversion of the heathens. This to him was their cardinal sin.

The Lutheran Church was no different to the Reformed Church. When the first Lutheran minister in the colony, Rev Johannes Phaff, remarried in 1749, he became the co-owner of four plantations. Just like their Reformed colleagues, slaves were part of the remuneration of the Lutheran ministers. However, the Lutheran Church went a step further, when it acquired the plantation Johan en Margaretha in 1757. The church bought slaves and started a coffee plantation to maintain the church financially. Due to mismanagement, the plantation suffered a significant loss and was given to creditors to repay the Chruch's debts.

The Church of England, the Reformed Church and the Lutheran Church were established to meet the needs of their members who were in the colony. The Moravians, on the other hand, came to the colony to see if it was possible to win some 'Wilds' (Natives) and 'Moors' (Afro-Surinamese slaves) for the Lamb. They did not discourage slavery but, contrary to the Lutheran and Reformed Churches, they preached the gospel to the slaves. They practiced what Kals advocated, that slaves do not need to be free physically, as long as they were spiritually free. They had to endure physical suffering in the footsteps of their Lord and Master and submit themselves to human institutions. After a synod in 1769, the Moravians applied another method. They bought slaves to work on their plantations. Even though these slaves remained slaves, they were treated as free members of the church. The missionaries lived in the same plot with their slaves, worked intensively with them to support both themselves and the slaves. Acquiring slaves was then for the Moravians a missionary activity. The slaves were taught a trade and they received the gospel. In 1848 the Moravian Church leader Otto Nelis Tank wrote a circular letter to all the owners, directors and administrators of plantations in Suriname. Tank, who was the leader of the Moravian mission in Suriname, visited different plantations and saw how slaves were treated. He pleaded for improvement of their lot and for missionaries to be given more opportunity to visit plantations. Tank felt that the missionaries were treated by plantation owners as puppets. These plantation owners cared only for the economic benefits of their companies. Tank's letter caused a commotion in the colony. Three very influential gentlemen, Egbert van Emden, Henri Guillaume Roux and Jean Frouin called the Moravians to account. Van Emden was a Jew. Roux was the treasurer of the Reformed Church and president of the Reformed commission for the orphans. He was also the administrator of 28 plantations. Frouin was a deacon in the Reformed Church. They requested an answer to fifty-nine questions that they put before Tank's successor. The response of the church was disappointing. New missions leader Pfenninger distanced himself from the circular letter. According to him, Tank got involved in political and civil issues, which was contrary to the rules of the mission. Even the Haagse Maatschappij in the Netherlands, which supported the work of the Moravians among the slaves, distanced itself from Tank. This was not surprising, since the names of Roux and Frouin appeared on the list of board members of the Haagse Maatschappij in Paramaribo. It was clear that the Moravians were not ready for people like Tank, who dared to speak against injustice in society.

The Roman Catholic Church also had slaves. It founded an organisation called Liefde fonds, to buy freedom for slaves.

Christianity in Suriname accepted slavery as an institution and helped maintain it. It participated in the mistreatment of slaves and the making of laws that dehumanised them. Slaves on the plantation of a Lutheran minister, for example, complained in 1751 that they were mistreated daily. Among the Moravians, who accomplished a lot for the slaves, there were some who held the Afro-Surinamese people in contempt. They punished their slaves and sometimes abused them physically. They did not spare these slaves the rod, the chain or the neck-iron. They considered them to be ignorant children, who needed discipline. The following words that Sister Schmidt spoke when she was in an argument with a Maroon lady give an indication of that: 'Bear in mind that I am White'. In the course of time there was a clear distance between the White Moravian and the Afro-Surinamese Moravian. The White Moravian was the 'master', 'teacher'. The Afro-Surinamese was 'our house Negro' or 'our Negro in the bakery'. In their own eyes the slave was 'a poor person', 'a weak person' and 'wretched'. These names may have contributed to the fact that the Afro-Surinamese lost his own self-esteem and underestimated his own ability and knowledge. In the era after the abolition of slavery there was an incident in which a Moravian sister from Europe indicated that she wanted to marry an Afro-Surinamese brother. Most of the White missionaries opposed the idea.

At the same time, Christianity has done much more than any other institution to improve the lot of the Afro-Surinamese slave. It educated slaves even though it was forbidden in the colony up to 1844. Up to 1857 it was still forbidden by law to teach slave children how to read. Yet, the Moravians successfully taught Maroons how to read as early as the late eighteenth century.

7.3.2. The relation between Afro-Surinamese people and Whites

The first question in the relation between slavery and Christianity was whether the (Afro-Surinamese) slave was a human being, equal to the (Christian) White. This simple question received different answers. Some Whites made it clear, even before the law of 1828, that slaves were human beings just like the Whites. They were created by the same Supreme Being. The Creator however, shone the light of the gospel on the Whites and that privilege was not given to the Afro-Surinamese people. This 'enlightened' group of Whites was a minority in the colonial society. The majority had a different view.

Some described the Afro-Surinamese people as 'beasts', who were rude, barbarian, wild and stupid. According to one writer, some of them had brains, but the majority did not (Hartsinck 1770:906). They were lazy, bloodthirsty and revengeful. They were inclined to steal, lie and to become addicted to alcohol and women. This inferiority according to some was due to the fact that they served idols. These views that were supported by Christianity in the colony influenced the law-makers, who were also considered to be Christians. Slaves were not considered to be human beings. The following citation from the West Indian Company (WIC) contract with Berbice makes it clear:

> The colonists may sell their plantations, slaves, beasts and other goods at any time; they may also take their slaves, beasts and other goods from the colony with them wherever they want to go (Article 9, quoted in Hartsinck 1770:347).

Slaves were treated as commodities, things or goods and not as human beings. In the seventeenth and eighteenth centuries one could speak about 'merchandise' that was necessary for the colony, such as 'slaves, horses, oxen, cows, and donkeys'. Slaves were personal goods. It was taken for granted that the Afro-Surinamese people were inferior to the Whites and were seen as a kind of 'creature in-between'. They were there to provide the Whites with what they needed, including profit. The laws at that time supported the notion that Afro-Surinamese people were inferior to Whites. In 1698, a law was passed that stated that, when Afro-Surinamese people came across Whites on the street, they had to get out of the way to allow the Whites to pass. In 1769 it was stated that Afro-Surinamese people were not allowed to wear shoes or socks. Furthermore, they were not allowed to put on bridle hats. Officially, Whites were not allowed to marry the Natives or Afro-Surinamese. In 1686 during the time of the devoted Christian governor, Van Sommelsdijck, a law was passed that the 'inhabitants' (meaning the Whites), were not allowed to have sexual intercourse with Afro-Surinamese or Native women. If such a thing happened, the White had to pay a fine of two thousand pounds of sugar. This of course did not prevent White men fathering children with Native and Afro-Surinamese mothers. Many Whites lived together with slaves; even members of the police department committed this 'sin'. In 1711, another law stated that, if a White woman had sexual intercourse with an Afro-Surinamese man, she would be whipped and sent out of the colony. The man was to be killed.

7.4. Biblical and theological motives used in support of slavery

In the Netherlands, where the Surinamese Reformed Christianity originated, there were a few voices against slavery. Slavery itself was forbidden in the Netherlands. A well-known voice from the seventeenth century was undoubtedly Jacobus Hondius (1629-1691). In 1679, he published a work entitled *Swart Register van duysent Sonden* (Black register of a thousand sins). He labelled the slave trade as the biggest sin of their time. He warned Christians not to participate in it.

> Church members who buy and sell slaves and trade in these miserable people commit a sin. For these are people of the same nature as them not mere animals. Even so such slave trade is conducted not only by Jews, Turks, and Pagans, but so-called Christians, indeed, Dutchmen, as well. Reformed members should not taint themselves with such uncompassionate trade.

Instead, they should act fully in fear of the Lord, in order that the money they make will be a blessing rather than a curse (Vink 2003).

This voice was a minority. Christianity in those days gave at least three biblical-theological arguments in support of slavery.

1) The general teaching of the Bible. In 1718 the historian Herlein, who lived in Suriname at the beginning of the eighteenth century, argued that the Old Testament clearly stated that one could buy slaves from surrounding nations and from foreigners in their midst.[4] He referred to Lev 25:44 and Exod 21:20 to support his idea. The passage in Lev 25:44-46 reads:

> As for your male and female slaves who may belong to you – you may buy male and female slaves from the nations all around you. Also you may buy slaves from the children of the foreigners who reside with you, and from their families that are with you, whom they have fathered in your land, they may become your property. You may give them as inheritance to your children after you to possess as property. You may enslave them perpetually. However, as for your brothers the Israelites, no man may rule over his brother harshly (NET).

He therefore argued that it was not wrong to buy slaves and keep them.[5]

---

4. Godefridus Cornelis Udemans who defended this thesis before Herlein referred also to Josh 9:21 (cited by Paasman 1984).

5. It is remarkable that Herlein used these verses to justify slavery, as it was found in Suriname. The Old Testament did not institute slavery, but regulated it. It would have been much better if Christian leaders in Suriname had looked further into the Old Testament regarding this issue. 'If a man strikes his male servant or his female servant with a staff so that he or she dies as a result of the blow, he will surely be punished' (Exod 21:20, NET). The phrase *nāqôm yinnāqēm* translated 'he will surely be punished', probably refers to the death penalty. The principle of an eye for an eye was applicable here. Another reference is to the book of Job. 'If I have disregarded the right of my male servants or my female servants when they disputed with me, then what will I do when God confronts me in judgment; when he intervenes, how will I respond to him? Did not the one who made me in the womb make them? Did not the same one form us in the womb?' (Job 31:13-15) The argument in these verses is that with God there is no respecter of persons. The slave and his master are equal in the sight of God.

An important voice regarding the relationship between Christianity and slavery in the Netherlands in the eighteenth century was the Ghanaian Jacobus Elisa Joannes Capitein (1717-1747).[6] In an oration that he held in Leiden in 1742, he indicated that slavery was not against the teachings of Scripture. According to him, spiritual liberty was more important than physical liberty. He quoted, among others, 2 Cor 3:17: 'Now the Lord is the Spirit, and where the Spirit of the Lord is present, there is freedom' (NET). In his understanding, the slave masters had a responsibility to Christianise their slaves, set them free spiritually and to keep them in physical bondage. This however never happened in Suriname.

2) The 'Ham-ideology'. Another argument that was used in favour of slavery was the so-called 'Ham-ideology'. The point of departure of this view is Gen 9:25, the curse of Ham's son Canaan:

> Ham, the father of Canaan, saw his father's nakedness and told his two brothers who were outside. Shem and Japheth took the garment and placed it on their shoulders. Then they walked in backwards and covered up their father's nakedness. Their faces were turned the other way so they did not see their father's nakedness. When Noah awoke from his drunken stupor he learned what his youngest son had done to him. So he said, 'Cursed be Canaan! The lowest of slaves he will be to his brothers' (Gen 9:22-25).

On the basis of this curse, many theologians believed that the descendants of Ham, whom they equated with Africans, were cursed. Africans therefore had to take a lower place in comparison with the other peoples, especially the Whites. The 'Ham-ideology' and the spiritual freedom theory were only used to justify slavery biblically.

---

6. Capitein was probably born in 1717 in the present-day Ghana. This young slave was freed and given to a Dutchman. The Dutchman brought him to the Netherlands in 1728, where he was educated. From 1737 to 1742 he studied theology at the University of Leiden. He completed his studies with a dissertation. On 10 March 1742 he presented his dissertation. In the same year he returned to Africa and resided at Elmina. He served there as chaplain. In 1745, the West Indian Company sent him a bride from the Netherlands, whom he married. Capitein died two years later (see Kpobi 1993).

3) The providence of God. A theological justification for slavery was that God in his providence used slavery to bring gentiles to the knowledge of the gospel. Slavery, then, was a means to Christianise the slaves. According to Johann Picardt, the all-governing providence of God decided on the destiny of the sons of Noah. Ham's 'prosperity lay in slavery' (Picardt 1660:9). Georgius de Raad agreed and stated that both the heathen Africans and the Christians (Europeans or Whites) lived under God's providence (De Raad 1665). When by the providence of God slaves became the property of Christians, including through the slave trade, then the Christians had the responsibility to bring the slaves to the true religion, the Reformed faith.[7]

The negative effect of slavery on the Afro-Surinamese people in Suriname was not recognised. The leadership of Christianity in Suriname was White throughout the entire period of slavery and almost a hundred years afterwards. These leaders, who came from Europe, were not able to address the issues that the Afro-Surinamese people faced. Even though in 1863 slaves were liberated physically, there was still a mental slavery.[8] The first independent black preacher in Suriname, the Rev Carel Paulus Rier, was the first Christian leader to address the issues faced by Afro-Surinamese people as a result of slavery. He did that forty years after its abolition. His approach was very radical and was misunderstood.

7.5. Conclusion

Why did the Whites choose the Blacks as slaves? Was it because they were of the impression that the Blacks were inferior? David Bosch argued that colonisation made slavery an issue of race. According to him, after the discoveries of the fifteenth century 'slaves could only be people of colour. The fact that they were different made it possible for the victorious

---

7. One former slave, Olaudah Equiano, who wrote an autobiography in 1789, agreed with this theological argument. According to him, being brought to the New World as a slave allowed him, by God's providence, to become a Christian.

8. This problem was faced in the rest of the region. It was addressed among others by Bob Marley in his Redemption Song: 'Emancipate yourselves from mental slavery; None but ourselves can free our minds'.

Westerners to regard them as inferior' (Bosch 1991:227). Bosch identified the problem of 'colour' and 'inferiority'. This was certainly the case in Suriname. White colonists made sure that the people of colour were afraid of them. In the seventeenth and eighteenth centuries for example the ratio of Whites to Afro-Surinamese in the Colony was 1:20 or 1:25, and yet, the Whites abused them. Even though this observation was correct, in the case of Suriname, 'colour' and 'inferiority' were not the only reasons for enslaving people.

1) Both the British and the Dutch colonisers used Natives as slaves to work on their plantations. The Natives fought against this and both the British and the Dutch had to sign a peace treaty with them.

2) White 'servants' were recruited in the Netherlands to be sold to plantation owners in Suriname. These servants were thieves, who were sentenced in the Netherlands and were deported out of the country. Some were wanderers, deserters, gullible people and adventurers. Governor Van Sommelsdijck called them drunkards, liars and people who were good for nothing. Other parts of the Caribbean also made use of White slaves. These slaves were promised, among other things, a new beginning in the colony.

3) Enslavement was a way of getting a cheap labour force. With the abolition of the slave trade at the beginning of the nineteenth century and the closure of the 'Black-market' a decade later, the colony faced some serious challenges. The number of plantations dropped from 452 in 1791 to 210 in 1863. The slave population had dropped from 53,000 in 1787 to 36,484 in 1863. Just before the abolition of slavery in Suriname in 1863, the colonial government looked for 'migrant' workers in Asia. Indians, Chinese and Javanese replaced the African slaves.

4) Free Afro-Surinamese and Coloured people, who were well-to-do in Suriname, kept slaves. There were Afro-Surinamese slave owners in Suriname, as early as 1731 and probably already in 1685. Thomas Herman, one of the first free Afro-Surinamese, held a land title of twenty acres and was counted among the 'small sugar lords' in 1685. Elisabeth Samson (1715-1771), had 40 domestic slaves, not including those who worked on her plantations.

The Trinidadian historian Eric Williams said the following:

> Slavery was not born of racism: rather racism was the consequence of slavery, unfree labour in the New World was brown, white, black and yellow, Catholic, Protestant and pagan. . . The reason was economic, not racial; it had to do not with the colour of the labourer, but with the cheapness of the labour. As compared with Indian and white labour, Negro slavery was eminently superior (Williams 1944:7, 19).

Christians used biblical arguments to defend the institution of slavery, even in its cruel form in Suriname. The motives for maintaining slavery in Suriname were economic.[9] Slaves worked to provide an income for their masters. Women were forced into prostitution to provide additional income for their masters. Old slaves, who could not give their full strength anymore, were condemned to receive severe punishment. It was more beneficial for the plantation owner to kill them, than to keep them alive.

Christianity failed to address not only the fruits of the inhuman practice of slavery, but also its root cause, 'the love of money'. Christian governments, Christian churches and Christian leaders supported and maintained an evil system for their personal, material gain and enrichment.

Despite the efforts of the Moravians and the Roman Catholics to do missions among the slaves and their descendants, Christianity as a whole was blindly supporting slavery in Suriname. Slavery was officially abolished almost 150 years ago. However the motives that led to this inhuman enterprise and its dehumanising results are still prevalent in today's Surinamese society. In 1982 Pope John Paul II asked the Africans for forgiveness for the slave-trade. In 1992, he asked the Africans who were deported as slaves for forgiveness. The example of the Roman Catholic Church was followed by the Anglicans in 2006. The Church apologised for its role in slavery and acknowledged that the church was part of the problem and that the church should be part of the solution. The Reformed Church in the Netherlands, the official church in Suriname during the time of slavery, has never apologised for its slavery past. During a meeting in 2004 in Accra Ghana, leaders of the World Alliance of Reformed Churches

---

9. This was also true for the Africans who were involved in the slave trade.

(WARC) prayed prayers of repentance, for among others things, slavery and present-day economic exploitation. There have been individual church leaders from the Netherlands who came to Suriname and felt that they must confess the 'slavery sins' of their ancestors. However, Surinamese churches have not yet had an organised, national activity to confess this sin.

If an economic motive or human greed for wealth has been the main motive of the transatlantic slave trade, then Christianity should address the root cause of the problem. This is critical since the transatlantic slavery was abolished but 'the demon' that led to this enterprise is still around.

CHAPTER 8

The Era of Growth: 1830-1863

8.1. Introduction

The 1830's were a turning point for Christianity in Suriname in a number of ways. By this time, a few churches had settled in Suriname. The Protestant churches, Anglican, Reformed, Lutheran and Moravian were getting along well. The Roman Catholics were in the colony but were only tolerated by the Protestants.

On 28 April 1828 major-general Johannes van den Bosch, Commissioner of the Dutch West Indies possessions arrived in Suriname. His mission was to prepare new rules and regulations to guide the government's policies for the Dutch West Indies. There was a need for major changes in the colonies. There was no confidence in the financial situation of Suriname and agriculture was struggling. There was no independent judiciary and the rich influenced every sector. It was therefore not possible to develop the colony. Abraham de Veer (1822-1828), who was governor at that time, was not a match for the attorney-general Evert Ludolf van Heeckeren.

The situation of the slaves and the free Afro-Surinamese people however was worse than the social economic situation. The government wanted to address the destiny of these slaves and the free Afro-Surinamese people. Van den Bosch had the responsibility to see what could be done to improve the morality and marriages among the slaves. This would improve the fertility-rate among them. Since the slave trade was abolished, it was important to improve the conditions under which they were living. Van den Bosch did his work very well and without regard to persons. He finalised the new regulations on 21 July 1828, and they became operational on 1 August 1828. The governor received more power under the new regulations, while the court of police and justice was replaced by a high council, which consisted of four people.

Furthermore, the regulations were aimed at improving the living conditions of all civilians in the colony. All free people were to have equal rights. Jews and Coloured people were allowed to be appointed in prominent public offices. What about the slaves? The new law declared that slaves were 'persons'. Van den Bosch also had the view that the treatment and the feeding of the slaves had to be improved. A permanent change had to be brought about in the behaviour of the slaves through the gospel.

Some people paid attention to his recommendations, including the recommendation that encouraged the preaching of the gospel to the slaves to change their behaviour. In 1828, five prominent men founded a 'Society to propagate religious education among the slaves and Coloureds in the colony Suriname'.[1] Even though the Moravians were not part of the governing board, the society supported their mission work. A counterpart of this society was established in The Hague, the Netherlands, which became known as 'The Hague Society' (Haagse Maatschappij). Both societies decided to support the work of the Moravians, who had proven to be able to change the 'rude heathens' into useful people. The society took the initiative to give financial support so that the Moravians could acquire boats, increase the number of missionaries, the possibilities for education, establish more mission posts outside of Paramaribo and distribute the New Testament in Sranantongo. This led to a significant growth of the work of the Moravians between 1830 and 1863.

Another important event for Christianity in Suriname at the time was the establishment in 1829, of a subsidiary of the Dutch Bible Society to distribute scriptures in the colony.

In 1832, new laws that were passed made things more favourable for Christianity. According to this law clergymen must be allowed to visit the plantations. Those who owned slaves were compelled to allow teachers,

---

1. In Dutch, 'Maatschappij ter bevordering van het Godsdienstig Onderwijs onder de Slaven en Kleuringen in de kolonie Suriname'.

clergymen or missionaries to their plantations to minister among the slaves. Furthermore, they had to allow children under the age of fourteen to be educated in religious or other forms of education. Plantation owners were not allowed to set slaves free if they were not baptised. Only a baptised and free person was given the right to be his own boss or a private craftsman. It was stated clearly that no free civilian should be prohibited from occupying a post because of his religion or colour.

In 1833, slavery was abolished in the British colonies, including Suriname's western neighbour, Guyana. However, the Netherlands had not yet started the discussions about the abolition of slavery. Activist groups started to raise their voices after the 1840's. In Suriname, except for a major complaint in 1848 by the Moravian pastor, Otto Tank, the issue was not raised.

The political developments in Suriname after 1828 were very positive for the growth of Christianity. The support of the government and the help of the societies that were established, helped the Moravian Church to grow and to become the largest Christian church in the colony at the time of the abolition of slavery.

8.2. *The Growth of Christianity*

Thousands of slaves joined either the Moravian or the Roman Catholic Church. Between 1835 and 1862, the Moravians were working in 190 plantations, ministering to 27,548 slaves. In 1830 the church only had 2,000 members. The Lutheran and the Reformed Churches were 'Churches for the Whites' (*Bakra kerki*), even though a small number of Afro-Surinamese people joined them.

The total population of Suriname in 1862 was about 52,963 excluding the Natives and the Maroons. Of these, about 47,582 claimed to be Christians and 1,394 Jews. This meant that about 3,987 people in the colony were not connected to Christianity. Among the group of Christians there were between 5,000 to 6,000 who belonged to the Reformed Church and between 1,800 to 2,500 to the Lutheran Church. Thousands of slaves joined the churches when the abolition of slavery was getting close.

Table 19 *Religious population of Suriname in 1862*

Moravians	27,548
Roman Catholics	11,753
Reformed and Lutheran	8,281
Jews	1,394
Non-Christians	3,987
Total population (excluding the Natives and Maroons)	52,963

When slavery was abolished in 1863 more than 90 per cent of the population were adherents of Christianity. Most of the slaves joined a Christian church because of the new regulations and their desire to be free persons one day. There were also people who joined the church and accepted Christianity as a result of missionary preaching. The growth of the church took place in various parts of the country.

8.2.1. Growth of the Lutheran Church

In the period 1840-1862, one clergyman, the Rev C M Moes, served the Lutheran Church. Moes contributed a lot to the growth of the church, even though it was not involved in missions outreach among the slaves. In the second half of the nineteenth century slaves and free Coloured people became members of it. Some slaves chose the church of their masters to meet the requirement of the government. At the time of the abolition, the membership of the church was between 1,500 and 1,800. The number of White members was around 300. This meant that the majority of the members were either Afro-Surinamese or Coloured people. Membership however did not mean equal treatment of all in the church. Afro-Surinamese people and Coloureds were marginalised and were baptised for example on Wednesdays, while the Europeans were baptised on Sundays. This was unfortunate, since the European members of the church were not faithful to it. Because of their lack of attending the church services and activities, the celebration of the Lord's Supper was reduced to twice a year in 1858. Earlier it was three times a year.

8.2.2. Growth of the Reformed Church

The membership of the Reformed Church in 1847 was 1,600. The number of people who attended the church or made use of its services however was 3,600. The majority of the members at that time were Sranantongo-speakers, Afro-Surinamese people. The services however were held in Dutch, which meant that some did not understand the messages. In 1845, Willem Boekhoudt, a young man who studied theology, came to the colony to find a private job. When he realised that there was a need for Sranantongo in the church services, he studied the language. Within a short time he was able to preach in Sranantongo. The church tried to secure his services, but the government was not willing to pay the salary. The church knew that Sranantongo would contribute more to its growth and to the devotion of its people. It however did not want to pay the price for it. When the government rejected their request the church could have considered paying the clergyman from its own funds. This did not happen. In 1858, the church published a hymnbook in Sranantongo that consisted of songs that were translated from Dutch.

The membership of the Reformed Church in Suriname grew also when a group of Dutch peasants arrived in the colony in 1845. The plan was initiated by three Reformed clergymen in the Netherlands, Rev Jan Hendrik Betting, Rev Arend van de Brandhoff and Rev Dirk Copijn. The intention was to bring 1,000 people, approximately 200 families to Suriname. In order to join the group, one had to submit proof of baptism or church membership. The plans however were not successful. Instead of 1,000 peasants, 384 arrived in the colony with two of the clergymen, Brandhoff and Copijn. They settled in Groningen in the district Saramacca. In less than five months, 189 died. They suffered from tropical diseases. At the end, only one clergyman, Brandhoff, remained. His wife had also died and he had a large family to take care of. Because of this he could not give leadership to the group. Furthermore, he was not a good team player. The problems of the group continued when their first crop failed. The second harvest was a great success. And yet, because of the distance between their plantation and the city, they could not sell their produce. Again this turned out to be a disaster. The group decided to leave their settlement in Groningen and move closer to the city. Others returned to the Netherlands.

8.2.3. Growth of the Roman Catholic Church

The Roman Catholic Church grew, not only in Paramaribo but also in the districts.

First of all, there was growth in the three western districts, Nickerie, Coronie and Saramacca. Father Wennekers started a work in Coronie around 1823. At that time he baptised 141 people, including slaves. Between 1824 and 1840, no Roman Catholic clergyman visited that district. Because of the influence of the Moravians in that area, the church stationed Father Theodures Kempkes there permanently in 1841. Kempkes worked tirelessly to convert the slaves. However, the quality of discipleship left much to be desired. The plantation owners did not give the slaves enough time to attend the church services. Due to an accident with his horse, Kempkes was not able to visit the members at home. Once, a person tried to poison him and another time he drank poison by accident. The number of Catholics in Coronie grew to 750 in 1861. In 1849, a chapel was built in Paradise in Nickerie.

Earlier, work started in Batavia in the Saramacca district, where there was a leprosarium. Father Martinus van der Weyden had baptised 120 people there in 1826 and in 1836, Father Jacobus Grooff dedicated a chapel. By 1843, the number of people who were baptised there grew to 1,034. Batavia however was better known for the tireless and sacrificial work of Father Petrus Donders. Donders arrived in Suriname in 1842. After serving in various places for fourteen years, he settled in Batavia in 1856. He served the lepers there for twenty-six years. He preached to them, cooked for them, cleaned their houses, and served them in whatever way they needed service. Above all, they learned to love Christ.

Secondly there was expansion in Paramaribo. In Paramaribo, the church started a school. For that purpose Sisters from Roosendaal came to Suriname in 1856. The next year, they started two schools for the poor and two for those who could afford payment. The schools were well attended because of the quality of the education. In 1861, the Sisters were also entrusted with the care of the orphan girls.

Thirdly, the work among other plantations continued to grow. In 1861, the number of places where the church was active grew to twenty-three. This did not include the places where there was a permanent presence, such as Paramaribo, Batavia, Coronie and Nickerie. In 1843 there were 4,000 Roman Catholics in Suriname. This number grew to 11,753 in 1862.

8.2.4. Growth of the Moravian Church

8.2.4.1. Paramaribo

The church that grew the most in this period was the Moravian Church. As indicated earlier, it received support from the government and other organisations. As such it was very privileged. It grew in Paramaribo, but more so in the districts. In 1830 about 90 per cent of the members of the church lived in Paramaribo. In 1863, this was only 24 per cent. Membership in Paramaribo grew from 1,800 to 5,600.

The so-called 'helpers' played a critical role in the growth of the church in Paramaribo. They were volunteers, who inspired other members to become active participants. In 1844 they started a burial fund and health service and in 1847 a fund to support the poor. One of the workers, Magaretha Elisabeth Raatgever, started a missionary fund in 1859. Her intention was to expand God's work through financial support and prayer. Within a year membership of the organisation grew to fifty-one: thirty-three Sisters and eighteen Brothers. In 1860, the fund sent an amount of one hundred and five guilders to support the work that was done in Oskraal in South Africa by missionary Philipp Heinrich Meyer. The local workers also took the initiative to collect money for the Netherlands when it was flooded.

The 'helpers' served in other capacities as well. Through their activities, they offered both the missionaries and the slaves a warm Christian fellowship in the difficult slave society. Some of the activities that they initiated are still being carried on in the Moravian Church. Just like Alabi and Jephta among the Saramaccans and the Natives, they played a key role in the work of Bible translation. Some of them were counsellors to the missionaries. One of these counsellors was Catharina Ulrik. She was appointed as helper in the church in 1815, when she was in her fifties. She may have heard missionaries such as Kersten preaching in her plantation from 1779. Because of this she knew the church very well. She saw missionaries coming and going. She was a personal counsellor and a spiritual mother to missionary Wilhelm Treu, who served as the *praeses* (general secretary) of the church from 1839-1846. She died in 1847.

The Christians were comforted, encouraged, strengthened and edified by fellow Afro-Surinamese believers, who knew their situation and who could understand them very well.

8.2.4.2. Districts

From 1840-1863, the work grew significantly in the districts. In 1863, 76 per cent of the people who were under the spiritual care of the Moravians were in 190 plantations. The period was rightly called the era of missions to the slaves.

8.2.4.2.1. The western districts

The Moravians started their missionary activities in Nickerie in 1817, on two plantations. Due to a lack of workers, they stopped their work in 1821. In 1859, they established a new mission station on the plantation Waterloo.

Missionary Wilhelm Treu visited Coronie in 1837, after an incident with a slave called Tata Colin. Colin claimed to have received visions from God. He called upon his fellow slaves to stop their work. The slaves were meeting in secret to hear what Colin had to say. This however came to an end, when a fellow slave revealed the secrets of the group, including a conspiracy, to the owner of the plantation. Colin and two of his close associates were brought to Paramaribo for trial. There they were visited by missionary Treu. Colin rejected the message of Treu, but his two friends, Denmark and Franklin, accepted it. When they were brought back to Coronie, after the trial, Treu went with them. He preached the gospel to more than 1,200 slaves. In 1840, a missionary settled permanently there. At the abolition of slavery more than 1,000 slaves were baptised, including a former Muslim. Around 85 per cent of the population of Coronie were adherents to Christianity at the abolition of slavery. The majority of them were Moravians.

In 1853, 1,300 slaves were ministered to by the Moravians in Saramacca. The church settled there permanently in 1855, with a mission station in Catharina Sophia.

8.2.4.2.2. The eastern districts

In 1856, the missionaries were able to preach the gospel to more than 9,000 slaves in the eastern part of the country, in six mission stations. Further growth however was hindered by at least two factors. In the first place, the missionaries could not visit all the plantations that were open to the gospel. They could also not provide spiritual care to all the slaves adequately. The second factor was the lot that the Moravians were using. The lot had to decide if a person was ready to be baptised or accepted as a member of the church. Sometimes people were waiting for more than two years to receive an answer.

More positive was the support that the missionaries received from some plantation owners. They allowed the missionaries to preach the gospel and to provide education for their slaves.

8.2.4.2.3. The central and southern districts

The work in Para was more difficult than the other districts. Work started there in the 1830's. The results were meagre. Missionaries continued to battle against the traditional religion of the slaves. One missionary destroyed the shrines of their gods. In 1854 and 1856 two missionary stations were set up, in respectively Berlijn and Hannover. A third station followed in 1858, in Bersaba. The seemingly successful battle of the missionary against the shrines of the gods of the slaves seemed to have impressed some of the slaves and they became Christians. The traditional religion however did not lose its power. The outward destruction of shrines did not take the belief out of the hearts of the people.

The upper and lower Suriname districts followed the same pattern as Para. In 1841, a missionary station was built in Berg en Dal. The widows, Catharina Voigt-Dittmar and more so Maria Hartmann-Lobach did much work on this station. Even though Hartmann-Lobach was not allowed to preach, because she was a woman, she witnessed to many people on the station. Through her work a church started in Koffiekamp, a surrounding village. Many slaves in the area became Christians and joined the Moravian Church before the abolition of slavery.

In 1859 a station was built in Clevia, in the lower Suriname district. From this station the missionaries visited plantations in the neighbourhood.

8.3. Conclusion

The growth of the church in this period was numerical and geographical. This however was not always accompanied by spiritual growth, leading to maturity in Christ. Not all converts, or should we say proselytes, were properly discipled. The zealous missionaries and their committed 'helpers' were not able to provide the necessary pastoral care to all the new converts. Because of this a kind of Christianity was developed, which included membership of a Christian church and adherence to the traditional religion. This problem became more evident after the abolition of slavery when the regulations no longer forced slaves to join a Christian church.

CHAPTER 9

The Church in Paramaribo after the Abolition of Slavery

9.1. Introduction

After the abolition of slavery, many changes took place in the colony. Changes took place in the way in which it was governed and in the economy. Furthermore, many people either left the plantations or the colony. After a brief description of these issues (9.1), this chapter will describe the development of the Creole Church (9.2) and the arrival of new churches (9.3).

In May 1863 districts-commissioners and districts-secretaries were appointed. Their task was to keep order among the slaves and to provide them with a family name. Before that time, slaves did not have a family name.

In 1866, the colonial parliament was established. It consisted of thirteen members, nine of whom were elected by a group of people who had the right to vote. Four were appointed by the governor. The right to vote was connected to a certain amount that was paid in taxes. This amount was too high for the average Surinamese at that time. Only 2 per cent of the population were able to pay it and receive the right to vote.

The governor represented the Dutch government. So even though there was a parliament, the government was still in the hands of the Netherlands. The economic dependence of Suriname on the Netherlands was one of the possible reasons for this.

Often, there were misunderstandings between the governor and other public servants, who were sent from the Netherlands on the one hand, and the general population and parliament on the other hand. The 'Surinamese' (parliament and population) did not trust the Bakras or 'Dutch people' (governor and Dutch public servants). Some of the Dutch people looked down on what they considered to be the inferior Surinamese people. Among the 'Surinamese' there were also tensions. A large group of the Surinamese elite was Jewish. They looked down on the rest of the population. Even though slavery was abolished, the problem with superiority and inferiority based on ethnicity was still present in the colony. Racism was still and still is an issue in Surinamese society.

After the abolition, the slaves were to work for ten years on the plantations under supervision of the government. They had to sign contracts with plantation owners in order to be able to work. A number of them left the plantation and moved to the city, Paramaribo. Many plantation owners sold their plantations and assets. With the proceeds from their sales and the money that the Dutch government paid them, as a compensation for liberating the slaves, they returned to the Netherlands. They did not trust the labour of the emancipated slaves. According to them Afro-Surinamese people would not be able to produce without pressure.

The exodus of the plantation owners influenced the economy negatively. Between 1 July 1862 and 1 July 1864, 95 plantations were sold. This process continued after 1864. This was one of the reasons the economy of the colony was bad and depended on Dutch support. Another reason for the weak economy was the decline of sugar exports, which started in the first half of the nineteenth century. The European market had replaced sugar from sugar cane with beet sugar. Furthermore, the cotton industry in the United States of America was a threat to the Surinamese industry. The number of cotton plantations before the abolition was 400. This reduced to less than 100 in 1896. Finally, the cultivation of cocoa failed because of diseases on the plants that were not expected.

9.2. The Creole Church

The post-emancipation Suriname was confronted with urbanisation. The process started during the ten years in which the slaves had to work under the supervision of the government, and continued afterwards. In 1860, 34 per cent of the population lived in Paramaribo and the surrounding area. The number grew to 47 per cent in 1880 and 63 per cent in 1950. This of course had its impact on the development of the colony in general and on Christianity in particular. Many of the stations that were established in the period leading to the emancipation had to be closed. These included Clevia (1899) and Catharina Sophia (1902). New posts were established such as Domburg (1892), Saron (1900), Nieuw Amsterdam (1901), Groningen (1902), Albina (1894) and Potribo (1895).

Due to the growth of the population, the church had to expand its ministry in the city. This development led to the founding of the Creole Church. The Creole Church was characterised by large numbers of people who joined the church for 'political' reasons. Their choice to join the church was not always motivated by true discipleship or commitment. For some, it was in order to receive freedom. Those who joined the church for this reason did not take responsibility for the maintenance and growth of the church. The generation that came after them, their children were automatically connected with the church of their parents. Their names were in the church's registers, but they did not participate in church life. The church blamed external factors for this lack of commitment. It was under the impression that the emancipation came too early and that the slaves did not know how to go about their newly-gained freedom. The fundamental reasons may have been 'political' conversions and the lack of discipleship.

9.2.1. The Moravian Church

Table 20 *Membership of the Moravian Church*

Year	Paramaribo		Other places		Total
	Number	Percentage	Numbers	Percentage	
1868	6,500	28%	17,000	72%	23,500
1882	9,500	42%	13,000	58%	22,500
1913	14,000	52%	13,000	48%	27,000

In 1868, 28 per cent of the members of the Moravian Church lived in Paramaribo. In 1913, it was 52 per cent.

In 1868 the church started what was called the Stadszending (City Mission). The aim of this arm of the church was to minister to the Coloured people in Paramaribo, who were not yet Christians or who had turned away from Christianity. This work presented challenges because the people living in Paramaribo did not live in one place. They were in different townships. Those who left the districts for the city did not always provide their new details to the missionaries. Because of this the administration of the church was unreliable and the pastoral task could not be performed adequately.

New townships in and around Paramaribo were organised into new churches. With support from friends new church buildings were erected to serve the members in Rust en Vrede (1882), Combé (1884), Wanica (1886), Saron (1900), Noorderstad (1906) and Zuiderstad (1912/1913).

A major problem in the churches after the abolition was the marriage of the former slaves. Before the abolition slave couples were allowed to make a *ferbontu* 'covenant' in the presence of a church officer. The government however did not accept this covenant as a legal marriage. After the abolition, the Moravian and the Roman Catholic Churches took the side of the government and requested that the couples marry for the second time. The marriage had to take place in the presence of a public servant and followed by a celebration in the church. Members who were not willing to do that would be placed under church discipline. This led to 3,100 leaving the Moravian Church and 5,000 put under discipline. Those who left joined the Roman Catholic Church. This exodus caused problems within the Moravian Church. The decision to excommunicate members was taken by the board without consulting the missionaries, who were involved in the day-to-day running of the church.

Another challenge that the Moravians faced had to do with education. After the abolition, the number of pupils in their schools grew. In 1874, about 62 per cent of the pupils in Paramaribo attended a Moravian school. The results of the schools were often not satisfactory. The teachers were not qualified for their job and this can be explained. The Moravian schools were conducted in Sranantongo. However, the government made a language policy that stated that education had to be given in Dutch. The Moravian missionaries came mostly from Germany and Dutch was a problem for them. They were also not trained teachers or academic theologians. The changes in the education system also affected the curriculum. Bible education, the heart of Christian education, could only be taught after school time and because the government was subsidising the education the Moravians had to comply. The changes were motived by the desire to secularise education. A similar battle was going on in the Netherlands. Supporters of public education did not want to include special (Christian) education in a government-supported school system. In 1866, the church appointed a Dutchman as the superintendent of the schools. This however did not upgrade the level of the schools. Yet, in the interior and the districts, the Moravians were the only providers of education for many decades, even after the abolition of slavery.

Between 1860 and 1870 the Roman Catholic education on the other hand grew significantly. In 1870, there were 3,043 pupils in Paramaribo and 2,481 in the districts. The subsidy given by the government should be credited for this growth, besides the effort of the Redemptorist educators.

9.2.2. The Roman Catholic Church

On 30 July 1865 Pope Pius IX offered the Surinamese Catholic Mission to the *Congregatio Sanctissimi Redemptoris* (C.SS.R), Congregation of the Most Holy Redeemer, better known as the 'Redemptorists'. This allowed for members of this congregation to serve the mission in Suriname. The growing mission needed more workers. Just like the Moravian Church, the emancipated Afro-Surinamese people flocked to the Roman Catholic Church. The growth did not happen only because of the effort of the missionaries. As indicated earlier, some Moravians who were not happy left their church and joined the Roman Catholics. Most of them however returned to the Moravians when the Catholics also changed their regulations regarding marriages.

On Sundays mass was celebrated in the Sint Petrus en Paulus Church in Srananantongo (06.00) and for children in Dutch (07.00). At 08.30 high mass was celebrated and a homily was delivered in Dutch. During the week mass was celebrated once or twice every day.

The arrival of the Redemptorists allowed the church to pay more attention to the education of its members. Just as with the Moravians, slaves joined the church because of the benefits they received. When these benefits fell away after the abolition, the churchgoers needed education in the Christian faith. Various groups and fraternities in the church organised weekly activities and retreats to educate the people. The church issued pastoral letters to address problems that members faced. The purpose of these meetings and letters was to promote holiness among the members, especially in families. And even with all these things in place, the church lamented regularly about the participation of its members in heathen activities. Besides the problems with the traditional religion the church had issues with the practices surrounding death. The Afro-Surinamese people had an extraordinary respect for the dead. They displayed that in the way in which they conducted themselves at the burial ground and the things they did for the deceased. On top of their own ceremony they welcomed that of the priests. When a person who was not a member of the church was sick, the family would invite the priest to come and convert him, so that if he died the priest would give him a good funeral. Often the bishop would deny these so-called converts a 'good funeral'.

The third problem that the Creole Church faced had to do with poverty. Most of the church members were poor and did not come from a strong social background. Slaves did not enjoy strong family ties, because they were separated from their families by the colonial plantation owners. They depended on help from their owners or the colonial government. The abolition brought a change to this situation. The declining economy of the country caused many people to become poor. This in turn caused the average lifespan to continue to reduce, with a high rate of child mortality. Many of the poor belonged to the group of illegitimate children. Despite the fact that child mortality increased, the number of children who were born, compared to the era of slavery, also increased. Many parents therefore left the care of their children to the church. This mentality is still seen among some Afro-Surinamese members of Christian churches today. They expect the church to take care of their children. The churches continued to suffer financially, because the members were not supporting their churches. Finance was always a major problem for the Surinamese church. However, the Afro-Surinamese people are willing to make major sacrifices when these are required within the traditional religion. Did this attitude grow because the churches used their financial support to attract people to their churches? Was it because the leadership of the churches got support from abroad to maintain the churches? Studies have to be conducted to find the answer to this major problem within Christianity in Suriname.

The Roman Catholic Church provided care for the orphans. The number of orphans grew from 489 in 1862 to 762 in 1868. Before the abolition, the church was only responsible for the 'free' orphans. The orphans of former slaves were taken care of by the slave masters. After the abolition the churches had to take care of all the orphans. The church is still seen as an institution that has to take care of orphans.

In 1863 workers of the church used to visit 30 plantations. This number grew in 1866 to 40 and 50 in 1880. This did not include the districts and the villages of the Natives. In 1870, the priests were visiting 16 Native villages, with approximately 565 people. These villages lay scattered throughout the country in Upper Suriname, Upper Saramacca, Orleane Creek, Kalebas Creek, Tibiti and Wayombo. In 1875, the church had baptised 500 Natives and in 1883 the number grew to 800. This represents a significant growth. The number of Natives who lived in the lowlands, the coastal area, at that time was estimated at 1,000.

Because of the growth of the church, new buildings were erected. On 10 July 1885 it dedicated its largest church building in the country, Sint Petrus en Paulus (Saint Peter and Paul). In 1958 when Suriname became a diocese the building became a cathedral. Sint Petrus en Paulus is the largest wooden building in the country and probably in the Americas.

9.3. Beginning of the Baptist, Adventist and Methodist Churches

The post-emancipation era saw the arrival of new churches in Suriname, including one established by a Surinamese. These new churches had strong ties with churches in Guyana. Christians from Guyana started the Adventist and Methodist Churches and even though the founders of the

Baptist Churches were Surinamese, they all became Christians in Guyana. The small Plymouth Brethren Assembly that was established also had strong ties with Guyana.

9.3.1. The Vrije Evangelisatie

The Vrije Evangelisatie was the first church that was established by a Surinamese. The founder was Meyer Salomon Bromet, a Jew who was born in Paramaribo in 1839. He became a Christian in what was formerly British Guyana.[1] In 1860, he returned to Suriname and started to preach the gospel. In 1864, he left for England to study theology. When he completed his studies he preached in Europe for a few years, before he returned in 1885. He served in the Reformed Church for a little while, but felt that he was not free to preach the gospel there. At that time liberalism entered the Reformed Church.

Bromet, who was influenced by the Moody Revival, started to preach in a building that a Jew made available to him. He set up a committee that had to look for means to buy a church building. He raised funds in the Netherlands, England and Scotland. On 10 November 1887, the first stone was laid for a building for the *Gemeente van Gedoopte Christenen* (Church of Baptised Christians). The building was dedicated on 11 March 1888. The *Vrije Evangelisatie* (Free Gospel) was established in Suriname. Many Jews became Christians as a result of Bromet's ministry and joined the church. The church started a Sunday school that was attended by many children. By 1901, 100 children were attending the Sunday school. Bromet also started a street-preaching ministry and Bible studies. In 1897 he started, with support from the Netherlands, a Christian primary school. Bartel de Jong came from the Netherlands to head up the school. De Jong was supported by three Surinamese teachers W M Knoch, ThJ Asdot and M E Stuger and four other assistant teachers. Bromet died in 1905. Before

---

1. Probably through the ministry of believers from the Plymouth Brethren Assemblies who were in Guyana since 1827. The Baptists did not arrive in Guyana before 1861. The church in Suriname included the words Free Gospel Hall in its name. This was the phrase that was normally used by the so-called Open Plymouth Brethren Assemblies. Bromet was also baptised by John Rhymer, a Brethren missionary in Guyana.

he died however, he saw the first church split in Suriname. One of his disciples left the church to start another, independent church.

9.3.2. The Surinaamse Baptistenkerk

Carel Paulus Rier was born in 1863 in Paramaribo. In 1888, he left Suriname for Demerara in Guyana where he joined the American National Baptist Convention. This denomination belonged to the Afro-Americans in the United States of America. Rier became a Christian there. On his return in 1890, he attended the Vrije Evangelisatie Gemeente of which Meyer Salomon Bromet was the founder. In 1893, he was baptised and became a full member of the Vrije Evangelisatie. Rier was a beloved disciple of Bromet, who encouraged him to study. Bromet lent him some of his own theological study books and allowed him to help in gospel preaching on the street. Rier was not satisfied with things in the Vrije Evangelisatie; this caused a separation between the two preachers. According to Rier he could not get the freedom to evangelise in Sranantongo, the language of the common people, especially the Afro-Surinamese people. Taking into consideration that Rier was converted in an Afro-Guyanese church, this may explain his struggle. Others attributed the split to the fact that the members in the church belonged to the middle class, and that women were allowed to preach. Whatever the case may have been, around 1898 Rier and some of the people who attended the Bible studies of Bromet left the Vrije Evangelisatie and founded a new group, which was called Surinaamse Evangelisatie and afterwards *Surinaamse Baptistenkerk* or *Doopsgezinde Gemeente*. The work of Rier was very successful, but by the end of 1901 and the first part of 1902, the church experienced problems. Most of the male members left. Despite these problems, Rier continued his work. In 1903, he left for the USA to do an examination and be ordained as a clergyman.

Rier was very active among the Afro-Surinamese people. He translated various Old Testament books into Sranantongo. The death of his wife in 1909 was a severe blow to him. After her death, he was no longer the energetic man he used to be. Although he continued his work, it was with less zeal. He died in 1917.

The Surinaamse Baptistenkerk was confronted with two breakaways. In 1902, a few of the male members in the church left. They were not happy with the way in which Rier led the church. The breakaway group founded the new church *De Evangelisatie Ebenhaezer*, under the leadership of N C J Neus. Fortunately, in 1924 the members of Ebenhaezer returned to the Surinaamse Baptistenkerk. In later years, the members of the Surinaamse Baptistenkerk returned to the Vrije Evangelisatie.

There was however another group that broke away from the Surinaamse Baptistenkerk around 1907. This group started meetings similar to the Plymouth Brethren Assemblies. One of the leaders of the group was E Byron. The services included the weekly celebration of the Lord's Supper, which stopped in 1911. After that, the group remained very small, until Byron passed away in 1936. A new attempt to start a Brethren assembly in Suriname took place in 1983.

9.3.3. The Seventh-day Adventists

The beginning of the Seventh-day Adventist Church in Suriname was in 1894. Warren G Kneeland met with a group of Sabbath-keepers in Nickerie. Their numbers grew, due to the work of colporteurs who distributed Adventist literature. The work was supported by the Adventist mission in Guyana. In 1903, the superintendent of the Guyanese mission, D C Babock, visited Suriname. He preached to the Natives in the interior. After many years of mission activities, the first person was baptised in 1909. She was Mrs Beck-Durban. Ten years later, A E Riley was invited to come to Suriname. On 6 March 1919, Riley baptised six people in Nickerie. The first church of the Adventists in Suriname was organised on that evening. The church started with six members. These members spread the Adventist message in Suriname. The church grew and started branches in various parts of the country.

9.3.4. The African Methodist Episcopal Church

The African Methodist Episcopal Church (AMEC), an Afro-American denomination, started their church in Suriname in 1912. The Guyanese AMEC clergyman, the Rev Dr D P Talbot, visited Suriname to conduct services in Nickerie and Paramaribo. The services were held in English and focused on Guyanese. The church started the Bethel congregation in Paramaribo. The AMEC Church services followed in the tradition of the so-called Black churches in America. Members expressed their agreement with the preachers, by exclaiming phrases like 'Amen, hallelujah, this is my Jesus', during the sermon. Their clapping of hands during the singing was also new in the colony. AMEC remained a small congregation and was only able to reach a small group of Afro-Surinamese people.

9.3.5. The Salvation Army

The beginning of the twentieth century also saw the introduction of the Salvation Army in Suriname. Henriette Alvares, who was a member of the Vrije Evangelisatie Church, went to the Netherlands for her education as a nurse. In the Netherlands, she came in touch with the Salvation Army. When she returned to Suriname in 1924, she and her sister introduced the Salvation Army to Suriname. The work received a boost when Captain and Mrs Jos Govaars arrived in 1926. The army then started its organised activities in Suriname. The work of the Salvation Army spread to various parts of the country. It is especially known for its social work among the less privileged.

9.4. Conclusion

The post-abolition Surinamese society saw the development of the Creole Church. Besides their faithful members, churches were confronted with members who continued to practice the traditional Afro religion, the Winti. Furthermore, these members were not supportive of their church, but were expecting the church to provide for the needy. This new form of Christianity presented the Moravian and Roman Catholic Churches with new challenges that were difficult to deal with at that time. Adding to that problem was the arrival of workers from Asia.

This era saw the arrival of newchurches, most of which had a Guyanese influence. Even though their number was small, the Baptists, Methodists, Adventists and Salvation Army established themselves in the colony. Before we can continue with the history of Christianity in Suriname, attention must be given to the arrival of the new inhabitants of the colony, the migrants from Asia.

Appendix to chapter 9: Jehovah's Witnesses

One religious organisation should be mentioned here in this brief survey, the Jehovah's Witnesses. They differ from other Christian churches in many ways, even though they use the Bible as one of their theological sources.

It was difficult to trace when the Jehovah's Witnesses established themselves in Suriname. The first official visit made by a Witness was in 1915. A certain Mr Coward visited the country, followed by Mr Rainbow and Mr Young. It is not certain if they came to Suriname as a result of previous interactions with Surinamese.[2] Archival documents found so far, seem to suggest that a permanent establishment took place in Paramaribo in the 1940's.[3] Activities of the organisation soon spread to other parts of the country. By the end of the 1950's it had a strong presence in the eastern part of the country, among the Ndyukas. Activities are still taking place along the Marowijne, Tapanahony and Lawa rivers. In February 2006, it dedicated a congress hall in that area with a seating capacity of 800 people. In Paramaribo where it all started, the organisation has a congress hall and a multifunctional office complex. In 2011 the complete Bible was published in Sranantongo (*Nyun Grontapu Vertaling*). The organisation has members throughout the country. According to its 2011 statistics, it has 49 congregations, 2,520 peak witnesses and 9,008 memorial attenders.

---

2. See the brief description in *De Vraagbaak. Almanak voor Suriname* 1955 (1954).
3. The address in 1947 was 50 Zwartenhovenbrugstraat, in 1948, 80 Gemenelandsweg and in 1950, 141 Rusten Vrede Straat.

CHAPTER 10

Missions to the Ethnic Groups

10.1. Introduction

Starting from 1853, immigrants came from Java and Madeira. Eighteen Chinese came from Java and 120 Portuguese from Madeira, with an additional 155 Portuguese from Madeira in 1854. In the ensuing years, more immigrants came from the following countries: there were 500 from China (1858), with more in the following years; 526 came from Barbados (1863). Immigrants also came from India (1873) and Java (1890). Initially they came as contract labourers. After their contracts expired, most of them remained in the colony. Towards the end of the nineteenth century Lebanese migrants came to the colony. Contrary to the other migrant groups, they came voluntarily with the purpose of setting up businesses and they were associated with a branch of Christianity in their country of origin. Most, if not all, of them were Maronites and joined the Roman Catholic Church after their arrival. They remained a close group in Suriname.

Suriname became a mixture of different ethnic groups with diverse languages, religions and cultures. The presence of the immigrants changed the landscape completely. This was a challenge to the colonial church. It had its discipleship problems with the Afro-Surinamese people and had to work among people of other faiths, for which it was not prepared. Missions among the migrants and the different ethnic groups that were created by the colonial government took place along ethnic lines. The church had missions to the Indians[1], Chinese, Javanese, Natives and Maroons. This went on until the last half of the twentieth century. This chapter will present a brief survey of the Indian, Javanese and Maroon missions.

10.2. *The Indians*

In June 1873, 410 immigrants from India arrived in Suriname. The majority of them came from North India, particularly from the districts of the United Provinces, and from Bihar. Between 1873 and 1916, more than 34,000 immigrants came to Suriname. At the end of their contracts, most of them remained in Suriname and made it their home.

The immigrants were given freedom of religion. The majority (84 per cent) adhered to Hinduism. With the coming of a new group, the *Arya Samaj*, the more traditional group of Hindus called themselves *Sanatan Dharm*, 'The Eternal Religion'. Among the Hindus the Sanatan Dharm has more followers. A small number of the Indian immigrants were Muslims. Scholars differ in their opinion whether the Indians practiced the cast system, since all had to do the same work in the sugar cane fields.

Most of the immigrants spoke either *Bhojpuri* or *Awadhi*, two vernaculars of North India. The descendants of the migrants consider their language to be Sarnami Hindostani. This present-day language however differs from the Hindi language.

The Indians became very influential in every aspect of life in Suriname. When these immigrants arrived in the colony, the Moravians and Roman Catholics competed for their souls.

---

1. The Indians are also known as 'East Indians' to distinguish them from the so-called 'Red Indians', the Indigenous (Native) people of the Americas. In Suriname the Indians are known as Hindostanen (Hindostani). In this work we call them 'Indians'. See the two detailed monographs written by CJM de Klerk (1951) *Cultus en Ritueel van het Orthodoxe Hindoeisme in Suriname*. Amsterdam: Urbi et Orbi and (1953) *De immigratie der Hindostanen in Suriname*. Amsterdam: Urbi et Orbi. The history of missions among the Indians in Suriname and the Southern Caribbean was well presented in JMW Schalkwijk (2011) *Ontwikkeling van de zending in het Zuid-Caribisch gebied 1500-1980 in het bijzonder onder de Hindostanen 1850-1980*.

10.2.1. The Moravians

The first Indian convert of the Moravians was baptised in 1870. In 1873 two others followed. These early converts were immigrants from the British West Indies and not from India. Afterwards more converts were baptised, including those from India. They had learnt Sranantongo or knew some English. It was difficult to maintain contact with these converts. The missionaries did not know their language, religion, and culture. Because of this, the church decided to appoint Christian immigrants to labour among their own people. Abraham Lincoln, who became a Christian through the influence of the American Methodist missionary activities, was one of them. He came to the Caribbean as a nurse in an immigrant ship. In Guyana he taught migrants to read, write and taught the Bible. He worked as an evangelist in a few Caribbean islands. In 1897, he was appointed as an evangelist by the Moravian Church in Suriname. Through his work the missions made real progress. He advised that the church should recruit specialised missionary preachers and, should start a church and a mission school for the Indians. The Moravian Church followed that advice and brought in the first missionary to work among the Indians.

In 1901, Julius Theodoor Wenzel who was able to work with both Urdu and Hindi speakers came to Suriname and the first Indian church was formed. The second missionary Christian Johannes Voigt arrived in 1906. He served the Indians for eight years before he was transferred to the Stadszending (City Mission). The Danish missionary Peter Martin Legêne replaced him in that same year. In later years Danish missionaries played an important role in the upbringing of Indian children in especially the boarding school Sukh Dhaam that Legêne established at Alkmaar.

The mission started to expand. This was due to the work of both the Indian workers and the European missionaries. One of the influential local workers was Theodoor Gangapersad Lachman. He was born in Trinidad in 1887, and migrated to Suriname when he was eight. He attended the mission school of the Moravians and enjoyed the Hindi and Bible lessons from Lincoln. He attended the home church meetings secretly and when he was 18, he was baptised. After taking the evangelist course, he became an evangelist and faithfully preached the gospel among the Indians. His offspring contributed in different ways to Surinamese Christianity, first among the Moravians and later on among the Pentecostals.

In 1930, the Indian branch of the Moravian Church had 300 members, two church buildings, six mission stations, two mission schools and a boarding school. Due to the expansion the work faced challenges. Often there were not enough leaders. Some mission stations e.g. Saramacca, district Suriname, and Commewijne had to be closed down during the 1940's. There were other aspects of the work, such as the schools and the ministry among women that were growing.

In the 1950's workers from Suriname started to take more leadership positions in the work. A group of women was trained as evangelists to serve in house visitations and catechesis among women. In 1963, the church started an Indian mission's department with its own conference, and representation in the mission and provincial boards. The department grouped the work in the various districts according to jurisdictions. The church membership grew to 1,250.

In the 1970's and 1980's, academically-trained workers such as Johannes Rambaran (see 15.2.5), Frederik Rambaran (see 15.2.10) and Freddy Lachman were ordained to serve the mission. However, during this same period the Indian mission lost some of its workers, through emigration, repatriation and death. There were no replacements for most of them. Because of these phenomena, the workload of the remaining workers became heavier.

How should the missions to the Indians be evaluated? The answer to this question will only be given after a brief survey of the other churches which were also involved in missions to the Indians.

10.2.2. The Roman Catholics

The Roman Catholics started their mission among the Indians at almost the same time as the Moravians. The church baptised a few Indians in 1872. Different to the Moravians, some of the priests in those early days knew Hindi. In 1874 Engelbertus Odenhoven gathered the first family among the Indians and in 1879 a work started among orphans. The Indian mission was intensified from 1904 onwards and much effort was put into the work. The mission erected a building for the Indian mission and started its first school in 1910. The Catholic priests were better prepared than the Moravians for their task, because several priests studied the language and culture of the Indians very well.

In 1931, the Roman Catholic mission had baptised 1,000 Indians. It had nineteen schools and two boarding schools, with more workers than the Moravians.

10.2.3. Other Churches

In the 1990's the influence of the Moravian and the Roman Catholic missions among the Indians decreased. Other groups took over. Miss Barbara Erb of the International Mission started study groups among the Indians.

In 1993, Shekinah, now associated with Christ Gospel Church, started a fast-growing mission among the Indians. Within a short time, it founded churches in many places.

At the beginning of the twenty-first century, an interdenominational workgroup was formed under leadership of Mrs Usha Schalkwijk-Doerga to foster cooperation in missions among the Indians. This is a very promising initiative.

10.2.4. Conclusion

Missions among the Indians have been going on in Suriname for more than one hundred and thirty years. However, the results were meagre. According to the census figures of 2004, only 6.48 per cent of the 135,117 Indians in Suriname claimed to be Christians. In earlier years, as in missions among other groups as well, rivalry was prevalent between the Moravians and the Roman Catholics. According to the Moravians, Catholics gave children and adults, who had already been educated by the Moravians, money and promised them other things if they become Roman Catholics. Despite these human shortcomings, God in his grace worked among the Indians and some of them came to know Jesus Christ as Saviour.

Some Indians, although they were not converted to Christ, boast of their Christian education and the good teachings of Christianity. Christianity influenced their morals. Indians had no problems with the influence of Christianity in their life and thought. Hinduism can easily adopt features from other religions. The teachings of Christ should move beyond the sphere of influence to accepting the person of Christ as Lord and Saviour of all. Missions among the Indians in Suriname still have to see the great harvest.

10.3. *The Javanese*

The colonial government had to depend on the British government to bring in immigrants from India to the colony. Because of this and other reasons, the Dutch government decided to bring immigrants from its own colony. In 1890, the *Nederlandse Handelmaatschappij* received permission to bring in migrants from Java. Ninety-four immigrants arrived in Paramaribo in 1890 to work on the plantation Marienburg. Because of good experiences with these immigrants, the government brought other groups. The number of immigrants from Java between 1890 and 1938 was 32,956 of which 26 per cent returned to their country after their contracts expired.

The immigrants who remained were involved predominantly in farming. Contrary to the Indians, they did not try to get the ownership of the lands on which they were farming. Their activities were on a small scale, largely for their own consumption. They tried to keep the traditions of Java alive, including the style of their houses. This however was only for a short period. The generations that were born in Suriname, were no longer keeping the traditions. Javanese were losing some of their cultural heritage and were taking on new ones. Integration of the Javanese into the community of Suriname in the early 1900's was not easy. The position of the Javanese immigrants was different from the Indians because the British government protected the latter. Life was generally much harder for the Javanese. Nowadays the Javanese are integrated in the Surinamese society, with some of them involved at the highest levels of political life.

All the Javanese immigrants claimed to be Muslims. Religious activities among them however proved the contrary. Pre-Islamic Javanism activities such as *jaran képang* (horse dance), and other rituals such as *slametan* (a sacred fellowship meal), *sajèn* (sacrifices) and *nyekar* (visiting the grave of dead ancestors) are still prevalent among them. This Javanism is a religion based on a belief in spirits that live in houses, trees, rivers etc. A Javanist is a Javanese, who keeps the *adat* (fixed traditions concerning lifestyle) and strives to live in harmony with the spirits.

The language of the immigrants was not homogenous because they came from different locations. It is not clear how these different languages developed in Suriname. Nowadays the descendants of the immigrants consider their language to be Surinamese Javanese and it differs from the language of Indonesia.

10.3.1. The Moravians

The beginning of the Javanese mission of the Moravians started with missionaries who shared the gospel with immigrants in Sranantongo. The results were poor. In 1903, a boy named Radjiman was baptised as the first fruit. He, however, left his faith and died very young.

The second conversion in 1908 was more effective. Niti Pawiro, a former Muslim leader, became a devout evangelist, who preached the gospel to his people. Sadly he died in 1914, only six years after his conversion.

Hermann Moritz Bielke came to Suriname in 1909 to work among the Javanese. He studied the Javanese language in Indonesia for eighteen months. He worked for twelve years at Leliendaal. In 1918 he was encouraged by the government to start a boarding school there at Leliendaal. He had to leave Suriname due to illness. Missionaries who came after him started churches in Rijnsdorp, Meerzorg, Tamanredjo, Domburg, Saramacca, Wageningen, and Nickerie. The first Javanese church in Paramaribo was built in 1934 and a boarding school in 1943. This boarding school started to accommodate the first 'students' from the Leliendaal boarding school who had to attend secondary school in Paramaribo.

In 1957, the first Javanese pastor, Soekoer Mingoen, was ordained followed by the second, Toekiman Remanuel Wongsodikromo (see 15.2.6), in 1965. Both served the Javanese mission in various posts until their deaths respectively in 1996 and 1986. The third pastor Ramin Djamin, was ordained in 1974. He also served the church in various positions and died in 2006.

The Moravian Church restructured its mission, so that their mission is no longer divided along ethnic lines. There is no longer a Javanese or Indian mission's board or church. A person living in a particular area has to visit a church in that area. In so doing, churches can no longer focus on a particular ethnic group.

10.3.2. The Roman Catholics

The first Javanese was baptised in the Roman Catholic Church in 1901. A major boast was given to this work when Gerardus Wilhelmus Maria Ahlbrinck started his work among the Javanese in 1924. He opened an agricultural project at Copieweg. His idea was to draw Javanese through this project to the mission station. The agricultural project was successful until its closure in 1951. A boarding school was also started in 1925. The mission at Copieweg was more than a Javanese mission station. It served as a base for various ethnic groups. Different priests ministered to each ethnic group separately, but used the same lectionaries and the same hymn books.

In 1968, a presbytery for Javanese started in Paramaribo. At that time there was a discussion going among the church whether there was a need to continue with separate missions among the ethnic groups.

10.3.3. Other Churches

The Pentecostal Church, Pinksterzending, started a ministry among the Javanese in the 1970's. In 1975, the leader of the ministry, Willem Wongosemito, left for the Netherlands. Antoon Sisal, a converted Muslim, became the leader of the Javanese mission of the Pinksterzending. Under the leadership of Sisal, the ministry grew and became an autonomous non-denominational church. The name of the new group was called Christengemeente Dian. This denomination now has various churches in Paramaribo and in the other districts. It is very successful in its ministry among the Javanese.

In the 1990's, Johannes and Dorothea Martoredjo of the Christian and Missionary Alliance Church (C&MA) started their church-planting ministry among the Javanese. At present, this church also has various branches in Paramaribo and the surrounding districts.

10.3.4. Conclusion

According to the census figures of 2004 about 14.46 per cent of the 71,879 Javanese in Suriname claimed to be Christians. The number included converts among all the Surinamese churches. This number was reached after more than a century of missionary activities. The number seems to have increased in recent years. However, a lot still has to be done among this group in Suriname.

The language that was used by the Moravians was the so-called 'High Javanese'. The pastors followed the Javanese tradition by using the 'sacred' language in addressing God. Both Christengemeente Dian and C&MA use Surinamese Javanese, in preaching, Bible-reading and singing in their churches. Undoubtedly the language is one of the factors that contributed to the success of these newer churches.

10.4. Maroons

Christianity among the Maroons will be studied in three groups. The first group comprises three smaller groups of the Matawai, Kwinti and Paramaccan (10.4.1). Around 1900 their numbers were approximately 600, 200 and 400 respectively. In 1960 the numbers grew to 2,000, 500 and 2,000 respectively.

The second group is that of the Saramaccans (10.4.2). In 1900 their total number was estimated at around 4,000. In 1960 the number was between 15,000 and 20,000. The third group is that of the Ndyuka (10.4.3). Their numbers were equal to that of the Saramaccans.

10.4.1. Matawai, Kwinti and Paramaccan

10.4.1.1. Matawai

The work among the Matawai people started as a result of the conversion of Johannes King.[2] King visited the Moravian missionaries in Paramaribo in 1857 as a result of a dream. He was baptised during his second visit in 1861. In 1862, he was appointed as the leader of the church that he

---

2. For details, see the work of Dr Hesdie Zamuel (1994) in Part II of this book. Christofel de Beet and Miriam Sterman (1981) wrote in detail about the Matawai people in their doctoral dissertation entitled: *People in Between. The Matawai Maroons of Suriname*. Meppel: Krips Repro.

founded among his people in Maripaston. Due to the work of primarily King, the evangelists Charles Edward Bern and Johannes Hiwat, most of King's tribesmen were converted to Christianity.

10.4.1.2. Kwinti

The Kwinti Maroons originated from a group of slaves who escaped slavery in the middle of the eighteenth century.[3] They hid themselves in the area of Para and maintained a good relationship with the Matawai people. Due to problems with the Matawai people they left that area in 1880 for Coppename. In 1887, they were recognised by the government as an independent Maroon group.

The Kwinti people came into contact with Christianity through the ministry of Johannes King, when they were still with the Matawai. Alamu, the leader of the tribe in Coppename however, was still a follower of the traditional religion. A missionary threw his god Koffiemakka away in 1890. In 1892, Aron Olensky, a worker from Berg en Dal was appointed as worker for that area. Due to mistrust from the Kwinti and his own ineffectiveness, he was replaced in 1894 by Christiaan Kraag. Kraag's ministry was very successful. Around 1910, the Kwinti were converted to Christianity.

The church however was not without its own problems. Some members left because of family feuds. The members who left invited the Roman Catholic Church to settle in their village. From that time on, the two Kwinti villages on the Coppename were divided along denominational lines. The villagers of Bitagron belonged to the Catholic Church and those of Kaaimanston to the Moravians. As was the case with other tribes, not all church members were dedicated Christians. The traditional religion continued to be practiced alongside Christianity.

---

3. These Maroons are also known as: Koffimakka-negers, named after their leader Koffi. Wim Hoogbergen (1993) wrote on the history of the Kwinti people in 'De geschiedenis van de Kwinti'. *SWI Forum*. Jaargang 10, nummer 1. Juni 1993. Paramaribo: Stichting Wetenschappelijke Informatie. See also Christofel de Beet & Miriam Sterman (1980): *Aantekeningen over de geschiedenis van de Kwinti en het dagboek van Kraag* (1894-1896). BSS 6. Utrecht: Universiteit van Utrecht.

10.4.1.3. Paramaccan

The early history of the Paramaccans is uncertain.[4] Around 1830, they moved to the Paramaccakreek, from whence they got their name. In 1894, a Moravian missionary visited them for the first time. During a visit in May 1896, the tribal chief Apensa was baptised. According to his traditional religious belief he had committed a serious offence because he had killed another Maroon. He tried to pacify the spirit of the deceased man through offerings and sacrifices without results. He therefore needed to be delivered from the avenging spirit that was haunting him. When he heard about Christ and the deliverance that he could give, He gave his life to him. He continued in his Christian faith and was admitted to communion two years later. The Moravians were not the only denomination interested in the Paramaccans. The Roman Catholic Church was also involved there. Probably Catholic missionaries from French Guyana were the first to visit the Paramaccans. The presence of two competing denominations caused much harm to the cause of Christianity among the Paramaccans. For the most part, Christianity among them remained an outward religion.

10.4.2. Saramaccans

10.4.2.1. Moravians

The Saramaccan Christians, who remained after Alabi and Grego passed away were not able to continue with the church and therefore requested a new missionary from Paramaribo to come and live with them. In 1835, a missionary visited the group at Ginge Bambai. He asked them to erect a new church building. This was done and it was inaugurated in 1837. The missionaries who visited in 1835 and 1837 were both attacked by malaria. Because of this the church became reluctant to send a missionary to live there permanently. The two sons of Johannes Alabi, Johannes Alabi II and

---

4. See the doctoral dissertation by John D LeNoir (1973), *The Paramacca Maroons: a study in religious acculturation*. New School for Social Research. Michigan: University Microfilms. See also his paper (1975) 'Surinam national development and maroon cultural autonomy'. *Social and Economic Studies*, Vol. 24, No. 3 (September 1975), pp. 308-319. Sir Arthur Lewis Institute of Social and Economic Studies, University of the West Indies.

Hiob were encouraged by the visit from Paramaribo and became active again in the work of the mission.

Missionary Rasmus Schmidt, who visited Ginge, was again attacked by malaria. Nevertheless, in December 1840, he and his wife went to Ginge to live there. He served the believers there for about four-and-a-half years and died in 1845. In response to his request before his death, his wife carried on the work. She later married missionary Johann Gottfried Meissner and both continued with the work. In 1847, the group moved to a new village called Ganse. Due to the illness of the husband, the couple had to leave Suriname in 1849. Missionaries, who came to Ganse after them, died shortly after arrival or had to leave due to illness. From 1854 on, the church was left without a missionary. Local leaders such as Johannes Alabi II, Franz Bona, and Samuel Kwakoe Treu were again leading the church.

In 1860, Gottlieb, the first Saramaccan to serve as an official evangelist of the Moravians, was sent to the village Guyaba, where a revival had started. Gottlieb served there for a short time and had to leave. Due to a family feud, some of the people also left Guyaba and started a new village called Aurora in 1891, followed by Nieuw Aurora in 1901. Christianity seemed to have been one of the sources of tension among the Awana people, a clan within the Saramaccan tribe. The modus operandi of the Moravians was to move the Christians away from their non-Christian relatives. Often, the Christians were not willing to do that. Some continued to maintain relationships with their 'heathen' families, including the use of their traditional medicinal knowledge. This practice was not approved of by the missionaries.

Another revival was experienced at the village Sofibuka in 1892 when Paulus Anake cleansed the village from objects that were worshipped by the villagers and started a new church. He wanted to associate his church with the Moravians. Members of his family left and started a new village called Botopasi (1895). So far, the Moravians had been working among one of the twelve clans among the Saramaccan tribe, the Awanas. With the work started in Botopasi, Christianity was brought to another group, the Dombis. Other villages that were started due to problems around Anake were Futunakaba and Abenaston. In that way, the Christian faith was spread to other areas as well.

In 1890, Daniel Yvelaar, the first Saramaccan to serve as a missionary teacher, was sent to Ganse. This was a new direction for the church. From this period onwards local leaders were sent to be missionaries to their own people.

In 1950, the Moravians were involved in six Saramaccan villages with 2,000 baptised adults and children. The six villages were: Ganse, Nieuw Aurora, Botopasi, Futunakaba, Abenaston and Pokigron. The church is still active in these villages. Medical and school work is also done in Debike, Djumu and Kajana. Due to the shortage of ordained pastors the work is now done by trained pastoral co-workers. From time to time an ordained pastor visits the area to serve communion, baptise and confirm new members. The commitment of the church members in this area had always been an issue of concern for the church leaders.

10.4.2.2. The Roman Catholic missions

In 1907, two Roman Catholic priests, F Bazelmans and L B Luykx, accompanied by a Saramaccan captain Dirifowru, made a visit to the upper Suriname River. The purpose of this visit was to get to know the area and the Saramaccans. After a few visits Franciscus Petrus Morssink suggested that the church should set up a mission station in that area. A school was built in 1919 at Sonté, near Kabelstation, followed by the church in 1921. The school had to be closed because its building burned down in 1922. In 1925, a new opportunity was given to the church. A delegation from Gran Rio, upper Suriname River, came to the capital city requesting priests to come and build a school in their area. Following this, the church responded and built a mission station and a school. The station was called Ligorio.

In 1935, the church built a new centre. It was called Lombe. Lombe however had some challenges. In 1957, Nicolas Johannes Spruyt moved to that area, but drowned in the same year. Piet van der Pluym and some Sisters of Tilburg who gave attention to the school and medical work moved to the area. Sadly, Van der Pluym also drowned in 1961. This for the Saramaccans was a sign of bad omen. Due to the lake that was created in that area, the station had to be moved to a place closer to the city. The new station was also called Lombe.

The tradition of the Roman Catholics not to have priests living among the people was also carried on among the Saramaccans. Fathers Spruyt and Pluym and the school personnel, who normally lived among the people, seemed to be the exception to this rule. Their presence was very short. Currently catechists drawn from local people are trained to live and work among their own people. From time to time a priest visits these villages.

10.4.2.3. Other churches

In 1969, leaders of the Pentecostal Evangelisch Centrum Suriname (ECS) visited the Saramaccan villages at the Suriname River. Among them were American missionary James Cooper and the Jamaican Franklyn Sephestine and a few Saramaccans. A villager from Futunakaba had told the two missionaries about a prophecy that was apparently given by Paulus Anake. According to this prophecy, White people would come to Futunakaba to preach the gospel to the villagers.

The activities of Pentecostals in the area were not welcomed by the churches that were there before them, particularly the Moravians. Some of the people who joined ECS were members of the Moravian Church. Despite the protests from the leaders of the Moravian Church and the Moravian-dominated villages in that area, by 1970 ECS had established itself in Futunakaba. The work expanded to other villages such as Guyaba, Tjalikondré and Godo.

Church of the Living God International has churches or mission activities in Pikin Slee, Ko Sindo and Semoisi.

10.4.3. Ndyuka

The early history of the Ndyukas has not been studied sufficiently to give information of their formation period.[5] The beginning of their history should be sought in the invasion of the French, under the leadership of Jacques Cassard in 1712. Many slaves used the invasion to flee into the bush in search of freedom. A large group of people joined the Ndyukas in 1757, when a few hundred slaves revolted in the Tempati area. As a result of this revolt, the colonial government was forced to sign a peace treaty

---

5. See the oral version of the Ndyuka historian Andre Pakosie (1999).

with the Ndyukas under the leadership of the paramount chief Fabi Labi Beyman in 1760. From that time on, the Ndyukas lived as a free people, primarily in the eastern part of Suriname.

The religion of the Ndyukas, like the Saramaccans, has a complex pantheon of gods, including the ancestors and certain reptiles.

10.4.3.1. The Moravians

In 1847, the Moravian missionary, Otto Tank, visited the Cottica area in the north-eastern part of the country to see what the possibilities were for mission activities there. In 1850 the mission leader, Heinrich Rudolf Wullschlägel, spoke with the paramount chief of the Ndyukas, Manyan Beyman, about the possibility of starting missions among them. Beyman denied the missionaries access to his people because he felt that Christendom was for the White people. The Ndyuka people had to serve their own gods. Beyman made it very clear that he, and probably his people also, would not let go of his own religion and religious practices. His reaction was based on what he had heard about the work of the Moravians among the Saramaccans. According to Beyman the Saramaccans who accepted Christianity were those who most of the time suffered sickness and death. This was so, because they were no longer using the powerful herbal medicines that were given to them by the gods.

The attitude of Beyman changed when the Matawai prophetic preacher, Johannes King, visited him at his residence in 1865. King preached the gospel to the Ndyukas and it impressed Beyman to the extent that he would no longer stop anybody from accepting Christianity. His only restriction was that he would not allow that the people be baptised in his area, in Marowijne. Before King could arrange for the people to be baptised at a visit two years later, he was denied access to the Ndyuka area, the reason being that Beyman died in 1866. A witchdoctor said that Beyman died because he opened the area to King. The people tried to kill King by poisoning him, but God delivered him miraculously.

The Moravians were allowed to start missions among the Ndyukas in 1892, in the village Wanhatti and in 1894 in Albina. Due to the lack of interest from the Ndyukas, the mission station of Wanhatti was closed in 1919. Even the new station, started in 1926 at Gaanman Staalkondre, with school and medical work, was closed in 1934. In 1938, the work at Wanhatti restarted. After World War II, a new station started at Stoelmanseiland, which became the centre for the work among the Ndyukas. The Moravians had churches, medical centres and schools in various villages of the Ndyukas. Due to the civil war, between 1986 and 1992, much of what had been built up was lost.

10.4.3.2. The Roman Catholics

In 1895, the church built a station at Albina from where a priest visited some Ndyuka villages. In 1898, the Ndyuka paramount chief Oseyse visited the mission station at Albina. By this Oseyse gave his recognition of the work of the Catholic Church. The church was established among the Ndyukas.[6]

10.4.3.3. Other Churches

Besides the Roman Catholics and the Moravians, other churches worked among the Ndyukas as well.

10.4.3.3.1. Wesleyan Church

In 1945, the Rev Leonard Leitzel of the Pilgrim Holiness Church (Wesleyaanse Gemeente) came to Suriname. He started, with the help of William Parris, a work at the village which they called Pelgrim Kondre (Pilgrim Village) in the district Marowijne. The work grew and a new church started in the nearby village Akale Kondre. Besides the church, there was also a school and a boarding school at Pelgrim Kondre. The civil war has also caused much damage to this work, but it is still going on.

10.4.3.3.2. Baptist Church

In the 1960's, Rob and Els Sussenbach from the Vrije Evangelisatie (Baptist Church), continued a work in Albina, Marowijne. This work had been initiated by Jan Kool and his wife (1959-1965), and also by the family Van Stormbroek (1962-1963). It focused primarily on the Natives (Arawaks and

---

6. Vernooij wrote a detailed history about this work, of which I will give a survey in the third part of the book (see 16.4.5.2.4.4).

Caribs) but gradually also included the Ndyukas. The work also suffered from the effects of the civil war of the 1980's.

10.4.3.3.3. Pentecostal Churches

In the 1970's and 1980's the Pentecostal Churches, especially Evangelisch Centrum Suriname (ECS) and Gods Bazuin, started missionary activities among the Ndyukas. At first they held evangelistic crusades in various villages. The message of salvation was preached and prayers were offered for healing and deliverance. The response of the people to this new approach led to the formation of centres for Pentecostal Church activities, in two villages: Snesi Kondre and Nyun Libi. Graduates from the training school of Evangelisch Centrum Suriname started churches in various Ndyuka villages. After the civil war, people were more open to the message of the gospel, and especially the Pentecostal Churches profited therefrom.

The Church of the Living God International and Bribi Ministries also have churches among the Ndyukas.

10.4.3.3.4. Others

The Seventh-day Adventists started a branch in Moengo. In the 1990's the Plymouth Brethren started a work in the village of Peto-Ondro. Recently a team from the Southern Baptists started to work among Ndyukas as well.

10.4.4. Conclusion

According to the census figures in 2004, there were 72,553 Maroons in Suriname. Almost 60 per cent claimed to be Christians. The statistics revealed that in the Sipaliwini district, where the Maroons traditionally lived, only 35 per cent of the population claimed to be Christians. Most Maroon Christians live in the capital city. The worldview and traditional religion of the Maroons continued to be a challenge to all the Christian churches working among them. After more than 245 years of missions among the Maroons they remained among the least-reached groups in Suriname. Growth in some churches often takes place at the cost of others.

There is a need for evangelism among villages and families that have not yet been associated with any church. Churches should consider combined evangelistic activities instead of proselytising each others' members. The attitude of churches towards each other may have contributed to the lack of conversions among the Maroons. Christianity has been a dividing factor among the Maroons, where families are divided along denominational lines. Also, as the former Roman Catholic bishop Aloysius Zichem once said: 'all the churches are laying their eggs in the same nest. When the eggs hatch out, they are fighting about the chicks'.

CHAPTER 11

Christendom in the Autonomous Suriname

11.1. *Introduction: Nationalism*

Before the arrival of the Baptists in the 1880's, all the Surinamese churches were led by foreigners. All the workers and leaders came from outside of the country. The foreigners were sometimes assisted by local 'helpers'. This was parallel to the political development in the country. The country was governed by Dutch public servants, who were sent from the Netherlands. After the 1880's people started to protest against this. These protests were suppressed brutally. In July 1902 the colonial army killed more than twenty and wounded dozens of protesting workers in Marienburg.

11.1.1. Killinger, Doedel and De Kom

In 1910 the Hungarian Frans Pavel Killinger who was an inspector of police in Suriname, hatched a plot against the government. Together with a few Surinamese, he planned a coup to overthrow Dutch rule in Suriname. The plans were discovered and it caused turmoil in the country. Many people responded to the event, including the leaders of the Christian churches. According to the Roman Catholic paper *De Surinamer*, Killinger was a psychopath. The Lutheran clergyman A E Boers gave a talk on the 'movement in our days'. Boers' message was not well accepted by people in society. According to Boers, the majority of Surinamese preferred not to be ruled by Jews or Coloured people. The Coloured people preferred Dutch rule. Surinamese according to him were not willing to accept leadership from each other. The Dutch people were the only ones who could lead the nation. The people felt that Boers placed the Dutch above the Afro-Surinamese people, when he said the following in his lecture: 'You will not become like the Dutch people... We are more [higher, better] than you are'.[1] The Afro-Surinamese people did not accept this, especially from a Dutch clergyman. They protested strongly against this. However, their protest did not lead to an uprising. They did not support Killinger.

An uprising came in the 1930's under Anton de Kom. The nation was plagued by great poverty. A number of Surinamese left for the Dutch island of Curacao. At that time, there was a flourishing oil industry there. Under the leadership of Anton de Kom and Louis Doedel, the Surinamese people protested against the colonial government. This protest was suppressed by first expelling Anton de Kom out of the country and subsequently placing Louis Doedel under restraint in a psychiatric institution.[2] These two leaders however did not want to work with the church. De Kom advocated a separation of church and state. He wanted the government to stop supporting churches and to close down Christian schools. The labour organisation Doedel and others established was abandoned in 1932 under suspicion of 'antireligious propaganda'.

11.1.2. Rier, Comvalius, Rijts and the Nimrod beweging

The first half of the twentieth century saw the appearance of Christians from Afro-Surinamese descent who protested about their status in society. They emphasised the characteristics and the special features of the Afro-Surinamese. At that time, many Afro-Surinamese people in the colony were unemployed. According to them this was because of the poor government of the colony and the arrival of the migrants from Asia. The emancipated Afro-Surinamese people were not prepared properly for life after the

---

1. The Dutch phrase was: 'Wij zijn meer dan gij zijt' (Boers 1911:18).

2. Doedel died on 10 January 1980. See Scholtens B (1986). *Opkomende arbeidersbeweging in Suriname. Doedel, Liesdek, De Sanders, De Kom en de werkiozenonrust 1931-1933*. Nijmegen: Transculturele Uitgeverij Masusa. See also: Scholtens B (1987). *Louis Doedel, Surinaams vakbondsleider van het eerste uur: een bronnenpublikatie*. Paramaribo: Universiteit van Suriname.

abolition. One could not expect that a people who have been in slavery for many centuries would suddenly become independent. Among the Afro-Surinamese people there were a few prophetic figures who stood up to preach a message about a better future for the descendants of the Africans. This movement was influenced by the Black Awareness or Consciousness Movement that was emerging at that time.

The Baptist clergyman Rier was one of the advocates of the movement. His Surinaamse Baptisten Gemeente existed to look after the interests of the Afro-Surinamese people. In the Surinamese society of the twentieth century much attention was given to the birthday of King Willem III and Queen Wilhelmina of the Netherlands. However, the abolition of slavery was only remembered in churches. In a message to remember the abolition on 1 July 1904, Rier argued that the Old Testament prophet saw the African (Ethiopian) on the upper level of society. He had to wait, because the rule of Japheth (the White) would come to an end. He called upon the Afro-Surinamese people to esteem themselves highly and to help each other. He asked that better education be provided for the Afro-Surinamese and that scholarships be given to them. He further asked that labour protection should be put in place. Rier was the first to call upon the Afro-Surinamese and society to protect women.

As a minister of God's Word, he also addressed the Afro-Surinamese. He spoke about their shamelessness, lack of respect and lack of desire to find employment. He disapproved of their polygamy, polyandry, lawlessness, lack of mutual confidence, worship of money instead of God and idle folkdances. Sunday became a day for sins. Lesbian relationships (mati) were also prevalent.

Rier was a prophetic voice to the Afro-Surinamese people. He wanted the Afro-Surinamese to deal with their traumatic past. The abolition of slavery set them physically free but mentally they were still in bondage. As a theologian Rier believed that the Africans came into the New World in the providence of God. He therefore felt it necessary to thank those, who under God's permission brought their ancestors from Africa to the New World. They taught the Afro-Surinamese through punishments, as much as they could. They taught them: soundness, humanity, freedom, activity, brotherhood and citizenship.[3]

The Americans, Booker Taliaferro Washington and William Edward Burghardt Du Bois, influenced the so-called Black awareness. Their message was preached in Suriname by the Afro-Surinamese school teacher Theodorus Adriaan Charles Comvalius. Comvalius (1877-1950) called upon the Afro-Surinamese people to stop looking down on their own condition. That attitude would only bring them down. Afro-Surinamese people must recognise and respect their origin. Thousands of them denied that they were 'Negroes', because the colour of their skin was lighter than that of those whom they called 'Negroes'. Afro-Surinamese people must not be ashamed of who they are. Comvalius pointed to what an 'Afro' person can achieve by pointing to the respected Afro-American doctor Booker Washington from Alabama.

The message to uplift Afro-Surinamese continued with the two brothers Rudolf and Johan Rijts. They preached in public and published a magazine called *De Nimrod Beweging* (Nimrod Movement). They called on the full-blooded 'Negroes' in the colony to return to Africa.[4] Rudolf Rijts (1880-1949) was called a crazy person and was placed in a mental institution. This method was a popular one of the colonial government.

The traditional churches in Suriname were not ready for these nationalists or the Black Consciousness Movement. This can be understood, because the leaders of those churches were 'white'.

Minor changes had started to take place within the churches and Surinamese leaders were appointed for ministry. The Roman Catholic Church ordained Henri Francois Rikken (1863-1908) as a priest in 1891. Rikken studied in the Netherlands from 1877-1891. He returned to Suriname in 1892. In 1902, the Moravians ordained Cornelis Winst Blijd (1860-1921) as a clergyman. Blijd was first trained as a teacher and became

---

3. Theologians will disagree with some of Rier's views. Did the Dutch teach the Afro-Surinamese people the things that Rier referred to? No theologian will question the providence of God. However, when human beings acted in a brutal way towards another person and applied cruel methods of punishment, one should attribute that behaviour to the sinfulness of men. That kind of behaviour cannot be attributed to God.

4. The brothers Rijts represented Marcus Garvey's international movement: Universal Negro Improvement Association (UNIA).

an assistant missionary in 1899. The Reformed Church and the Lutherans were not ready yet to appoint Surinamese.

The churches could not respond to the Afro-Surinamese nationalist movement of that time. They could not provide the leadership in the process of spiritual and mental liberation, because they did not understand the Afro-Surinamese people. The Surinamese church needed more leaders like Rier.

11.2. Autonomy

Suriname received a form of autonomy in 1948. However, it remained within the kingdom of the Netherlands. The autonomy allowed for a general right to vote. Because of this, 54 per cent of the population were eligible to vote. Suriname was now able to organise free and general elections. Various political parties were set up and churches participated directly or indirectly in these parties.

In 1946, Father Leonardus Josephus Weidmann founded the Progressive Surinamese People's Party (*Progressieve Surinaamse Volkspartij*, PSV). The PSV was a party for all who believed in one God. In 1948, Weidmann founded the Progressive Labourers' Organisation (*Progressieve Werknemers Organisatie*, PWO). Through these two organisations, the Roman Catholic Church wanted to contribute to the political and social development of the nation.

The Moravian Church did not found a party but members of the church saw the leader of the National Party of Suriname (*Nationale Partij Suriname*, NPS), Johan Adolf Pengel as their leader. Pengel was a member of the Moravian Church. The Moravian William Emanuël Juglall from Indian descent was not only a member of the NPS; he first served as a member of parliament and then as a minister in cabinet. The co-founders of the NPS were the Rev Christoffel Alexander Paap and Johan Ferrier, both of whom belonged to the Reformed Church. The NPS was the political home of the Protestants.

The 1950's experienced a new development. A group of young Surinamese, who went to the Netherlands to study, rediscovered the value of that which belonged to them. In 1951 they started a movement that was called *Wi eygi sani* (WES, our own things). These young Surinamese discovered during their studies in the Netherlands the impact that colonialism had on the way Surinamese think. If they wanted to bring change to Surinamese society, they had to think in a nationalistic way. In the Netherlands they 'discovered' what was their own. They had not responded to the call of the pioneers such as Rier and Comvalius a few decades earlier.

The Indians saw the Wi eygi sani movement as a threat to their culture and started their own movement in the Netherlands to emancipate their own language, Sarnami Hindostani. The movement was known as *Hindostani Nawyuak Sabha* (HNS, Indians' Young People's Association). WES and HNS were not able to develop one Surinamese view, but represented their ethnic supporters.

The Christian church did not share the views of the nationalists. The emphasis of some members of Wi eygi sani on the traditional religion was a thorn in the flesh of the church leaders. Wi eygi sani was thankful for all the efforts of the church to educate the Afro-Surinamese people. The church took care of the religious and social development of the Afro-Surinamese people. However, mentally and spiritually the Afro-Surinamese people were still not liberated.

The nationalistic movements forced the church to re-evaluate its own mode of operation. From its beginning in Suriname, the church worked along ethnic lines. In the 1960's a committee suggested to the Roman Catholic Church that it should abandon the practice of doing missions in that way. The committee recommended a radical integration of the different branches of missions. The Moravians were also confronted with this question. In the 1970's the Roman Catholic Church started to abolish its ethnically-based missions. As stated in the previous chapter, this process started much later in the Moravian Church.

11.3. The Committee of Christian Churches

The Christian denominations had a long history of opposition to each other. At the beginning of the nineteenth century, the Protestants joined forces and opposed the Catholics. This battle was for the souls of the people. It appeared however that all the churches were losers in this battle. This was clearly seen in the results of it. In the 1930's the churches realised they could not carry on in the same way. The arrival of Protestant church leaders with a liberal theological persuasion made collaboration easier. They were open to work with people from other theological streams. On 4 July 1937 a partnership was established, *Het Comité van Christelijke Godsdiensten* (Committee of Christian Religions). The committee was responsible for a radio broadcast via the first radio station in the country, *Algemene Vereniging Radio Omroep Suriname* (Avros). The churches moved on and founded the *Comité Christelijke Kerken* (CCK, Committee of Christian Churches), on 23 November 1942. The founding members were the Moravian Church, the Evangelical Lutheran Church, the Reformed Church and the Roman Catholic Church. The Salvation Army was an associate member. The Baptists, Adventists and Methodists did not participate in this committee.

The goal of CCK was to promote the common interests of the churches. It studied questions in the field of individual and corporate ethics that the churches found important for the nation. It took the lead in these matters by giving its opinion publicly and assisting in solving these matters in a practical way, if its assistance was required. At its establishment, CCK protested against the immoral lifestyle of the American soldiers who were in the country to protect Suralco, an American aluminium company. Church leaders were of the opinion that the movies, parties, drinking sprees and sexual immorality of the Americans, had a negative effect on the population. The CCK leaders called upon the government to take steps against this moral decline. In the years that followed its establishment, CCK continued to address important issues in the nation through its publications.

11.4. Developments within the Moravian Church

The responsibility of the Moravian Church in Suriname was in the hands of the mission board in Herrnhut (Germany). Herrnhut was also responsible for the finances of the work in Suriname. This changed in 1928. The *Zeister Zendingsgenootschap* (ZZg) in the Netherlands took over this responsibility. It appointed a chairperson and an administrator for the Surinamese church board. Locally, a church conference was responsible to select three more members for the board. Most of the workers were still Germans. In 1940, all the German missionaries were put in camps. The church had to make changes to its board. It appointed a Swiss missionary as the chairperson with Surinamese and Dutch workers as members. This development made it necessary for the church to work towards its independence.

In 1957, the church received the status of a 'Synod Province of the Unitas Fratrum'. The church became independent on 1 January 1963. The Surinamese, Rev Rudolf Eduard Constantijn Doth was consecrated as bishop on 11 February 1962. He became the first chairperson of the province. The board of the new province consisted of various departments. These departments were responsible for the missions among the ethnic groups and the missions in the city.

11.5. Developments within the Roman Catholic Church

Stephanus Joseph Maria Magdalena Kuypers led the Catholic Church in Suriname from 1946 to 1971. He first served as the apostolic vicar from 1946 to 1958. From 1958-1971, he served as the bishop of Paramaribo. The church expanded its work under his leadership in various ways and became the largest Christian denomination in the country.

In 1946, the church started with the training of four young men to become catechist teachers. Two of them completed their training and served among their own people in the interior. Arrangements were also made with the regional seminary in Trinidad, for the training of clergymen.

In 1955, two Surinamese, Andre Berenos and Rudolf Lim A Po, were consecrated as priests. However, they did not serve in Suriname but in

Brazil where they were trained. Father Harry Moesai, who studied in the Netherlands, was consecrated in 1956. He remained in Suriname and served the church in various places and capacities. For many years, he was the leader of a boarding school.

Due to the lack of local workers, the church continued to receive workers from abroad. In 1949, Fathers and Frères from the Oblates of Maria came to Suriname. These leaders contributed much to the work in the interior among the Natives and the Maroons. In order to take better care of the deaf and mute and the blind people, Franciscan Sisters from Oudenbosch started an institute.

The church grew significantly in numbers between 1859 and 1964.

Table 21 *Numerical growth of the Catholic Church between 1859 and 1964*

Year	Number
1859	9,500
1955	40,000
1964	71,166

The growth of the work brought financial challenges to the church. In order to continue with most of its activities, it had to close seven schools among the Maroons. It closed its paper *De Surinamer* in 1955 and replaced its weekly *De Katholiek* with another weekly, *Omhoog*.

On 24 August 1958, the Surinamese vicariate was elevated to a diocese. The first bishop was Mgr Kuypers. This marked a new beginning in the history of the Catholic Church in Suriname. This bishop started with the process of making the church a Surinamese church. He continued to encourage the training of Surinamese priests and that Suriname religious workers would take over the work. In order to train local priests the Petrus Donders Seminarie, a small seminary was established in 1961.

Mgr Kuypers' new direction towards a Surinamese church received a major boost. The Second Vatican Council (1962-1965), gave clear instructions as to the direction the church should take. It emphasised that religion and culture had to engage each other. The European culture and church model that dominated the church was foreign to the Surinamese situation. In 1965, suggestions were made to the church to move towards a Surinamese liturgy that would include Surinamese ideas, materials and style.

In 1966, a pastoral centre was established. Its goals were to prepare pastoral policy decisions for the care of the souls and to serve as a training institute for people who were involved in the care of souls. Furthermore it had to promote communication between the bishop, the priests and the members of the church. The church started to imitate local practices, such as celebrations at special anniversaries and care during the time of mourning. Instead of the traditional focus on conversion from heathenism and non-Christian religions, the message of the church focused more on keeping faith alive and the practice of love. The attitude of confrontation was replaced by dialogue.

In 1968, the church started with a socio-cultural training centre, *Ons Erf*. It also established the *Pater Albrinck Stichting* (PAS) that focused on missionary renewal and social activities in the interior.

On 5 November 1969 Pope Paul VI gave the diocese permission to consecrate the first Surinamese, Aloysius Zichem, as an assistant bishop.

11.6. Conclusion

Christianity had to respond to the developments in Suriname. The rise of Creole and Indian nationalism compelled the church to reconsider its own mode of operation within the Surinamese society. The church did not find it necessary to revisit its ethnically-based missions. The process of nationalisation however received attention during this process. The leadership of the Moravian Church, for example, came into local hands. The Roman Catholic Church also took the first steps in that direction. It consecrated a Surinamese as assistant bishop and started to train Surinamese to become priests.

Within the Moravian Church, young Surinamese theologians started to respond critically to the theology and mode of operation of their own church. This will become evident in the summaries of their works in part II of this book. There was a clear call for renewal in the academic documents they produced. The church itself however chose for consolidation instead of renewal. The era of nationalism therefore only started the process of developing a Surinamese church.

CHAPTER 12

The Beginning of Pentecostal Churches

12.1. Introduction

In the 1950's and the 1960's Full Gospel and Pentecostal Churches established themselves in Suriname.[1] Contrary to what was found among the other churches, Pentecostals did not write their history or theology. It is therefore difficult to describe their history because of the lack of written sources. There were personal testimonies but very few systematic written histories.[2]

12.2. Full Gospel Church in Suriname

12.2.1. Introduction
The Full Gospel Churches in Suriname can be divided into three main groups: Assemblies of God, *Stromen van Kracht* and *Evangelisch Centrum Suriname*. Other churches came forth from these three groups. In recent years, new churches were planted, which will not be included in this chapter.

---

1. Some theologians differentiate between Pentecostal churches (which started around 1901) and charismatic churches (which started in the 1950's as a renewal movement within the traditional churches). In Suriname most Pentecostal leaders refer to their church as a Full Gospel Church. Some prefer to speak about 'Pentecostal', to avoid the impression that they are the only ones who preach the 'full gospel'.
2. This chapter therefore is a tentative attempt to do so, based on the resources that were available and personal interviews.

12.2.2. Assemblies of God

12.2.2.1. The First Assembly of God

In November 1959, missionary John Tubbs of the Assemblies of God arrived in Suriname. Earlier he had served as a missionary in Venezuela and Guyana. He started to minister to children. Because of his language barrier, he could not reach as many people as he wanted to. Tubbs did not master Dutch, the official language of Suriname. He started The First Assembly of God with a small group of people. As the church started to grow, he felt that it was necessary to have a Dutch-speaking minister. John de Cock and his wife, from the Netherlands, came to Suriname for that purpose. The church met at the house of De Cock at the Grote Combéweg. In September 1962 it bought its own property at 24 Hayariestraat in Rainville, where the church still exists.

When De Cock left Suriname in 1962, John and Donna Verbarendse came to serve the church. At that time the number of believers grew to between 250 and 300 people. The Verbarendse ministered there from 1963 to 1967. With their arrival the church started to experience friction. The precise reasons for the problems could not be established. However, a group of between 200 and 250 believers left the church and started a new church called Pinksterzending. Before Verbarendse left the country in 1966, things were discussed and resolved between him and the group that left. However, the group never returned to the mother church.

12.2.2.2. The Stichting Pinksterzending

The events that led to the beginning of the *Pinksterzending* took place in 1964/65. On 8 March 1965, the first official meeting, a prayer meeting, was held at the house of the family Parisius. About ten brothers and sisters came together for prayer. This was after they left because of the problems within the Assemblies of God. When Pinksterzending started, a group of between 100 and 150 believers joined the group.

On 24 March 1965 the group officially founded the Stichting Pinksterzending. Johannes van den Bergh, who came from the Netherlands, was its first pastor. The church started new ministries for children, youth and a radio programme. The ministry of Van den Bergh in Suriname was short-lived. He was put out of the country on 6 May. The day before he left, he consecrated Mrs Kitty Uyleman as the new pastor. This decision was not easy, because in those days it was not usual for a woman to stand behind the pulpit. Mrs Uyleman however persevered and served the church well. She continued with the radio ministry and personally presented a programme for children. The number of broadcasts of the church grew to five programmes per week. In May 1971, the first television broadcast of the Full Gospel churches in Suriname, *De Stem van het Volle Evangelie* (the voice of the Full Gospel) was inaugurated. Pinksterzending contributed to the broadcast as well.

Pinksterzending was very active in evangelistic work in the interior. It held evangelistic crusades in Brokopondo, Gran Kreek, Pikin Saron, Tapuripa, Klaaskreek and Balingsula and established outposts in these places. Other places were visited 'once off' without a permanent settlement. The work of Pinksterzending caused problems with especially the Moravian Church, because some of the areas that the Pinksterzending visited were traditionally Moravian areas. This led to tension between the two churches.

Besides the work in the interior, Pinksterzending also ministered in areas close to Paramaribo, where they established churches or Sunday schools, such as Lelydorp, Dessa, Menckendam, Nieuw Weergevondenweg, Latour and Blauwgrond.

On 1 May 1966, two Dutch nurses, Lammy Krol and Lucky Hartenberg, started *Kinderhuis Samuel*, a home for children. The Pinksterzending and other Full Gospel churches supported the idea, but the leadership of the home remained in the hands of the two sisters. Krol and Hartenberg provided a home for dozens of orphaned and underprivileged children.

The 1970's were very difficult for the church. After its initial growth, the church started to experience a decline after some leaders had left the country to settle in the Netherlands. Pinksterzending was not the only one who faced this problem. Because of the approaching autonomy many Surinamese left for the Netherlands. Pinksterzending also suffered a loss of leaders and members to other Pentecostal churches. On top of that Mrs Uyleman, the pastor, left for the Netherlands in 1977. She was very ill and suffered from the effect of the brutal violence that she suffered, when robbers came into her house. Although she recovered well and came back to Suriname, in 1983 the family left permanently. Mrs Uyleman died on 12 February 1985.

On 23 January 1983 Willem Ngatmin Wongsosemito was consecrated as the new pastor of the church and a new board of directors was established. The church started with new evangelistic activities, including door to door evangelism in its neighbourhood and an evening Bible school. It started to grow numerically again and expanded its ministry to the growing number of Haitian immigrants in the country. In order to accommodate the Haitian ministry, Pinksterzending started a foundation in 1984 called *Stichting Evangelisatie Zending tot Uitredding der Schare* (EZUS). One of the board members of Pinksterzending, Achmed Rickets was appointed as the pastor for this ministry. He was assisted by another board member Glenn Kranenburg. After a few years, EZUS was able to consecrate a Haitian, Dèjean Fleurentin, as pastor of the church.

12.2.3. The Movement Stromen van Kracht

12.2.3.1. Stromen van Kracht

The beginning of the *Stromen van Kracht* (Streams of Power) in Suriname goes back to a crusade held by Karel Hoekendijk. The Dutch Pentecostal preacher Hoekendijk came to Suriname in September 1961. He started to hold meetings in a house at the Gongrijpstraat in Paramaribo. Because of the growing interest he rented a bigger facility. Karel Hoekendijk started his revival meetings on 16 October 1961 in the Thalia theatre. He preached the Word, prayed for the sick and ministered deliverance to the demon-possessed. His wife Elizabeth 'Bep', son Johannes Franciscus (Frans) and daughter-in-law Yvonne joined him later to support the work. The services in Thalia were attended by almost 2,000 people and that was unique in Suriname at that time. Many Hindu pundits came to these meetings. Within a few months, Hoekendijk baptised 667 believers by immersion. In order to be able to continue with the services legally, Hoekendijk started the foundation *Stichting Suriname Volle Evangelie Gemeente Stromen van Kracht* on 19 February 1962.

The established churches in Suriname criticised the mode of operation of Hoekendijk. They had to watch how their members were leaving and being re-baptised by Hoekendijk. Rev Christoffel Alexander Paap of the Reformed Church did all that was in his power to get the Hoekendijks out of the country. Paap was successful and the attorney-general decided to expel the Hoekendijks.[3] Karel and his wife left in 1962, on the same flight with Rev Paap. Frans and his wife followed soon. The Prime Minister Johan Pengel had sworn that Hoekendijk would not enter the country anymore during his lifetime.[4]

The new church was left in the care of four young Surinamese believers. Ludwig van Kanten, Ilse van Kanten-Reeberg and Bernadette 'Detta' Hewitt-Guda were responsible for the music and the singing. Pudsey Meye led the prayers. Sermons were sent on audio from outside the country and were played during the services on Sunday. The number of people who were associated with the church was 800.

With such a large number of believers and a lack of proper organisation, the church started to experience problems.[5] There were also problems between Meye and the other leaders. It was not possible to establish the nature of the problems. Pudsey Meye left the movement and started *Gods Bazuin* with a group of believers that joined him.

The Surinamese Stromen van Kracht wanted to become independent from the Dutch organisation. When this happened, Mrs Van Kanten-Reeberg assumed the leadership of the church. In 1965, Stromen van Kracht experienced a new split. The Van Kantens and Hewitt-Guda left and started *De Gemeente van Jezus Christus*. The group that remained with Stromen van Kracht continued under the leadership of Wenzel and Wies Lachman and Mr and Mrs Hermelijn. Wenzel was the son of the Moravian

---

3. The Ministry of Health in the Netherlands is alleged to have communicated to the Surinamese authorities that Hoekendijk was a fake.
4. Eight years later the new prime minister apologised to Karel Hoekendijk and invited him to visit Suriname again. The day after Karel's arrival in Suriname, the previous prime minister, Pengel, died. A few days later Karel Hoekendijk was walking behind his coffin.
5. There were also problems within the movement in the Netherlands. In 1968 there was a split between Karel and his children. The movment also owed the printer of the monthly Stromen van Kracht a lot of money. The crusades that were held in foreign countries cost a lot of money. Karel and his wife emigrated to Indonesia, where he continued with his evangelistic ministry.

evangelist Theodoor Gangapersad Lachman. When Hoekendijk came to Suriname, Theodoor was 74 years old. At that time he was very sick. However, at the prayer of Hoekendijk, he was healed instantaneously and baptised in the Holy Spirit. Wenzel and Wies played an important role as leaders of the church. At the age of sixteen their daughter Soecila 'Sila' Prabhoede Lachman joined the evangelistic team of Hoekendijk. After a period of training in the Netherlands, she returned as a missionary to her own country in 1966. In 1985, she and her husband Roy Wong Swie San became the pastors of Stromen van Kracht.

A number of churches came out of Stromen van Kracht in Suriname. Two of them will be treated separately, because of their own impact on Pentecostalism in Suriname (Gods Bazuin and Gemeente van Jezus Christus). They were founded by the original leaders of the movement after the Hoekendijks left.

In 1993, Ramon Manbodh started Gemeente Shekinah. Earlier he had an Indian-speaking ministry within the church. Shekinah started with members of that group. The church started at the home of Manbodh but had to move to a larger hall within six months. In 1995, the church bought its own property at the Oude Charlesburgweg in Paramaribo. Shekinah expanded its ministry to Meerzorg (Commewijne), Indira Gandhiweg (Wanica) and Saramacca. Initially the church focused on Indians. Gradually it moved away from that. The church is currently affiliated with Christ Gospel Church.

Roy Wong Swie San who had pastored Stromen van Kracht since 1985, left it to start an independent ministry. In 1991, he and his wife 'Sila' founded *Lob Makandra*. Lob Makandra developed a broad ministry with a church and retreat centre. Since 1996, it provided a space for *In De Ruimte*, a Christian ministry that looked after people with bodily handicaps. Gloria Lie Kwie Sjoe-Wong Swie San, a daughter of the Wong Swie Sans, and her husband, Winston Lie Kwie Sjoe, started *Weid Mijn Lammeren*, a ministry that focused on children. Weid Mijn Lammeren provides training for children's workers nationwide and it is making an impact on the ministry of churches to children.

In 1980, Irma Gimith-Woerdings started the church *Bribi* in Albina (Marowijne). She came to the Lord in 1968, through a radio programme of Stromen van Kracht. Bribi started in Albina where Stromen van Kracht had a church that was dying. At the time that Bribi started, 'Ma Irma' was a widow with six children. The church started to grow in Albina. Due to the civil war in the second half of the 1980's it relocated to Paramaribo. In Paramaribo it grew significantly and started branches in different parts of the country. In 2003 'Ma Irma' was appointed as an apostle to oversee all the eighteen churches of Bribi.

12.2.3.2. Gods Bazuin

Pudsey Meye came to the Lord in 1961 during the crusades of Hoekendijk. When the Hoekendijks left Suriname in 1962, Meye was one of the four leaders who were appointed. Due to problems with the other leaders, he first left his position of leadership and later the church. Knowing that God had called him to ministry, he founded the church Gods Bazuin in 1963. The first services were held after a crusade in October 1963. Within a short while the number of believers grew to two hundred. After almost five years later, the church inaugurated its own building on 31 March 1968 at the 37 Verlengde Keizerstraat (Paramaribo).

Gods Bazuin started to expand its ministry to the interior. It conducted evangelistic crusades in Albina, Bigiston, Maimakondre and Cottica. It visited Natives in Kalebaskreek, Corneliskondre, Donderskamp and Tapuripa. In Corneliskondre, the crusade was held in the building of the Roman Catholic Church. Hundreds of people attended the crusade and dozens came to the Lord. In Paramaribo and surrounding areas, crusades were held and churches were started at Boonweg, Menkendam and Flora.

In 1993, the church changed its organisational structure. All its churches were united under the name: *Gods Bazuin Ministries*. In 1994, the founder of the church Pudsey Meye was recognised as its first bishop. He consecrated his son Stephanus Meye, who was one of the associate pastors in the ministry, as his successor in 2002. Currently there are sixty-two churches operating under the umbrella of Gods Bazuin Ministries in Suriname and seven outside of the country.

A number of churches broke away from Gods Bazuin. The first group left under the leadership of Ronald Ronde. It started a new church called *Eenheid in Christus*.

The second was the group from Boonweg under the leadership of Naifa Saling. In 1987, Saling founded the *Stichting Evangelisatie Gemeente Handelingen*. This church had a strong outreach towards the Maroons, since Saling himself was an Ndyuka Maroon. The church grew significantly and was able to acquire its own property in less than eighteen months. It started a branch in Moengo, in the eastern part of the country. Due to some personal problems Saling stepped down and Johannes Pinas became the new pastor.

In 1993, the third church, that of Menkendam, separated itself under the leadership of Ferdinand Waakzaam. It began to operate under the name *Gado Genade*. It planted a branch in Moengo. Just like Handelingen, this church has a strong focus on the Maroons.

The fourth group that left was the church in Flora. Under the leadership of Milton Carbiere it started *Gemeente Petra*. A gospel group of this church, *Stem fu prijs* under the leadership of Marcia Dalfour became well-known in Suriname.

The fifth group to break away was under the leadership of Izaak Jabini, who was the leader of the Sranantongo ministry of the main church at the Verlengde Keizerstraat. He started *De Rank Ministries*. After a few years, the church joined Bribi Ministries.

A sixth group broke away from the main church in 1998. Eric Tjin Kon Kiem, who was the senior pastor, left the church and more than 75 per cent of the members followed him. He started Tabernacle of Faith and Love. Currently the church has branches in Saramacca and Wanica, and it runs an interdenominational Bible training programme and a drug rehabilitation centre.

12.2.3.3. *Gemeente van Jezus Christus*

Ludwig van Kanten and Ilse van Kanten-Reeberg returned from the Netherlands to Suriname in 1953. In the Netherlands, they were members of a Baptist Church. When they arrived, they maintained good contacts with David Neff, a missionary of the West Indies Mission. The two families started a prayer meeting for a revival in Suriname.

The Van Kantens and their friend 'Detta' Hewitt-Guda started to attend the meetings of the Assembly of God. They received the baptism in the Holy Spirit during the Hoekendijk crusades and joined the Stromen van Kracht movement. When the Hoekendijks left, they became the Surinamese leaders of Stromen van Kracht.

Under the leadership of Ludwig van Kanten, Ilse van Kanten-Reeberg and Detta Hewitt-Guda, a group of believers left Stromen van Kracht. On the 13th of July 1965 they founded De Gemeente van Jezus Christus and Ilse Van Kanten-Reeberg became the pastor of the new church. She pastored the church until she died in 1991. Many of the well-known Surinamese Pentecostal leaders came from under her ministry. She led them to the Lord and played a role in their early beginnings, including Purcy Blackson, Detta Hewitt-Guda, Stanley Hofwijks and Benny Macnack.

Detta Hewitt-Guda left De Gemeente van Jezus Christus in 1978 and started a new church, Logos. In the early years of Logos, Hewitt-Guda worked under the wings of the Assemblies of God. Later on the church became independent. She was the pastor of Logos until she died in 2009.

Van Kanten-Reeberg and Hewitt-Guda were both active in evangelistic ministries nationally. None of them however planted other branches of their church. Their ministry influenced many Christian leaders.

12.2.4. Evangelisch Centrum Suriname

In September 1968, the former Dutch Baptist missionary Jan Kool and the former American Baptist James Cooper started the foundation Evangelisch Centrum Suriname (ECS). Kool and Cooper both became Pentecostals at that time. On 1 January 1969, ECS started with a three-year Bible school called 'Hebron'. It welcomed its first students on 3 March 1969. Hebron was a residential school on the former plantation Slootwijk in the district of Commewijne. Kool came to Suriname in 1952 and served the Baptist Church. Because of his experience of the baptism in the Holy

Spirit, he left the church in 1965 and joined the Pentecostal movement. Philip Mohabir, a Guyanese Pentecostal pastor, brought Kool and Cooper, who shared similar experiences, together. The first group of students of Hebron consisted of the following people: Henry Macnack and his wife, Benny Macnack, Joan Mangroe, Gladys Zarks, Haidy Tjon A Jong and Carmen Pengel. They were followed not long after their arrival by Enid Marman, Stanley and Celeste Dissels, John W Slagtand and Kala Debie. Some of these students became Christians through the ministry of Ilse van Kanten-Reeberg.

The graduates of the school planted new churches in the districts and the interior, since the other Pentecostal churches were in the city. Graduates of Hebron became leading figures in the Pentecostal movement in Suriname and abroad. The leaders of the foundation led the movement by example. They were also actively involved in evangelistic crusades.

Just like that of the other Pentecostal churches, the activities of Evangelisch Centrum Suriname met with serious resistance from the older churches. The Moravian Church especially raised serious complaints about the method in which Evangelisch Centrum Suriname operated. ECS was accused of sheep-stealing.

Jan Kool was involved in the Bible school up to 1973. In that year, he returned to the Netherlands. The idea came up to give the leadership of the organisation to the Surinamese. In the late 1970's the organisation established a new leadership model. The leadership consisted of seven people, with James Cooper as the leader. In 1981, Benny Macnack became the director of the Bible school and when Cooper left for America in 1984, Macnack also became the leader of the team. In 1989, he handed over the leadership of the Bible school to the American missionary Chester Oliver, who came to Suriname in 1970.

Table 22 *Pentecostal Churches in Suriname*

1. Assemblies of God 1959	1.1. Pinksterzending 1965	1.1.1 Dian 1975 (Independent)
		1.1.2. Ezus 1984 became Church of the Living God in 1995
2. Stromen van Kracht 1961	2.1. Gods Bazuin 1963	2.1.1. Eenheid in Christus (?)
		2.1.2. Handelingen 1987
		2.1.3. Gado Genade 1993
		2.1.4. Tabernacle 1998
		2.1.5. De Rank (?)
		2.1.6. Petra (?)
	2.2. Gemeente van Jezus Christus 1965	Logos 1978
	2.3. Bribi 1980	
	2.4. Shekinah 1993	
	2.5. Lob Makandra 1991	
3. Evangelisch Centrum Suriname 1969		

12.3. Conclusion

Starting in the late 1950's to the early part of the 1970's, the Pentecostal movement established itself in Suriname. The membership of the movement at that time was estimated to be around 1,500. This estimate was not based on accurate information, because in the early days, the Pentecostal churches did not have a membership administration. Most of the members of the church came from the other established churches, but they remained members in the records of their former churches. This made it very difficult to give accurate statistics.

The Pentecostal movement was not a united organisation. A few years after it started in Suriname, it consisted of three groups, with a few breakaway churches. In the early years of their presence, there was a revival in Suriname. Currently, most of these churches have however lost their early zeal for missions and evangelistic activities. Most are consolidating what was achieved.

CHAPTER 13

Bible Translation Organisations

13.1. Introduction

Bible translation has been going on in Suriname for many years. The first translation dated back to the 1740's, when portions of the New Testament were translated into the Arawak language. Missionaries of the Moravian Church translated the entire New Testament or major portions of it and Old Testament books into Sranantongo, Saramaccan and Arawak. This chapter will not include these older translations. It will only focus on the contribution of the Bible Society and on translation work done since the 1960's.

Table 23 *Bible Translations published in Surinamese languages after 1960*

Language	Type	Publication date
Carib	New Testament	2003
Javanese	New Testament	2000
Ndyuka	New Testament	1999
Saramaccan	New Testament	1991
Sarnami	New Testament	1998
Sranantongo	Lectionary	1998
Sranantongo	New Testament	2002
Sranantongo	Complete Bible	1998
Trio	New Testament	1979
Wayana	New Testament	1979

13.2. The Bible distribution agencies

The Netherlands Bible Society, which started in 1814, had an auxiliary in Suriname as early as 1829. The work of the auxiliary was to distribute Bibles. This work had some success, but not among the Natives and slaves. In 1815, the Society inquired at the possibility of translating the New Testament into Sranantongo. The Moravians had already translated the New Testament. The Dutch Society published a harmony of the gospels in 1816. In 1829, the British and Foreign Bible Society printed the full New Testament in Sranantongo. The Dutch Bible Society continued to provide Suriname with Bibles throughout the nineteenth century.

In the first half of the twentieth century, the Netherlands Bible Society carried out its Bible distribution in Suriname through the *Vereniging tot Verspreiding van Bijbels en Traktaten in Suriname*. This was an association for the distribution of Bibles and tracts in Suriname. The members of this Protestant association came from the Reformed, the Moravian, the Lutheran, and the Baptist churches. The association did more than distributing Bibles and tracts. It organised joint activities to promote the cause of Protestantism.

The Netherlands Bible Society intensified its relationship with Suriname in the 1950's. In 1956, it sent Jan Voorhoeve as linguist to Suriname with the primary task to revise the existing New Testament. Voorhoeve started but did not complete the project. He revised the gospel of Luke and the book of Acts.

In 1966, Karel Zeefuik founded the *Surinaams Bijbel Comité* (Surinamese Bible Committee). During his studies in the Netherlands, he received a gift of one thousand guilders from the Netherlands Bible Society for that purpose. The goal of the Society was to distribute Bibles and to promote their use. According to the bylaws of the foundation, only Protestants were allowed to become members of the board of directors. The board of directors of the committee came from the following churches: Moravian, Reformed, Lutheran and Salvation Army. In 1969, a member of a Pentecostal church joined the board.

In 1971, the foundation changed its name to *Stichting Het Surinaams Bijbelgenootschap* (Foundation of the Suriname Bible Society). Due to ministry responsibilities and his embarking on further education, Zeefuik left the ministry of the Bible Society and a new board of directors was elected. At that time, the Society started to become more involved in the work of the United Bible Societies, the internal partnership of Bible Societies. Suriname became a national office in 1973. In 1978 Paul Doth of the Moravian Church was elected as chairman of the board, a position he held up to 1989. It was during his leadership that the first full time members for the society were employed. The Guyanese pastor Cedric Singh was appointed as General Secretary of the society. Within a few years a few more people were employed, including Erle Deira. Under the leadership of Rev Singh and Rev Deira, the Suriname Bible Society took over the responsibility for Scripture distribution in all the three Guyana's.

In 1985, the Society moved to a new property that it rented at 39 Gravenstraat, which it bought a few years later with the board under Rev Detta Hewitt-Guda as chairperson. The Society further amended its bylaws so that other denominations could participate in its board, including the Roman Catholic Church. In 1987, the Society became an associated member of the United Bible Societies, followed by full membership in 1994. In 1998, the Rev Cedric Singh who had served the Society since 1985, retired and the Rev Erle Deira became the General Secretary. Under Deira's leadership, the Suriname Bible Society and SIL International (Summer Institute of Linguistics International) under leadership of Nico Doelman signed partnership agreements to work together in the cause of Bible translation and publication in Suriname. This was done successfully in all the projects in which the cooperation took place. The Rev Deira resigned from his position in 2006 and became more involved in the work of the American Bible Society in many capacities. The Suriname Bible Society is the main distributor for scriptures not only in Suriname, but also in Guyana and French Guiana.

13.3. Summer Institute of Linguistics

13.3.1. Introduction

Members of SIL International and the Wycliffe Bible Translators (WBT) did language studies and Bible translations in most of the languages of Suriname. Their work in Suriname started in 1967, after Dr Joseph Grimes did the preparatory work in 1966. SIL International signed a contract with the government of Suriname which allowed the organisation to work in the country. The goal of the organisation was to do a systematic scientific study of the languages of Suriname and to translate books of high moral value. Members of these organisations, together with Surinamese co-workers, did language studies in nine languages and translated scriptures into six languages. For more than 30 years, various people were involved in the Suriname branch in the translation department and also in support services.

In 1967, Joel Warkentin and his wife left their work in the Bolivian branch of SIL to come to Suriname. Joel became the first director of the new branch. In September 1967, the first translator Naomi Glock arrived, followed by Sara Rountree in January 1968. As a para-church organisation, the SIL translation programmes were not part of a larger evangelistic or church ministry. Translation was their mission. Members of the organisation had to go and live among the people they were planning to work with, to learn their language and culture. If the language had never been written before, an orthography had to be developed.

13.3.2. Saramaccans

In September 1968, SIL received approval from Agbago Jozef Daniel Aboikoni, the paramount chief of the Saramaccans to allow their members to live among the Saramaccans. Naomi Glock and Sara Rountree left Paramaribo for the interior and lived among the Saramaccans and learned their language and culture. With the help of some Saramaccans, they translated the New Testament. The Saramaccans who contributed in one way or another to the project were Dawsen Petrusi, Asoinda Haabo, Francis Pansa and Jajo Asodanoe. In 1991, the International Bible Society printed

2,000 copies of the New Testament under the title *Gadu Buku* (God's Book). In 1998, a revised edition was published.

13.3.3. Ndyuka

In 1968, the Ndyuka paramount chief, Matodja Gazon, gave Dr George and Mary Huttar permission to live in Diitabiki and to learn the Ndyuka language. The Huttars learned the language quickly, but they could not start work on translations because George was appointed as the director of SIL operations in Suriname. James 'Jim' and Joyce Park took over the responsibility of the translation project. They continued with the translation until 'Jim' became the director. The coordination of the project was given to Louis and Lisa Shanks. With a team of Ndyuka speakers, primarily Carlo Velanti and Evert Koanting, the New Testament was translated into Ndyuka. In 1999, the International Bible Society published *Beibel*, the New Testament in Okanisi Tongo.

13.3.4. Sarnami Hindostani

In the 1960's Dr George Huttar conducted research on the Hindostani (Indian) language in Suriname. This research showed that a translation in the Hindostani language of Suriname was needed. The Surinamese Hindostani language differed from the Indian Hindi in many ways. SIL International therefore decided to start a translation. Albertine Laura Bosch and Anna Bernada Huiskamp worked with various Sarnami Hindostani speakers on the project.

In 1998, the International Bible Society published the New Testament in two editions: *Parmeswar Ke Náwá Pustak* (government orthography) and *Parmeswar Ke Naawa Poestak* (SIL orthography).

13.3.5. Carib

SIL International initiated Bible translation into Carib when Ed and Joyce Peasgood came to Suriname. In 1970, they went to live among the Caribs in Bigi Poika in the western part of the country. Upon arrival, Peasgood started with the study of the Carib language. The translation project faced many difficulties. Due to the civil war in Suriname (1986-1992), it was not possible for the team to visit Carib villages to work with mother-tongue speakers in their villages. There were also misunderstandings within the team. In 1998, Cornelis van der Ziel who coordinated the team to translate the early books and his family left Suriname for the Netherlands. He continued to serve the project as an advisor. Henk Courtz continued as the coordinator, with Lienke Pane and Charles Maleko as main translators. In March 2001, SIL International handed over the project to the Surinaams Bijbelgenootschap. The translation was finalised in August 2002. The New Testament *Asery Tamusi karetary* was printed in Suriname and dedicated in August 2003.

13.3.6. Sranantongo

The new translation project in Sranantongo started in 1977. The idea was to work with three teams. The first team consisted of Frits Mastenbroek and Mrs H C Tiendali, the second team consisted of Miss Flora Brul and the third of Mr and Mrs John and Marilyn Nickel. This idea did not work, due to lack of time in the case of the Mastenbroek and Tiendali team and the fact that the Nickel team still had to learn the language.

In 1980, John Nickel was asked to become the 'Administrative Assistant coupled with the role of computer applications coordinator' for the whole SIL branch in Suriname. Brul became the main translator and the Nickels continued with linguistic support for the project. She translated most of the books of the New Testament.

Unfortunately in 1992, Brul had an accident, which caused one of her legs to be amputated. Besides that, she had also developed cataracts in her eyes. Therefore, SIL recruited a new translator, Conrad 'Robby' Anijs, to help Brul. Anijs, however, had to leave the project for family reasons. The administration of SIL suggested that John Wilner and his Old Testament team should help with the completion of the New Testament. Lucien Donk and Hertog Linger who also joined the team, translated the remaining books. Linger left the project before the final revision was complete. Donk became the main translator and reviser. John Wilner, Norbert Rennert, Flora Brul and Franklin Jabini provided exegetical and linguistic support.

In 2001, the Suriname Bible Society and SIL International agreed that the SIL team would be transferred to the Suriname Bible Society, and that the Suriname Bible Society would provide the consultant to check the quality of the translation. In 2002, the project was approved and the translation was published. On 10 October 2002, *Nyun Testamenti*, the New Testament was dedicated. An Old Testament project is currently underway under the leadership of Lucien Donk. Conrad Anijs joined the team again.

13.3.7. Surinamese Javanese

Edward and Linda Speyers came to Suriname in 1979, to work among the Javanese. Javanese-speaking churches in Suriname were using Bible translations from Indonesia. There was an up-to-date translation available in Bahasa Indonesia. The Speyers tested the Indonesian materials with various people and found out that many did not understand the text. The Surinamese Javanese language was creolised and modified. In 1979, Edward Speyers met Antoon Sisal. Antoon Sisal was a Javanese pastor, who worked among the Javanese in the Pinksterzending Pentecostal Church. The Javanese church under the leadership of Sisal became an independent church and operated under the name Dian. The church was no longer linked with Pentecostalism. In 1982, Sisal left his job as teacher to become a full-time Bible translator. Sisal was able to complete the New Testament translation and it was published by the Bible League in 2000, as *Kitab Sutyi Prejanjin Anyar, ing Basa Jawa Suriname*.

13.4. Gijsbertus Roest and Eddy van der Hilst

In 1976, the Roman Catholic theologian Gijsbertus J Roest and the Surinamese linguist Eddy van der Hilst started a Sranantongo translation of the readings from scriptures, taken from the *Lectionarium Romanum* of 1970. The readings consisted of 550 portions from scriptures over a period of three years. The translation was not in the chronological order in which the texts appear in scripture, but according to the order in the Lectionarium. The book was therefore very practical to use in the church service since all readings for one Sunday were on the same page. After twelve years of translation, the work, *Leypisi fu den sonde nanga den fesadey* was completed in 1988. During the twelve years that the work was in progress, portions of translated scriptures were made available for use in the parishes.

Although this translation was intended for the Roman Catholic Church, the bishop did not initiate the project. The translators had the liberty to translate the Word of God from their own 'motive, inspiration, insights and responsibility'. The main goal of the translators was to present the scripture readings in Sranantongo as it is used by present-day speakers. According to the translators, translation work was thus far done primarily by foreigners, who were not able to 'feel' the language. Although Roest is a foreigner, the input of van der Hilst, a mother-tongue speaker was decisive in the translation; therefore, this translation aimed to use all the possibilities of the Sranantongo language. The translators state clearly that they were not working from the Latin, but from Hebrew and Greek. The translated text met with resistance from some catechists, who disagree with the translation of the Holy Spirit as Santa Winti. The word 'Winti' was used for the traditional religion.

13.5. Robert Patton

American missionary Dr Robert Patton came to Suriname in August 1986. He worked in the academic hospital in Paramaribo and taught medicine, while he was involved with the Bijbel Baptist Kerk in Suriname. His church worked primarily with people from the interior, who could not speak Dutch.

Since coming to Suriname, Patton felt the leading of the Lord in preparing a translation of the Bible into Sranantongo. He became more convinced to work on a translation when he was preparing to start the Bible Institute of the Bijbel Baptist Kerk. Since there was no translation of the Old Testament available, a translation was necessary. In 1991, Patton decided to start with the translation of the Bible. His goal was to produce a study Bible based on the KJV text. Patton received help from three of the young Surinamese preachers of the Bijbel Baptist Kerk. When he completed the translation, Bearing Precious Seed in America printed the Bible at a nominal cost. This translation was the first complete Bible printed in Sranantongo (1998). According to Patton, in the translation process he was not only committed to the verbal plenary inspiration of Scripture, but also the doctrine of divine preservation, therefore, he wanted to use the Masoretic text and the Textus Receptus. Since his knowledge of the original languages was limited to searching out specific words or looking up uses in a dictionary, he used the King James Version as his base text.

The spelling and the vocabulary used in the translation are the same as that of the New Testament printed in the nineteenth century. This choice had one weakness, in that most Evangelical churches were no longer using this language in the pulpit. What was even worse, was that most people were not able to read major portions with comprehension in that old language. Many people from different churches purchased this Bible since it was the only complete Bible ever to be published in Sranantongo.

13.6. Conclusion

Bible translation was an important part of Christianity in Suriname. Most of the initiatives were taken by foreigners. The translations were therefore not owned by the Surinamese churches. A lot has to happen for the translated scriptures in these different languages to become the scriptures of the Surinamese churches.

CHAPTER 14

Christianity, Autonomy and Revolution

14.1. Introduction

The 1960's were difficult years in Suriname.[1] Many were dissatisfied with issues in the country and this led to major strikes of teachers in 1966 and 1969. The cabinet under the leadership of Johan Pengel resigned in February 1969. A new cabinet, led by the predominantly Indian party (VHP) and *Progressieve Nationale Partij* (PNP, a group of dissatisfied Blacks who left the national party of Pengel), came to power. A strike in 1973 brought the government down again. At that strike, the police killed one of the leaders of the union, Ronald 'Abaisa' Kitty. The police jailed two other leaders, Fred Derby and Eward Naarendorp. The strikes demonstrated that trade unions were a power that could no longer be ignored.

In 1973 a new coalition called *Nationale Partij-Kombinatie* (NPK), came to power and had the support of the main trade unions. The prime minister of the coalition, Henck Arron, announced on 15 February 1974, that his government was working towards the independence of Suriname no later than the end of 1975. The nation was not prepared for independence at such short notice. Many remembered the riots between Indians and Afro-Guyanese people in the neighbouring Guyana when it became independent. VHP, the Indian-dominated party, was not part of the coalition. Due to

---

1. This chapter provides an initial response to Christianity in the post-independence Surinamese context. Much more research has to be done, since many issues in that era are still waiting to be solved. This is especially true for the period after the 1980's.

fear of violence, about a third of the Surinamese population migrated to the Netherlands on the eve of independence.

Surinamese independence, just like the abolition of slavery, was a big celebration, and the predicted ethnic riots stayed away. However, the country faced other problems. It appeared that in 1969, around 61 per cent of the population lived in poverty. In 1974, 24 per cent of the working population was unemployed and yet the average annual per capita income of the population was US $1,100. The majority of the working population worked for the government. The situation developed like this despite investments that were made in the first five-year plan (1967-1972) and the second five-year plan (1972-1976).

The country was also confronted with a new group of young people who studied in the Netherlands and returned in the early 1970's. In the Netherlands, they learned a new kind of freedom. They did not only go against the moral rules of those days but supported the freedom struggle in countries like South Africa, South and Central America. These new Surinamese had serious problems with the exploiters in Suriname, such as the bauxite companies that were supported by the political elites. They were more radical than the Wi eygi sani movement of the 1950's. Some of them chose to serve their nation through the media.[2] Others formed political parties that took part in the general elections.[3] Because they were not united, they were not a strong opposition to the traditional political parties. In 1977, the *Nationale Partij-Kombinatie II* (NPK II) won the election again. The economic problems of the country continued. The new government started to take on more people as civil servants. In 1979, more than 60 per cent of the national budget was spent on salaries of civil servants. The old political parties were not working towards a renewed or a

---

2. Different papers were published such as: Pipel, Mokro, Sonde Spikri and De Vrije Stem.

3. Such as *Democratisch Volksfront* (H Keerveld), *Progressieve Socialistische Partij* (A Kamperveen), *Surinaamse Socialistische Unie* (Henk Herrenberg), *Communistische Partij Suriname* (Bran Behr), *Volkspartij* (R Lie Pauw Sam) and *Palu* (Krolis). Others among these who contributed in different ways to the development of Suriname were, Eddy Jharap (Petrol company of Suriname), Frank Playfair (member of parliament), Winston Caldeira (auditor's office), Henk Goedschalk (governor central bank of Suriname), Harold Jap A Joe (university of Suriname), Cynthia Rozenblad (director of a government hospital) and Marie Levens (minister in government).

truly independent Suriname. At its independence, the Dutch government gave Suriname three billion Dutch guilders as development aid. This money was not used for development but to keep political friends and party loyalists happy.

Between 1970 and 1980, around 149,000 Surinamese migrated to the Netherlands. This had a negative influence not only on the society as a whole but also on the church.

14.2. Independence

14.2.1. Churches and Independence

The process of independence started earlier among the traditional churches. However, most of them remained connected and dependent on their foreign mother or sister churches. Churches from different denominations used independence as a way of demonstrating their solidarity with each other. A joint service was held, but the solidarity did not continue after the service. Christianity in Suriname at that time was not a unity, but a diversity of different independent churches and denominations.

The churches that formed the Committee of Christian Churches (CCK) were united in their attempt to provide guidance for the nation. CCK sent out a pastoral letter to encourage the people to take a positive attitude towards the political independence of the country. It called for the creation of a righteous society, in which the whole nation enjoyed the riches of the country. The abuse of power was to be stopped.

In another document, CCK called on the government to guarantee the human rights of the people in the constitution. It also called for free education and prepared a document on development-cooperation between Suriname and the Netherlands. It appeared that the church took a critical attitude towards the government, and it complained against the fact that the government and parliament were not doing their work as they were supposed to.

In 1978 and 1979, CCK wrote to both the government and parliament about the abuse of the development money: The rich in the nation became richer and the poor became poorer.

The government had problems with the attitude of the churches, especially when CCK held a seminar in 1978 together with left-wing groups about Christianity and socialism. Earlier, churches were followers of the government and now the churches started to speak out against government policy and practices. This changed attitude should be attributed to the fact that the leaders of the CCK churches were now trained academics. As will be seen in the review of their works in part II of this book, they did not only criticise the government, they criticised their own churches as well. The government did not pay attention to the call by the churches.

14.2.2. Population and religion

The census of 1964 and that of 1972 revealed that the Roman Catholic Church was the largest Christian church in Suriname. Christians consisted of 44 per cent of the population.

Table 24 *Religions in Suriname 1964*

Religion	Census 1964	
	Total	Percentage
Hindu	87,575	26.9%
Roman Catholic	71,166	22.0%
Muslim	63,809	19.7%
Moravian	54,392	16.8%
Reformed	11,911	3.7%
Lutheran	4,764	1.5%

The census did not include all the Christian churches that were in Suriname at that moment. In the census of 1960, the following churches that appeared in the table below were included, but did not appear on the 1964 list.

Table 25 *Churches not included on the 1964 census*

Church	Number in 1960
African Methodist Episcopal	500
Vrije Evangelisatie (Baptist)	318
Gereformeerde	284
Adventists	283
Methodists	163

The Pentecostal churches, Salvation Army, the Wesleyan Church and other smaller churches were not seen on the map of churches in Suriname.[4] In 1972, we see the following situation.

Table 26 *Religions in Suriname in 1972*

Religion	Census 1972	
	Total	Percentage
Hindu	112,095	29.5%
Roman Catholic	81,871	21.5%
Muslim	74,170	19.6%
Moravian	59,837	15.7%
Reformed	9,788	2.6%
Lutheran	3,931	1%
Vrije Evangelisatie (Baptist)	940	0.3%

The number of Christians in percentage of the total population was 41 per cent. The division of the members among the different Christian churches should be interpreted carefully. As indicated earlier, members of the Pentecostal churches remained as members of the traditional churches. It was also normal for parents to indicate their religion as the religion of the house, even though some members were actively attending other churches.

---

4. If 50 per ent of the people who were put under the categories 'Others' and 'Unknown', with a total of 4 per cent on the census lists, then another 2 per cent should be added to the total number of Christians. About 50 years ago the number of Christians was 64 per cent.

Another issue that created problems was that the census form did not include the new churches.[5]

The churches in the independent Suriname were clearly part of the ethnically, religiously and politically plural society and had to decide on their own direction. The era in which the churches received preferential treatment was gone. In 1971, for example the name 'idolatry' was taken out of the constitution as the name of the traditional religion of the Afro-Surinamese people.

The churches had to start with the process of decolonisation. They did much to develop the Surinamese through education and medical care. Now, they had to work on the fact that the Surinamese church was a foreign institution. It still depended on personnel and finances from abroad. Churches that stood against each other in the past had to contribute together towards a new, unified nation.

14.2.3. Christian movements

14.2.3.1. Renewal among the Moravian Youth

The years after independence saw revival movements among the young people in various churches. On 1 January 1976, Paul and Coby Doth came to Suriname to lead the Stadszending of the Moravian Church. This ministry focused on the young people and services were held that targeted them. Young people came together for these meetings and many of them became active Christians, with many testifying of their conversion. The youth wing of the Moravian Church, which was led by leaders such as Leo and Maarten Schalkwijk, Carl Breeveld, Glenn Blom, Guno van Engel, Constance Landvreugd and Eveline Schotsborg, also conducted youth camps. In later years, the activities were decentralised to the local churches. This movement clearly led to the conversion of many young people. It cannot be denied that the Holy Spirit worked in the lives of the young people, which led to radical conversions and a desire for holiness in their lives.

---

5. If a person indicated 'Full Gospel' as his religion, the question was asked: Are you Roman Catholic or Moravian?

Some of these young people were more attracted to the church services in the Pentecostal churches, since those services seemed to speak more to their own experience. For unexplained reasons some young people did not remain in the Moravian Church because they were not taken care of spiritually and pastorally by the church. The problems were probably on both sides. Some young people despised the leadership of the church at that time, because in their opinion, the leaders were not 'converted' or 'born again'. They did not see some of the manifestations that were visible among them in their pastors. Some pastors on the other hand did not endorse the Pentecostal influences with their 'questionable theology' that they saw among the young people. These and other human factors led to estrangement between the youth and its church leaders.

14.2.3.2. Renewal in the Catholic Church
The Roman Catholic Church also experienced a renewal. The church took a different approach than the Moravians. The *Katholieke Charismatische Vernieuwing* (KCV, Catholic Charismatic Renewal) started in Suriname in 1974. In 1979, Father Herman van Nimwegen was delegated to lead the movement within the diocese of Suriname. In that year, he had experienced the renewal at a conference in Trinidad. He spoke in tongues and fell 'in the Spirit'. He led the services of the renewal movement in Suriname, and organised conferences and weekends for contemplation. In 1988, he started with Marriage Encounter meetings for couples. He saw many people whom he prayed for fall over and experience the 'rest in the Spirit'. The renewal remained a movement within the church and did not become an independent movement as with the youth meetings in the Moravian Church.

14.2.3.3. The Jesus Students
A third movement that started among young people in 1977 was the Jesus Students. The movement started in response to a verse read by Erle Deira, a Pentecostal believer, on 17 October 1977, during his quiet time. The verse read as follows: 'Deliver those being taken away to death, and hold back those slipping to the slaughter' (Prov. 24:11 NET). Deira felt that Christian students should do something to rescue their fellow students.

He shared the idea with his Moravian friend Carl Breeveld. Breeveld who was at a Christian pedagogical institute at that time supported Deira and they spoke with church leaders and pastors about their vision. On 11 November 1977, they started the Christian student organisation *Christelijke Studenten Organisatie*. At the recommendation of Breeveld, the name of the organisation was changed to 'The Jesus Students'. This movement started at a strategic time in the history of Suriname. In the years after independence, young people demonstrated against the age at which one was entitled to vote. They demanded that this be brought down from twenty-one to eighteen. Young people wanted to have a say in the way in which they were going to be led. The Jesus Students was a movement that worked with young people from all denominations and ethnic groups. It did not want to be a church or have specific dogmas, but wanted to use the Bible as its basis. Its main purpose was to call upon all to repent of their sins and to accept Jesus as their personal Lord and Saviour. Those who came to the Lord should meet for prayer, Bible studies and service in a church of their own choice. The movement started to expand to other secondary schools. It organised gospel concerts that were a great success. Hundreds of young people came to the concerts and gave their lives to the Lord.

14.2.4. Towards Surinamese leadership in the churches

The call for local control of the churches had been heard in Suriname for almost thirty years. The process started in the 1960's. At that time, the Moravian Church appointed Surinamese as leaders of the church. The Catholics also took initial steps. In the 1970's the development continued in the Catholic and the Lutheran churches.

14.2.4.1. Roman Catholic

Father Aloysius Ferdinandus Zichem was consecrated as the first Surinamese bishop of the Catholic Church in Suriname on 8 February 1970. He was installed in his office on 24 October of the same year. The motto that he chose for his episcopacy was *Amore traxit omnia* (through love he draws all to himself) and Mgr Zichem lived according to that motto.

The church however did not become a 'Surinamese church' with the consecration of one Surinamese. The personnel of the diocese consisted mostly of Dutch missionaries and the liturgy still followed a Dutch model. To help solve the problem of finding more local workers, a new training programme was started for catechists under the leadership of Father Toon te Dorsthorst and sister Egno Monk. In 1981, Mgr Zichem commissioned a group of eighteen catechists to do the work of missions in the interior. Some of these catechists worked in churches that became known as the 'base churches'. The 'base churches' used Surinamese instruments and local songs in their services, which resembled those of the Pentecostal churches. This led to tension among the catechists, as some were not willing to follow that model.

Besides the catechist programme for the interior, a new programme was started for workers in the capital. The first group from this programme graduated in 1982. The 1980's saw a few academically-trained Surinamese becoming clerics in the church such as Karel Choennie, Esteban Kross, Patrick Koole and Kenneth Vigelandzoon (see part II of this book). Mgr Zichem resigned from his office due to a stroke on 9 August 2003. Father Wilhelmus Adrianus Josephus Maria de Bekker was appointed in 2004 and ordained as the new bishop of Paramaribo in 2005. His episcopal motto was: *Tesimonium Domini Fidele*, 'the testimony of the Lord is faithful'.

14.2.4.2. Lutheran Church

The idea to start training Surinamese clergymen for the Lutheran Church originated with Rev Johan Hendrik Hanneman, who served the church from 1949 to 1960. In 1952, the first Surinamese was sent to the Netherlands for his theological education. Unfortunately, he did not return after he completed his studies. The second student chose a different direction and also remained in the Netherlands. In 1973, the first Surinamese, Leo King, was appointed as an assistant preacher and in 1974, he was ordained as clergyman. However, it was not before 1990 that the leadership of the church came into Surinamese hands. The second Surinamese Lutheran member of the clergy was a woman, Lucretia van Ommeren. After preparatory study at the Moravian seminary in Paramaribo, she continued her studies in Jamaica. On 12 July 1987, she was ordained as the first woman into the ranks of the clergy. The third Surinamese Lutheran member of the clergy, Marjorie Slagtand also a woman, was ordained in 1990. In 1995, Pearl Gerding, a woman, and Steve Stewart, a man, were also ordained. The Lutheran Church however, did not change its liturgy to reflect the Surinamese reality and the church still depends on financial support from outside the country.

14.2.4.3. New structures in the Moravian Church

Almost thirty years after the independence of the Moravian Church in the 1960's, it approved a new structure in 1993. At the synod of 1996, it was agreed that the restructuring should be carried out. The church started with that process in 1998. One of the important decisions in the new structure was the discontinuation of the difference between church and mission. This brought an end to the church's missionary activities along ethnic lines. The church was governed according to regions and no longer on an ethnic basis. The new structure has to prove itself. The church also has to work on its financial independence as it continues to depend on support from the Zeister Zendingsgenootschap (ZZg) in the Netherlands.

14.2.4.4. The Reformed Church

The process of appointing Surinamese leaders started much later in the Reformed Church. The first Surinamese clergyman, Max Lieveld was appointed in 1987. After moving to the Netherlands he joined the Moravian Church, where he serves as a pastor, first in Rotterdam and now in Utrecht. After Lieveld, the church appointed two Surinamese women, Diana de Graven in 1995 and Naomi Neslo-Claver in 2001.

14.3. Christianity during the era of the revolution

14.3.1. Introduction

The political situation in Suriname did not improve after the time of the independence. Instead, things became worse. Corruption was out of all proportion, civil servants were not working, even though they were on the payroll of the government. Those responsible for the cleaning of the city for example, never turned up. Because of this, the city was dirty. The poor and especially the elderly did not receive their monthly social grants regularly. The grant was not even enough to live on. The main old-age home at that time fell into despair and attracted vultures. The situation in the country was not pleasant. The ideals of independence were not achieved, even though Surinamese were responsible for the government. Because of this and the fact that the government did not allow them to start their own union, members of the Surinamese army overthrew the government on 25 February 1980. The military intended to save the country from decline and called for a change of mentality, so that the people would work towards the development of the country. Renewals were propagated in four areas: political-governmental, social, social-economic and educational. The purpose of these renewals was a complete renewal of the mentality and the human relations in Surinamese society. This should have led to a new Surinamese person. The population who were tired of the 'old politics' quickly welcomed the military, who enjoyed nationwide popularity. The military brought about some changes and developments. It paid attention to the needy and took care of them. Civil servants had to work or be at their workplace in order to receive a salary. During school holidays, young people had to work to clean the city. For this, they received some payment.

Some of the nationalists and revolutionaries who came back from the Netherlands in the 1970's thought that the new direction would allow them to realise their ideals. This however, did not materialise. On 8 December 1982, some of them were killed. The political parties Palu and Volkspartij chose to support the military and in 1983, some of them took part in government under the direction of the military. The killings in 1982, cast a shadow on a period that started with a new and great ideology. What was the response of the church?

14.3.2. Christianity and revolution

The census of 1980 indicated that membership of the Christian churches declined. This can be attributed to emigration to the Netherlands in the 1970's. The number of Christians in percentage of the population however grew by 1 per cent. The numbers of Christians, according to the denominations, in a total population of 354,860 was as seen in the following table.

Table 27 *Christians in 1980*

Adventists	1,061
Vrije Evangelisatie	944
Lutherans	2,695
Reformed	6,265
Moravians	55,625
Roman Catholics	80,922

The Roman Catholic Church remained the largest Christian group in the country. This census did not include some of the other smaller churches.

14.3.2.1. *The Committee of Christian Churches (CCK)*

When the military came to power, the CCK gave them the benefit of the doubt. The CCK however regretted the fact that some civilians died. It called on the military to respect human rights and democracy. The nation was called upon to play its role towards the new future of the nation. This was necessary because the nation as a whole was responsible for the decline of the country. It was therefore necessary to work together to bring about a change.

The CCK was of the opinion that the churches also needed conversion and had to undergo their own revolution. This positive attitude towards the revolution changed in 1982. CCK took part in a march of a group called the 'Association of Democracy'. Things became worse when a group of opponents of the military regime was killed in December 1982. CCK felt that at that time it was called to sound the prophetic word of God, even if it meant criticism of the policies of the military government. The military did not pay attention to the prophetic voice of the CCK.

Some individual members of CCK churches became a severe critic of the military regime. The Roman Catholic Father Martinus Noordermeer was one of them. In December, he would normally remember those who died on 8 December, pray for them specifically and burn a candle for them. Because of this, this Dutch priest was thrown out of the country as *persona non grata*. Father 'Bas' Mulder, another critic, was abused physically. He criticised the military policy on how they treated the Guyanese. The military wanted to put Guyanese out of the country in an inhuman way.

A group of women started an organisation for justice and peace, *Organisatie voor Gerechtigheid en Vrede* (OGV) in the late 1980's. The Moravian clergyman Rev Rudy Polanen was the chairperson of the organisation and was also a severe critic of the military. Polanen had to leave Suriname for the Netherlands in 1989. Mrs Ilse Labadie of the Lutheran Church became the new chairperson, until she passed away in 1999. Betty Goede became the chairperson of the organisation.

14.3.2.2. Pentecostal churches

The military leaders seemed to have developed a more open attitude towards the Pentecostal churches. These churches did not criticise the military as the CCK churches did. Military leaders attended crusades that were organised by the Pentecostals.

In 1986, a major crusade was held that was supported by individual leaders from the Moravian Church and the Baptist Church. A team of foreign Pentecostal evangelists led the interdenominational evangelistic crusade. The crusade received much attention and many people attended. The invitations for the crusade announced signs and wonders that were going to take place. The slogan of the crusade was 'God visits Suriname'. Some criticised the slogan, since they believed God was always in Suriname.

Another major activity that was held simultaneously with the interdenominational crusade was the School of Ministry of evangelist Morris Cerullo. In the following years, the school continued under the leadership of some Pentecostal leaders.

The nation felt the presence of Pentecostal and Charismatic Christianity through their strong media activities. Church services and specifically recorded programmes were broadcast on national radio and television stations. Some churches sponsored programmes presented by foreign preachers such as Robert W Schambach, Ernest Angley, Johan Maasbach and Benny Hinn.

14.3.2.3. The Agape-beweging

An organisation that played an important role in evangelisation during the time of the military was the Campus Crusade for Christ (CCC). A branch of the organisation was founded in Suriname in 1980. In March 1981, Henk and Tiny Veltman came from the Netherlands, to serve the organisation. The Surinamese branch operated under the name Agape-beweging. Its first activity was a large-scale national evangelistic crusade called *Ik heb 't gevonden* (I found it). The crusade started in 1983, just two months after the December killings. Many people came to the Lord during the crusade that was supported by forty local churches. Members of these churches went door to door to explain the gospel of Jesus Christ, with the help of the booklet 'Four Spiritual Laws'. After that event, the Agape-beweging started with a discipleship programme for churches. In 1986, 1987, 1991 and 1997 it organised a conference called EXPLO. During the conference, in which the Dutch evangelist Henk Binnendijk spoke, around 700 believers went door to door in different areas of Paramaribo to preach the gospel. The movement was also responsible for the translation of the Jesus Film into different languages. In 1989, it started a ministry at the campus of the University of Suriname. Now, a Surinamese team under the directorship of Armand and Bianca Morsen, leads this ministry.

14.3.2.4. New churches

14.3.2.4.1. Christian and Missionary Alliance Suriname

The *Christelijke Alliance Gemeenschap van Suriname* (Christian and Missionary Alliance, CAMA) started its work among the Chinese in Suriname with the arrival of Rev Gabriel Tsang and his wife. Rev Tsang, who was the pastor of a church in Canada, came to Suriname in 1979. He held the first service on 4 February 1979, with 62 adults and 11 children. The work grew and new churches were initiated among the Chinese in French Guyana (1991), Venezuela (1992), Guatemala (1992), Brazil (1996), Panama (1998) and the Netherlands (2002). In the 1980's CAMA Suriname started a Dutch division and in the 1990's a Javanese division, with Johannes and Dorothea Martoredjo as overseers.

14.3.2.4.2. Plymouth Brethren

On 14 September 1983, the Dutch missionary couple Gerard and Roeli Elbers and their family came to Suriname. The family started to hold services in their living room not long after their arrival. Other people soon started to join the services. A few Guyanese brothers and sisters started to attend the services. Because of this, the meetings became bilingual: English and Dutch. In 1987, around a hundred people attended the meetings in Paramaribo. Elbers was also involved in outreaches among the Natives in Powakka, Wit Santi, Domburg and Bigi Poika. The work among the Natives did not see the planting of churches. Outreaches to the Ndyukas in Peto-Ondro and the Saramaccans in Brokopondo saw the beginning of new churches in those areas.

14.3.2.4.3. Church of the Nazarenes

In August 1982, a group of believers from the Church of the Nazarenes came together for prayer. In October 1984, the church was officially launched and started to hold meetings in 1985. Not long after that, the work expanded to the Haitian immigrants. This expansion was easy because many of the immigrants were already members of the church in Haiti. Currently, the church has five branches in Suriname.

14.3.2.4.4. Southern Baptist Mission

The Southern Baptist Missionary couple Harold and Martha Lewis started their work in Suriname in 1971. Missionary Leo Waldrip followed them. After they completed their language studies, the team started their work in Rainville. The work expanded to Doekie project. In 1979, there were nine Southern Baptist missionaries in Suriname.

14.3.2.4.5. Independent Faith Mission

In 1974, the family Champlin founded the Independent Faith Mission in Suriname. The Champlins came to Suriname in 1965 and started to work with the Methodists. In 1974, they left the Methodist Church and founded a new mission. In 1986, Dr Robert Patton came to Suriname to serve as a medical missionary. He worked at a government hospital and lectured at the medical university. In 1987, he founded the Bijbel Baptist Kerk. The mission focused primarily on the Ndyuka Maroons, both in the interior and in the city.

14.3.3. Christianity and the civil war

In July 1986, a civil war started in Suriname. A group of seven Maroons made a raid on a military post in Commewijne and took the military hostage. The leader of the group was a former member of the military, Ronnie Brunswijk. The group was later named Jungle Commando and received support from the Netherlands, from opponents of the military regime in Suriname. The attack in 1986, was the beginning of a civil war. Hundreds of Maroon young people joined the Jungle Commando. The military conducted a few mopping-up operations to take revenge. During these operations, many civilians were killed, including those of the village *Moiwana* and a group at *Tjongalangapasi*. The Surinamese government was ordered by the Inter-American Court of Human Rights to pay compensation to the survivors.

The Jungle Commando, supported by foreign mercenaries, killed many military, including a group of seven at *Kraka*. It also attacked companies such as those of Suralco, Bruynzeel and Victoria. Thousands of Maroons and Natives who lived in the interior had to flee from their villages. Some went to Paramaribo, while others went to French Guyana and lived there as refugees. The civil war had a devastating impact on the living area of the Maroons and the Natives. The medical care and educational infrastructures were destroyed. Families were divided on the basis of their loyalty to either 'Brunsi' (Jungle Commando) or 'Bouta' (military). Supporters of 'Brunsi' did not hesitate to burn down the village Pokigron and Wakibasu, because the village allegedly supported 'Bouta'. Women were also brutally raped. Besides the physical and material damage, the civil war created emotional problems. Many are still suffering from post-traumatic stress syndrome. This applies to civilians as well as to former Jungle Commando fighters and military. They have not received professional trauma counselling. Some of these former fighters on both sides became lunatics. After the civil war ended in 1992, the country saw an increase of violence and the use of force. The use of drugs grew both in the city and in the interior.

The churches experienced serious damage from the civil war. Members of the Jungle Commando especially raided the buildings of the churches in the interior. Stoelmanseiland, where the Moravians had a mission post, was a headquarters of the Jungle Commando. The churches lost valuable goods, including theological resources of clergymen.

The Moravian and the Roman Catholic churches played a critical role among the refugees. Leaders of these churches provided pastoral care to the refugees in French Guyana and in the city. Many refugees became Christians or took their Christian belief more seriously. A number of churches were started in areas that were affected by the war after it ended. People became more receptive to the gospel. Clergymen from the CCK churches, in particular Father Toon te Dorsthorst and later on Rev Wilfred Sumter, also played a critical role in the negotiations that led to the signing of a peace agreement in 1992 to end the civil war.

14.4. Conclusion

The process of independence of the Surinamese churches is still ongoing. Except for the Roman Catholic Church, Surinamese lead most of the churches. The liturgy and the form of worship still reflect those of the colonial era in most of the churches. Pentecostal churches do not have a colonial background. However, Dutch or American Pentecostalism heavily influences them. There is a need for an independent Surinamese Christianity, in different ways. The process that started from the 1960's should continue and it must be strengthened. Migration in the period around the independence of the country had a major influence not only on the membership of the churches, but also on their leaders. The effects of the civil war also affected the churches. The Moravians and the Roman Catholics especially suffered the most from it. New movements within Christianity, such as the Jesus Students and Agape-beweging continue to be a source of encouragement to especially the evangelical churches.

What is the future of Christianity in Suriname? Will Christianity in Suriname be able to transform itself from a foreign institution to a truly Surinamese branch of the worldwide Christian movement? Even more so, will it become the source of transformation, hope and vision for the future of Suriname? Suriname has many issues that have to be addressed. Christianity, which is the dominant religion, has a critical role to play. It must overcome its own weaknesses to be the beam of hope to a great country with many opportunities. Above all, through its testimony Christ the Son of God must be made known in Suriname and the world.

Appendix to chapter 14: The Church of Jesus Christ of Latter-day Saints (Mormons)

The Church of Jesus Christ of Latter-day Saints (Mormons) should be mentioned here. They differ from other Christian churches in many ways, even though they use the Bible as one of their theological sources.

The Mormon family Jay and Shirley Bills lived in Suriname from 1969 to 1972 and held services at home. It is not clear if there were converts at the time. In 1988 John and Beverly Limburg came into contact with people in Suriname.[6] A few months later a few people were baptised. On 24 February 1990, elder M Russell Ballard gave official permission to teach the doctrines of the Mormons in Suriname. In 1991 the first Surinamese leader, elder Paul Levie was appointed with Selma Armaketo as head of the Relief Society. In 1997, there were one missionary couple and eight elders in Suriname. At the beginning of 2000, there were 454 Mormons in Suriname with two chapels.

---

6. See Garr et al. 2000, s.v. Suriname.

PART II. THEOLOGIANS

CHAPTER 15

Survey of Surinamese Theological Scholarship

15.1. Introduction

This second part of the book provides a summary of academic work that was done by Surinamese scholars from the Moravian (15.2), Roman Catholic (15.3) and Lutheran (15.4) churches. These theologians started their academic journey in the 1950's. Their work interacted with the European form of Christianity that was established in Suriname. They criticised the way in which the church functioned in Surinamese society and called for a Surinamese 'version' of their churches. Certain themes were addressed across denominations such as marriage (Kent, Moravian; Choennie, Roman Catholic; Stewart, Lutheran), Hinduism (Kross, Roman Catholic; J Rambaran, Moravian), Saramaccans (Kent, Moravian; Choennie, Moravian; Stewart, Lutheran) and other Maroons (Zamuel, Moravian; Misidjang, Roman Catholic). Other writers engaged a combination of different topics related to African Christianity (Zeefuik, Darnoud, Jones, Kent, Loswijk, Choennie and Vigelandzoon). Most Surinamese theologians reviewed here, were trained in the field of Missiology or Practical Theology. There was one in the field of the Old Testament (F Rambaran) and one in the New Testament (Kross).

The purpose of this overview is to provide a brief summary of the content of the works which were mostly written in Dutch. The summary may serve as an introduction to Surinamese theologians and their theological works. The writers of these works are not responsible for the way in which their work is summarised here. As the writer, I have done my utmost to summarise the works as best as I could. I present their views as I have understood them, without agreeing with every aspect of them. I have chosen not to enter into a debate with any of them.

15.2. *Surinamese Moravian scholars*

In 1946, Bishop Johannes Raillard took the initiative to train new leaders for the church. In the 1920's the church had to close its training school, because there were not enough candidates. The new initiative was necessary to prepare the church since it wanted to become an independent province. Jan Marinus van der Linde and his wife Anna van der Linde-Rijksen came to Suriname to take on the responsibility to train leaders. They started general theological studies with twenty-two students on 15 November 1951 in Paramaribo. Besides the theological subjects, they taught Greek, Latin and English. Later on they were joined by Bert Graafland who taught Biblical Hebrew. Due to the illness of Mrs Van der Linde, the couple had to leave Suriname. Seven students, who passed an entrance exam, followed them to Zeist in the Netherlands, where they continued their education. The seven students were Ronald Berggraaf, Alexander Darnoud, Leonel Dielingen, Heinrich Hessen, Johan Jones, Soekoer Mingoen and Emile Ritfeld.[1] They completed their studies and returned to Suriname in 1956.

Van der Linde was an authority on the missions of the Moravians in Suriname.[2] With his publications, he set a high standard for his students to imitate.[3] Some of his students continued their studies to write an academic

---

[1]. A DVD was prepared to commemorate the 50th anniversary of these seven ministers. *Leviticus 25:11a. Moravian Church Suriname* (www.ebga.nl). There is also an accompanying book that was completed by Agnes Ritfeld, 1956-2006. *Jubileumfotobook predikanten 50 jaar geleden in dienst getreden.* Paramaribo, 2008.

[2]. See his dissertation which he defended in 1956 (see the third part of this work).

[3]. Besides his work on the Moravian Church he published on the Reformed Church. His bibliography appeared in a farewell book entitled: *Gods wereldhuis. Voordrachten en opstellen over de geschiedenis van zending en oecumene* (Amsterdam: 1980). He continued to publish after his retirement, including a work on the so-called *Ham-ideology: Over Noach met zijn zonen: de Cham-ideologie en de leugens tegen Cham tot vandaag* (IIMO, 1993). He

or a major paper.[4] Some completed their *Baccalauriaat Theologiae* and did not produce an academic thesis (e.g. Dielingen, Hessen, Mingoen and Ritfeld).

After the group of seven returned, other candidates followed such as Humbert Hessen, John Kent, Ferdinand Lachman, Edgar Loswijk, Rudy Polanen, Johannes Rambaran, Frederik Rambaran, Max Vlijter, Toekimin Wonsodikromo, Hesdie Zamuel and Karel Zeefuik. They have all served their denomination in one way or the other.

In the late 1970's, clergymen of the Moravians were trained in Paramaribo again. The seminary offered programmes up to a level that was comparable to a bachelor degree. The graduates completed their studies with a thesis. I will not include their work in this review. The scholars included here were all born before 1950. I will treat them in chronological order of birth.

15.2.1. Theodorus Alexander Darnoud

15.2.1.1. Introduction

Theodorus Alexander Darnoud was born in 1920 in Commewijne. He was encouraged to go into the ministry by the Rev Gilly Polanen. He started his preparatory theological studies in Suriname in 1951. Following that, he went to the Netherlands to study under Jan van der Linde. He completed his training in 1956 and returned to Suriname.

He served his church as a pastor in Nickerie, Coronie, Wanica, Paramaribo and the Netherlands Antilles. In 1977, he was elected as praeses (general secretary) of the Surinamese province. He served in that capacity until 1987. Darnoud was consecrated as bishop on 4 December 1994. He taught missiology for many years at the seminary in Paramaribo.

---

also published a book on Comenius: *De wereld heeft toekomst: Jan Amos Comenius over de hervorming van school, kerk en staat* (1980).

4. The work of the Surinamese who studied at Utrecht are discussed by Jan Jongeneel (2012). This includes the following Moravian theologians: Zeefuik, Loswijk, J Rambaran, Wongsodikromo and Zamuel.

15.2.1.2. *African people and power*

In 1971, he wrote a thesis in the field of Missiology (Darnoud 1971). It was entitled 'African people and power'. The focus of the thesis was on the figure of the medicine man in Africa. Darnoud was triggered to study this phenomenon based on his own experiences in the interior of Suriname.

After an introduction (chapter 1), the thesis studied three 'holy people in Africa' (chapter 2): the medicine man, the priest and the prophet.

In chapter 3, it studied messianic people and movements such as William Wadé Harris (Liberia), Simon Kimbangu (D R Congo), André Matswa (Brazzaville Congo), the Kimbangu Movement, Enoch (South Africa), Isaiah Shembe (South Africa) and Hendrik Witbooi (South Africa). The chapter concluded with a discussion on messianic expectations.

Chapter 4 discussed the Church of the Black Christ. It started with Isaiah Shembe and provided a detailed study of his person and the structure of his Nazareth Baptist Church. It continued with a similar detailed study about Edward Lekganyane and the Zion Christian Church.

In chapter 5, the thesis studied African religion and Native movements in South America and the Caribbean. Among the African religions, it studied *Voodoo* in Haiti, Bedwardism and Rastafarians in Jamaica and the Umbandistic movement in Brazil, which was analysed in greater detail. It continued with Messianic movements among the Negroes in Brazil and among the Natives in Brazil, Columbia, Argentina and Peru.

The final chapter (6) studied the Surinamese church and the African inheritance. It started with prophetic messianic figures in Suriname: Tata Colin, Atjarimikoele, Wensi, Paulus Anaké and Johannes King. Besides these religious leaders it studied two political figures from the coastal area who played a significant role in the whole country: Johan Adolf Pengel and Eddy Bruma. The second section of this chapter is a critical evaluation of the role that the church played in Suriname. It studied the life of the Moravian Church and the African (religious) inheritance. One of the problems that the Moravian Church was experiencing was the loss of members to other churches and religious organisations.

> It is almost unbelievable to see, that people who did not want to have anything to do with the church in the past, are now active members of these groups (p. 104).

This observation agreed with what was seen in many African churches. The Moravian Church had to pay more attention to the issue of healing.

In the third section attention was given to the missions among the Bush Negroes. This group had many similarities to the African religions.

The fourth section studied 'Christ and the (spiritual) powers' from a biblical-theological perspective. All the spiritual powers are subject to the crucified and risen Christ, even against their own will. Christ should be honoured. Messianic movements seemed to glorify man and were expecting a new era. But that never happens.

The fifth and final section called for renewal in the Surinamese church. Following John Mbiti it listed five things that were important and applied them to the Surinamese situation: the Bible, the teaching hour on Sunday, catechism, Christian literature and the use of African (local) languages. The Moravian Church seemed to have taken up some initiatives that were never finalised, including a study on their hymnbooks. What about dance during worship?

> We have the task to keep on looking for new ways and forms,
> so that the work may be done in more efficient ways (p. 120).

15.2.2. Johan Frits Jones

15.2.2.1. Introduction

Johan Frits Jones was born in 1932 in Paramaribo. He started his theological education at the theological school in Paramaribo. He completed his studies in Zeist, the Netherlands, with a Baccalauriaat Theologiae (BTh) in 1956. He continued his education and earned the licentiate degree in divinity at the *Facultas Theologiae Evangelicae Bruxellencis* in Brussels, Belgium in 1966. The degree was awarded with distinction. In 1975 he received his doctorandus degree (MTh equivalent) and in 1981 he completed his *Theologaie Doctorum* (ThD) with honours at the same institution. Jones started his theological career as a pastor in 1956. He served the church in Groningen (Saramacca) and Zorg en Hoop (Paramaribo). His main ministry however was as a missionary pastor and leader of the so-called interior missions (Boslandzending). In 1974, he started his teaching career at the Moravian Theological Seminary. He taught missiology and the science of religions. He supervised many theses in his field.

He continues to teach at the seminary, but has also served as an external examiner for the South African Theological Seminary. Since 2011, he served as a guest lecturer at the Evangelical School of Theology in Suriname.

15.2.2.2. *Christianity and West African religions*

In his licentiate thesis, Jones selected a topic that dealt with African religions. He wrote on the encounter of Christianity with the West African religion in Suriname (Jones 1966).

After an introduction, his thesis discussed the encounter between God and human beings in the Bible. It started with the Old Testament and concluded with the New Testament. The encounter in the old covenant took place through the deeds of God in history. In the new covenant the encounter took place in Christ, who became man.

In chapter 2 Jones discussed the West Africans' journey to the Americas, the New World. The chapter argued that folk religion in West Africa was not primitive as some scholars maintained. There were clear relationships of gods, goddesses, sons of gods and divine figures, which reminded one of the Greco-Roman pantheons. The chapter concluded with the slave trade and slavery.

In chapter 3, he discussed the religion of the Afro-Surinamese in Suriname. This resembled the West African religion, including its pantheon.

Chapter 4 discussed the involvement of various churches in missions. These were the English Church, the Reformed Church, the Roman Catholic Church and other smaller churches and religious groups. The remainder of the chapter was devoted to the work of the Moravian Church. It discussed fellowship, *koinonia*, *kerygma* with attention to the preached, written and sung word and finally *diakonia* with attention to the social-economic, medical and educational services. The chapter closed with a study of the prophetic figure Johannes King.

In chapter 5 Jones studied the response of the Afro-Surinamese people to the gospel. It studied their response within the walls of the church and outside of the church. The final paragraph is entitled 'The dualistic attitude of the Christian Negro'.

In chapter 6, the study answered the following question: 'Is the Moravian Church in Suriname a closed paradise?' The thesis suggested that the church should use the local languages in its ministry. It also argued that Christian literature and the Bible should be made available in these languages. Religious instruction was crucial for the Surinamese church. The study called for a review of the existing model. The church needed supporting materials. This required research on the part of the church. Christian literature that addressed the Surinamese situation was a must. Besides the Bible, daily reading guides, a church paper and hymnbook, the church did not have other reading materials. The church paper focused mainly on information from the various churches within the denomination.

The language of communication was also critical. There was a need to address each people-group in their language. Sadly, during church services, some people preferred to be addressed in the official 'church language' even though that was not the language that they best understood. The Surinamese church should also translate its own scriptures.

The final section of the chapter called for a spiritual renewal of the church. This was based on the work of Dr Visser 't Hooft, called 'The Renewal of the Church'. This renewal however was not based on the church's own way. Renewal had to be based on a fresh hearing of the word of God and rebuilding through the Holy Spirit. The church also had to rediscover its missionary character.

The work ended with seven theses and eight sub-theses.

15.2.2.3. Kwaku and Christ

In 1981, Jones received his doctorate based on a dissertation that dealt with the relation between *Kwaku* and Christ (Jones 1981). Kwaku in the title of the dissertation was the personification of the Afro-Surinamese slave, his descendants, his Afro-American religion and culture. Christ on the other hand referred to the Protestant Christianity of the Moravian missionaries.

Chapter 1 dealt with the cultural inheritance of the Afro-American person and the attitude of the church in Suriname. The chapter started with an *Anansi* (spider) story, which was told by an African professor and an *odo* (proverbial saying) told by a Surinamese paramount chief. This

Anansi story and the odo placed the theme in an historical context. In the words of Jones:

> The important thing for us was that West African persons came under the grip of foreign people. They were transplanted to another continent namely America (p. 10).

In the new continent, the African person developed his own worldview and an Afro-Surinamese religion. This religion encountered a marriage between the state and the Calvinistic branch of the Christian church. The slaves were not confronted with the Christian faith, but with 'laws and regulations'. These laws and regulations were not the result of biblical exposition, but the products of the marriage between state and church. What was the response of the slave to this? The slave responded with proverbial sayings called odo, songs and drama. But there was also another side to the encounter. The slave protested and offered resistance. The government responded by issuing more laws and regulations.

Chapter 2 studied the relationship between the Moravian Church and the slave. The introduction dealt with the role of the missionaries in helping Kwaku to get rid of his idols. The missionaries were successful in taking away the physical idols, but Christ did not get permission to take possession of the entire house of Kwaku. In the words of Jones:

> Man cannot be set free or redeemed from a belief system or false ideology [idols] by another human being such as a missionary, but by the Liberator, Christ himself (p. 38).

However, in spite of many shortcomings, in general the missionary was still respected by the slave. He was seen as a father figure. On the day that slavery was abolished an Afro-Surinamese Christian said the following to the missionaries: 'You are our fathers and we are your children' (p. 39).

After the abolition of slavery and the compulsory ten years of paid service (1863-1873), the relationship of father and child became difficult. The Afro-Surinamese became a free person and a process of awakening started. How did the Moravian missionary view slavery? He did not publicly protest against it. Instead, he welcomed the slave as his brother and fellowshipped with him. In that fellowship however, the slave was prevented from singing his own songs. He had to sing the songs from Herrnhut. In those songs, the suffering and death of the Lamb were the central themes. The Herrnhut Brethren did not allow Jesus to say a word about liberation from the horrible situation of slavery in which the Afro-Surinamese people were.

The Afro-Surinamese had to accept his fate. This was seen in songs that portray the Afro-Surinamese Christian as a 'poor, weak and underprivileged' person. The missionaries ignored the religious world of the Afro-Surinamese people completely, in their songs, catechism and pastoral work. The Afro-Surinamese people therefore interpreted Christian concepts in the light of their own worldviews. They saw the angels, who according to the missionaries were given to serve the saints, as the attributes that they kept from their previous traditional religion. The gospel of the missionaries was not sufficient to meet the needs of Kwaku. Therefore Kwaku kept elements from his traditional religion.

Chapter 3, dealt with 'Creole nationalism'. Jones published a brochure on this issue a few years before he completed his dissertation (see under National awakening). One of the key mechanisms of the Creole nationalism in Suriname was the Sranantongo. It was the communication language since the days of the British in Suriname, in the second half of the seventeenth century. The Moravian missionaries used that language for the furtherance of the gospel. They preached in it and published many works in it, such as translations of scripture, hymn books and missionary reports. Chapter 3 contained a discussion of different forms of theology and nationalism, including Black theology and Liberation theology. After a study of prophetic figures and movements in Africa, the study focused on a few prophetic figures in Suriname (e.g. Tata Colin, Paulus Anake, Carel Rier, Rudolf and Johan Rijts). The research did not find a clear answer from the official church on the issue of nationalism. Through its work however, the church contributed, unknowingly, to the emancipation of some of the Surinamese people.

Other Surinamese played a more significant role in the issue of nationalism. There were those who were associated with the church (e.g.

Koenders and Trefossa) and those who were critical of the church (e.g. Slagveer and Dobru).

Chapter 4 discussed the present-day society and the Christian church. Religion is an important part of the present-day society. The law stipulates that equal protection should be given to all religious and ideological communities. Suriname is a multi-religious nation. Religions are practiced along ethnic lines. The Afro-Surinamese is Christian, the Chinese is Confucian, the Indian is Hindu or Muslim, the Javanese is Muslim and the Bushnegro is an adherent of an African traditional religion.

Religion also plays a significant role in politics, which is practiced along ethnic lines. This shows that the church has a role to play in society. This role is called the priestly function of the church. This focus of the church on society is made effective through its intercession, testimony, relief work and prophecy.

In the past, the church fostered what has been dubbed the *sakafasi* (humble) attitude. It would not raise its voice against evil in society or evil done against her. That was clear when the colonial government confiscated two premises that the church had recently purchased. A prominent and well-respected advocate, who was a Moravian, offered to sue the government and defend the case for the church free of charge. The church rejected the offer. It accepted the injustice done to it by the government without complaining. The church should do more than its priestly function. It had neglected its prophetic task.

> It had not critiqued forms and structures in society openly ... it continued to play the role of Good Samaritan without making efforts to find out what led to the suffering of the Surinamese person and to eliminate those causes (p. 102).

What was the role of the church in the development of Suriname? One critical question that was set before the church was the issue of 'one-people'. Churches, including the Moravian Church, worked along ethnic lines in the past. In the pluralistic society of Suriname the Christian church must propagate by all means the notion of unity, in accordance with the Christian message. According to Jones, the church has to take on a new attitude and not protect old structures or maintain the status quo. It had to find new ways to change the old order. One way in which the church tried to do that, was through CCK, the Committee of Christian Churches. This committee exercises the prophetic role of the church very well. It raised its voice against what was unjust in society and supported what was right.

What was the response of Kwaku to his encounter with 'Christ'? Kwaku represented three groups: the two Maroon groups who fled slavery and lived in the interior (Ndyuka and Saramaccan) and the group that remained in the plantations (Creoles).

The Kwaku from the Ndyuka group who encountered 'Christ' added elements of 'Christ' to his worldview. When he prayed to his gods, he would also add the name of Jesus to the list. The Saramaccan experienced the same things as the Ndyuka. Much more than the Ndyuka, he accepted the message, but 'Christ' did not answer all his questions. This, despite the fact that 'Christ' provided medical care and Christian schools.

So what was the relation between the Maroon and the church? In those villages where there was a church building and a residential pastor, the Maroons attended church faithfully. This was done out of conviction, to build up the faith and due to social control from the community. Baptism was also seen as an important step, a 'must' in the life of the Maroon. It belonged to the Christian community. The water of baptism had divine power and worked as such on human beings. It could protect against evil spirits and evil influences and heal certain forms of illnesses. The Lord's Supper on the other hand was something that is reserved for the 'elite-Christians'. It was a secret meeting that could only be attended by special Christians. This idea was supported by the fact that the Moravian Churches among the Maroons, celebrated the supper with closed doors and in white clothes.

Yet, Christianity had influenced the Maroon societies positively. The so-called Christian villages were better developed and had more facilities (e.g. medical, educational and economic) than the other villages. The 'Christ' of the Maroon must be delivered from European church colonialism. The church should stimulate the Maroons to start appreciating their own things and people. Accepting oneself and the other in a pluralistic society was a necessity.

The 'Christ' of the Creole group was not different from that of the Maroon. Their responses were mixed. There were people who were members of the church and were participating in activities of the Winti (traditional religion). This group lived in two worlds. They were participating actively in Winti activities, while serving faithfully in the church.

There was also another group. It called for the nationalisation of the Afro-Surinamese people. It responded differently to 'Christ'. The group that consisted of young and educated Afro-Surinamese people saw the church as a foreign institution, a colonial appearance that oppressed the people. This group strove for the recognition of the traditional religion in its own right.

A third group of intellectuals considered the church to be a functional group that had a certain role to play.

The Pentecostal churches criticised the Moravian and the more traditional churches. According to them, these churches were not able to set the people free from bondage by evil powers. In their understanding, changed people will bring about changed structures.

In the biblical and theological comments on the issues that were raised, the study highlighted four issues.

1) A Christian cannot have a dualistic attitude or lifestyle. He cannot live in two worlds. Jesus said that he is the truth, the way and the life. This message was normative. Every other message must be evaluated in the light of the Divine Message.

2) Churches needed an urgent spiritual deepening. The Moravian Church may no longer be a community church, in the sense that membership was taken for granted. Membership must be a conscious choice, in which the member-to-be focused on the one Truth, Christ.

3) Services of the church to society should not be divorced from the church's relationship with God. The Christian church served society through its living knowledge of God. Its service was because of its relationship with God. Services done by the church should be seen from that perspective.

4) The church should serve the whole person. It calls people to repentance, serves their material needs, raises its voice against unjust structures in society and it cannot ignore political issues of its day.

It is hoped that the new attitude of theologians will lead to the birth of a Surinamese theology. This theology will continue to appreciate what the Moravian Church has done for Suriname in these past centuries.

15.2.2.4. National awakening

Jones published a few smaller works. One of the first works, written in the 1960's or early seventies was a twenty-two page pamphlet about Surinamese nationalism (Jones nd). This work raised some thoughts on 'national awakening'. The awakening of the 'Creole' of Suriname in the 1950's led him to knowledge that he was not a European, but a Surinamese. He became self-conscious and started to realise his self-worth. The Creole received his freedom back. He could explore his culture, express himself in his own language and propagate the Winti as his own religion. Jones acknowledged that this freedom was necessary. However he also made the point that freedom has its borders. The Winti religion for example was not a typical issue for all Afro-Surinamese people. It was a general phenomenon that the Bible condemned as unbelief, superstition and lack of faith.

Society in those days condemned the churches for following the colonial ethnic lines in their missionary work. The population that was divided along ethnic lines by the colonial government was also kept apart in the churches. Jones defended the position of the church on this issue as follows. The church needed specific tactics to approach each ethnic group. Each group had to be confronted with the gospel in a different way. The church had to bring the gospel message in a language that each group understood best. Despite these differences in approach, there was a spiritual unity among the believers. Jones therefore argued for a national unity and not a Creole nationalism. The message of Christianity defied all group ideologies. Isolationism within groups was completely against the spirit of the biblical message. In the final part of this brochure Jones called for a national awakening. Politics should be done in the nation in accountability to the Lord and for the benefit of the land and nation. This will be for the benefit of Suriname.

15.2.2.5. *Jesus Christ, Bonuman*

Jones taught a seminar on Jesus Christ and the *Bonuman*, a religious figure in the Winti religion. The seminar's notes were published afterwards in a series issued by the Roman Catholic Catechetical Centre (Jones 1984). Jones said the following about this figure:

> In this system of the *Winti* belief there is the *obiaman* or *Bonuman* who plays an important role. His position can be typified as the man who has contact with the world of the spirits and the gods. He stands between the gods and men. One could say that he is a priest (p. 2).

As he had done earlier, Jones again disputed the notion that Winti was the religion of all the Afro-Surinamese. It is the religion of some of them. However, people who have nothing to do with the Winti-religion could be influenced by it, for instance when someone 'sends a Winti' to that person. He made it clear that the world of the Winti was a powerful reality. People live under the power of these spiritual forces, whether they like it or not. This should not be strange for the Christian, since Christians know that there is another force, besides God. However, there is a way out of the power of these forces. Deliverance is possible.

15.2.2.6. *Contextual theology*

In 2000 the Moravian seminary published a booklet written by Jones on 'Contextual theology in Suriname' (Jones 2000). The booklet had three short chapters and it was based on classes that were given at the Moravian seminary. Contextual theology was recognised as essential, especially in the Surinamese context. The reason for this was that Surinamese churches were still copying without questioning what was happening in other churches. It was important for Surinamese theologians to do their own theological work, in their multi-religious and cultural context. The main question however was which context should be taken into consideration: 'an 'authentic' or a global context or both'?

Chapter 1 dealt with the notion of 'theology in context'. It conceptualised a few key terms and a phrase: 'theology', 'context', 'globalisation' and 'biblical theology'. It argued that biblical theology is contextual theology. God addressed people in different life situations. He gave them a message based on that specific context. This was true in both the Old and the New Testaments. The names that people gave to Jesus were born out of their context. The apostle Paul for instance called Jesus of Nazareth differently in his missionary work. The Messiah became *Kurios* (Lord) in the non-Jewish context. In the letter to the Hebrews Jesus of Nazareth was seen as the High Priest, in Revelation, the Bright and Morning Star.

Chapter 2 addressed the cultural, religious and ethnic diversity of the Surinamese society. The book of Revelation spoke about the people from different language groups who will stand before the throne of God to glorify him. The gospel should be heard in every language.

> We hear them speaking in our own languages about the great deeds God has done! (Acts 2:11)

The Bible does not know of the notion of one sacred language. In principle all languages are sacred. Theology in Suriname should be multiform to accommodate the diversity of the pluriform society. It should also listen to the global language, since globalisation has not stopped at the door of Suriname. The context of theology has become international. Therefore it is useful for theology to earn its place in the world of the Surinamese university among the other academic disciplines. Surinamese theology should also interact with other cultures and religions, such as Winti, Hinduism and Islam. The study called for a dialogue between theologians from these different confessions. As proposed the topic for discussion is: dealing with questions that live within everyday human life. The discussion then should be about issues related to anthropology and not theology. At a later stage, discussions about theology can take place.

Chapter 3 argued that contextual theology should not be an academic theology. It should be a theology developed from the grass-root level, not prefabricated in the academic world. The academic theologians, all of whom studied outside of Suriname, have a role to play. But, according to Jones, the contextual theology should receive the 'data' from the 'popular theology', developed by the people. He argues that a theology that wants to be a servant to the world of Suriname therefore has to be tilled and nurtured on Suriname's soil.

15.2.2.7. Other publications

In 1976, a team of Surinamese theologians published articles about the church and the independence of the country. Jones contributed an article on 'Christ and Kwaku' (Jones 1976). He said that the church had lost its privileged position in Surinamese society. For a long time that position has been an uneasy inheritance of the colonial period. But now, according to Jones, this loss should be seen as gain for the church. The church did not have to depend on the government to issue so-called Christian regulations. The church must learn to depend on Christ, who promised: 'I am with you'.

Jones (1997) contributed a chapter to a festschrift for SIL on the celebration of its 30th anniversary in Suriname. Jones described the contribution made by the Moravian Church in Bible translation in Surinamese languages. He also discussed the use of the Bible within the Moravian Church.

He also contributed a chapter to a book, which consisted of papers that were delivered in 2000, to commemorate the 300th birthday of Count Nicolaus Von Zinzendorf (Jones 2004). He spoke about the theology of Zinzendorf that was Christocentric and Zinzendorf's openness to people of other religions.

In 2003, he published another booklet on the phenomenon of religion in the multi-religious society of Suriname (Jones 2003). It was written to commemorate the centenary of the Moravian theological seminary in Suriname. It is an introduction to the theology of religions within the Surinamese context.

True to what he argued in his licentiate thesis, Jones wrote a booklet in one of the local languages entitled: *Joe Findie Gadoe ka?* (Have you found God yet?)[5]

---

5. This work was not available to me and was not consulted.

15.2.3. Ronald Ewald Berggraaf

15.2.3.1. Introduction

Ronald Berggraaf was born in 1934 in Paramaribo. He belonged to the group of seven young Moravians who started their theological educational journey in Paramaribo with Jan van der Linde. He continued his studies in the Netherlands and earned his Baccalaureaat. After serving various churches in Suriname as pastor, he went to Belgium to continue his education. He earned his licentiate and doctorandus at the Facultas Theologiae Evangelicae Bruxellencis in Brussels. He served as a pastor in several churches of his denomination (Zorg en Hoop, Nickerie, Coronie and the Noorderstadskerk). For a short while he was the study coordinator of the theological seminary and the chaplain of the Diakonessenhuis in Paramaribo. Berggraaf left Suriname for the Netherlands Antilles in 1978, where he served the Moravian Church up to 1995.

15.2.3.2. Sranantongo hymnbook

In 1968, he wrote his licentiate thesis on the Sranantongo hymnbook (*Singi-buku*) of the Moravian Church (Berggraaf 1968). Berggraaf started with an introduction, sketching spiritual songs in biblical perspective and historical perspective. He discussed Zinzendorf's views and the so-called 'Singstunden' that were introduced in Herrnhut. The purpose of these 'Singstunden' was to sing about Christ's redemption. The fifth section studied the song and confession. In section six, it raised the issue of the song of Herrnhut in Suriname, followed by the object of study, the 'singi-buku' in the seventh section.

In chapter 1, Berggraaf studied the language of the Singi-buku. It discussed the beginning of the language and its use. Sranantongo started as a contact language and grew to become a full language.

Chapter 2 explored how the Moravian Brethren used this language. It appeared that the Moravians used a special form of Sranantongo that they 'created' in their mission's context.

Chapter 3 described the history of the Singi-buku. The hymn book was used in handwritten manuscripts until it first appeared in print. The songs in the hymn book were Christocentric. Their theology opposed various 'isms' that were prevalent in Europe (rationalism, orthodoxism, mysticism, Methodism and 'existentialism/sensualism'). None of these 'isms' however were relevant in Suriname (in the context of the Afro-Surinamese).

Chapter 4 was an analysis of the Singibuku. The Singibuku consisted of 655 songs that were divided into 39 sections. There were 16 litanies and liturgies. The hymns were translated and or reworked European hymns, with some that were composed in Suriname by the missionaries. The thesis provided examples of 53 songs that had a strong focus on the theology of the cross (*theologia crucis*). The empty grave received only 19 songs. This proportioning was not a good balance between suffering-death and victory. There was a limited view of the new man in Christ. Was the church able to appropriate the gifts that it received through salvation?

> The song of Herrnhut in Suriname made use of every opportunity to show how man was *poti* (poor) and *mofina* (miserable) (p. 56).

The study provided numerous references to these two concepts in the hymns. It referred to 19 hymns that emphasised the notion of believers being 'poor' and 49 hymns that spoke of them as being 'miserable'. These were just a few references and not a complete list. Often there were combinations such as 'poor soul', 'poor sinner', 'poor man', 'poor weakling', 'poor lost person' and 'poor beggar'. Other words that were used to describe the condition of man were 'slave', 'evil one' and 'lost'. The hymn writers probably used these words as a way of describing man in relation to God Almighty. In the slave society of Suriname, prior to the abolition of slavery in 1863, the plantation owners preferred to keep the slaves as 'poor and miserable' people who had to display 'patience', another word that was often used in the hymns. Without intending to do that, the one-sided and meagre presentation of the work of Christ and the Holy Spirit in some hymns contributed to the negative view that the slaves developed about themselves. Was this the reason why most tried to find their maturity outside of the church, in national politics, education and science?

Chapter 5 discussed the function of the hymn book. The hymn as a tool of transmission served two purposes. 1) It evoked new belief, inspiration and hope in man. It mobilised in him the strengths that were necessary for his struggle in life (e.g. 'We shall overcome'). 2) It brought all movement in him to a standstill and called for a resignation to one's fate or a quiet surrender (e.g. 'Wait O my soul, wait on the Lord').

The hymn served three purposes in the church. 1) It served as a tool for preaching and teaching. The Moravians used song to communicate the content of the Bible. Many hymns were based verbatim on portions of scripture. Others summarised the content of scripture. The hymns communicated the theology of the Moravians very well. 2) It served as a mission and revival song. Many hymns called upon the church as a whole to testify to the saving act of God in Christ. 3) It served as a source of comfort. The church was suffering. Johannes King expressed it in the following way: 'In the depth of our being we are crying and the pastors do not know that'. The hymns were used to comfort and encourage the church. They taught the church not to value the world and that man had to suffer. They also taught *how* man had to suffer. Man had to accept his life of suffering patiently until he died. This way of looking at life did not help the church to take decisive actions.

Hymns were also used outside the meetings of the church. Three of these usages were discussed. 1) '*Singi*' and '*Begi*' (literally: singing and praying). These two were groups or committees. They served a group of people of the same family or background. The Singi or Begi included a health insurance and a burial fund. Sometimes it also included a savings fund. During Christian festivals, the group came together to sing and celebrate. Hymns played a critical role in all their gatherings. 2) *Dedeosu* and *Aitideisingi* (literally: 'house of mourning' and 'song of mourning on the eighth day'). When a person died, the family normally stayed in the house for eight days to comfort those who remained behind. During that time the mourners sang hymns. On the eve of the eighth day the family and friends would meet to sing in honour and remembrance of the deceased. A meal was prepared for the deceased. It was put in a quiet place. The hymns were used to express deep human suffering such as death and mourning. 3) The hymns also functioned in the political arena. People of Protestant churches sang hymns at political gatherings, including one or more hymns from the hymn book. Hymns were also used during election campaigns. How should the use of the hymns outside of the church meetings be evaluated? Is it an expression of a Christian perception applicable to every aspect of life? This probably was the intention of the Afro-Surinamese. However, this was not the reality.

> The encounter (Afro-Surinamese versus the White person) took the Afro-Surinamese by such surprise, that he became ashamed of his own feelings of dignity, right and wrong, pure and false (p. 82).

His own insights could not stand in the New World. His own forms of expressions, e.g. language and dance, could no longer communicate his intentions. He looked up to the Whites and tried to imitate them. He was no longer able to be creative. Is the use of the church hymn as indicated above not an indication of his lack of creativity? The missionaries were aware of this lack of creativity. They therefore created two hymn books for the Afro-Surinamese church.

In conclusion: the hymn books of the Moravians served their purpose. They compensated for the lack of creativity among the locals.

In an epilogue the thesis presented two requirements for a good hymn book. If the church wanted to be relevant in its own time, it should consider the following facts. 1) In the current hymn books, Herrnhut was speaking. Most of the hymns were translated from German and other European languages. In a new hymn book, the voice of the Afro-Surinamese people must be heard clearly. 2) The gospel was not only for the individual. God had people-groups in mind. The church should have a Suriname focus with Christ as its centre. A good hymn book must be a representation of the church's own response.

The thesis concluded with eight theses and five sub-theses.

15.2.4. Karel August Zeefuik

15.2.4.1. Introduction

Zeefuik was born in 1934. He went to the Netherlands in 1957. In 1964 he completed his studies with the degree of doctorandus (MTh) in theology. His main field of study was history of religion. During his studies, he also completed courses in African languages. He returned to Suriname in 1964 and served the Moravian Church in many capacities. At the request and with the help of the Dutch Bible Society, he founded the Suriname Bible Society in 1966. When he returned to Suriname in 1973, after obtaining his doctorate, he served as the director of the Moravian seminary. He taught the biblical languages and homiletics. In later years his contribution has been in the political arena where he served for many years as a member of the Council of State.

15.2.4.2. The Winti

In 1963, Zeefuik wrote his doctorandus[6] thesis at the *Rijksuniversiteit van Utrecht* about a topic that was and still is very controversial in the Surinamese Christian community, namely the 'Winti'. Winti is the name of the traditional religion of the descendants of the African slaves in Suriname. The title of his thesis, when translated into English reads: The Winti and the complex magical and religious actions and the phenomena that are closely related with it in Suriname (Zeefuik 1963). Even though his focus was on the phenomenon in Suriname he looked for parallels in West Africa.

After the 'Preface' (Chapter 1), he discussed the phenomenon Winti and the different kinds of Wintis (Chapter 2). In chapter 3, he raised the question: How does one 'receive' a Winti and how is it venerated? In chapter 4, he discussed 'dance' and in chapter 5, he explained sicknesses that are caused by the Winti and their cure. Chapter 6 studied Obia and Wisi, two methods that are used by religious leaders in the Winti to achieve their purposes for their patients. In chapters 7 and 8 he studied the *Yorka*

---

6. A degree that was common in the Netherlands and its colonies and which is approximately equivalent to a Master of Theology.

(spirit of the deceased) and Soul respectively. After a summary (chapter 9), he concluded his study (chapter 10).

Zeefuik argued that the church had to engage the world of the Winti seriously. This world was one of supernatural powers and forces (p. 60). People in society accordingly preferred to discuss life's problems with the *obiaman* (medicine man in the Winti) instead of the clergyman. The clergymen did not seem to understand the problems of the Afro-Surinamese. They were very judgemental about the 'spiritual/magical' issues. People therefore preferred the obiaman, because of the more positive and effective results that he achieved. Zeefuik raised the following question:

> How can the church in Suriname come to a correct approach to this world, that differs so from the world of Christianity? Or, to put it differently: how can the church enter into the world of these forces through the preaching of the powerful gospel? (p. 62).

Zeefuik concluded that members of the church, who were baptised and registered in the books of the church, should be brought to the understanding that Christ conquered these forces.

15.2.4.3. *The Hague Society*
In 1973, Zeefuik earned his doctorate degree at the Rijksuniversiteit van Utrecht. His dissertation was on the Moravian mission and the Haagsche Maatschappij from 1828 to1867 (Zeefuik 1973). The purpose of the study was to tap into a source that was unknown up to that moment. The Haagsche Maatschappij assisted the Moravian mission in Suriname in the nineteenth century. The dissertation was based on an archival research.

Chapter 1 discussed the issues that led to the formation of the Haagsche Maatschappij. It discussed slavery in Suriname, Suriname as a plantation colony, the merchant churches and the Moravian Church and slavery.

Chapter 2 studied the establishment of the Haagsche Maatschappij in 1828. It explained how and why the company started in Suriname and took shape in the Netherlands, in The Hague.

Chapter 3 studied the Haagsche Maatschappij and the missions of the Moravians. The Maatschappij was willing to provide technical assistance to the missions, so that the missions would have the opportunity of reaching more plantations. It would campaign to bring about a change of mind-set among the public in the Netherlands.

Chapter 4 studied the confrontation between the Haagse Maatschappij and the plantation owners.

Chapter 5 discussed the relationship between the Moravians and other churches and groups. This chapter discussed the attitude of Christians in the Netherlands towards slavery (e.g. a committee of ladies and the Dutch society for promoting the abolition of slavery).

Chapter 6 discussed the famous circular that the Rev Otto Neils Tank wrote in 1848. This was the first and most critical response of a member of the church in Suriname to slavery. Tank's ideas however were not supported by the leadership of the Moravian Church in Suriname.

Chapter 7 explained the Moravians' attitude towards emancipation. The celebration of the emancipation day on July 1, 1863, from the perspective of the church was studied in detail.

Chapter 8 was on 'The Haagsche Maatschappij and the attitude it adopted towards emancipation' and 'Other movements in the Netherlands' in favour of the emancipation. The chapter studied five movements.

Chapter 9 was on the role that the Maatschappij played in education in Suriname.

Chapter 10 was a critical evaluation of the work of the Haagsche Maatschappij from 1828-1867 and comprised the conclusion of the dissertation. And, as usual, an English summary drew the work to a close.

Zeefuik was critical of the attitude of some of the people involved in the society. They considered the missionary message of the Moravians unsuitable for themselves but highly suitable for the uncivilised Coloured people. By adopting this attitude they did a profound disservice to missions. The work of the Maatschappij itself was highly praised. Zeefuik mentioned two important results of the work:

> The work of the Moravian Brethren in Suriname was singularly blessed and gave to that country a practical example of a new

kind of living and thinking, and secondly, ... the work of the Haagsche Maatschappij was used in the providence of God to advance the work of the Moravians in Suriname at a critical time in the development there (p. 191).

15.2.4.4. Church and politics in Suriname

In 1976, Zeefuik wrote a paper about the church and the political situation in Suriname, at its independence in 1975 (Zeefuik 1976). He argued that the church should accentuate the equality of all people and their common humanity. People in Suriname should live together. It was important to avoid an 'island mentality' in order to build the nation. From a Christian perspective he gave the following key terms as guidelines for the new Suriname: unity, mutual acceptance, solidarity and tolerance.

15.2.5. Johannes Rambaran

15.2.5.1. Introduction

Johannes Rambaran was born in 1935. His father Daniel was converted to Christianity, through the influence of Hindi Christian songs. Daniel became an evangelist of the Moravian Church in Nickerie. His sons Johannes and Frederik followed in his footstep by also entering into Christian ministry.

After he was trained as a teacher, Johannes felt called to go into Christian ministry. He received a scholarship to study theology in the Netherlands. He and his family left for the Netherlands in the 1960's. Just like other Surinamese theological students before him, he stayed in Zeist, the home of the Moravian Church in the Netherlands. Rambaran studied theology at the University of Utrecht. In 1967, the Zeister Zendingsgenootschap deployed him to India to study Hindi and Urdu. Furthermore, he had to do research into the best ways to preach the gospel to the Indians in Suriname. He stayed there for one year and studied at the Leonard Theological College in Jabalpur, India. In 1968, he returned to the Netherlands and from there to Suriname. He became the first Surinamese Indian to be ordained as a clergyman. He served at the *Soesamatjaar* Church, but also ministered to other Indian congregations in Alkmaar, Nickerie and Saramacca. He also conducted services in the houses of people, as was the religious tradition of the Indians in Suriname. When he and his wife Soemintra Sansaar started to run the Sundar Singh boarding school they had five of their own children, three girls and two boys. Johannes himself grew up at that same boarding school after he had to leave Nickerie, his birthplace, to study in Paramaribo, the capital. In 1974, he and his family went on furlough to Europe, where he visited the work of the Moravians in Germany and Switzerland. Rambaran tried to integrate the culture of the Indians into Surinamese Christianity. In 1979, he returned to the Netherlands to complete his education at the University of Utrecht. He wrote a thesis on the ways to salvation in the *Rāmāyaṇa* of Tulsidās. He returned to Suriname in 1980. He served the Moravian Church for another three years, until his untimely death at the age of 47.

15.2.5.2. Ways to salvation in the Rāmāyaṇa of Tulsidās

Rambaran wrote his doctorandus thesis on the ways to salvation in the Rāmāyaṇa of Tulsidās (Ramabran 1980).

In the introduction, the thesis started with the question: what is salvation? Salvation is an important concept in religions. It is described in different ways, e.g. spiritual welfare, prosperity and deliverance in this or the life to come. Deliverance is achieved through self-activation and self-realisation or through divine or superhuman intervention. The superhuman can manifest itself through different powers. God can manifest himself in different forms: stone, fire, dance, sacrifice, book, human beings, etc.

In Hinduism, the world with everything in it is governed by the principle of the cosmic moral order, the *Ṛta*. This cosmic order brings about the recurring cycle of life and death. The dead will be rewarded according to his works and his fate depends on his attitude in this life. As he sows in this life, so he shall reap. This is the *karma*, which is closely connected with the doctrine of the reincarnation. Depending on one's deeds, one will be reborn in the heaven of the gods or in a higher or lower caste, or even as an animal or plant. The cycle will end when salvation is achieved, the *mokṣa* or *muktī*. The individual soul, the *ātman* reaches salvation when it becomes conscious and identifies itself with the All-soul, the Brahman.

Theistic movements in Hinduism play an important role in the teaching of salvation. The divinity allows the worshipper to serve him through sacrifices, love and devotion. The divinity accepts this glorification and answers by helping and saving the worshipper by his grace.

The thesis studied the most important ways to salvation in the Rāmāyaṇa. These are the *karmā-mārga* (the way of works), *jnāna-mārga* (the way of knowledge) and the *bhakti-mārga* (the way of love and devotion).

In chapter 1 the thesis stated its purpose. Its intention was to bring greater awareness of the work of Tulsidās among Dutch-speaking people. It will provide insight into the Hindu way of thinking. An understanding hereof will aid dialogue in encounters with Hindus. Christians, preachers of the gospel, argue that Jesus Christ is 'the Way, the Truth and the Life'. He is the only way, in a singular and absolute form. In the Hindu way of thinking there are many ways. They do not speak about 'one way' but about 'various ways' to salvation. One is allowed to choose for example between the three ways identified earlier: the karmā-mārga (the way of works), jnāna-mārga (the way of knowledge) and the bhakti-mārga (the way of love and devotion). The second part of chapter 1 (pp. 5-14), studied the life and influence of Tulsidās, the author of the Rāmāyaṇa.

Chapter 2 studied the Rāmāyaṇa of Tulsidās in detail. Section one (pp. 17-20) focused on its origin, name, place and function. Section two (pp. 20-21) gave a summary of the seven *Kāṇḍas* (chapters). The third section (pp. 22-31) gave a detailed analysis of the *Ayodhyā-kāṇḍa*.

Chapter 3 described *Rāma* as the incarnation of *Viṣṇu*. The first section discussed the birth and life of Rāma, the bringer of salvation (pp. 35-37). The second section (pp. 37-43) explained the relationship between Rāma and Viṣṇu.

Chapter 4 discussed the three ways to salvation. Section one (pp. 47-53) studied the karmā-mārga (the way of works). Section two (pp. 54-55) studied the jnāna-mārga (the way of knowledge) and section three (pp. 56-60) the bhakti-mārga.

The study drew eight conclusions. 1) The three ways of salvation seemed to be interrelated in the Rāmāyaṇa. 2) The bhakti-mārga seemed to have a more prominent place in both the bhakti-mārga and the *Bhāgavad-Gitā* (an ode to the Lord). Much of what is found in the bhakti is also found in the Christian's relation with his God, e.g. grace, devotion, love, inner peace, worship and unification. 3) *Rāma-kathā* (reading) and *kirtan* (group singing) are means for the bhakti. Through the many repetitions people go into a trance to achieve unification. 4) In the Rāmāyaṇa one is confronted with the great flexibility in the Hindu way of thinking. It opposes the fixed, schematic way of thinking within Christianity. 5) Unfortunately, in daily life there is little tolerance among Hindus. This is because of the lack of knowledge of their religion. Their response to Christians would simply be: 'why do we have to discuss this? Everything is the same'. All rivers flow to one sea. 6) There are similarities and differences between Rāma and Jesus.

Table 28 *Similarities between Rāma and Jesus*

Rāma	Jesus
Human, righteous and good	Ditto
Preacher of peace and justice	Preacher of the kingdom of God
Full of compassion	Ditto
Saviour of mankind	Ditto
Destroyer of Rakṣasas	Conqueror of Satan
Sufferer in exile	The suffering servant
King of the kingdom of peace, Rāma-rāja	Jesus is King

The differences are:
- The suffering of Jesus was for the whole world (all nations).
- The suffering of Jesus went beyond humiliation, banishment and hardship. He was slaughtered as a means of atonement.
- Jesus is exalted as the risen Lord of heaven and earth.

7) Rāma acts as redeemer. He will judge and destroy the sinful world in which adharm (unbelief, immorality and guilt) takes place. Those who keep the dharm will not be judged. It should be re-iterated that in Hinduism, 'sin' is not the same as in Christianity. Sin is *a-vidyā* (ignorance). Christianity will have to translate concepts in such a way that the Hindu will understand it. This is necessary for dialogue. 8) Tulsidās was a man of his own time, the sixteenth century.

15.2.6. Toekiman Remanuel Wongsodikromo

15.2.6.1. Introduction

Toekiman Remanuel Wongsodikromo was born in 1936 in Domburg. His father was a Muslim, born in Java. He converted to Christianity a year after Toekiman was born. Toekiman grew up in the home of this new Christian family. He started his preparatory theological studies in Suriname after which he went to the Netherlands for his studies at the University of Utrecht. He completed the first part of his studies in 1962, and his doctorandus studies in 1964. Wongsodikromo spent four months in Indonesia, where he visited churches and universities. During his studies in the Netherlands, Wongsodikromo married Jenny Flier. In 1965, the couple returned to Suriname. Wongsodikromo was ordained in 1966. He served churches of the Javanese mission of the Moravians in many capacities. In 1967, he and his wife were entrusted with the care of the Siswa Tama boarding school. Wongsodikromo died suddenly at the age of fifty in 1986.

15.2.6.2. *The word* amṛta *in the old Javanese*

Wongsodikromo wrote his doctorandus thesis on the word *amṛta* in the Old Javanese literature (Wongsodikromo 1964). The thesis consisted of an introduction, five chapters, a conclusion and an appendix.

The introduction started with an explanation of the battle for existence. It was a battle for 'bread and water' and in particular 'the water of life', which signified existence in the world of the gods after a person died. The water was often guarded by demonic forces. This of course led to a battle against these evil forces. The word used for this complex concept is amṛta: 'nectar of the gods, nectar of immortality, a state of permanency and immutability, a state of security in which the cycle of being born and dying no longer exists'. The thesis intended to investigate if the word amṛta in the Old Javanese literature had any relationship with parallels in the Indian literature.

Chapter 1 was an orientation to the Old Javanese literature. Indian literature influenced those in Old Javanese. The influence was described in three periods. The first period produced prosaic documents. These were written in Sanskrit, followed by a paraphrase in Javanese. One such example is the *Mahābhārata*. The second period saw a poetic (*kakawin*) reworking of epic material, such as the *Arjuna wiwāha*. In the third period the poets (kakawins) were no longer prominent.

Chapter 2 studied amṛta in the story of the churning of the milk sea. The purpose was to discover the relation between this story in Old Javanese and in Sanskrit. The study discussed this event in the Old Javanese *Ādiparwa*, *Tantu Panggĕlaran* and *Manik Maja* and *Rāmāyana*.

Section one. In the Old Javanese Ādiparwa the story of churning the milk sea was described. Winatā was cursed by her son Aruna, because she acted prematurely. She became the slave of her sister *Kadrū*. The gods met at the top of a mountain to discuss the way by which they would achieve amṛta. The demons were also there. At the end, the gods achieved amṛta and the demons did not. This story was found in the Sanskrit version of the Mahābhārata. The Old Javanese version of the story was different. The history of *Winatā* continued in the story of the mythical bird *Garuḍa*, the son of Winatā. It was also clear that the ransom paid for Winatā to be freed from slavery was the amṛta that was found by the gods through churning of the sea. Garuḍa was able to take the amṛta away from the gods, after he conquered the protecting host of gods. And the history of how Garuda returned to heaven, after he redeemed his mother, is very purifying for those who hear it.

Section two. The Tantu Panggĕlaran and Manik Maja were partly based on the story of churning the milk sea. They can be compared with the Indian *Purāṇas* even though there are major differences between the two.

Section three. The story of the churning of the milk sea was also found in the Old Javanese Rāmāyana. This story had agreements and differences with the Indian version.

Chapter 3 studied the amṛta that was part of the consecration ceremony, in the *Nāgarakṛtāgama*. The Nāgarakṛtāgama was an ode to king *Rajasanagara*, *Hayam Wuruk*. King Rajasanagara was that of the well-known *Majapait*, the capital city of the mighty Javanese kingdom. The Nagarakṛtāgama contained a consecration ceremony in which the amṛta (sacred nectar) was an important element. A priest presided over the ceremony. He sprinkled the king with solidified milk, honey and pure butter. He gave him water to drink that was mixed with various elements. The water represented amṛta. The literature indicated that the word amṛta was known in the Old Javanese world. It was used in various passages in old documents. Amṛta was one of the influences of Hinduism on Java. The meaning of the word however went through different stages in Java.

Chapter 4 studied amṛta that came from the *Jambu* tree. This was described in the Brahmāṇḍa-purāṇa, one of the eighteen Indian purāṇas, which was also available in Old Javanese. The text of the two versions seemed to be identical. The amṛta from the Jambu tree had an indescribable taste. Those who took it were not plagued by old age, death, suffering and hunger. They were not troubled, weary and sad. Accidents were not known in their land.

Chapter 5 studied the jar with amṛta, as an attribute of Çiva. This was discussed in the *Korawāçrama*. In this document Çiva became the centre of the universe. As such he took over that role from the Jambu tree and the Meru hill. He took over the role as the source of the 'water of life' from them. This was clearly seen in the description of the jar with tīrthāmṛta as one of his attributes. This part of the document was clearly from Javanese origin since it was not found in the Indian literature.

The conclusion indicated that the Indians influenced the Javanese in different ways. There were Hindu-Javanese kingdoms, societies and literature. The word amṛta in the Javanese literature was not local. It came in with the Sanskrit literature, but developed itself into different independent directions.

15.2.7. Edgar Loswijk

15.2.7.1. Introduction

Edgar Loswijk was born in 1944. He completed his teacher-training at the *Kweekschool* (teachers' training college) and did the *hoofdakte*, a certificate that entitles one to become a headmaster. After preparatory studies at the seminary in Paramaribo, he went to the University of Utrecht. The first two years in the Netherlands were devoted to the classical languages (Greek and Latin). After that, he started with his studies, a combination of theology and Caribbean literature. He completed his doctorandus degree in 1979 and returned to Suriname in that same year.

Upon his return he served the church as pastor in Nickerie, the *Grote Stadskerk* and *Combé kerk*. At the *Diakonessenhuis* he served as a chaplain for ten years. Loswijk served in the provincial board for five terms of three years each. He was lecturer in church history at the theological seminary for many years. From 1 November 2011, he has been serving at the Moravian archive in Paramaribo.

15.2.7.2. Nationalism and gospel
Edgar Loswijk wrote his doctorandus thesis on nationalism and gospel in the modern Surinamese literature (Loswijk 1979).

Chapter 1 explained the meaning of nationalism. The word 'nation' was first used in the universities of the Middle Ages. Students from the same region grouped themselves gradually into a 'nation'. This use of the word differs from the modern usage. The modern meaning can be described as idolatry, 'the glorification of the collective 'I' '. European nationalism was exported to Africa and Asia. The subordinated 'elite' of Africa and Asia, who studied at European institutions, started nationalistic movements in their own countries.

> In general, nationalism is the pursuit of a country (people) to liberate itself from the rule of another country, so that it can take care of its own business independently (p. 6).

The second section discussed forms that nationalism accentuates. These included culture and ideology (pp. 6, 7). The third section raised the following question: 'Is there a biblical view on the phenomenon of nationalism?' A brief survey of the Old Testament studied the calling of and promises to Abraham (Gen 12:1 ff), the beginning of the fulfillment of the promise (Exod 12:29-42) and the fulfillment when Israel crossed the Jordan river (Josh 1:1 ff). Particular attention was given to Deut 10:19, which was a warning against an excessive love for one's own country. The survey of the New Testament referred to Mark 12:13-17 and Rom 13:1-7. A government that is not good cannot lay claim to the obedience of its people. The people will rise up against it. Men must obey God more than human beings.

> The Bible calls upon us to be good citizens of our native country, that is to be nationalists in the good sense of the word. But the Bible warns us against an uncritical lifestyle that does not agree with the Word of God (p. 9).

Chapter 2 discussed the beginning of Surinamese nationalism in the Netherlands and its effect in Suriname. Surinamese nationalism in the Netherlands and Suriname was connected with an association called Wie Eegie Sanie (WES, Our own thing or that which belongs to us) and the person of Eddy Bruma. While studying law in the Netherlands Bruma, together with others, founded Wie Eegie Sanie. Wie Eegie Sanie criticised the dominant position of the West European culture, the Christian religion with its many norms and values and the Dutch language taught at the schools. When Bruma returned to Suriname, he established an association with the same name. Later on, he founded a political party, Partij Nationalistische Republiek (PNR, Party of the Nationalistic Republic). The association was distrusted by the established politicians. They believed PNR and WES would lead to their loss of power among the people. The non-Creole people thought the association and the party would lead to the dominance of the Afro-Surinamese people. The 'Creole nationalism' failed for three reasons. It underestimated the influence of the West European culture; it had a simplistic view of the complex problems in Suriname and its expectations of itself were too high. Bruma did not publish much. He will be remembered as one who fought for the independence of Suriname.

Section three discussed three forerunners of Bruma. They were Anton de Kom, Julius Gustaaf Arnout Koender and Lodewijk (Lou) Alphonsus Maria Lichtveld (pseudonym: Albert Helman). De Kom published a book called *Wij slaven van Suriname* (We, the slaves of Suriname) in the 1930's. De Kom's view was the wellbeing of Suriname as a whole. Koenders was the editor of a Sranantongo magazine called *Foetoeboi* (messenger) in the 1940's and 1950's. He propagated that the Afro-Surinamese had to be proud of the colour of his skin, history, language and culture. To disprove the fable that Sranantongo was not a literary language he translated poems from Dutch into it. Was it necessary for Koenders to prove the value of the Afro-Surinamese culture by comparing it to that of the 'White'? Music by Bach is good but cannot be taken as criterion for African or Asian music. The problem with the church members is not the lack of creativity (contra Berggraaf) but the sacralised European form in which the gospel came to us.

De Kom focused on the social-economic problems, Koenders on the spiritual-social factors and Bruma on a synthesis of both.

Albert Helman was a prolific writer. He refused to participate in the Surinamese nationalism movement. He was disappointed in both Suriname and the Netherlands. Symbolic of his position towards the Netherlands and Suriname was that he lived on the Caribbean island of Tobago from the 1960's. What was the attitude of these writers towards the gospel? Bruma was not interested in the church, but wanted to use it to achieve his political ambitions. De Kom would allow the church as a necessary evil in society. Koenders preached a return to the Creole culture, which would include the Creole religion. Helman started to be trained as a Roman Catholic priest. At a later stage he renounced his faith. In one of his writings he indicated that the gospel has value in itself and that everybody should see what he or she can use from it. It can be concluded that none of these nationalists were Christians. However, they have not rejected the gospel in their writings.

Chapter 3 was devoted to the poet Trefossa (H de Ziel). He published a collection of nineteen poems called *Trotji* (1957). These poems were written in Sranantongo. They expressed his faith, doubt, joy and sorrow. One of his poems was *Kalfaria*, which was a good report of the encounter of a Surinamese nationalist with the gospel. Trefossa also confronted the Winti religion of the Afro-Surinamese people, but did not give a clear-cut answer. The gospel of Jesus Christ demands a clear 'yes' or 'no' and not 'yes and no'. Trefossa composed the second couplet of the Surinamese national anthem. That poem expressed the unity of the Surinamese people and connectedness with the Surinamese territory. He also 'created' the word *srefidensi* to express the notion of independence. Trefossa expressed his disapproval of corruption among the civil servants in his poems *nanga wan ai* and Srefidensi. He inspired many Surinamese to write in their own Surinamese way. His nationalism was a cultural nationalism.

Chapter 4 discussed the place of Sranantongo in the process of national awakening. The chapter discussed the beginning and growth of the language. It was developed into a social-cultural language. Due to the work of Koenders, Bruma and Trefossa, Sranantongo became a literary language. Sranantongo had been the language of the church since the second half of the eighteenth century. Now it was used in the communication of the gospel, the education of the Afro-Surinamese people, translation of scripture, writing of hymns, sermons and other literature. The Creole Church member did not participate in the creation of hymns. Due to the excessive fear of heathen influences the church members became passive instead of active participants in the religious happenings. It is hoped that soon this will change in the church.

Chapter 5 discussed the notion of modern Surinamese literature. The term 'modern' is used to mark a new era of Surinamese literature. This period came after Trefossa. Due to his contribution, poets and writers started to use Sranantongo and the Surinamese Dutch language freely. Which ethnic group is most represented in the Surinamese literature? Three Indian poets were identified: Shrinivasi (Martinus Lutchman), Bhai (James Ramlall) and Dew Ramboens. The other poets and writers belonged to the Creole group. Despite these it is better not to speak about Creole nationalism, but of Surinamese nationalism, a nationalism that has representatives among all the groups of Suriname.

Chapter 6, the main part of the thesis, discussed nationalism and gospel in modern Surinamese literature. Writers and poets were divided into four groups. The first group (A) discussed writers and poets who were older than fifty years. The second (B) group was between forty and fifty years. The third group (C) consisted of writers who produced prose only or prose and poetry. The fourth group (D) consisted of authors who were younger than forty. Four authors were selected for each group.

Group A. The first author was Jozef Johannes Rudolf Berrenstein. In his poem *Anana na fesi*, he expressed his involvement in the folk culture of the Afro-Surinamese people. His poem *Den Jos josi foe Sranan* was a call for national unity. In another poem he criticised the abuses in Surinamese society. The gospel had a special place in his poems, but his involvement in the Winti religion was also prevalent. Both religions were important to him. He had a dualistic attitude.

> This phenomenon appears everywhere where the gospel is brought in West European form and the people do not get the opportunity to substitute West European forms with local forms (p. 39).

The second author was Adolphina Zwennicker-Groenefelt. Her poem *Watra-Mama angan joe goutoe kam* is an example of the interwovenness of religious and nationalistic feelings. The Watra-Mama was the water goddess of the Creole folk religion. In her poems she used the words *Anana*, God and *Here* (Lord) for the Upper Being. In one poem she referred to *Gado* (God), *Mama Sranan* (a reference to *Aisa*, the mother goddess in the Winti pantheon), and Anana. Just like Berrenstein she was dualistic.

The third author was Johanna Schouten-Elsenhout. In her poem Kodyo she referred to the mother of the ground (*gronma*), God and Aisa. The poem indicated that Winti was part of her identity as a Creole woman. Her poem *Afrikan kondre* (land of Africa) expressed her love for her origin. In *Kresnete-stare* (Christmas star), she expressed her desire to live close to that star. She expressed the value of the gospel and the desire to partake of it. Her life was characterised by both the gospel and the Winti.

The fourth author was Eugène Willem Eduard Rellum. Rellum lived for many years outside of Suriname. Nationalism in his poems was characterised by his longing for unity among the Surinamese people. In contrast to the previous writers he was consciously a Christian. In his poem *Het gebed van een Surinamer* he expressed his desire to be used by God to serve his fellow human beings.

Group B. The first author in this group was George Humphrey Nelson (Pieter) Polanen (pseudonym: Kwame Dandillò). He started as a nationalist. He called upon the Surinamese to dedicate themselves to build their native country. Later on, due to an incident with the prime minister, he turned his back on everybody. He grew up with Christianity in his youth. However, he turned away from it. He expressed his doubts about belief in God in his poem: *Is God dood?* (Is God dead?) His answer was: God lives invisibly in the eyes of a child and dies when the person becomes older.

The second author of this group was Michaël Arnoldus Slory (pseudonym: Asjantenoe Sandodare). He was a nationalist with his eyes open to what was happening outside of his own country. He called upon the Surinamese people to unite. This unity was based on a love for Suriname and a struggle against exploitation of the people by foreign multinationals and corrupt leaders. The gospel was not evident in his writings. The same was true for the traditional religion. He had an indifferent attitude towards religion.

The third author was Robin Ravales (pseudonym: Dobru). He was the most well-known Surinamese poet, nationally and internationally. He criticised wrongdoings in the Surinamese society. He called upon the Surinamese people of all ethnic groups to join forces and 'clean up the mess'. He wanted to see a new type of people, which he described in his poem *Eén Ster* (One Star). He called for this unity even though he acknowledged his own ethnicity in his poem *Ik ben een Neger* (I am a Negro). Dobru never hid the fact that he was a Winti believer, even though he was not against Christianity. He was tolerant of all religions. He expressed that in his poem *Wan* (One). One line said: 'one God, many ways of worship, one people' (p. 61).

The fourth author in this category was Martinus Lutchman (pseudonym: Shrinivasi). He loved Suriname, even though he resided in the Netherlands. His poems expressed that unity was still lacking in his country. This was clearly seen in the contrasts between the Indians and the Afro-Surinamese people. He contributed to a better relationship in his poem *Negers* (Afro-Surinamese people). He wrote: 'Afro-Surinamese people are God's warm shadow in the grip of the sun' (p. 63). His works spoke of hope for a better future. In one of his poems he said: 'I would have loved to bind you together to be one people, not hoping that this will remain a fairy tale'. He was a Roman Catholic believer. He never denied his Christian faith, not even among the Indians, the people of his ethnicity. He was also very tolerant to people of other religions. One of his poems ends: 'In the name of Shri Krishna, Allah and the Lord of Nazareth' (p. 65).

Group C. The first author in this group was Leo Henri Ferrier. He was not a nationalist. His wrestling with his identity, that is the search for a harmonic coexistence of the African and Indian part of him, may serve as an example for the cooperation of the various ethnic groups. He rejected Christianity as something foreign and unprofitable for Suriname.

The second author was Bea Vianen. Vianen did not focus on nationalism, but on the individual who was limited in his scope to develop himself. The strong ethnic bondage hindered the unity of Suriname. Key people in her books were those who detached themselves from the Surinamese society and lived like individuals. In her presentations, she said that the church did much harm to the Surinamese people. The missionaries robbed people of their identity and placed them in 'boxes'.

The third author was Astrid Roemer (pseudonym: Zamani). She expressed her love for Suriname in her works. Her nationalism was connected to her being an Afro-Surinamese. Roemer grew up in the Roman Catholic Church. While searching for her identity as an Afro-Surinamese, she let go of her faith. She identified the Winti as the religion of the Afro-Surinamese people.

The fourth author was Edgar Cairo. He did not address nationalism directly in his writings. He referred to his identity as an Afro-Surinamese. Because of this identity he was emotionally attached to the Winti. He had a dualistic religion. His attitude towards Christianity should probably be characterised as indifferent.

Group D. The first author in this group was Dew Rambocus. Even though this author was a Marxist, he should be classified as a revolutionary nationalist. There was no room for the gospel or any religion in his worldview.

The second author was René Mungra. Nationalism was interwoven with identity crisis in his works. The gospel did not have a right to exist, since it was associated with the culture of the exploiter.

The third author was Glenn Sluisdom. Sluisdom was associated with his country emotionally. However, he cannot be classified as a nationalist. His attitude towards the gospel was not clearly articulated.

The fourth author was Alphons Levens. Levens was an outspoken nationalist, who loved his country and aspired to a common future for all Surinamese. He recognised the value of the gospel but did not want to be identified with a church denomination.

Finally, as a result of his research Loswijk drew a few conclusions: 1) Nationalism existed among all groups. 2) All nationalists called for unity among the people. 3) The attitude towards Europe differed among the nationalists. Group A accepted both Christianity and the Western culture. 4) Groups B to D criticised Christianity and the influence of the Western culture. 5) Nationalism received more attention in the thesis than the gospel. 6) What should the church's attitude be towards its critics? The church should start to incorporate cultural elements into its activities, while keeping the content of the gospel the same. 7) The church should pay attention to the following issues: a) an open and honest analysis of every aspect of life in Suriname; b) a reorientation of the tradition from which the church was established; c) a self-motivated, independent interpretation of the Bible in the specific Surinamese context; d) reflection on the church's ministry towards those outside of its orbit of influence; 8) The Moravian Church contributed towards the well-being of society at large, towards the development of Suriname and its people. As Loswijk concluded, it made a contribution in three specific areas (kerygma, diakonia and koinonia): a) preaching the gospel to all the ethnic groups in Suriname; b) it served the people through education, socio-economic and medical services; c) it established fellowship with the people in and outside its church services. The Moravian Church has always attempted and still attempts to contribute towards the building of the Surinamese nation.

15.2.7.3. Winti and Christian religion

In 1988, Loswijk conducted a seminar on the Afro-Surinamese religion. His presentation was published afterwards (Loswijk 1988). His focus was on the Afro-Surinamese people (Creole) of the city. He started by asking the question: 'Is Winti a religion?' If people are given the opportunity to believe what they choose then Winti is a religion. During the colonial era, the slaves were denied the right to practice their religion openly. The appeal of the Winti religion was very strong and the colonial era could not wipe it away. 'In order to meet their religious needs slaves retreated to the bush'. Dance was an important medium to come into contact with the gods.

In the past the Moravian Church worked primarily among the slaves from Africa and came in touch with the Winti. The people realised that the preaching of the gospel did not meet their needs. When the clergyman left, they returned to their old beliefs.

To remedy this problem partially, the church started conducting dedication services to consecrate people's houses. The slaves did not have to use a *tapu* (an amulet for protection) any more to protect their houses against evil spirits. Christendom as it was brought to the slaves did not fit into the experience of the people. Just like John Kent, Loswijk was of the opinion that the gospel was brought in a 'European package' to Suriname. He goes on to say:

> An important feature of Winti is the dance, but in our churches the people have to sit obediently and listen. We have problems with the clapping of hands in the church. The result is that the people start to live in a split world (p. 10).

Elements from the Winti should be used during Church services. The *apinti* (a drum to convey messages) should take over the place of the organ. This should not be a problem because in the past the organ was considered a pagan instrument. The radical rejection of the Winti comes out of fear. The Christian faith should get the opportunity to be integrated with the Surinamese culture. Winti is both a religion and the culture of the Afro-Surinamese.

15.2.8. John Kent

15.2.8.1. Introduction

John Kent was born in 1944. He started his theological journey in Suriname in 1965. After a preparatory year, he went to the Netherlands, where he studied for three years at the *Nederlands Bijbel Instituut*. After his studies in the Netherlands, he studied another two years in Jamaica at the United Theological College of the West Indies. There he received his licentiate in theology, in 1971. In 1984, he left for the United States of America to do follow-up studies at the Moravian Theological Seminary in Bethlehem. He completed his Master of Arts in Pastoral Counselling in 1986.

From 1971-1984, he served as a pastor in several villages (Stoelmanseiland, Botopasi/Futunakaba and Klaaskreek). In Stoelmanseiland he served as the head of the boarding school as well. From 1987-2008, he was the chairman of the Saron boarding school in Paramaribo. In 1987 he was elected as the praeses (general secretary) of the Moravian Church in Suriname. He served in that capacity until 1999. After a sabbatical of almost a year, most of which was for research purposes in the Netherlands, he was appointed as the principal of the theological seminary. He served the seminary from 2000-2008. In 2004 he was elected as the chairman of the Committee on Theology of the Unity Board of the worldwide Moravian Church. On 2 February 2003, he was consecrated as bishop of the *Unitas Fratrum*, the worldwide Moravian fellowship.

15.2.8.2. The Saramaka Church

Kent wrote a monograph on the historical development of the Moravian Church and its influence in the Saramaccan Community in Suriname (Kent 1978). This work was done in English, and it will not be summarised. Here I shall limit myself to a brief overview of its content.

Chapter 1 dealt with the Maroon society. It discussed the escape to the forest and the division of the Maroon tribes. Chapter 2 discussed three aspects of the Saramaccan community, namely the social structure, religious and economic life. Chapter 3 discussed the history of the Moravian Church among the Saramaccans in two parts. The first part was the period of instability (1765-1848) and the second, that of stability (1848-1950). Chapter 4 studied the changes in the Saramaccan community as a result of the introduction of the gospel. It discussed three areas: culture, religion and economy. Chapter 5 concluded the research.

15.2.8.3. Botopasi

In 1979 Kent wrote a monograph about the village Botopasi (Kent 1979). He based this work on the diaries and annual reports of the church in the village between 1916 and 1978. Besides these archival resources, interviews were conducted with a number of people in the village. This made the monograph an important work for the knowledge of this Moravian village. It includes pictures of the village and some of its senior people.

Kent wrote this monograph as part of his work to develop the church in the village. He saw it as an obligation, because: A good citizen of a country, city or village, is supposed to know the beginning and the development of that area where he is privileged to live.

In chapter 1 and 2 he described the founding of the village in 1895 and the names of the leaders and the number of people living in the village in 1978. Chapter 3 discussed the beginning of the Dombi, the group that lives in that village. These people escaped slavery from a plantation owned by a certain Mr Domin, in the area of Carolina. The group went to the upper Suriname River and settled there among other Saramaccans. Chapter 4 described the problems that led to a separation within the clan. This was due to the work of a prophetic figure, called Anake. During a funeral ceremony in 1892, he became possessed. He destroyed the trees and other objects that were venerated by his people. He started a new religion, his own church. His religion, contrary to what was normal among the Moravians was not 'Christo-centric' but 'Anake-centric'. He became the central figure, he was the redeemer. This led to the separation from the clan.

Chapter 5 described how a group of people left Sofibuka, their original village at the time of Anake. Some members of the clan went to a village called Slee and the other group started a new village Botopasi. Anake and some of his followers settled in Futunakaba. Botopasi was founded as a Christian village. In 1898, Izaak Albitrow, settled in the village as the first missionary. During that time Anake was baptised by a Moravian missionary. The chapter continued with an overview of workers in the village up to 1940.

Chapter 6 discussed the developments in the village from 1940-1958, when the missionary Monsels served there. Because of his input in the development of Botopasi, this period was given much attention. Monsels identified himself with the people of Botopasi. He paid much attention to the economic development of the village, perhaps at the expense of the spiritual aspect. He saw the low spiritual level of the church members and tried to explain it from the poor socio-economic condition of the people. By changing the socio-economic condition he wanted to bring the spiritual life to an acceptable level. The church services and Bible readings did not receive due attention. Despite this, it can be concluded that the Monsels family played an important role in the development of the village.

In chapter 7 he discussed the era after Monsels, from 1958-1978. The new leaders took a different approach to that of Monsels. The situation was also different. The workers who served during this period served both the school and the church. When Kent himself arrived in 1973, he took a holistic approach. Preaching the gospel has to focus on the whole person, man in his spiritual, social and economic situation. The spiritual was the basis. Much attention was given to the work in the local church. Besides the regular church services, there were prayer meetings and Bible studies. Attention was also given to the youth. Social activities that were introduced included Boy Scouts and draughts competitions. Despite many meetings and sessions for information and discussion about the development of the village, it was not possible to do certain projects successfully. Contrary to what was hoped, the construction of a new church building should be included in the unsuccessful projects, because of the lack of cooperation of the people.

Chapter 8, a critical review of the work, was entitled: 'the unfruitful ground'. Why were Monsels and his predecessors successful in mobilising the people? 1) The people did not have much contact with the outside world at that time. 2) The number of people in the village was very small and there was social control. 3) The village did not suffer from the influence of political parties. 4) There was leadership in the village. The period after Monsels experienced its own problems. The people were not taught to be self-active. Monsels was the motivating force of the community upon whose energy all depended.

The missions to the people in the interior did not have a clear policy to guarantee continuity of the work. A continual lack of plans for the future haunted the church in the post-Monsels era. Three important factors had an influence on this village. 1) The political changes, which among others gave the Maroons the right to vote. Political parties influenced the villages with their empty promises. The unified village was divided along political lines. Dissension within the village (and families) means weakened society. (2) The plan to build a dam along the Suriname River, the Brokopondoplan, was the reason for some men leaving the village. They went to Afobakka to work and earned a lot of money. This changed their lifestyle completely. When the workers returned to Botopasi, they could not continue with the new lifestyle. Many therefore left the village for the city, Paramaribo. (3) However, the improved education system in the interior improved the interaction with the world outside of the village.

Politics added to the problems by creating an elite group in the village. This group that was loyal to a political party in the capital city was given jobs. Because of this they felt powerful and were no longer willing to submit themselves to the village leaders. This situation had a negative impact on village life. The church also played a role in this situation. The study revealed that throughout its history the spiritual life of the members in the church was very low. The church and its ministers were also responsible for this situation. The liberation that the gospel brings should become a reality for the people. The people should also learn that they have a responsibility. The village should however not become pessimistic, it has potential. There is a need for repentance. Kent stressed that things cannot go on as they are going right now.

Chapter 9 gave the foundational principles towards a healthy development of the village. These were 1) self-respect, 2) belief in one's own ability, 3) cooperation, 4) and love for one's own village. Furthermore, 5) the various institutions active in the village (church, school and government) must find common goals, 6) Education should be recognised as the heart of the development, 7) Finally, there was a need for unity and self-sacrifice among all the members of the village. All this was propagated as the foundation of a living faith in Jesus Christ. Faith in Christ breaks down all walls and brings people together. Faith in Christ allows one to know himself, who he is and who he should be. Without faith in Christ nobody will do well.

In an epilogue Kent gave three points that were given as an update in 1979. 1) A group of women became very active and organised activities for women in the village. 2) Eighteen young people who were studying in the city came during their Easter holiday to help the village. 3) A group of young people took the initiative to repair the broken bridges in the village.

15.2.8.4. Ancestor veneration

In 1984 Kent gave a series of lectures at the Catechetical centre of the Roman Catholic Church, entitled 'The veneration of saints and ancestor cult' (Kent 1984). His lectures were published afterwards. The first part discussed the issue of the veneration of saints, from the perspective of the Roman Catholic Church. Veneration of saints is often associated with the Roman Catholic Church. However, the book argued that the annual celebration of Reformation Day with Martin Luther at the centre was nothing else than a veneration of the reformer. The book started with the Roman Catholic position on the saints. The Roman Catholic Church divided the saints into three categories: (1) the church militant, (2) the church triumphant and (3) the church suffering. A Roman Catholic theologian argued that a bond of holy fellowship encompasses the living and the dead, the militant on earth and the crowned in heaven and unites those on earth who are striving for righteousness. The saints live in another domain but they are part of the one fellowship. Outsiders however, get the impression that the departed Christians (saints) are minor gods and that prayers are offered to them. What is the role of these saints in the church and in the life of the believers? The saints are not gods, but yet they are believed to mediate between God and man. They have the task of intercession. Veneration takes place through prayers, by asking the saints to pray to Christ and God on our behalf, by following their example and through the relics.

The book continued with an explanation of ancestor veneration. When a person dies, according to the Western worldview, that means the end of the person. The traditional person has a different view on that issue. The person who dies continues to live in another situation, in the land of the dead. The people living in the land of the dead and those living on earth are one unified society. The living depend on the dead.

Veneration of the ancestors is supported by the notion that the ancestors know both the world of the living and that of the dead. The ancestors also know the world of the gods and are able to mediate between the gods and the world of the living.

How is the relationship between the living and the dead maintained? From the side of the ancestors there are two ways. (1) Ancestors appear in dreams. (2) Some ancestral spirits will come back and take possession of a living person. This spirit can be an avenging spirit. From the side of the living there are also two ways. (1) Those living offer water or rum as a libation. (2) Some will evoke the spirits of the ancestors, either directly or through the medium.

What is the role of the ancestors in the relation between God and man? Depending on the issues that the living are facing, ancestors may be seen as mediators between God and man or ancestors will be venerated. They are never considered to be gods. At the best they are mediators between God and man, since they know both worlds very well. They are called 'the living-dead', the dead who are still nearby.

After this presentation, the book reviewed both 'saints' and 'ancestors' in the light of the Bible. In the Old Testament covenant, it was God who established the relationship with his people, through the king, prophet and priest. In the veneration of both saints and ancestors, their role as mediators was established by men. The Old Testament seems to prohibit the consultation of the dead (Deut 18:11; Ps. 115:17; Eccl. 9:15). 'Why consult the dead on behalf of the living?' (Isa 8:19) The New Testament also does not support the idea of the so-called fellowship of all the saints, as discussed earlier, and the veneration of ancestors and saints. In the New Testament, all Christians are saints. The role of human mediators, such as the priest, is no longer necessary in the New Covenant, with the arrival of Christ (Heb. 8:6). Paul said Christ is the mediator between God and man. He is the way to God. Through the sacrifice of his blood He opened the way to God (Rom 5:12; Heb. 10:20). He reveals God (Joh 1:18; 6:46; 8:32). Prayers will be answered when they are offered 'in the Name of Jesus'. Acts 4:12 sums up the whole idea:

> And there is salvation in no one else, for there is no other name under heaven given among people by which we must be saved.

The book included a summary of the discussions that took place after the lectures.

15.2.8.5. Forms of reconciliation in family counselling

In 1986, Kent wrote a thesis on family counselling for his Master of Arts degree in pastoral counselling (Kent 1986).

Chapter 1 is the introduction to the study. The purpose of the study is first to identify several family problems and their causes as they occur in different types of families and secondly to discuss several forms of reconciliation. The study followed a mixed type of literature review and surveys. The surveys were conducted in two areas: the surroundings of the Saron and Latour in Paramaribo, Suriname and Egeboro Moravian Church and Moravian Theological Seminary in Pennsylvania in the United States of America. The introduction concluded by conceptualising the terminologies of the study: church, family and reconciliation.

Chapter 2 provided the theological understanding of both the family and reconciliation. The family is a formation centre for human relationship. It reflects an intra-family relationship and a relationship to the environment. Family was part of God's creation. It is impossible to think of the family apart from God's involvement with and in it.

The words 'leave' and 'one flesh' in Gen 2:24, express the concept of 'dis-union and union'. The union is characterised by mutual love and trust and is expressed in the sexual relationship of man and woman. The most important purpose of the family is 'pro-creation'. The family is that agency in creation that has as one of its purposes, the continuity of the human community. The family also has relationships with the body of Christ. The church is compared to a family and families must function within a church.

Human beings have a special place in the context of creation. Man is created in the image and after the likeness of God (Gen 1:26). He was given authority to subdue creation and to have dominion over everything on earth (Gen 1:28). A further relation of man is expressed in the words 'it is not good for man to be alone, I will make him a helper fit for him' (Gen 2:18). Only in community can he and she be a true human being. This relationship was part of what God saw to be very good (Gen 1:31). Gen 3 and 4 explained how the relationship between God and humans and between fellow human beings has been affected. This disturbance resulted in alienation or estrangement: sin. Humans turn away from

God to other creatures, idolatry. This stage of human existence called for change, re-creation.

> Re-creation means the re-establishment of man and woman in the original state as God wanted them to be from the beginning of creation; man and woman in a harmonious relationship with God, themselves and fellow humans, so they can become fully human as they ought (p. 31).

This process of re-creation is called reconciliation.

> The basic affirmation of the New Testament message of reconciliation is that in the life of Jesus, God himself stepped into the breach with the purpose of reconciling sinful and therefore ruined creation by making the Son himself, sin. ... Since this peace between God and human beings is established on the cross, reconciliation in our human world means our calling, our mission to establish peace (pp. 33, 34).

Reconciliation has a relation to fellow humans. The dividing wall between the far-off and the near has been broken (Eph 2:11-22). Reconciliation has a universal scope (Col 1:20). There is also a relation to oneself, a good relation to all systems of the human personality. Reconciliation of the interpersonal relationship can fully take place when the person enters into a new relationship with God in Christ.

Chapter 3 studied the sociological understanding of the family. Whereas the theological understanding (chapter 2) focused on the vertical dimension, the sociological understanding focused on the horizontal. One of the characteristics of family is that within families there is an interchange both within the family and with those outside the family. A second characteristic is openness. A third characteristic is the triangular system of father, mother and child. The chapter continued with a discussion of different types of families. These include: the nuclear, the single-parent, the extended and the polygamous family.

Chapter 4 which is based on the empirical findings, discussed the family crisis. It identified its problems, causes, solutions tried and professionals consulted.

Chapter 5 studied the pastoral counsellor as a reconciler. It answered the question 'what are the forms of reconciliation that can be pursued in Surinamese society?' The study identified interpersonal, intrapersonal and economic relationships and the relationship to God. Reconciliation has to take place in these areas. The thesis called for the institution of the role of pastoral counsellor in Suriname. The counsellor should dedicate himself or herself to the creation of: 1) A family life education group; 2) A genuine safeguard to protect the interests and needs of the members of the church who are single, widowed or divorced. Furthermore, the counsellor in Suriname has a prophetic role.

15.2.8.6. The Winti religion in the interior

In 1988, John Kent presented papers on the topic: 'Winti: the encounter of the Afro-Surinamese religion and Christianity' (Kent 1988). The papers were published in book form. The book focused on the manifestation of this religion in the interior among the Maroons. The book started with the story of a person who conveyed to Kent that he would not attend his presentations. He preferred to spend the time praying. The book argued that a clergyman should broaden his knowledge of other religions to be able to serve the people much better. That does not mean one has to practice the Winti religion. Winti is defined in different ways: (1) primitive religion, (2) traditional or tribal religion, (3) idolatry, (4) Winti and (5) Afro-Surinamese religion. There are two groups of gods and spirits in the Winti pantheon: (1) gods of nature and (2) spirits.

Among the spirits, the kunu is predominant in the interior. The kunu is the spirit of a person or an animal that was killed or mistreated while it was alive and when it died, it became an avenging spirit to the matrilineal family of the person who killed or mistreated it. The kunu will possess someone and will move on to another when that person dies. It is said to haunt the family forever. Each Maroon family or clan has a kunu.

The book continued with a confrontation between the Winti and the gospel. It argued that four approaches can be taking in the dialogues about

Winti: (1) The Winti can be accommodated. By doing that not much is damaged. One takes the Winti in the form in which it is manifested and then brings Christianity into it. (2) The second approach is a syncretistic approach. This approach blends together various religious views and practices, so that they form a unity. (3) In the parallel approach, Winti and Christianity live side by side: the so-called bedroom and living room approach. (4) Finally Winti can be dismissed radically.

The book differentiated between Christendom and the gospel, because Christendom has shortcomings, but the gospel can function in all cultures. It referred to the European form in which Christendom was brought to Suriname. According to the early European missionaries, everything of the people in the interior was wrong. The people who became Christians have done away with their arts because they were idolatrous. The book observed that practitioners of the Winti kept some positive elements that one cannot deny. A herbal bath brings healing. In that religion however the 'deliverance' is temporary, one remains bound. The gospel brings in a dimension in which one is fully set free. When a kunu is washed away through a herbal bath, that spirit stays away, but another one comes into the scene. However, the gospel gives total deliverance, in which no spirit will be able to influence one negatively.

The book emphasised the need to reflect about the way in which the gospel should be preached and translated so that it will take over the place of the Winti in the lives of the people.

15.2.9. Hesdie Zamuel

15.2.9.1. Introduction

Hesdie Stuart Zamuel was born in 1946. In 1963, he received a scholarship to study in the Netherlands. After completing his secondary education, he started his theological studies in 1968 and graduated in 1975, with his doctorandus (Masters equivalent) degree from the University of Utrecht. In that same year, he returned to Suriname to serve as a pastor in the Moravian Church in Moengo. He worked there up to 1976. He served as the chaplain of the Surinamese army from 1976 to 1991. From 1981 to 1996, he served as the chairman of the mission board of the Moravian Church in Suriname.

In 1990, he became the principal of the Theological Seminary. Zamuel received his doctorate degree in 1994. In 1999, he was elected as praeses of the church. From 2007 to 2009 he was a lecturer at the *Theofilo Kisanji University* in Mbeya, Tanzania.

15.2.9.2. Bible translation

While working in Moengo, in the eastern part of Suriname, Zamuel started to work on a translation of the Old Testament. He did that because he felt that there was a need for the Old Testament in Sranantongo. He worked on the translation of the Minor Prophets from the Hebrew text. In 1984, he published a translation of the book of Hosea with explanatory notes, followed by Joel, Obadiah, Amos and Micah in 1985 (Zamuel 1984; 1985a; 1985b). In 1986, he continued with Zephaniah, Nahum and Habakkuk (Zamuel 1986). He completed the series in 1996, with the translation of Haggai, Zechariah and Malachi (Zamuel 1996a). The book of Jonah was not translated since an older translation was available.

15.2.9.3. Johannes King

In 1994, Zamuel received his doctorate at the University of Utrecht. His dissertation was on the life and work of Johannes (John) King, a prophet and apostle of the Surinamese interior (Zamuel 1994). The dissertation is divided into five parts, apart from the foreword and the introduction. These parts are followed by five appendices, and a summary in English.

In the 'introduction' Zamuel explained the research problem of the dissertation. Much has been published about King. A summary of his life and work however is missing. The same is true for the deeper background, motives and characteristic features of King. The purpose of the dissertation is to place the person and work of Johannes King against the background of his own times. Furthermore, Zamuel studied the relevance of the theological meaning and coherence of King's words and deeds for present-day Suriname. Zamuel belongs to the same tribe as King, therefore he cannot guarantee a purely objective historical account of the events. The work is an attempt to reconstruct an important episode of his own history. This approach is important since descriptions by outsiders missed important nuances of the history. The introduction concludes with a description of the primary and secondary sources on King.

The first part consists of two chapters (chapters 2-3). In chapter 2 he discussed the colony of Suriname, including life in the city and on the plantations. In chapter 3 he focused on the interior, the domain of the Maroons. In the eighteenth century the colonial government signed peace treaties with the Maroons. These treaties were signed in 1760 (with the Ndyukas), in 1762 (with the Saramaccans) and in 1767 with the Matawais, the tribe of Johannes King. The Maroon community consists of six independent tribes: The Aluku or Boni, Ndyuka, Paramaccan, Saramaccan, Matawai and Kwinti. These tribes maintain contact with one other. Contacts are supported as long as they do not threaten the order of one's own group. Zamuel mentioned the similarities and differences between the different tribes.

The second part consists of four chapters (chapters 4-7). In chapter 4 Zamuel presents a biography of King. King was born around 1830 and died on 24 October 1898. His mother was of Matawai and his father of Ndyuka descent. Because of the matrilineal system among the Maroons, he was reckoned to be a Matawai, the tribe of his mother. He spent his early years on plantations close to Paramaribo. King was married to two wives according to the Maroon tradition. One wife belonged to the Matawai and the other to the Saramaccan tribe. He settled with his family in the Matawai village of Maripaston.

In chapter 5, Zamuel discussed the conversion of King in detail, using King's own words. King became very ill in Maripaston. Because of his licentious lifestyle, including sleeping with other people's wives, King believed he was poisoned. His illness went on for more than two years. At the point when all thought he was going to die, King received a vision which he wrote down in detail. In his illness, Jesus came to him and healed him. In the vision he was brought to the gates of heaven. There he saw men and women clothed in white robes. In the vision he saw himself as being completely well. He was taken to another gate, the gate of hell. He saw a fire that was burning, and it became very hot there. He was told that that place would be his eternal home if he did not repent. The messenger told him to go back to earth and to preach the message to everybody. He was also told to be baptised, because God did not want him to die as a heathen. He also received guidelines to build a church in Maripaston. King also received a vision from the ancestors who encouraged him to carry on the mission that he received from the Lord namely, to preach the gospel. The visions contributed to a new lifestyle by King. He started to drive out demons from people, to heal the sick and to clear out idol temples.

Chapter 6 discussed his ministry at length. It speaks about the church in Maripaston. The church grew between 1861 and 1867. King undertook a few mission trips, in which he visited Maroon villages. He visited the Upper Saramacca, Upper Suriname and Marowijne River. He preached the gospel to the Maroons in all the villages along these rivers. The responses were not as he expected. Among the Saramaccans he met with resistance, which could be due to a specific historical reason, for some time before the Matawai people had killed a paramount chief of the Saramaccans. King also preached at plantations in the Para area.

In chapter 7 Zamuel discussed the crises in King's life and ministry and his death. King faced a few crises in his life and ministry. The visions that guided him were a source of some of the conflicts with the church. In 1867, the leadership of the Moravian Church forbade King from continuing to use his visions as means of God's revelation. A certain Nicolaas Manille, who lived in Maripaston complained to the leadership about King's usage of visions. According to him King used his own ideas and fantasies which he attributed to God. King had problems from another side as well. His own brother Noah Adrai denied him the right to serve in the church. As the paramount chief, Adrai did not want the people to think that King was the leader of the tribe. He expelled King from Maripaston. Just before Adrai died he allowed King to return and take up his work in the church again. Other areas of dispute were the fight against the *grantata* cult and the battle to become the paramount chief, the *gaama*. He won the battle and became the chief. Not long after that, he resigned from that position, probably under pressure from the Moravian leadership. King died in 1898.

Part three consists of two chapters. In chapter 8 Zamuel discussed the theology of Zinzendorf, the theology of the Moravians after Zinzendorf and the theological situation in Suriname. In chapter 9 he looked at King as an independent theologian. King's preaching resembled that of the Moravians, since he was one of their disciples. However there were elements that seem to be based on King's own understanding. According to him, the *sweri*[7] is a good gift from God to the Afro-Surinamese people, to order their society. Even the *obias*[8] were a gift from God. However, they were changed because God cursed them and made them powerless.

King was also positive about the *dresi* (herbal medicine). He wrote a *dresibuku*, a book about herbal medicines. The Moravians had a different view of all these three issues. King therefore was not just a follower of the Moravians. He used his knowledge of the African-related way of existence among the Afro-Surinamese people and tried to contextualise the Christian message. He was an independent interpreter of the gospel according to the basic principles of Moravian theology.

Part four which discussed the memories about King and his relevance, consisted of two chapters. In chapter 10 Zamuel discussed the memory of King. He was not only remembered among the Matawai, but also among other members of the Moravian Church. The oral tradition kept some of these memories alive. One of these was when King crossed the river under water.

In chapter 11 Zamuel discussed the relevance of King. Who was King? Was he a prophet, an apostle, a Pentecostal or liberation theologian? He discussed his relevance with regard to contextualisation, faith and the preaching of the gospel. He continued to discuss four issues about the continuity or discontinuity of King, based on a question raised by Kraemer.

Part five discussed the works of King. In the first part of chapter 12, Zamuel discussed the works of King in detail. The second part consisted of four missionary journeys undertaken by King. The final part consisted of fragments from the dresibuku (medicine book) of King.

The five appendices included 1) a chronological overview, 2) some pictures, 3) manuscript fragments, 4) a list of Surinamese words and concepts and 5) a list of abbreviations. The work has a summary in English.

---

7. 'An oath, vow, a friendship pact' (see p. 226).
8. 'Magical or prevention medicine; knowledge and skills given by a divinity' (see p. 225).

The dissertation was published as part of the series Mission (Missiological Research in the Netherlands) under the final editorship of Professor Jan A B Jongeneel, who was Zamuel's doctoral promoter.

15.2.9.4. Mission of the church

In 1997, Zamuel published a book on the mission of the church (Zamuel 1997a). Following the introduction, he divided the book in three parts. The first part presented a biblical orientation (chapters 2-6). The second part (chapters 7-11) studied aspects of missions. The third and final part studied people in mission (chapters 12-14).

In chapter 2 he studied the Old and New Testaments as the canon of the Christian church. Section 2.1 studied the relation between the Old and New Testaments. Zamuel identified three approaches that he characterised as follows: 1) The Old Testament is the real Bible and the New Testament is an explanatory dictionary or appendix to it. 2) The New Testament is the most important part and the Old Testament was a preparation for the New. 3) The Old and New together form the Bible. This is the approach that Zamuel supported.

Section 2.2 asked whether there are differences in approach between the two Testaments? This point is explained based on a discussion of evil in both Testaments. With regard to evil, the Old Testament does not have a problem with the idea that it comes from God or that it happened with his knowledge (1 Sam 16:14; 1 Kings 22:19-23; Job 1:6-12; 2:1-6; Isa 45:5-7; Lam 2:20; 3:17). In some parts of the New Testament one get the impression that two powers are competing with each other (Mat 13:19; Luk 11:15). This 'dualism' goes against the testimony that YHWH is the God of the gods (Deut 10:17; Ps 50:1). In his presence, all powers are nothing. The dilemma can be avoided by a study of the image of light and darkness.

Section 2.3 concluded with Zamuel's defence of the unity of the Old and New Testaments.

In chapter 3 he studied Isa 61:1-3. The messenger of God's salvation in Isaiah is identified with Christ in Luke 4:16 ff. And via Jesus, the church is called, just like the messenger to announce glad tidings today. Those who mourn, or those who are enslaved, imprisoned and without hope receive new courage through the proclamation of the church.

In chapter 4 he studied Acts 15:12-21. The early church reached a conclusion on four non-negotiable issues that were sanctioned by the Holy Spirit. The church argued for freedom in Christ. Zamuel raised the question whether we in our days should decide on non-negotiable issues that should be kept under all circumstances. If so, what should they be?

In chapter 5 he studied John 21:1-14, under the title: 'The stranger at the seashore'. It deals with the challenge of the gospel to continue to enter into new territories even though they seem strange to us.

Chapter 6 studied Matt 25:14-30 under the title: 'Working capital'. The story of the talents calls us to not only to save (preserve), but also to recruit by investing that which was entrusted to us, by being active.

In chapter 7 Zamuel posted four theses on missions.

1. Following Israel, the church sees itself as a community that is elected to be a testimony in the world of God's merciful involvement with his creation (7.1).

2. The primary task at the execution of the missionary command is not that we should be successful in convincing others (proselytise). We should function in the world in a consistent manner as a relevant sign of God's saving love (7.2).

3. A missionary church can be described as follows: it is a fellowship of people who, in obedience to and in imitation of her Lord and Saviour Jesus Christ, have no other aspiration than to be the mediator of God's salvation for mankind and the world (7.3).

4. Making the biblical message real is of vital importance for the church to be able to carry out its missionary command in a correct manner. This can only take place through contextualisation (7.4).

In chapter 8 he studied the diaconate of the church. The example of a diakonos (servant) is Jesus Christ, who according to Mark 10:45 'did not come to be served but to serve, and to give his life as a ransom for many' (NET) (8.1-2). The church as the body of Christ should represent him and follow in his footsteps (8.3). Jesus' approach was comprehensive (8.4). In missions, preaching (*kerugma*), praise (*leiturgia*), fellowship (*koinonia*) and service (*diakonia*) should always be present. The one should not be done without the other (8.5). Diakonia can be described as 'the ministry of the church that is focused on the wholeness of mankind and society, as a sign of their being 'part of' God's salvation for this world' (p. 29).

In chapter 9, he studied contextualisation and dialogue as an ongoing task. Should the messenger of God's salvation accept the context of the people uncritically, when he carries out his calling and if so, to what extent? Section 9.1 discussed the problem of contextualisation. Can the cultural forms of non-Christians be taken and given a new meaning in the light of the gospel (e.g. Christmas as the feast of light)? This approach has been criticised because it is impossible to separate completely form and content, since they influence each other. Obviously, there is a danger of syncretism, in which important elements of the message can be affected. However, the revelation of God in itself was contextualisation. The climax of the revelation was the incarnation of Jesus Christ. Zinzendorf explained this as follows: Because man was not able to learn God's language, God adapted himself to man's language. European cultures contextualise the gospel. Why should the Germanic form of praying with the hands folded be more respectful than lifting up the hands, which is often used in the Psalms?

Plurality in society calls forth problems in contextualisation and communication (9.3). The church should recognise that God is the creator of heaven and earth and everything in it (Ps 24:1, 2; Isa 40:12-31; 48:12,13). He is also the God of the gods (Deut 10:17; Ps 50:1; 82; Job 1:6-12; 2:1-6). This, according to Zamuel, cannot mean anything else than that the people of the earth, no matter which god they serve, should be considered as his creation and his own. The church should therefore continue to work towards a society of peace and harmony.

In chapter 10, he discussed the issues of folk religions and ecumenism. Folk religions are characterised as 1) an adjusted interpretation by the people themselves; 2) an integration of the social and spiritual world and 3) a contextualisation of religious values (9.1). Section 9.2 argued that there is a need for a distinction between adaptation, contextualisation and syncretism. Section 9.3 discussed two historical developments in folk religions. The first was prevalent in the time of Jesus in the New Testament and the second during the time of the Reformation. Section 9.4 ended with a discussion on the Afro-Caribbean religions and ecumenism. There is a need for an interreligious dialogue as people who live in the one world created by God.

In chapter 11 Zamuel studied the Winti religion. Section 11.1 raised the question of 'who or what is man?' Man is seen first as a living soul (*nephesh*) and then as spirit (*ruach*), which is defined as a working active power. Section 11.2 discussed God and the gods. The gods were intended to be executers of God's will; at least that was the original intention (Ps 103:20-21). Some of them tried to withdraw themselves from that and wanted to go their own way. God calls them to give account (Ps 82), corrects them (Matt 9:31-32; 17:18) and finally destroys them (Matt 8:29; Rev 12:1ff; 20:7-10). Section 11.3 studied the role of the Holy Spirit in the history of the Moravian Church. Section 11.4, started the discussion on the Winti religion. It demonstrated clearly that Moravian leaders have always disapproved of their church members who participate in Winti practices (11.5). This has been the case, at least until 1971, when the law on Winti as idolatry was abolished. The nationalists argued that Winti should not be considered as a religion but as culture. According to Zamuel this is an ambiguous assumption. If Winti is not a religion but a culture, then Christians should not have a problem to participate in it. But, according to Zamuel, religion is also culture. Then one needs to ask, 'Is everything that is culture also acceptable?' Zamuel does not give an answer to this question but presents it as a challenge to the readers. On the other hand, it is true that Winti belongs to the culture of the Afro people. It will be impossible to reach the Afro people with the gospel, apart from their concrete way of thinking and feeling. Zamuel agrees with his predecessors that the gospel as it was preached in Suriname came in a European form. He raised a few questions that the church (the Moravian) needed to answer prior to the formulation of a position about the Winti. One needs to ask: (1) What is cultural lumber in the life of the church and what is the core of the gospel? Intensive and thorough Bible study can help to give us some insights in this. (2) What part of the Winti-system can help the church to have a better understanding of the Afro-Surinamese person, as a prospective practitioner of the gospel, and what should be seen as purely religious? The answer to these questions should not be clear to the church leaders alone, but also to the church members. Zamuel does not give a clear-cut answer to the question of what should be the attitude towards the Winti now, because according to him a few assumptions, which he clearly identified, need to be answered before one can take a clear position.

Chapters 12 to 14 studied three important figures in the Moravian Church. In chapter 12 Zamuel studied Jan Amos Comenius, the theologian, philosopher, educator and the last bishop of the old United Brethren. In chapter 13, he studied Count Nicolaus Ludwig Von Zinzendorf. Chapter 14 studied John King, the subject of his doctoral dissertation (see Zamuel 1994).

15.2.9.5. The missional church

In 1997, Zamuel published a study guide for the extension programme of the theological seminary. This work dealt with the missionary church (Zamuel 1997b). It explained the grounding (chapter 1), purpose (chapter 2) and nature (chapter 3) of the missionary church. Chapter 4 discussed the new situation in the twenty-first century. The new challenges included secularism, rationalism, individualism (4.1), and syncretism (4.2). The latter contained gnostic (4.2.1), mystic (4.2.2.) and New Age (4.2.3) elements. The next challenge is Pentecostalism (4.3). The missionary church in the twenty-first century should be a diaconal church to serve as the salt (chapter 5) and a dialogical church to serve as the light (chapter 6). It should dialogue with the religions (6.1), authorities (6.2) and with culture (6.3). The work concluded with summaries and conclusions (chapter 7).

15.2.9.6. Caretakers of God's creation

In 2010, Zamuel published his class notes for a course on mission and ecumenism that he taught at a theological university in Tanzania (Zamuel 2010). The book consisted of two parts, missiology and ecumenism. Each part consisted of five chapters. The work was written in English.

In chapter 1, the introduction, he introduced the field of missiology. He interacted with the works of two missiologists of the twentieth century, David Bosch and Jan Jongeneel.

Chapter 2 is a biblical foundation for mission. Zamuel argued that three methods can be used to find the biblical foundation for missions. 1) Find certain books or chapters in the Bible which speak of mission. 2)

Look at the Bible itself as being missionary. 3) Look for keywords that can illustrate the meaning of mission in the Bible. He studied mission in the Old Testament (2.1), the New Testament (2.2) and keywords (2.3). He summarised his findings in sixteen points (2.4).

In chapter 3 he studied mission as representation. The missionary is a representative of the one who sends him. He speaks and acts on behalf of his sender. The chapter studied the mission of God (3.1), of Christ (3.2), the church (3.3) and peoples (3.4). He summarised his findings in eight points (3.5).

In chapter 4 he studied mission strategies, with attention to strategy (4.1), contextual adaptation (4.2) and tactics (4.3). The chapter concluded with a six-point summary (4.4).

In chapter 5 Zamuel summarised his study on missiology in the previous chapters in nine points.

In chapter 6 he started his studies in ecumenism. Ecumenism is defined in a broad (large) and narrow (small) way (6.1). 'Large ecumenism' is defined as follows:

> Ecumenism is the pursuit of the church (church-denominations) to establish the understanding that the whole (visible and invisible) creation belongs together and was meant to form an organic entity, to the glory of God, the Creator (p. 68).

'Small ecumenism' is defined as follows:

> Ecumenism is the pursuit to establish unity among the church denominations as part of the one body of Christ; each with its own gifts and functioning, but all contributing to the perfection of the total body (p. 68).

The chapter continued with the history of the ecumenical movement (6.2) and the ecumenical bodies (6.3). The ecumenical bodies are divided into three categories: global bodies (6.3.1), Christian world communions (6.3.2) and regional ecumenical bodies (6.3.3).

In chapter 7 Zamuel studied two of the major global bodies, the World Council of Churches (7.1) and the Lausanne Committee for World Evangelism (7.2).

In chapter 8 he studied the All Africa Conference of Churches (AACC). He discussed its vision (8.1), motives and objectives (8.2), Africanisation (8.3) and Assemblies (8.4).

In chapter 9 he studied ecumenism in the Caribbean. Chapter 10 concluded with a study on God's caretakers.

15.2.9.7. Minor publications

In 1993 Rev Johan van der Veer interviewed Zamuel (Zamuel 1993). That interview was published under the title: 'This country does not stimulate you to go to church' (Zamuel 1993). Church attendance of Surinamese in the Netherlands is low. Zamuel explained the possible reasons for it.

In 1995, Zamuel gave a paper entitled 'Popular Religions and Ecumenism'. It was published as a chapter in the book *At the Crossroads* (Zamuel 1995).

In 1996 Zamuel published two articles about theological education in the Moravian Church of Suriname. The articles started with the beginning of formal theological education in the 1890's (Zamuel 1996b; 1996c).

In 1998 he published a basic introduction to the Bible as a study guide for the extension programme of the theological seminary (Zamuel 1998).

In 1999, he published an article on Winti and the Christian church in Suriname (Zamuel 1999).

15.2.10. Frederik Muktisahai Rambaran

15.2.10.1. Introduction

Frederik Muktisahai Rambaran was born in 1949 in Nickerie. In 1973, he went to Brussels to study theology at the *Universitaire Protestantse Theologische Faculteit*. After completing his candidature, Rambaran taught religion part-time at a secondary school in Belgium. In 1981 he completed his licentiate degree for which he wrote and defended a thesis on fellowship offering. At that time, the World Council of Churches offered him a one-year scholarship for further education in India. However, the provincial board of the church in Suriname asked him to return home. From 1982-1984, he served at the Sadhu Sundar Singh boarding school in Paramaribo. In 1984, he was appointed as the pastor of the Immanuel Church in Zorg en Hoop. Rambaran served as a lecturer at the theological seminary in Suriname, where he taught the history of Israel, archaeology, pastoral theology, liturgy and biblical theology. In 1988 he returned to Belgium, where he took his doctorandus examination. Due to family circumstances he emigrated in 1992 to the Netherlands. In 1993 he took up office with the Hervormde Kerk in Scheveningen (Netherlands). He served as the chaplain for two nursing homes. Fifty per cent of his time was devoted to the service of the Moravian Church in Rotterdam. He was appointed to work among people in diaspora in Noord Brabant, Limburg and Zeeland in 1994. He served the Moravian Church in Curacao from 1999 to 2003.

15.2.10.2. Fellowship offering
Rambaran wrote his licentiate thesis on the fellowship offering in the Old Testament (Rambaran 1981).

In chapter 1 he introduced the concept of the sacrifice. The study focused on the fellowship meal that took place at specific times and certain places (1.1). It was believed in the ancient world that the gods participated in those meals. These were sacred meals. Rambaran focused on the Old Testament šᵉlāmîm (peace offering). He studied it in the different literary redactions, such as the Deuteronomistic history, the Chronicler history and the Priestly codex. The developments of the sacrifices in the Old Testament were divided into three stages. The first stage was the one in which the notion of fellowship and social belonging was intensive. This was described by the Deuteronomist. The second stage was when the cultic sacrifice took place in a sanctuary at set dates. In the third stage, the sacrifice was separated from other cultic elements. The priest did everything. The Chronicler and the Priestly codex described this. The intention of this study was to describe this development.

In section 1.2 he gave a detailed and technical study of the Hebrew word šᵉlāmîm. He studied the root word *šlm* and the derived verb, noun (*šālôm*) and adjective (*šalēm*). The word šᵉlāmîm appeared eighty-six times in the Old Testament. Forty-nine of these appearances were in combination with a form of the word *zebaḥ* (sacrifice).

In chapter 2 he discussed the use of šᵉlāmîm and zebaḥ šᵉlāmîm. The double phrase zebaḥ šᵉlāmîm is used in the Priestly texts. It follows after the ʿôlâ (burnt offering). In some texts only the word šᵉlāmîm is used. Section 2.1 studied the use of the word in various passages. It started with various phrases that were used in Lev 7:11-21 and 7:28-34. It continued with Lev 9:4 and 22, Num 6, the Holiness code (see Lev 17), Ezek 40-48. In section 2.2 he studied šᵉlāmîm in various literary genres. Section 2.2.1 studied the word in the non-Priestly texts. In these contexts šᵉlāmîm had to do with important events. These events included when David brought the Ark of the Covenant to Jerusalem (2 Sam 6:17-18); when he was at the threshing floor of Araunah (2 Sam 24:25); furthermore, when Solomon started to reign (1 Kings 3:15) and at the consecration of the temple (1 Kings 8:64). In these passages šᵉlāmîm can be seen as a major public sacrifice. Section 2.2.2 studied šᵉlāmîm in the Priestly texts. Here, it was connected to the altar (Lev 6:5 and Lev 9). Furthermore reference was made to specific things, e.g. fat was to be burned on the altar (Lev 6:5), the blood was to be sprinkled on the altar (Lev 7:14,33). In the Deuteronomist the notion of eating and rejoicing in the presence of YHWH was prominent. In section 2.3 he studied the concept of zebaḥ šᵉlāmîm which appeared often in the Priestly Codex.[9] Section 2.3.1 studied the phrase in the non-Priestly texts. It identified the unusual forms of the phrase in 1 Sam 11:15 and Exod 24:5. In the Priestly texts (2.3.2) where the normal phrase appeared, two independent types of offerings were combined. It was not clear whether this was an actual combination of two offerings or just a literary combination. A bloody rite (šᵉlāmîm) was added to the zebaḥ. The priests were responsible for this sacrifice.

In chapter 3 Rambaran studied the Deuteronomistic historiography. Section 3.1 described the historical situation. Judg 20:36 and 21:4

---

9. In Lev 3:1,3,6,9; 4:10,26,31,35; 7:11,13,15,18,20,21,29 (bis), 32,34,37; 9:18; 10:14; 17:5; 19:5; 22:21; 23:19; Num 6:17,18; 7:17,23,29,35,41, 47,53,59,65,71, 77,83,88; 10:10. In the Deuteronomist: Josh 22:23.27; 1 Sam 10:8; 11:15; 1 Kings 8:63; In 2 Chron 30:22; 33:16; in Prov 7:14 and Exodus 24:5 and 29:28.

described the first stage of Israel's history after they possessed the land (3.1.1). The people built an altar to sacrifice and did not use an existing Canaanite one (21:4). Earlier they may have used an existing one. Section 3.1.2 explained 1 Sam 10:9, 11:15 and 13:9. It dealt with the time of Saul and Samuel. Section 3.1.3 studied 2 Samuel. David brought the ark to Jerusalem (2 Sam 6:17-18). Because of this Jerusalem became an important place. Later on, David offered sacrifices at the threshing floor of Araunah. Probably David took over a Jebusite sanctuary on that occasion. Section 3.1.4 studied 1 Kings. It focused on Solomon and Jerusalem. Solomon went to Jerusalem and offered sacrifices there (1 Kings 3:15) and he built the temple there (2 Sam 7). It was remarkable that the people in the Northern part of the country almost never used the temple, even though they recognised it. First Kings looked at the division among the Israelites as the result of Solomon's unfaithfulness to YHWH. Chronicles on the other hand attributes the division to Israel's apostasy from the true cult in Jerusalem. In 1 Kings 8:63-64 Solomon consecrated the temple and served as a priest by offering sacrifices. Solomon brought sacrifices to the altar there three times a year, including šᵉlāmîm. Section 3.1.5 studied the book of 2 Kings and in particular Ahaz and Jerusalem. Ahaz had to make changes to the temple and the cult under the influence of the Assyrian king Tiglath-Pileser (2 Kings 16). He commanded that a new altar was to be built and sacrifices were to be brought on it, including šᵉlāmîm (2 Kings 16:13). In 2 Chron 28:22-25 it was said that he shut the doors of the house of YHWH and built altars in every corner of Jerusalem. In conclusion, it can be said that šᵉlāmîm was used in connection with a sanctuary. It had to do with special events and happenings, such as the conquering and taking over of the land, selecting a king and the bringing of the ark to Jerusalem. A special happening was also the consecration of the king's temple in Jerusalem.

Section 3.2 studied the cultic acts of the šᵉlāmîm sacrifice. It started (3.2.1) with the šᵉlāmîm as a non-cultic event (Deut 27:6-7; Josh 8:31; 1 Sam 10:8; 1 Kings 3:15). Section 3.2.2 studied the šᵉlāmîm sacrifice. The character of the šᵉlāmîm as a sacrifice is seen in the passages that include David (2 Sam 24:25; 2 Sam 6:17-18). But it is also used as such in older passages (Judg 20:26; 21:4; Josh 22:23-27) and passages in Kings (1 Kings 8:64; 9:25; 2 Kings 16:13). The šᵉlāmîm was mentioned together with a burnt offering and an animal sacrifice. In this case the šᵉlāmîm may have been a specific type of sacrifice or a cultic meal. When it is used with other words such as ʿālâ (go up) and ʿāśâ (make), it definitely refers to a sacrifice.

Section 3.3 studied the places where šᵉlāmîm was included by the Deuteronomistic historian. This was seen in the following passages: 2 Kings 16:13; Josh 22:23,27; 1 Kings 8:64 and 9:25.

In chapter 4 Rambaran studied the Deuteronomist and the šᵉlāmîm. There seemed to be two views on šᵉlāmîm in the Deuteronomist. In the first view, there seemed to be a sacramental understanding with a cultic meal. In the second, the šᵉlāmîm was seen as a specific sacrifice. Section 4.1 discussed the sacramental aspects. In Deut 27:5-7 there was a cultic event. The ʿôlâ (burnt offering) was accompanied by a šᵉlāmîm, a cultic meal (see also Exod 20:24; Josh 8:31). Each cultic meal according to the Deuteronomist was characterised by celebration. Section 4.2 discussed the feast for the renewal of the covenant. Josh 8:30-35 seemed to be a short summary of that feast. Rambaran also referred to 2 Sam 6:17-18; 1 Kings 3:15 in connection with the Ark of the Covenant and Judg 20:26 and 21:4 in connection with knowing YHWH's decision. There were also some cultic practices connected with the šᵉlāmîm, e.g. weeping (Judg 21:26), waiting for a few days before certain actions can be done (1 Sam 10:8).

Section 4.3 studied the general aspects of the cult. Some cultic elements could not be derived from the traditions. In those cases, the šᵉlāmîm is first of all a sacrifice, and it is used in connection with the verb ʿālâ (see Judg 20:26; 21:4; 2 Sam 6:17 ff.; 24:25). Šᵉlāmîm was also found in some late additions to the Deuteronomistic work (Josh 22:23,27; 1 Kings 8:64 and 9:25). The word always appeared in these passages at the end of a list of sacrifices. Section 4.4 studied 2 Kings 16:13. It was a sacrifice in which, probably elements from the Assyrian cult were incorporated. For the Deuteronomist this was not an appropriate sacrifice. Section 4.5 concluded the chapter with a discussion of the transmission tradition. In the Deuteronomist, the šᵉlāmîm was part of the cultic events. However, Rambaran did not find the specific function of the šᵉlāmîm in his work. One should probably think of fellowship and in particular fellowship with YHWH.

In chapter 5 Rambaran studied the šᵉlāmîm in the work of the Chronicler. In the Chronicler the temple in Jerusalem was the only legitimate cultic place in Israel. The šᵉlāmîm was treated as a sacrifice, without the ambiguity that was found in the Deuteronomist. Section 5.1 explained the influence of the Deuteronomist on the Chronicler. The work of the Chronicler was dated at the time of the post-exilic community in Judah. In 1 Chron 16:1-2, the Chronicler took over the passage from 2 Sam 6:17-18 with some changes (5.1.1). Section 5.1.2 compared 1 Chron 21:26 with 2 Sam 24:25. The Chronicler added some new elements to the text, including the fact that the place for the future temple was given through divine revelation. Section 5.1.3 compared 2 Chron 7:4-7 with 1 Kings 8:62-64. The Chronicler seemed to indicate that the šᵉlāmîm was a sacrifice and not a cultic meal. It never discussed the precise meaning of šᵉlāmîm nor its function within the whole of the Israelite cult. Section 5.2 studied the Passover celebration of Hezekiah. At that celebration the šᵉlāmîm was one of the sacrifices that were brought. The event was a feast that was extended for another seven days. In 2 Chron 33:16, King Manasseh cleansed the Israelite cult from foreign elements. The šᵉlāmîm at that event was seen by the Chronicler as a cultic meal and not a sacrifice. The motive for this cultic event was gladness and thanksgiving. Even though there was an ambiguity in the work of both editors, the Deuteronomist and the Chronicler, the emphasis in their works can be identified. In the earlier work (pre-exilic), the Deuteronomist's emphasis was on the aspect of a meal. In the work of the Chronicler, which was of a post-exilic date, the element of a cultic sacrifice seemed to be in the forefront. In this phase, the notion of fellowship with God was replaced with that of reconciliation.

In chapter 6 Rambaran studied šᵉlāmîm in the book of Ezekiel. The word appeared only in chapters 40 to 48. It was part of the cultic happening and signified the notion of reconciliation. The notion of a cultic meal was absent. The šᵉlāmîm was a sacrifice.

In chapter 7 he discussed the only appearance of šᵉlāmîm in the Wisdom literature. It appeared in Prov 7:14 and should be seen as a sacrifice that was brought to fulfil a vow.

In chapter 8 Rambaran discussed the šᵉlāmîm in the Priestly literature. Section 8.1 studied the rites in Lev 3-4 and Num 6. Lev 1-5 contained a set of rituals for the various sacrifices. These were established among the circles of the deported priests in Mesopotamia and they were of late date. However, it can be assumed that they contained old materials, since the Chronicler seemed to have known them. The šᵉlāmîm and the burnt offering were probably the oldest sacrifices in Israel. It was clear from the language and literary form of Lev 3 that the šᵉlāmîm there was a sacrifice. It was a sacrifice for sin. The šᵉlāmîm in Num 6:13-20 that dealt with the vow of the Nazirite was also a sacrifice. According to the instructions in Lev 6 and 7, the šᵉlāmîm could be presented on account of thanksgiving (7:12-15) or as a vow or freewill offering (7:16-18). Section 8.2 studied the 'offering-torah' in Lev 6-7 and Num 15, which included various regulations. Provision was made for people who were unclean (7:20-21), and the portions of the šᵉlāmîm that belonged to the priests (7:31-33) and the high priests (7:34-36). Other collections of priestly regulations dealt with the building of the altar and the minḥâ materials that were given together with the šᵉlāmîm. These may indicate that in the early days of Israel the šᵉlāmîm was a cultic meal that was enjoyed in the sanctuary. The participants of the cultic meal shared in the holiness of the animal as soon as it had been sacrificed to God. This character of a meal was not lost during the exile, even though changes took place. The priest participated in the meal or enjoyed the portion that was allotted to him. The person who brought the sacrifice and those invited enjoyed the other parts. YHWH received the fat of it. Section 8.3 studied other regulations, such as the Priestly codex (8.3.1), the Holiness codex (8.3.2) and Exod 20:24 (8.3.3). Section 8.4 concluded with the Narratives in P. These regulations did not provide new instructions with regards to the šᵉlāmîm.

In chapter 9 Rambaran studied the meaning of the sacrificial system. The oldest word for the sacrifice was a gift. A special form of offering was the *zebaḥ* (slaughter, sacrifice). The unclean and inconsumable parts of the animal were burned. The family, the clan, the tribe or the wider circle of the tribe ate the sacrifice as a fellowship meal. YHWH received the most valuable part of the animal. There was fellowship between those who ate and with the *Deus praesens* (God who is present). When a sacrifice in the Old Testament was called a šᵉlāmîm, the notion of 'salvation' was present and this was restored by the meal. When zebaḥ and šᵉlāmîm appeared together they influenced the notion of *bĕrît* (covenant). All the sacrifices originated within a non-Israelite context. However, the God who said *'ănî* YHWH (I am the LORD), determined the meaning of the cult in its fullness. Because of this, the magical elements that were present in the non-Israelite context were taken out of these sacrifices. The majesty of YHWH gave the sacrifices new intention. The personal God was at the centre of the rites. The sacrifices in the Old Testament were characterised by, not only moment of silence, but also by moments of rejoicing, homage, thanksgiving and prayer.

In chapter 10, Rambaran drew conclusions in the form of summaries. Some passages gave the impression that the šᵉlāmîm should be viewed as sacrifices. Other passages however seemed to indicate that the šᵉlāmîm had the character of a cultic meal that was associated with a sacrifice. When the 'Ritual' regulations were given, probably already during the time of the kings, it was stipulated that the cultic event should take place in the sanctuary. Because of the holiness attached to this type of sacrifice it was seen as a sacrifice of reconciliation. In the work of the Chronicler, the šᵉlāmîm were seen as a meal, in which the notion of fellowship was emphasised. It was not possible to decide on the meaning of the cultic word. Probably the notion of 'fellowship' is the closest in meaning and is symbolised in the meal.

Meal and fellowship were closely associated. The šᵉlāmîm was a sacramental meal. The emphasis was on the confirmation of the joyful relationship with YHWH.

The summary gave a few translation options for šᵉlāmîm which included 'peace offering', 'salvation offering', and 'offering of thanksgiving'. What was the meaning of the šᵉlāmîm for the Israelite? In it the Israelite appeared before his covenant God. The translation 'peace offering' signified peace with YHWH and with fellow men. The šᵉlāmîm also spoke about the covenant between the worshipper and his God.

In his conclusion Rambaran made a few theological observations. The šᵉlāmîm was a special gift to YHWH. It was special because the worshipper did not have to give him anything. Everything belonged to him. The šᵉlāmîm was not a magical tool or a totem. It was also not a meal that was given to YHWH. He did not need any meal (Ps 50:12 13). The šᵉlāmîm was an act of prayer, a symbolic action. It was a complex action and one must be careful not to come with a simple explanation. The šᵉlāmîm was a sacrifice of joy, in which gifts and fellowship went together. This giving resulted in maintaining fellowship with YHWH. The work concluded with six theses.

15.3. Surinamese Roman Catholic theologians

15.3.1. Aloysius Ferdinandus Zichem

Zichem was born in 1933. He was ordained as a priest on 14 August 1960. He belonged to the *Congregatio Sanctissimi Redemptoris* (Congregation of the Most Holy Redeemer). He was appointed as the auxiliary Bishop of Paramaribo on 2 October 1969. On 8 February 1970, he was ordained as Bishop. He was appointed as the Bishop of Paramaribo on 30 August 1971 and installed on 24 October. Zichem resigned from his office due to a stroke on 9 August 2003. Zichem wrote a thesis on canon law in 1965. The work was in Latin and will not be summarised here (Zichem 1965).

15.3.2. Peter Sjak-Shie

Peter Sjak-Shie was born in 1941. He studied modern philosophy, New Testament exegesis and systematic theology at a Catholic theological institution in Dinhoven, Netherlands. He specialised in religious education. He taught religious education and philosophy in the Netherlands for a few years, before returning to Suriname in 1978. Upon his arrival he taught at the Catechetical Centre of the Roman Catholic Church. He also taught New Testament and philosophy for many years at the Moravian Seminary. Sjak-Shie died in 2009.

Peter Sjak-Shie edited the study guides of courses offered by the Catechetical Centre of the Catholic Church in Suriname, which were then published in a series entitled *Panda Cahiers*. The series consists of more than 40 titles and covered various theological issues. The study guides were written by theologians of the Moravian Church and the Roman Catholic Church, but also by people of other religions such as Hinduism and Winti. Most of the study guides however were written by Sjak-Shie himself, one of which was in English: *Be watchful; The Apocalyptic Discourse of Matthew*.[10]

---

10. See the bibliography for works edited by Sjak-Shie in the Panda series.

In this book I will not summarise his many publications. Sjak-Shie's works and contribution to Surinamese theology should be studied separately and may be taken up as the topic of a doctoral dissertation. He was the most productive Surinamese Roman Catholic theologian.

15.3.3. Karel Choennie

Karel Choennie was born in 1958. He studied theology at the Saint John Vianney and the Uganda Martyrs Regional Seminary in Trinidad (WI) from 1979 to 1984, where he earned his bachelor degree. He continued his education at the Catholic University in Leuven, Belgium, from 1995 to 1997, where he received a licentiate in theology. Choennie served his church as a parish priest at Latour, Boniface, Sint Clemence and Sint Alfons. He became the vicar-general in 2005.

15.3.3.1. Polygyny among the Saramaccans

In 1984, Choennie wrote a thesis on the practice of polygyny among the Saramaccans (Choennie 1984). It was an ethical appraisal. After the introduction, the work was divided into two main parts.

The first part is the main section of the study. Choennie studied the Saramaccan social structure and religion in the first half. The second half continued with polygyny, factors influencing polygyny, divorce and remarriage and sexual affairs.

In the second part Choennie gave a Christian ethical evaluation of polygyny. This he did in three sections. The first section studied the Old Testament, followed by the New Testament in the second section and the church's teaching in the third section.

Choennie continued with proposals towards an ethical position of polygyny among the Saramaccans. He argued that the Bible and the church stress certain other essential properties for marriage apart from exclusivity, without which it is impossible to speak of marriage. These are: love, indissolubility, mutuality, reciprocity and faithfulness. He disagreed with the harsh condemnation of *Gaudium et Spes*, which saw polygyny as being on the same level as 'the plague of divorce', 'so called free-love' and 'other disfigurements'. Adultery and fornication are clearly seen as disruptive elements in Saramaccan society and are not considered to be the same as polygyny. Unlike other polygynous societies, there exists no distinction between primary and secondary marriage. Every wife has the right to equal treatment. Choennie concluded his ethical position by indicating that Saramaccan polygyny possessed undesirable elements on which the church has to pass ethical judgement since Christian ethics is concerned with what the normative mode of existence is for all persons.

Finally he drew his conclusions and presented a future perspective.

15.3.3.2. *Pastoral theological re-evaluation of the Caribbean family system*

Choennie wrote his thesis for the degree of sacrae theologiae licentiatus (STL), licentiate of sacred theology, on the pastoral theological re-evaluation of the Caribbean family system among the folk Afro-Surinamese people in Suriname (Choennie 1997).

In chapter 1 Choennie conceptualised the Caribbean family system from the perspective of social scientific literature. In the first section, five reasons were given why it was necessary to re-evaluate the Caribbean family system. These were the renewed self-understanding of women, postmodernity, renewed interest by theologians in folk religiosity, the structural form of poverty and a preferred option for reflection from the perspective of the poor. According to him a pastoral theologian from the Majority World should not just accept what the Western anthropologist or theologian imposed upon them as scientific, objective, value-free and universal. Reality is often described from a White, male and upper-class perspective.

Section 1.2, discussed the concept of Caribbean (1.2.1) and family system (1.2.2). Caribbean refers not just to a geographical location, but has wider historical, economic, political, religious and cultural implications. Family system in the Caribbean should be defined within this wider context and not the Western core family of a man, a woman and children. The Caribbean type of family is found in all the Caribbean countries, despite the differences between the Spanish, British, French and Dutch colonisers. This family type is also found outside of the Caribbean. Section 1.2.3 provided a demographic orientation of Suriname.

Section 1.3, gave a historical background of the Caribbean family system. Slaves were not allowed to marry during the era of slavery. Some slave masters allowed a 'slave marriage'. In that case the man could visit his wife during the night or on Sundays. Husband and wife were not allowed to live together. The woman lived on her own, eventually with her children and grandchildren. The life of the White slave masters was not different (1.3.2). Slave masters were often single and had slaves as concubines, the so-called 'Surinamese marriage'. Often, these men depended on their concubines to survive economically and psychologically. In the third quarter of the eighteenth century, Elisabeth Samson was the first Black woman to marry a White person (1.3.3). This however did not change the status of Black women in the colony. They were often raped or forced into prostitution. What was the role of the church in this? (1.3.4). The churches were not able to break down the bastion of colonial political views on marriage nor establish a core family among their members. The expectation of the churches was that the concubine system of one man and one woman living together, without being married according to the law, would diminish. This, however, never happened. After the abolition of slavery in 1863, the churches tried to introduce Christian marriage to their members. The women opposed this, while the men, who were seen as the head of the family, were happy. This led to all kind of misconceptions about marriage.

The mining of gold that started from 1872 provided men with an opportunity to earn a living. However, they had to be away from their family for seven to eight months at a time. This situation was the same in the rubber industry. In the 1920's men emigrated to the Antilles to find jobs in the oil industry. They worked abroad and sent money home to support their mother, sister or wife in Suriname. From the 1960's, groups of people left for the Netherlands to find a living there. Often the man would go first, later on to be joined by his family.

Statistics indicated that marriage was never popular among the Catholics.

Section 1.4 discussed the relation between man and woman in the Caribbean family system. The relations are marriage (1.4.1), concubine (1.4.2) and visitation (1.4.3). Relationships may start with visitations. A man will be visiting a woman in her living unit, where she lives with family or sometimes alone. This relation may grow into a concubine relationship where the two will be living together. The next phase of the relationship is marriage. Marriage is not the first step in the Caribbean family system. It is often seen as the crown on a long relationship. Views around marriage also required certain privileges that can only come after a person is established. The concubine relationship in the Caribbean context is one where people are living together, just as two married people. The only difference is the lack of a piece of paper. The visitation relationship may grow into a concubine relationship but could remain temporary.

Matrifocality is the most important feature of the Caribbean marriage system (1.5). Women seem to be at the head of the household and play an important role in the family, while the position of the man is marginal. A household may consist of two or three or even four generations of mothers and their daughters and children and sometimes partners.

Section 1.6, discussed various theories that were designed to explain the Caribbean family system. These were the cultural historical explanation (1.6.1), culture of poverty (1.6.2), functionalist explanation (1.6.3) and institutional explanation (1.6.4). Scholars often refused to study the place of the woman in the family. Matrifocality is often explained by the absence of the father and an abnormal family model. It is blamed for many social shortcomings, such as crime among youth, drug abuse, AIDS, poor performance at school and teenage pregnancy.

Section 1.7, discussed the *mati*-relation (woman-woman relation). Apart from their relation with their husbands, Creole women of the folk culture in Suriname developed the culture of mati. The mati-relationship may include erotic, emotional, sexual and financial relations between two women. Surinamese literature avoided the term lesbian for this kind of relationship. The Caribbean family and the mati-relationships were heavily influenced by the economic circumstances, the folk culture and the folk religion.

Section 1.8 discussed the Winti, the Afro-Surinamese religion. The family has its ties with the Winti religion. When there are family or relationship problems, the family will consult the bonuman, the religious specialist in the Winti religion. The consultation is important because a personality may be influenced by spirits. A woman in different mati relationships may have a *motyo ingi* (a Native whore-spirit). This spirit enjoys pleasure, feasting, drinking and sex. A woman with a male *Apuku* spirit will have sexual relationships with that spirit in her dreams. It will be difficult for such a woman to develop and maintain a relationship with a man. The *Aisa* spirit is a head goddess in the Winti religion and demands a lot of respect. It is supposed to provide for offspring and to give the children wealth. Due to this central position of Aisa Choennie argued that the matrifocal family in Paramaribo is legitimised by the Winti religion.

Section 1.9 discussed recent evolutions in the social economic situation of the people of Suriname. In the 1980's Suriname was isolated politically and had a high inflation rate. Poverty grew, which affected women more than men. The number of teenage mothers grew as did youth prostitution. Globalisation also affected the people in one way or the other. It encouraged the matrifocal system. In this difficult social economic situation, the need for an extended family is critical. The core family concept does not help in this battle for survival. Section 1.10 concluded the chapter with a summary.

In chapter 2 Choennie discussed the church's view on 'non-marriage' relationships. He discussed the proceedings documents of *Vaticanum II* (2.1), the General Bishops' Conference of 1980 (2.2), *Familiaris Consortio* (2.3), the Latin American Bishops' Conferences (2.4), the Antillean Bishops' Conference (2.5) and the Diocese of Paramaribo (2.6). Vaticanum II was very tolerant towards non-western cultures. It stated that all cultures have a right to exist in the church if they do not go against the gospel. This positive approach was not applied to marriage and family, because according to Vaticanum II, sexuality between man and woman finds its most meaningful expression within marriage. By their essential make-up marriage and marriage love are focused towards the planting of a family. The Caribbean family system is not seen as part of the church's teaching about a healthy marriage and family life. At the Bishops' Conference in 1980, bishops from Africa and Brazil explained the family system in their contexts. Marriage according to them should include the extended family and not just the core family. The conference called upon the church to accept and love the rich diversity of cultures and life-styles in which Christian families find themselves. According to Choennie, the response of the Pope to the conclusions of the conference was disappointing. There were no different divine laws for different people and instances.

The Familiaris Consortio of 1981 shared a universal view of the family that was similar to the 'Western' view of marriage and family. Only the typical 'Western' type of family was seen as being faithful to the values of the family. Familiaris Consortio wanted to affirm this group. The second view related to those who were confused about or had become unfamiliar with the meaning and truth about marriage and family life. Familiaris Consortio wanted to counsel these people. The third group were those who were prevented from fulfilling their fundamental rights. Familiaris Consortio wanted to help these people. This document did not take the proposals of the African and Brazilian bishops seriously. The conferences of the Latin American bishops did not take the issue of inculturation seriously. One person summarised the conference of Santo Domingo where the issue of the family was discussed as follows:

> Thus on the whole, Santo Domingo shuns away from recognising a legitimate pluralism in Catholic theology, pays lip-service to an inculturation 'from within cultures', and prefers instead, under the influence of the Vatican, a (self-) glorification of a restorationist type of Catholicism.

At that conference the Pope emphasised the importance of the family. However, he rejected the 'free relationships' in Latin America unambiguously. He chose explicitly for the core family. At the conference, the only concession that the bishops gave was that they recognised the differences between the families in the rural areas and those in the city. The Antillean Bishops' Conference also did not bring changes to the views on marriage. Even though the bishops promised to study the situation of the Caribbean, this was not done. Instead they spoke about the 'non-legal unions'. There were a few positive words about these unions, since they were considered to be part of the experience on the road to marriage. As such they embodied promise and hope. However, the negative comments were more prominent.

> For many it is a cycle of exploitation where women are used time and again by different partners in short-term and irresponsible

relationships. This cycle cultivates a condition of mistrust and insecurity. Women become dependent on visiting partners for financial help to survive and for companionship. They are demeaned and often subjected to physical and psychological abuse. Children in many such homes have the same mother but different fathers. Infidelity and lack of commitment are rooted in this cycle. This, certainly, is not the gospel value proclaimed by Jesus (p. 86).

The diocese of Paramaribo followed the approach taken by the Caribbean bishops' conferences. However, it recognised the problems and challenges that families faced due to the historical situation and the cultural differences of the population.

The church only recognised the monogamous, exclusive and enduring marriages. Others, according to the church, live in an irregular situation. The family is the first and vital cell of society. The responsibility of the future of the world and the church depends on the health of the family.

In chapter 3 Choennie gave a pastoral theological re-evaluation of the Caribbean family system. Section 3.1 discussed the developing of a Christian identity. The church should develop an environment in which Christian development can take place in a Christian fashion. This includes in the first place that the church, in all humility, must accept its mistakes of the past and the present. It must confess that it did not show enough love to the poor. It looks down on the local institution, such as the Caribbean family system, in which the poor found shelter against the colonial violence of the past. After 500 years, the church has not changed its attitude. A pastoral approach to the family should respond to the historical trauma of the Caribbean person, if not it will fail. The issue of guilt can be approached from three perspectives: violation of a law, refusal of self-development and collective-wrong. The collective-wrong approach is the most helpful one. The benefit of this approach is that it indicates how something structural can be done against the injustice that stands in the way of a Christian family life. The disadvantage is that the personal guilt in private relationships is weakened. One can hide behind the cardinal sins of this age and avoid personal responsibility. However, man is never completely victim. He is also the author of sin and suffering.

The scars in the heart of the Caribbean person will only be removed by *metanoia* (repentance) and not by 'covering with the mantle of love'. Issues should not be glossed over by 'cheap forgiveness and grace'. The new form of evangelism should consider two important key words: compassion and reconciliation. It is important, in the re-evaluation of the Caribbean family system, to differentiate between an ethic of conviction and an ethic of responsibility. The first system operates with principles, while the second tries to find points of support in the given circumstances in order to move to a more ideal situation. The ideal Christian family can be described, in the light of the Sermon on the Mount, as 'a sacrament of God's kingdom'. That kingdom belongs to the poor of spirit, who are in the first place followers of Jesus. The gospel will criticise both the Western type of marriage and the Caribbean family system. It is possible to have a legal monogamous marriage without love, which is like a perfect prison cell. A maligned matrifocal family on the other hand, where the constitution of love is interpreted as justice, can be a cornerstone of the kingdom of God. A matrifocal family can serve as an ideal model of how a home church should function. Compassion however should not be reduced to a willingness to please the dominant culture. The gospel should demand explanations from the culture. The culture, especially the culture of the poor on the other hand, invites the church not the take up a too dogmatic position about the truth of the family. The Sabbath, according to the compassionate logic of Jesus, should not prevent us from doing what is good.

Section 3.2, discussed the prejudices against the Caribbean family. The source of criticism with those who have biases against the Caribbean family is not always clear. Does it result from a Euro- or ethnocentric perspective? Is it motivated by the gospel? The fact that women are working outside the home was criticised by the Caribbean bishops. This according to them is the cause of the malaise among families. This of course is not a Caribbean problem as such. It is not possible to imagine the world today without women in public life.

The term 'single mother' is also used to describe the matrifocal family. However, the two are not the same.

The third concern was that the matrifocal family contributes to the destruction of society. This view is based on the notion that the family is the first and foremost cell of society. In reality, however, it is society that dictates the kind of family that will exist. In the Caribbean context, globalisation with its individualism caused a lot of harm to society. The matrifocal family in the Surinamese context for example maintained the family by making sure that poverty does not end in a famine.

The third section (3.3) discussed the most severe criticism of the Caribbean family: unfaithfulness. Faithfulness is sometimes reduced to sexual exclusivity. In the Surinamese Creole family, marriage serves as a crown after a faithful relationship with a sacramental blessing. It is not uncommon in the West on the other hand to find many marriages that end in a divorce within three years. In Caribbean families there is a tendency to depreciate the uniting aspect of sexuality in favour of the procreative aspect. By doing that the body is reduced to an instrument of human culture. The church should re-appreciate the sexual body in Christian theology and protest against its exploitation. Relationships should be characterised by *chesed*. According to Choennie, a person displays chesed when he gives the other what the other may expect on the grounds of a mutual relationship.

It cannot be denied that in the Caribbean family men use crises to escape their responsibility. But faithfulness is more than not escaping responsibility during crises. Faithfulness required that the one partner grows with the other and continues to acknowledge the other in ever-changing situations.

The fourth section (3.4) discussed the challenge presented by inculturation. Choennie took the advice given by Gamaliel (Acts 5:38-39) and the decision of the first Council (Acts 15:19a) as his point of departure for inculturation. Unnecessary burdens should not be put upon the families during the process of advancing gospel values. The church should take the 'hidden theology' into consideration. It should defend the culture of the poor and not only pay attention to the seven sacraments, but also to the many rituals and folk devotions. The Caribbean families have a few deeply-rooted biblical values, such as community and solidarity. These should be taken into consideration. Inculturation should follow biblical patterns. On the day of Pentecost, the various languages (bearers of culture) were not united into one language. Everybody understood the apostles in their own language. This recognition of pluriformity is an important fact at the beginning of Christianity and should be a model for the church today. During the process of the inculturation of the gospel the following challenges should be taken into consideration: double religious system, 'the plague' of the sects, civil religion and spontaneous inculturation. In the context of Suriname, there must be a dialogue between Christianity and the Winti religion. There are conflicts between the view on man in Christianity and the Winti. Man in the Winti religion is free as long as the spirits allow it. In Christianity one is set free by Christ from the law, death and sin in order to live for the law of love (Gal 5). Human failure is often blamed upon the spirit world in the Winti religion. The mati and macho relations also need a re-evaluation. Mati relations do not necessary refer to a sexual relationship, even though it may be included. It refers to a relationship between women, who withdrew themselves from the male (macho) domination in the social and sexual spheres. As such matis can play an important role in the matrifocal setting. A biblical example that is close to the mati relationship is that of Naomi and Ruth. In the first place the relation was one of deep friendship in a situation of extreme poverty and desperation. Through the existing institution of a levirate marriage Ruth allowed Naomi to have a dignified existence. There is a need to interact with the macho and mati culture with a purpose of deliverance through the gospel.

Chapter 4 offers the conclusion. According to Choennie, the pastoral theologian must be moved with compassion for the plight of the poor. He will serve as a midwife at the birth and growth of the Christian identity. The family has been more the 'victim' of society than an agent of transforming it. Marriage in the Caribbean context is a dynamic process. The church has a primary responsibility in helping to heal the traumatic history of the Caribbean. The public confession of guilt by the Pope in Santo Domingo opened up the way for the people to cope with the wounds of the past. This can be a long journey. Finally the church is challenged by inculturation. The church should not force one family structure upon everybody. It must take steps towards the freedom of Pentecost where everyone hears God in their own language (culture).

15.3.4. Esteban Kross

Esteban Kross was born in 1963. He studied from 1982 to 1987 at the Saint John Vianney and the Uganda Martyrs Regional Seminary in Trinidad (WI), where he completed his bachelor's degree. Kross was ordained as priest in July 1988. He continued his studies at the Catholic University in Leuven, Belgium, where he received his licentiate in 1990 in the field of exegesis. In Suriname he taught Biblical studies at the theological programme of the diocese and served as the coordinator for the New Testament translation project of the Suriname Bible Society for a few years. Kross served as the pastor of the following parishes: Sint Rosa, Heilige Family, Sint Bonifacius and Paulus en Petrus Kathedraal.

15.3.4.1. Light and darkness at Diwali

In 1987 Esteban Kross wrote his bachelor's thesis on a Christian theological appraisal of the symbolism of light and darkness in *Diwali*, the Hindu festival of lights (Kross 1987). In a brief introduction, Kross indicated that he reviewed published materials in the daily newspapers and in special Diwali publications that appeared between 1966 and 1986. Reference is also made to classical Hindu scriptures. The study however focused on Trinidad and Tobago.

In chapter 1 Kross studied the concept of light and darkness in Hinduism. The first section of the chapter gave an ethical interpretation of these concepts. The concepts are related to the quality of life lived by the individual. This view was based on a review of articles written by Pundit Jankie Persad in Trinidad. Persad argued that Lakshmi is a manifestation of God, who reveals an aspect of the One who is beyond human comprehension. It is argued that invoking Shri Lakshmi on a pitch-dark night at Diwali with lighted *deyahs* signifies enlightenment of souls, when complete knowledge prevails so as to attain purity, peace and prosperity.

The symbolism of light and darkness is also related to the socio-political situation of Trinidad and Tobago. Diwali then is interpreted in the light of the whole human experience.

In the second section of the chapter Kross studied light and darkness in the Upanishad, a Hindi scripture. This scripture teaches a form of monism which states that there exists no ultimately independent reality apart from Brahman. There is also Atman in man, which is one with Absolute Reality, *Atman* is Brahman. The realisation of self-identity between one's Atman and Brahman is *moksha* or immortality. One of the prayers at Diwali is for moksha. Contrary to what is taught by Christianity, evil and sin are not accepted as metaphysical realities or entities. They are only consequences or manifestations of ignorance.

The third section studied light and darkness in Trinidad and Tobago. These concepts are interpreted differently in Trinidad and Tobago than in the Upanishads. In Trinidad and Tobago there is a more ethical, religious and perhaps more easily comprehensible approach. Secondly, evil and sin are seen as metaphysical entities or forces. Thirdly, growing into a life of moral virtue, devotion to God and commitment to others seems to be the path from darkness to light, not moksha.

In chapter 2 Kross studied Lakshmi and the symbol of light. Lakshmi is referred to in almost all the documents studied for this thesis. She symbolises immortality and embodies the goals of Hindu Dharma. She also embodied the virtues and attitudes that the light of Diwali calls one to. Lakshmi is the goddess of wealth and prosperity. Even though she provides wealth, prosperity, good health, success, happiness and peace it is also emphasised that material goods and wealth alone are not necessarily a sign of real human development and happiness. Prosperity should be placed within the framework of moral living and virtue and not become an occasion to forget them. During Diwali a *Murti* (picture or statue) of Lakshmi is often used as a source of devotion and a means to convey the truth.

In chapter 3 Kross gave a theological appraisal of the topic. Darkness and light are important symbols in most religions. Light symbolises that which is good and is associated with the divine. Darkness symbolises evil. In Christianity God is called light and salvation (Ps 27:1; 1 John 1:5) and Jesus is called the light of the world (John 8:12). Light and darkness are used as symbols of life and death (Ps 4:2; 56:13; 139:11). The Johannine literature carefully worked out these symbolisms. Life, light, love and truth are closely identified in Jesus Christ. Believers should respond to these in faith and live accordingly. There are three common perspectives in the ways in which light and darkness are used in religious traditions and secular thought. Firstly, light is a symbol for truth and darkness for falsity. Secondly, a moral interpretation takes light as symbol of moral truth and darkness as moral falsity. Thirdly, darkness is used as the symbol for the unknown and light of what is known. The concluding reflections compared and contrasted light and darkness in Hinduism and Christianity. Both traditions know of the search for a life in accordance with moral truth. The major difference is that in Hinduism the use of the symbols is theocentric, whereas in Christianity they are Christocentric. Christ is called by the Nicene Creed 'Light from Light, true God from true God'. Christ is claimed by Christianity to be the universal Saviour. Protestants like to refer to John 14:6 'no one comes to the Father except through me'. Catholics think along ecclesiocentric lines and its claim *extra Ecclesiam nulla salus*, 'Outside the church there is no salvation'. Both approaches emphasised faith in Christ as the light of the world. This knowledge should guide Christians in their dialogue with Hinduism.

15.3.4.2. Nakedness in 2 Cor 5:3

In 1990 Kross wrote his thesis for the Licentiate in Sacred Theology entitled *Nakedness in 2 Cor 5:3* (Kross 1990). The study explored four decades of exegetical interpretation.

The introduction identified the topic of the study, the concept of nakedness in 2 Cor 5:3. The thesis distinguished between the anthropological and soteriological interpretations.

The anthropological interpretation refers to a body-soul distinction. Kross identified two positions in this interpretation: the intermediate state and the eternal disembodiment. According to the first position believers will undergo a period of nakedness between death and the *parousia* or the resurrection. The second position refers to the Hellenistic idea of disembodied soul, a soul that will be freed eternally from the prison of the mortal body.

The soteriological interpretation argues that Paul was not concerned with a body and soul distinction. He was concerned with the salvation of the people. Two positions were also discussed under this heading: the fate of the wicked and lapsed Christians. The fate of the wicked is explained with the metaphor of nakedness, which is the same as condemnation. The lapsed Christians view argues that Christians who had put on Christ at baptism alienated themselves from him. At death or parousia they will be found naked, that is alienated from Christ.

In chapter 1 Kross provided a technical, text-critical and philological discussion of the problems in the text. This chapter requires a good knowledge of Greek for it to be understood properly. The first word that was discussed was *ependusasthai* (to put on). Because of the prefix '*epi*', some exegetes argue that word has the nuance of adding 'a garment on top of a previous one'. Others argue that 'epi' expressed continuity, while others did not add any value to the presence of 'epi'. The phrase *ei ge kai* at the beginning of verse 3, is accepted by most exegetes as the original reading instead of *eiper kai*. Among those who defend ei ge kai there are four different ways of interpreting the phrase: casual, concessive, a condition with a sense of doubt and a condition with a sense of assurance. The word *endusamenoi* (put on) is accepted as the correct reading in verse 3, instead of *ekdusamenoi* (take off). Some exegetes argue that *endusamenoi* (put on) and *ou gumnoi* (not naked) are to be interpreted as similar in meaning.

What is the metaphor 'nakedness' referring to in scripture? Kross argued that it can be used for economic poverty, distress, helplessness and destitution of the human being before God. Symbolically it refers to sin, judgement and guilt. In 2 Cor 5:3, the word may refer to the state of the wicked at the parousia or baptised people who were alienated from Christ.

In chapter 2 to 4 he studied the interpretation of this verse from the 1950's to 1980's. He studied 41 works, written by scholars from different backgrounds in Dutch, English, French and German. He presented his findings in two appendices. The second one is an overview of the positions, which will be presented here and taken as the point of departure for the rest of the survey (p.109).

Table 29 *Overview of exegetical interpretations of 2 Cor 5:3*

The anthropological interpretation		The soteriological interpretation	
A. Int. state	B. Disembodiment	C. Wicked	D. Lapsed Christians
Chapter 2 – The Fifties			
51 Cullmann	58 Masson	60 Ellis	
52 Dupont			
52 Robinson			
53 Sevenster			
53 Filson			
56 Feuillet			
57 Hettlinger			
58 Héring			
Chapter 3 – The Sixties			
61 Berry	62 Thrall		61 Wagner
64 Whiteley	65 Schmithals		69 Hanhart
66 Hughes	66 Moule		
	66 Hoffmann		
	69 Rissi		
	69 Demke		
Chapter 4 – The Seventies and Eighties			
73 Barrett	71 Bruce	72 De Boor	72 Collange
86 Martin	71 Harris		73 Baumert
86 Klauck	75 von der Osten-Sacken		84 Furnish
87 Kruse	77 Lillie		
87 Best	80 Gillman		
88 Craig	80 Fallon	**Difficult to categorise**	
	86 Lang	75 Ridderbos: nakedness present existence	
	89 Schnelle	89 Perriman: naked, death.	

Ellis was the only exegete in the 1950's who defended a soteriological interpretation. He concluded that being found 'not naked' which is the same as 'being clothed' referred to those who are incorporated into Christ's glory at the parousia. Masson expected the heavenly dwelling at death, which will exclude a possible nakedness of the soul between death and the parousia. Most of the other exegetes of the 1950's interpreted 'naked' as referring to an intermediate state between death and parousia.

In the 1960's exegetes continued to support the anthropological interpretation. However, they tended to move away from the intermediate state view. Only Hughes and Berry supported the idea fully. Whiteley, even though he agreed, argued that 'naked' referred to disembodiment. In a sense he was supporting the dominant view of the 1960's. The soteriological view was defended by Wagner and Hanhart. Among those who supported the anthropological disembodiment view there were different variants. Moule for example suggested that Paul feared that after being stripped of the body at death, there may in fact not be a new body awaiting him. Others saw a fight between Paul and his Gnostic opponents in the concept (e.g. Schmithals, Hoffman, Conzelman, Rissi and Demke). According to Schmithals Paul tries to convince his opponents that to be naked (the Gnostic ideal) equals non-existence, to be clothed equals existence.

The 1970's and 1980's continued to favour the anthropological interpretation. Contrary to what happened in the sixties, it appeared that more exegetes seemed to support the intermediate state view. The view was defended by Barrett, Martin, Klauck, Kruse and Craig. The disembodiment view is also well-supported. Bruce, Lille and Best argued that Paul expects the believer to experience no conscious time interval between death and parousia. Harris and Schnelle expected the heavenly dwelling immediately at death. Kross found it difficult to fit the views of Ridderbos and Perriman within one of the two broad categories. A small group of exegetes continued to support the 'lapsed Christians' soteriological view (Collange, Baumert and Furnish). De Boor seemed to have been the only one supporting the 'wicked' soteriological view.

As a conclusion, Kross argued in favour of the intermediate state. He drew supporting arguments from 1 Cor 15, where Paul clearly taught that the heavenly body will only be received at the parousia or at the resurrection.

The context of 2 Cor 5 also seemed to support this view. The passage does not seem to discuss the issue of the Gnostic opponents. The context seemed to be favouring the fact that Paul wanted to be clothed with the heavenly dwelling, not unclothed (v 4). When this has happened, Paul will not be found naked.

15.3.5. Kenneth Vigelandzoon

Kenneth Vigelandzoon wrote his bachelor's thesis on the Roman Catholic principles governing interreligious dialogue.[11] He did a case study on the Winti Religion in Suriname (Vigelandzoon 1997). Since the topic of Winti was discussed in detail by other theologians, I shall limit myself to a brief summary of his unique contribution. Vigelandzoon took a different approach to the Winti than the other theologians. He does not see the spirits in the Winti religion (which are also called Winti) as gods. According to him they are lower, immaterial beings created by Anana (the Creator God) to serve mankind. A Winti spirit may be used for good or evil purposes. Vigelandzoon argued that there is a need for a dialogue between Christianity and the Winti religion. The first step before that dialogue can take place, is that the Winti religion should be recognised as an official religion, just like Christianity, that works towards the wellbeing of creation. Since Vigelandzoon wrote his thesis laws in Suriname made it possible for the Winti religion to be recognised as an official religion. Vigelandzoon argued that when Winti is recognised, it will no longer be the religion of the Black person, but for all who want to show forth God's light in a unique way. In the dialogue it should not be about the conversion of the other person, but the sharing of values that will be beneficial to society as a whole.

15.3.6. Duncan R Wielzen

Duncan Wielzen was born in 1968. He studied theology at the St John Vianney and the Uganda Martyrs Regional Seminary in Trinidad (WI). He served the Pastoral Centre of the Roman Catholic Diocese, Paramaribo as an assistant to the director from 1991-1992. He continued his theological studies at the Radboud Universiteit Nijmegen where he received an MA

---

11. A biography was not available for inclusion in this review.

degree in theology in 1997 (Wielzen 1997). He completed a Master's degree in Educational Studies in 2007 at the Faculty of Psychology and Pedagogical Sciences of the Katholieke Universiteit Leuven. He earned his doctorate in theology in 2009 from the same university (Wielzen 2009). His dissertation was written in English. It builds forth on the MA thesis that he wrote in 1997. This work however was placed in the broader Caribbean context, whereas the previous work was limited to Suriname. Wielzen now has Dutch nationality.

The primary objective of his dissertation was to outline the contours of a theology of liturgical inculturation. Wielzen defends the view that such a theology can provide a proper framework for harmonising popular religiosity with the Roman liturgy, in the light of divine revelation. His five chapters discussed the following issues: contemporary theology in a postmodern context, popular religiosity in theological discourses and magisterial teachings, popular religiosity in the context of the Caribbean, inculturation in theological discourses and magisterial teachings and liturgical inculturation and popular religiosity.

15.3.7. Gerda Misidjang

15.3.7.1. Introduction

Gerda Misidjang was born in 1975. She studied economics at the Anton de Kom University of Suriname where she earned her doctorandus (Master of Science) degree in 2004. In 2005, she started with her diploma in biblical studies at the Catholic Bible Institute in Trinidad and Tabago. From 2006 to 2010 she studied at the Regional Seminary of Saint John Vianney and the Uganda Martyrs seminary in Trinidad and Tobago. Her studies at this seminary were done in association with the University of the West Indies, and she received her bachelor's degree in theology from that university.

She was the first woman among the Roman Catholics in Suriname to complete an academic theological study. Currently Misidjang serves in different ministries of the Catholic Church in Trinidad and Tobago. Her service includes a wide variety of ministries such as the Eternal Light Community, the Catholic Bible Institute, prison ministry, media ministry and Catholic Charismatic Renewal. She also works among the children at the Joshua Boys Home.

15.3.7.2. The Ndyuka culture and the Roman Catholic liturgy

Misidjang's thesis was a case study on the influence of the Ndyuka culture on the Roman Catholic liturgy in Suriname (Misidjang 2010). Misidjang's study is unique among the Surinamese theologians, because she is the first to engage the Ndyuka culture theologically.

In the introduction, the study gave a background of the Aucan Maroons, also known as *Okanisi* or *Ndyuka* people. The study focused on some of their cultural traditions that were kept alive: *puu-a-doo* (presentation of a new-born) and *puu-baaka* (ending of the mourning period). The case study was based on practices of two Catholic communities with a strong Nyuka membership: Basis Gemeente Hanna's Lust and Sunny Point.

In chapter 1 Misidjang studied inculturation in the liturgy and addressed methodological concerns. She identified the following positive elements about the principle of inculturation. a) Dialogue between the local culture and the gospel of Christ. b) The gospel of Christ must not be compromised. c) Good values of culture must be affirmed and if necessary purified by the gospel. d) Incorporation of the Christian message into a local culture and the life of the people. e) Integration of good values and cultural elements (that are compatible with the faith) into Christianity. f) Inculturation occurred over a period of time. g) It involves dynamic transculturation. She continued and answered the question how the Ndyuka culture finds expression in the Catholic liturgy. This was followed by an explanation of the methodology of the thesis. The researcher was interested in the way the catechists of the two Christian communities carried on the process of inculturation in their communities.

In chapter 2 Misidjang studied the puu-a-doo ritual. The first section studied the traditional ritual (2.1). At the puu-a-doo ritual the new-born child is officially brought outside the house in which it was born for the first time. This takes place on the eighth (girl) or ninth day (boy). In the first cycle, the *obiya-man* (medicine man) offers the child to the gods and then puts it on the mother's lap. He gives the child a name and the father will give the mother and child gifts. The obiya-man proceeds to do the libation for the ancestors and the gods. At the second cycle, a respected person in the village will do the *poti gogo a doti* (placing the buttock on the earth) ceremony. Following this, the child will be given to the father. The second section studied the Christianised version of the ritual (2.2). The child is presented to the church community on a Sunday. This normally takes place on the eighth day. If that day is not a Sunday, it will be done on the next Sunday. The parents and the child will take their place in front of the church. When the ritual starts, a catechist takes the child and prays for it. After the prayer a relative will take the child and walk with it from pew to pew, as a sign of welcome by the whole community. When the child is given back to the mother, the church takes up a special offering for the child. Section 2.3 analysed and contrasted the two rituals.

In chapter 3 Misidjang studied the puu-baaka ritual and followed the same format as in chapter two. The first step in this ritual is the *poti-a-baaka*, at which ceremony a widow(er) is placed in mourning. This period lasts for six months. The puu-baaka takes place at the end of that period.

The traditional puu-baaka (3.1) starts with a libation, in which it is announced to the spirits of the ancestors and the deceased person that the period of mourning is closed. At a *bookode* (night watch) celebration, villagers dance to traditional music from Friday 8:00 pm to Saturday 6:00 am. On Saturday a special meal is prepared to be offered to the ancestors (*towe-nyanyan*, food offering). On the Sunday, the *towe-wataa*, a libation of water for the soul of the deceased is offered. The mourner is then taken out of the *kee-osu* (mortuary, house of weeping). The mourning clothes are taken off and the mourner may go to the river to take a bath. After a few more rituals the mourner is then freed.

The Christianised version of the ritual takes place six weeks after the burial (3.2) at a church service. The mourners are invited to take their place in front of the church. The catechists pray for all the family members. The mourning clothes are untied and dropped on the floor. The mourners are then allowed to take a bath. The family shares refreshment with the community. Different music groups join in the celebration. Section 3.3, analysed and contrasted the two rituals.

The study concluded with a conclusion with recommendations for further research. Three appendices were included, with pictures of both puu-baaka and puu-a-doo rituals.

15.4. Others

Steve Michel Stewart was born in 1963. Stewart felt the calling to become an evangelist and at the recommendation of his pastor, Charles Leonard, he started his theological education at the Moravian Theological Seminary in Paramaribo. He studied here from 1987-1989. He received a scholarship to continue his education at the United Theological College of the West Indies in Jamaica, where he completed a Diploma in Theology. He did the Bachelor of Arts degree in Theology at the same institution. That degree was offered in association with the University of the West Indies. Stewart studied there from 1989 to 1993.[12] He left for the United States of America in 1993, to continue his education at the Wartburg Theological Seminary in Dubuque, Iowa. After completing one year at the seminary, he started with clinical pastoral education. He returned to Suriname in 1994. Stewart has since then served three churches of the *Evangelische Lutherse Kerk Suriname* (Evangelical Lutheran Church in Suriname) for thirteen years as a pastor. He also served as an army chaplain, from 1999. In 2006, he completed his Doctor of Ministry degree at the Columbia Theological Seminary, through the United Theological College of the West Indies. In 2008 Stewart and others left the Evangelische Lutherse Kerk Suriname and founded the *Trinitatis Lutherse Kerk*, an independent Lutheran denomination in Suriname.

Stewart wrote his doctoral thesis on pre-marital counselling (Stewart 2006). This thesis was intended to contribute to the development of models for the Evangelische Lutherse Kerk Suriname (ELKS, Evangelical Lutheran Church in Suriname) so that it can be equipped to serve as a

---

12. The title of his BA thesis was: *The Influence of Christianity on the Bush Negros in Suriname*. Unfortunately this work was not available for review. The major paper that he wrote for his diploma dealt with the influence of forced migration on the people of Ganse, due to a dam that was built. This paper was also not available for review.

church in the Surinamese context. Stewart argued for the necessity of premarital counselling and why the church must consider it a tremendous theological teaching moment to help people prepare for Christian marriage. He gave attention to what he considers to be the origin of premarital guidance.

The thesis gave a definition for the concept of marriage and paid attention to the theology of marriage based on Luther's point of view with the hope of influencing couples' understanding of marriage. Furthermore, it focused on the relationship between marriage and pastoral care. Finally, it offered a model for preparing couples for Christian marriages, emphasising the theological implications of marriage.

Stewart started by conceptualising the terminology that he used throughout the thesis. He defined marriage as a lasting covenant relationship ordered by God between a male and a female, who love each other and as such must share their lives in all the multidimensional reality consisting of affectional, legal, financial, procreative, cultural and religious realities. Premarital counselling he considered to be the process in which the church gets involved to help prepare partners 'to be' for the challenges of marriage and to educate them about the meaning of marriage. The working definition for pastoral care was taken from another scholar, who argued that:

> Pastoral care consists of helping activities, participated in by people who recognise a transcendent dimension to human life, which, by the use of verbal or non-verbal, direct or indirect, literal or symbolic modes of communication, aim at preventing, relieving or facilitating persons coping with anxieties (p. 10).

The first part of the thesis studied 'The journey to marriage'. This journey ends with the wedding ceremony. It discussed 'The origin of premarital counselling', 'Informal and formal teaching opportunities to premarital counselling'.

The second part discussed 'Martin Luther and Lutheran theology on marriage'. It appeared that the ELKS did not adhere to the pure Lutheran theology of marriage. This was due to the influence of the Dutch Reformed

Church, who made its pastor available to help with the shortage of pastors in the ELKS in past years.

The third part discussed 'Pastoral care and marriage'. What should be discussed during premarital counselling sessions? These according to Stewart would include issues like the meaning of the wedding, child rearing, celebration of the committed and growing relationship and birth control methods. On top of these he added general recommendations on the following issues for the Surinamese context: 'trust, second marriage, arranged marriage, age difference, long-distance relationship, having an own house, going into marriage with pregnancy, stepchildren, sexual and physical abuse and the 'macho' attitude of Caribbean men. This section also provided two case studies of couples who are married for years and are experiencing a serious crisis. It concluded with 'Caring in context for those getting married'.

In section four Stewart discussed models of 'Pastoral premarital work'. He started with a discussion of the different types of marriage which existed in Suriname at the time of writing: civil marriage, Asiatic marriage and religious marriage. Since Stewart wrote his thesis, the marital laws were changed and are more unified. The chapter discussed a model for pastoral premarital counselling, which consisted of six sessions. After the completion of the six sessions the rehearsal takes place. The next event is the wedding.

The thesis included an empirical component. It concluded with the 'Findings of data and recommendations'. The empirical component was a survey conducted among 73 Lutherans from three of the five Lutheran congregations in Paramaribo, Suriname. The total administrative population of the church is approximately 4,000 spread over the five churches in the country. The marital status of the respondents was as follows: 52.1 per cent are married, 16.4 per cent are single, 1.4 per cent are widowed, 6.8 per cent live in concubinage, while 23.3 per cent are divorced. One of the findings that the survey revealed was that of the 17 divorced people about 23.5 per cent said they received counselling, while 76.5 per cent did not receive any counselling. The findings were presented in graphs. The thesis has three appendices. Appendix 1, discussed the research method. Appendix 2, discussed the concept of preparing the service. Appendix 3 was the questionnaire, which consisted of 22 questions.

PART III. SOURCES

CHAPTER 16

Sources for the Study of Surinamese Christianity

16.1. Introduction

16.1.1. Approaches to the study of theological sources

In 1984 the South African scholar David Bosch published an article entitled *Missionary Theology in Africa*. Bosch's well-researched article presented the state of the art of missiological research in Africa south of the Sahara at that time and served as an annotated bibliography. This kind of article is a good starting point for researchers.

Almost ten years later, Hofmeyr, Millard and Froneman (1991) took a different approach when they presented a source book for the *History of the Church in South Africa*. They presented 'in book form some of the most important documents and sources of South African church history, from the early beginnings up to the modern period' (p. xiii). This work allows researchers to study the actual documents in Afrikaans, Dutch and English without going through the pain of working through archival documents. The editors provided a brief background and by so doing placed the various documents in their historical context. A work of such magnitude requires a broad cooperation of scholars. It also requires permission from authorities to publish their materials.

The work by Koschorke, Ludwig, Delgado and Spliesgart (2007) took a similar approach to that of Hofmeyr, Millard and Froneman. It provided actual documents of Christianity from Asia, Africa and Latin America, written predominantly by natives of these continents. The editors explained the approach in their work as follows:

> This volume documents the voices of indigenous Christians who address such questions as the colonial conquest, slavery and the demand for ecclesiastical independence. It also gives expression to the denominational and contextual plurality of these 'non-Western' churches (p. xxix).

16.1.2. Approaches in this study

Which approach was followed in this work? The method followed in this section of the book (16.3 and 16.4) was that of David Bosch (1984). The previous chapter took a different approach, which was similar to that of Koschorke, Ludwig, Delgado and Spliesgart (2007). The present chapter gives a systematic description of resources for the study of Christianity in Suriname, with a major focus on history. It should serve as a starting point for further types of research.

16.1.3. Issues for further research

A documentary sourcebook of Christianity in Suriname is still lacking. To facilitate this, further research and cooperation is desirable. Such a task requires a multilingual research team, because sources are available in different languages (see 16.2.3). As indicated earlier, most of what is written about Suriname is not known to the English-speaking world. An ideal document would be a sourcebook in which important documents are translated into English.

16.1.4. Limitations

To the knowledge of this researcher, this is the first attempt to present a survey of the literature for the study of Christianity in Suriname (see for a general review of Surinamese sources, Van Kempen and Enser 2001 and Van Kempen 2002).

Having studied Christianity in Suriname for more than twenty-five years, I know my limitations. I am not pretending to know all the works published on this subject, let alone the unpublished works such as letters, theses and dissertations. However, as much as can be done by way of introduction, this study identified the most important resources.

16.2. Challenges

Scholars who study Christianity in Suriname will face geographical (16.2.1), denominational (16.2.2), linguistic (16.2.3) and methodological (16.2.4) challenges.

16.2.1. Geographical barriers

The history of Christianity in Suriname is scattered in documents throughout many archives and libraries in different parts of the world. Suriname was under Dutch rule until its independence in 1975, except for 1651-1667, 1799-1802 and 1804-1816 when it was under British rule. Because of this colonial past, the history of Suriname can be found in archives in Britain and the Netherlands. There is a need for more research to be able to reveal Suriname's past. Since churches and church leaders in the colonial era came mostly from abroad, much of the history of the churches is hidden in archives in more countries than that of the two past colonial masters. Research in the past twenty-five years revealed that information about the history of Christianity in Suriname was scattered in Guyana, the Netherlands, the United States of America, Germany, Britain and South Africa. Information may be available in other countries as well, which were not researched. The history can be found in different books, written by authors from different backgrounds and continents for various purposes. An example of this can be seen in a work written by a South African about the Dutch peasants in Suriname (De Jonge 1996). This situation of scattered sources makes research into the full history of Christianity in Suriname a costly undertaking.

Due to the spread and presence of Christianity across the country, it might be necessary to conduct a study on the growth of Christianity along geographical lines. It can be argued that there is a concentration of Christianity in Paramaribo, the capital city. Studies should reveal the strength of Christianity's presence in the other districts (see Roest 1992b). A critical source for such an undertaking is the information about the population by place of residence that the census of 2004 provides.

16.2.2. Denominational barriers

The historiography of Christianity in Suriname was done along denominational lines. Although there has been an attempt to write an ecumenical history of Christianity in Suriname (Jabini 2000), this effort had its limitations: it was a collection of denominational surveys for theological students and did not include a study of Christianity within its historical and cultural context. A new and more in-depth effort will have to present a more comprehensive and ecumenical introduction of Christianity in Suriname.[1] There is a need for a more comprehensive, multi-disciplinary and collaborative study of Christianity in Suriname, from different angles. The challenge here is that some churches do not want to make their sources available to people outside of their denomination. In some cases even members did not have access to these sources. Because of this regrettable situation much of Surinamese history was lost or impossible to trace.

16.2.3. Linguistic barriers

The study of Christianity in Suriname requires an ability to consult works in different languages. Even though most of the works are in Dutch, there are important documents that require knowledge of other languages as well. The Huguenots were French-speaking. When they started their French section of the Reformed Church, they used French as the language of the liturgy and for their church records. Most of the Moravian missionaries were German-speaking. Their diaries were kept in German and their correspondence with Europe was also done in German. Without knowledge of German, it is practically impossible to uncover the early years of the Moravian Church in Suriname. The Anglican Church in Suriname remained an English-speaking church. Some of the Moravian

---

1. Jabini [forthcoming II]. A summary in English is presented in Part II of this book.

missionaries were also English-speaking. Some Roman Catholic resources are only available in Latin, without translation. Knowledge of Latin is therefore necessary to study these original documents. Both the Roman Catholic Church and the Moravian Church used the local languages to communicate the gospel and to carry out missionary activities. These include Arawak, Sranantongo, Saramaccan, Hindi, Javanese and Chinese.

The field of missionary linguistics or the linguistics of missionaries needs serious attention. Missionaries studied not only the official language of Suriname, but also the vernacular languages. They documented a number of these and published important works, such as the Bible or portions of it, grammars and dictionaries. The languages influenced the missionaries and the missionaries influenced the languages as well. In some case, a 'sacred language' was developed, which was used in the services of the church. Some monographs were written on Surinamese missionary linguistics (Kramp 1983; Esajas 2001). However other works remained to be studied in *Arawak* (Schumann 1882 [2x]; Van Coll 1892; Klinkhamer 1957), *Carib* (Van Coll 1887; Albrinck 1931; Klinkhamer 1952; Klinkhamer 1955), *Ndyuka* (De Groot 1984), *Saramaccan* (Schumann 1914; Riemer 1779; De Groot 1977; De Groot 1981; Donicie and Voorhoeve 1963), *Sarnami* (*Katholik-dharm* 1924) and *Sranantongo* (Wullschlägel 1856). Voorhoeve and Donicie (1965) prepared a detailed and annotated bibliography of works that were written in Sranantongo with an appendix on works in the languages of the Maroons. The work was published in French and is still very useful.

In the second half of the twentieth century, members of SIL International worked on most of the Surinamese languages (Wilner 2001).[2] Some members wrote dissertations on the languages (Pet 1987; Courtz 2008). Members of Worldteam worked on the Trio and Wayana languages (Wilner 2001). I (Jabini 2004) wrote a doctoral dissertation on the history of Bible translations in all the languages of Suriname. This work was done from a missiological historical perspective, with some attention to missionary linguistics.

---

2. Work done by SIL in Suriname is available online on the following website: http://www.sil.org/americas/suriname/index.html.

16.2.4. Methodological challenges

Christianity can be studied from different perspectives, according to different branches of theology or other sciences. There is a need for a theological history of Suriname in which the question will be asked: What has the church taught and believed throughout its history? Theologians from the Roman Catholic Church and some Protestant churches produced a combined work that tried to study the apostolic creed from a Surinamese perspective (Sjak-Shie editor 1988). These scholars also published a booklet on Christian faith and political actions (Sjak-Shie editor 1989). In 1992, Catholic and Moravian theologians met again to speak on different theological issues, to commemorate the centenary of the Roman Catholic Church in Nickerie (Roest 1992a). These works may need a follow-up and will have to address issues that have been a challenge to the Christian church in Suriname. These will include slavery, ethnicity[3], state and church, church and other religions, the marginalised, worldviews and independent Christian organisations (Agape-beweging [Boer 2001], Mission Aviation Fellowship [MAF 1978], Child Evangelism Fellowship, *Man Mit Man*, Bible schools and theological seminaries, Radio Shalom, *Comite Begi nanga Wroko* etc.). With a few exceptions, the fields of biblical studies and systematic theology are virtually lacking in Surinamese Christianity.[4] This serious omission has to be rectified. With a long history of Bible translation and a need for contextualisation, biblical studies should have had a more prominent place. The Roman Catholic Catechetical Centre did some work in this field, with Sjak-Shie, the director, contributing to most of the studies.

A biographical history of Christianity in Suriname or a dictionary of Christians in Suriname is still outstanding. There have been amazing people who contributed to Christianity in Suriname. Besides a general work, that covers the most important people, researchers should consider

---

3. Missions in Suriname were conducted along ethnic lines. It will be necessary to consult all the sources in the different denominations to have a clear picture of Christianity among the different ethnic groups.

4. Frederik Rambaran (1981) wrote his thesis in the field of the Old Testament and Esteban Kross (1990) wrote in the field of the New Testament. Johannes Martoredjo (2005) wrote a master's thesis on biblical theology. All the other theses referred to in this work were written in the field of practical theology or missiology.

academic monographs on key personalities, across all denominations (e.g. Vernooij 1969; 1990e). This will include among others the following people: Johannes Alabi, Cornelis Winst Blijd, Meyer Salomon Bromet, Petrus Donders, Rudolf Eduard Constantijn Doth, Detta Hewitt-Guda, Daniel Ijveraar, Ilse van Kanten-Reeberg, Theodoor Gangapersad Lachman, Pudsey Meye, Niti Pawiro, Gilly Polanen, Carel Paulus Rier and Paulus Antonius Wennekers.

As the survey in the previous chapter showed, most of the works done so far by Surinamese theologians about Christianity in Suriname were holistic. They looked at theological issues from different perspectives. Furthermore, they were often bound to a particular denomination, with limited or no reference to other denominations or ministries in the country. The problem of the Caribbean family system that Choennie addressed in his thesis is also applicable to the other churches.

There is a need for a major up-to-date history of Christianity in Suriname, written by Surinamese academics, from a Surinamese perspective and from a multi-disciplinary approach. The following sections will reveal resources that should be engaged in any comprehensive study of Christianity in Suriname.

16.3. General sources

The early period of Christianity in Suriname, produced little theological literature. Information about the period up to approximately 1850 is scattered in books about the general history of Suriname. Historians referred to incidents about Christianity in the early years, while discussing other events. Works of theologians that were preserved in those early days were their letters and church documents. The general resources that will be discussed in this section include writings on the general history of Suriname (16.3.1), church-related documents, such as letters, church books (16.3.2), papers and magazines (16.3.3). The final section will include political documents (16.3.4).

16.3.1. Writings on the general history of Suriname

Wolbers (1861), one of the main Surinamese historians, included extensive references to Christianity in Suriname. Even though some of the information presented by him has been superseded by further research, he is still one of the best Surinamese historians. Other works, earlier than his include Herlein (1718), Pistorius (1763), Fermin (1770), Hartsinck (1770), Nassy (1791) and Van Sijpesteijn (1854). These studies followed a chronological method, except for Nassy. Interesting, but often out-dated, is the ethnological information in these studies.[5] Scattered throughout the pages are references to Christianity. Most of these out-of-print resources are currently available online.[6]

Most modern histories followed a thematic (Bakker et al. [1998]; Buddingh [2000]; Van Lier [1971, 1977]; Hira [1982]), topical (Gobardhan-Rambocus [2001]; Kramp [1983]; Rens [1953]; Schalkwijk [1994]; Marshall [2003]) or ethnical approach (e.g. Zijlmans and Enser [2002], De Bruijne [2006], Tjon Sie Fat [2009]). These monographs contained detailed information on the role that Christianity played in their specific topics or among ethnic groups.

Gohardhan-Rambocus for example is the most detailed study on the role that Christianity played in education in Suriname. A theological study of Christian education however might be necessary for the church. Has Christian education in Suriname, including catechism, met the expected outcome? Should Christian churches continue with Christian schools? What should be done with its catechetical education?[7]

---

5. Deiros' (2002) article missed the richness of missionary ethnography in Suriname, since he limited it to the work done by the Moravians among the Saramaccans. The Moravians have not only produced ethnographical studies on the Saramaccans; they produced linguistic works on the Arawak, Saramaccan and Sranantongo (see section 16.2.3). Studies about missionary or theological ethnography were further published by Roman Catholic scholars such as Abbenhuis (1939), van Coll (1886) and de Klerk (1951; 1953).

6. See the following websites:
   http://www.dbnl.org/letterkunde/suriname/
   http://books.google.com/
   http://www.archive.org/

7. Joop Vernooij and Peter Sjak-Shie (1990) provided an initial answer to these questions for the Roman Catholic Church's catechesis.

Schalkwijk's study revealed some interesting relationships in colonial Suriname. Leaders of the Christian church were involved in various sections of influence in society. Schalkwijk studied these relations up to 1920. There is a critical need for a study of these relationships in the current Surinamese society.

Marshall's work gave some inside information on the role that Christian leaders played in the development of Surinamese nationalism at an early stage.

Suriname needs to rewrite its history. Its history is still based on the work of outsiders. A new history written by a team of Surinamese will play a critical role in the study of Surinamese Christianity. It will also provide Christianity with a stepping-stone as it imagines or dreams of a new Suriname.[8]

16.3.2. Church-related documents

16.3.2.1. Letters

Clergymen and missionaries wrote letters to church leaders and authorities in Europe. Some of these letters were preserved, others are no longer available. A small number of letters written by Saramaccan Christians was also preserved (see Arends and Perl 1995). In general the letters gave a picture of Christianity in Suriname as the European missionaries saw it. Even the letters written by Surinamese reflected a European approach to the issues. Since these letters were denomination-specific, they will be listed under the specific denominations. Those written during the period of Zeeland (1667-1683) are currently available online.[9]

The Roman Catholic bishops wrote pastoral letters. These letters are a source for contextual theology (see Zichem 2005). The same is true for the messages that were published by the *Comite Christelijke Kerken* (Council of Christian churches).

---

8. On the topic of imagining a new future, see the works of the Ugandese Roman Catholic theologian Emmanuel M Katongole e.g. *A Future for Africa: Critical Essays in Christian Social Imagination* (African Theology Today). University of Scranton Press, 2005; *The Sacrifice of Africa: A Political Theology for Africa*. Eerdmans, 2011.

9. See http://www.archieven.nl/db/0/toegang/239/GIDS102/.

16.3.2.2. Church registers

Important sources of information are the so-called church registers. These books consist of the registrations of baptisms, weddings, and confirmation of members. The books available covered the periods 1688-1730 and 1770-1792. These resources are currently available online.[10] Unfortunately, a number of these documents are missing. Those available are helpful for statistical studies. They also give a picture of the ethnic make-up of the church. Archives in Suriname and the Netherlands have church books of the Moravian, the Roman Catholic and the Lutheran Churches. Researchers sometimes complain about these resources, since they do not always give a clear picture. Members did not always communicate with the church authorities when they changed their status, e.g. left the colony. The information here has to be used with caution.

The Reformed Church's clergymen and lay leaders met for an annual general meeting, called the *Conventus*. At this meeting issues related to the wellbeing of the church were discussed and recorded. The records were sent to the political leaders of the colony and to the mother church in Amsterdam, Netherlands. Ort (1963, 2000) gave a summary of the main points of the minutes of these meetings. Further studies from a Surinamese perspective are still outstanding.

16.3.3. Church papers and magazines

The church papers and magazines still need to be explored by theological students. Often they were the medium for expressing theological differences. A comparison of these early interactions with the current Surinamese inter-denominational relationships, will reveal the ecumenical progress that has been made. The papers and magazines are also a source of contextual theology.

16.3.3.1. Moravians

The Moravian Church published a magazine in Sranantongo called Makzien *vo Kristen soema* zieli (1852-1906, 1912-1932) and *Zondeicouranti vo Anitriesoema (1907-1911)*. It published the following Dutch papers:

---

10. See www.nationaalarchief.nl.

De Christelijke Huisvriend (1888-1900), Zondagsblad (1907-1921), De Hernhutter (1906-1945) and Kerkbode (1945- present). The following missionary publications were also important: *Berichten van de zendingen der Evangelische Broedergemeente onder de heidenen (1798-1799, 1801, 1803), Berigten wegens de zendelingen der Broedergemeente (1820-1835), Berichten uit de Heiden-wereld (1835-1927), Ons Suriname (1929-1949)* and *De Surinaamse Zending (1950-).*[11]

16.3.3.2. Roman Catholic

The Roman Catholic Church published a paper called De Katholieke Waarschuwer (1891-1934), De Katholiek (1935-1955) and Omhoog (1956-present).

16.3.3.3 Reformed and Lutheran Churches

The Reformed Church and the Lutheran Church jointly published a weekly newspaper called *Protestantenblad* (1895-1897, 1904-1911, 1916-1919, 1921-1936), *Protestantenblad Weekblad voor Suriname* (1936-1970) and *Protestantenblad van de Hervormde en de Evangelische-Luthersche Gemeente in Suriname* (1970-1976). See also Jongeneel (1990:82).

16.3.3.4. Pentecostal Churches

The Pentecostal churches in Suriname started different publications. However, they did not last long. *Pinksterzending* published a paper called *De Regenboog* (The Rainbow). The paper appeared between 1969 and 1971. In 1972, it appeared under a new name *Onze Banier* (Our Banner). *Gods Bazuin* published a magazine called *Turning Point.* Tabernacle of Faith and Love published *Geloof en Liefde. Kandelaar* published *Kandelaar Nyunsu. Stromen van Kracht* published a magazine called *Op de Hoogte.* Roderick Hewitt and others published an interdenominational magazine, *One Way.*

These magazines (papers) often consisted of a biblical message, testimonies, poems and activities of the church. Some would also include information from ministries and churches outside of Suriname. These

---

11. Jongeneel (1990:15, 40, 100-102) discussed a few minor publications that I was not able to consult.

magazines should be explored for a contextual Pentecostal theology in Suriname.

Magazines that were published in the Netherlands contained articles on Pentecostal Christianity in Suriname. These included *Kracht van Omhoog*[12] and *Stromen van Kracht*.[13] Both magazines published articles on the beginning of Pentecostalism in Suriname. They included reports from Surinamese Christians as well.[14] The magazine *The Pentecostal Evangel* published by the Assemblies of God contained reports on their work in Suriname.

Maranatha Church in the Netherlands published a magazine called *Maranatha Ministries Magazine* (1999-). A few interviews with Christian leaders from a Pentecostal background were published in the magazine. The magazine is available online.[15]

16.3.3.5. Others

Stichting Boen Njoensoe published a monthly magazine, edited by the Plymouth Brethren Dutch missionary Gerard Elbers.[16]

Nyunsuplus of the Evangelical School of Theology published biographical interviews with Christian leaders across denominations.

The Dutch mission scholar Jan A B Jongeneel published a bibliographical catalogue for Protestant missionary periodicals from the nineteenth and twentieth centuries. Periodicals in Suriname were included in the catalogue.[17]

---

12. See http://www.krachtvanomhoog.nl. (September 2011). The magazine appeared from 1937-1996. Due to the Second World War, the magazine did not appear between 1940 and the first half of 1945. The first reference to Suriname in the magazine seems to be number 22 of 1945. The article was on Christmas in the jungle of Suriname. More articles about Suriname appeared in the 1960's.

13. See http://www.stromenvankracht.info.

14. Another Dutch Pentecostal Magazine that influenced many in Suriname is *Nieuw Leven* (New Life). It was published by John Maasbach. The magazine included testimonies from Surinamese as well.

15. http://www.maranatha.nl/content/blogcategory/0/35/.

16. *Hanoe Makandra*. The magazine orginally started in the Netherlands. Elbers published it in Suriname from 1983 untill his homecalling in 1994.

17. Jongeneel JAB 1990. *Protestantse zendingsperiodieken uit de negentiende en twintigste eeuw in Nederland, Nederlands-Indië, Suriname en de Nederlandse antilen: Een bibliographische catalogus met inleiding. IIMO research publication 30. Leiden: IIMO.*

16.3.4. Political documents

Early Christianity in Suriname was closely related to the state. Affairs of the Reformed Church, that was considered the church of the state, were discussed, approved or rejected by the political leaders of the colony. The church therefore had to submit all its important documents, letters, etc. to the political leaders for approval. The minutes of the political leaders therefore include references to church affairs.

The early laws that were passed in Suriname are critical for the study of the development of Christianity. Most of these laws were prepared in consultation with the Reformed clergymen. Schiltkamp and De Smidt (1973) published the laws that were passed between 1667 and 1816. A collection of laws that were published between 1816 and 1855 is available online (*Governmentsbladen*). There is a need for a critical monograph on the relation between Christianity and government in Suriname. Schalkwijk (1994) provided a starting point. An in-depth study is necessary, which must include Christianity and government after 1975.

A work that provided important information about different aspects of Suriname, including Christianity, was the *Almanak*.[18]

16.4. Denominational sources

This section will introduce sources according to denomination. The sources are presented in chronological order of arrival of the churches, except for the churches that arrived later.

---

18. It was first published as *Surinaamsche (staatkundige) Almanak* and then as *De Gids Almanak voor Suriname* and *De Vraagbak-Almanak voor Suriname*. See: http://surinaamsealmanakken.com/. This website also contains information about other important publications, such as the so-called *Heerenboekjes* (with the names of important officials) and the *Oost- en West-Indische Post*. The almanacs are available online (see: http://www.dbnl.org).

16.4.1. Anglican Church

16.4.1.1. Introduction

The Anglican Church or Church of England started in Suriname in 1651. It was founded by settlers from Barbados.

16.4.1.2. Historiography

16.4.1.2.1. Systematic history

The first systematic history of the Anglican Church in Suriname was a short five-page article written by Oudschans Dentz (1916). Oudschans Dentz gave a brief survey of the whole history of the Anglican Church in Suriname. He wrote one paragraph on the beginning of the church in Suriname. The rest of the article gave brief facts of the church after 1800.

Duke (2000) published a book about the Church of England in Guyana. She included Suriname in her presentation, because Suriname belonged to the Guyanese diocese. Duke wrote a paragraph on its beginning (p. 18) and a few paragraphs are scattered throughout the book on its history (pp. 77, 397-399). To the knowledge of this writer, Oudschans Dentz and Duke are the only ones who wrote systematic histories of the Church of England in Suriname. Duke (p. 444) referred to a booklet written in Dutch, that discussed the history of the church from 1651-1991. The booklet was not available in the church in Suriname. It was Duke's major source for Suriname.

16.4.1.2.2. Useful references

A survey of the early history of the church requires interaction with other general writings on Suriname's history. The writings of Bowdon (1850), Calamy (1802), Evans and Evans (1854), Palmer (1802) and Sprague (1854) contain some valuable references to the church in Suriname.

Two other branches of the church were also present at the beginning: the Quakers and the Puritans. Carroll (1973) published reports on the activities of the Quakers between 1658 and 1659. Information about the Puritans can be found scattered throughout the following works: Anderson

(1848), Bowdon (1850), Calamy (1802), Palmer (1802) and Sprague (1857). Some passing comments about English Christianity in Suriname are found in Jones (1966), Ort (1963, 2000), Rens (1953) and Van der Linde (1956).

16.4.1.2.3. General background

Williamson (1923) published a well-written book which included the period of the British in Suriname (1651-1667). There is a helpful annotated Dutch translation of the Surinamese section of this work (Williamson 1926/27). Between 1666 and 1668, Justinianus Ernst Von Weltz came to Suriname as an independent missionary. Sadly, nothing is known of his activities in Suriname at this time. His ideas are important from a missiological perspective. Scherer (1969) published a collection of his writings.

The writings of some of the early peasants in Suriname are available for exploration. The Rev John Oxenbridge, one of the first English clergymen in the colony, published a few works that provide valuable information on early Christianity in Suriname (Oxenbridge 1661, 1670, 1671).

Henry Adis (1664), a Christian belonging to the General Baptist Church in England, who lived in Suriname for a while, wrote about the situation of Christianity in Suriname. William Byam (1665) wrote about an incident with Allen, a member of the church at that time. Allen attacked Governor Willoughby with a cutlass at a prayer meeting.

Other documents written during that period indicate that there were tensions between the colonists. This raised questions with regards to the credibility of some of the documents (e.g. Behn 1688 and Byam 1665). It is also evident that all the literature available addressed the situation after 1660. This left a big gap in the early days of British Christianity in Suriname. Research so far in archives of the Church of England did not produce documents of that period. This probably is because the church in Suriname was not an official branch of the Church of England. Furthermore, the members of the church left the colony when the Dutch conquered it.

A critical study of the settlement of the Church of England in Suriname is outstanding; resources of the first decade are missing. A critical study should engage the Barbadian background of the settlers and their Christianity.

16.4.2. Dutch Reformed Church

Abraham Crijnssen conquered the British in Suriname in 1667. Suriname became a Dutch colony. The settlement of the Dutch in Suriname led to the beginning of the Dutch Reformed Church in 1668. The Dutch Reformed Church became the official, state church. The works listed under general sources will provide the historical background to this period.

16.4.2.1. Reformed Christianity in the seventeenth century

Between 1668 and 1676, the first Reformed clergyman in Suriname, the Rev Johannes Basseliers, wrote a few letters. Dr Jan van der Linde (1966) published these letters as an appendix in his book about Surinamese sugar lords and their church.[19] Van der Linde's work is a monograph about Reformed Christianity in the seventeenth century in Suriname.

An important person in the seventeenth century Christianity in Suriname is the Governor Cornelis van Aerssen van Sommelsdijck (see Oudschans Dentz 1938; Bijlsma 1930). Van Sommelsdijck was a committed Christian who promoted Christianity's cause in many ways.

Closely related to the history of the Reformed Church in Suriname is the history of the Labadists and the Huguenots. Their history is found in the works referred to above, but also in Berg (1845) and Koenen (1846). The first systematic description of the Labadists in Suriname was from Knappert (1927/1928). He also published an extensive summary of *De Reize der Labadisten* (the travels of the Labadists) that J W C Ort published in the *Protestantenblad voor de kolonie Suriname*. F Bubberman (1974) wrote a popular article about the Labadists for *Suralco Magazine*. The Huguenots became part of the established Reformed Church. Their history is included in general works on the Reformed Church.

16.4.2.2. Reformed Christianity in the eighteenth century

Dr Jan van der Linde (1981, 1987) wrote a well-researched article and monograph about Joannes Guiljelmus Kals, a Reformed clergyman of the eighteenth century. Van der Linde's monograph was done with the same

---

19. See the originals at: http://www.archieven.nl/db/0/toegang/239/GIDS102/.

scientific accuracy as his previous work on the Sugar lords in Suriname. Prof Aart Arnout van Schelven (1922/23) wrote about Kals in his article about Suriname in the eighteenth century. Kals was the first Reformed clergyman to openly advocate the cause of missions among the Natives and Negroes.

16.4.2.3. Systematic historiography of Suriname

It was during the second half of the nineteenth century that historians of the church started to write the history of the church in a systematic way.

16.4.2.3.1. Cornelis van Schaick

In 1855 the Rev Cornelis van Schaick (1855) published his contribution to the history of the Reformed Church in Suriname. This contribution was not intended to be a scientific presentation of the history. According to Van Schaick such a task was impossible for various reasons. The main reason was that due to the various outbreaks of fire in the city many important documents were burned or were lost. His work was the first contribution to the history of the Reformed Church in Suriname.

16.4.2.3.2. S Van Dissel

The Rev S Van Dissel (1877) took a different approach from Van Schaik. He used 'all the old documents, that were still to be found in the Reformed Church and the archives of the church council' (p. 4). He prepared an extract of the documents that he found. He discussed five main points in the history of the Reformed Church in the nineteenth century. These were issues related to the church itself, the building, the clergymen, the church council and the poor and finally the finances of the church.

16.4.2.3.3. L Knappert and S Kalff

Knappert (1928) wrote an informative monograph on what he called Handelskerken 'commercial/business churches'. These were Reformed churches that were planted by merchants or businessmen outside of the Netherlands. The church in Suriname was seen as one of them.

Kalff (1928/29) gave an overview of clergymen in the West Indies, including Suriname.

16.4.2.3.4. A W Marcus

The Rev A W Marcus (1935) published a thematic history of the church. He described the history of the church from its beginning up to around 1935. He discussed the beginning of the Reformed Church, the Jewish Church and the mission of the Labadists. He described the various branches of the church: Commewijne, Cottica and Perica, Torarica, French, Saramacca, Nickerie and Paramaribo. The section on Paramaribo included the words spoken by the governor on the laying of the first foundation stone of the church building in 1810. Much attention was also given to the service that was held after a fire destroyed that building in 1821. A brief survey discussed the church during the time when Suriname was under British leadership at the beginning of the nineteenth century. The church used the building of the Lutheran Church after the fire. In 1832, a new fire destroyed the building of the Lutheran Church. The Reformed Church erected a new building in 1835. The consecration took place when Prince Hendrik of the Netherlands visited the colony. The details of the service held on that day, 5 July 1835, including the full sermon, were given. The consecration of the church organ took place eleven years later, on 12 July 1846. He continued to discuss the church's care for the orphans, the various associations in the church, memorable events and the choir. He explained the organisation and management of the church, followed by a list of the clergymen who served the church in Paramaribo from 1668-1835. The book concluded with a list of memorable events.

16.4.2.3.5. D Mulder and Rev C A Paap

In connection with the 275th anniversary of the Reformed Church, the Rev D Mulder and Rev C A Paap published a brochure (Mulder and Paap 1943). This work consisted of four parts. Governor J C Kielstra wrote an introduction, in which he explained the relation between the government and the Reformed Church. Rev Mulder gave historical notes about the church. His work is based on that of Van Schaick (1855). The third part, written by Rev C A Paap, gave a detailed analysis of the liberal theological path that the Reformed Church took in the nineteenth century. He then continued with a discussion of various societies within the church. The final part of the brochure gave a list of the clergymen, which is also based on the work of Schaick.

16.4.2.3.6. J W C Ort

In 1963, the Rev J W C Ort published a major work on the settlement of the Reformed Church in Suriname from 1667-1800.[20] Ort critically engaged the work that was done before and defended the work of the Reformed Church up to 1800 against its critics.[21]

In chapter 2, he discussed the sources that were available for the study. He divided them into: church sources, political sources, letters, travel stories and journals of contemporaries about the events, general works and articles about Suriname and church historiographical works.

In the first part of chapter 3, he engaged the sources critically. He corrected many errors that were made in previous writings (e.g. Van Schaick [1855], Wolbers [1861], Buiskool [1914-17] and Knappert [1928]). Ort's critical historiography had a better presentation about the facts of Reformed history in Suriname. In the second part, he discussed in detail some of the wrong presentations about the location of the early Reformed Churches in Suriname. He presented well-argued evidences for the location of Torarica. His view seems to have the support of the old maps. He continued with the churches in Commewijne.

Chapter 4 gave a general presentation of Suriname. It discussed the country and its rivers, districts and churches, the distances, the climate and sicknesses and the population. The chapter concluded with a brief history of the colony.

Chapter 5 was a detailed history of the clergymen who served in the church up to 1800. Ort corrected some of the factual errors about the clergymen of the church and provided a new list for all the churches.

---

20. The original edition of the work was mimeographed: Ort JWC 1963. *Vestiging van de Hervormde Kerk in Suriname. 1667-1800*. Amsterdam: De Sticusa. This review was based on the printed edition (Ort JWC 2000). This printed edition has some typographical errors, including a few wrong dates.
21. Earlier, Oudschans Dentz (1949) wrote an article in which he corrected some of the errors about the beginning of the Reformed Church in Suriname.

Chapter 6 was the main body of the book. It was divided into four parts, dealing with the churches in (1) Torarica, (2) Commewijne, (3) Perica-Cottica and (4) Paramaribo. Most of the study was devoted to Paramaribo, which was divided into six periods. It studied the church from the arrival of the Dutch originating from Zeeland to the arrival of Van Aerssen van Sommelsdijck (1667-1683).[22] The next period studied the church under Van Aerssen van Sommelsdijck (1683-1688). Van Aerssen van Sommelsdijck was a great asset to the church. The third section studied the church after Van Aerssen van Sommelsdijck (1689-1700). After a brief review of the fourth period (1701-1730), he gave a detailed presentation of the fifth period (1730-1760). He studied six topics in this period: (1) the unrestricted power of the government; (2) protection of the colony and the protected church; (3) the privileged church; (4) the Lutheran Church; (5) The early historiography and the view that came out of that with regard to the Reformed Church in Suriname; (6) The life of the church from 1730-1760. Finally, the sixth period studied 1760 to 1800. This concluded the history of the settlement of the church in Suriname. An additional section included five studies. The first studied missions in Suriname. It included a review of the work of the Moravians. The second one gave a detailed summary of the important points from the minutes of the Conventus Deputatorum (the general meeting of the churches). The third study focused on piety in the colony during the period under study. The fifth and the sixth studied the church's social welfare work and finances respectively.

16.4.2.3.7. André Hendrik Loor

Two small brochures were also published to commemorate the church's 325th and 335th anniversaries. Both were probably written by Andre Loor (1993, 2003). These were the only contributions on the Reformed Church in Suriname that were written by a Surinamer.

There is a need for a critical history of the Dutch Reformed Church in Suriname, written from the perspective of a Surinamer.

---

22. Ort argued for the beginning of the church in Suriname at 1667. Van der Linde has since presented evidence against 1667. The correct date of the start of the church should be 1668.

16.4.2.3.8. Dutch migrants

There was a small Reformed congregation of Dutch immigrants in Saramacca. Julius Eduard Muller and Cornelis Atses Hoekstra (1895) wrote a book to commemorate the fiftieth anniversary of their settlement in Suriname (see also Hoekstra 1903). A book was also written to commemorate the seventy-fifth anniversary (De Vestiging). Their history is well covered by C de Jonge (1976, 1996). See also Loor (1995), who is a descendant of these Dutch peasants.

16.4.3. Moravians

The first missionaries of the Moravian Church arrived in Suriname in 1735. After a few attempts, the church settled successfully in Suriname in the second half of the eighteenth century. Their early missions focused primarily on the Natives and the descendants of the African slaves, in the city, districts and in the interior (the so-called Maroons).

16.4.3.1. Missionary letters and diaries

Fritz Staëhelin (1913-1918) published an important resource for the study of the work of the Moravians in Suriname. It contained a collection of letters and diaries written by missionaries from 1735-1813. This work was published in German, in three volumes, in three parts. The first volume (1735-1745) dealt with the first mission in Suriname. The second volume (1738-1765) dealt with the mission among the Natives in Suriname and Berbice. The third volume (1765-1813) deals with the mission among the Maroons and the Negro slaves in Paramaribo. The final section of this third volume included the last part of the missions among the Natives. This work was not translated. Mrs Annelies Vollprecht prepared a detailed summary of the most important events in Dutch (Vollprecht 1998-2000; 2010). Many of the letters however were published in Moravian missionary magazines in other languages, e.g. Dutch (*berichten*), English (periodicals) and German (*Missions-Blatt*).

These letters were not a systematic study of the history of the Hernhutters in Suriname. They described personal experiences of the missionaries. Just like most missionary letters in those days, these letters concentrated on the heroic deeds and struggles of the foreign missionaries. Little was said about the local workers. An exception was the detailed information given about two important local leaders, Johannes Alabi and Johannes King.

In the archives, researchers will find diaries that were written after 1800. The tradition of keeping diaries is still practiced among the Moravian pastors in Suriname. These diaries are an important source for the study of the church. Some of them were published (see below).

16.4.3.2. Systematic historiography

16.4.3.2.1. H Weiss
H Weiss (1911) wrote the first survey of the work of the Moravians in Suriname, in Dutch.[23] He wrote the history along ethnic lines. His work was the first detailed study of the work of the Moravians in Suriname.

16.4.3.2.2. Hermann Georg Steinberg
Hermann Georg Steinberg (1933) enlarged and updated the work of Weiss.[24] The work started with an introductory chapter that was written by G J Staal, former governor of Suriname. Staal gave a brief overview of the land, its people, history and government (chapter 1).

In chapter 2 Steinberg gave a background to the beginning of the Moravians (Hernhutters). He discussed the role of Zinzendorf and the beginning of the foreign missions of the movement. Finally he discussed the attempts of the church to settle in Suriname.

Chapter 3 was devoted to missions among the Natives in Berbice and Suriname. In detail he discussed the years of growth and the decline of the mission.

Chapters 4 and 5 were devoted to the work among the slaves before the abolition of slavery (pp. 81-155). Chapter 4 discussed the slaves in Suriname, their spiritual life and the beginning of the missions among them. Chapter 5 discussed the growth of the missions in Paramaribo and various districts between 1830 and 1863. The growth did not take place only because of the evangelistic activities of the church. There were also

---

23. This work can be consulted online at: http://ufdc.ufl.edu/ (August 2011).
24. This work can be consulted online at: http://ufdc.ufl.edu/ (August 2011).

regulations such as the requirement for slaves to join a Christian church if they wanted to become free. That requirement probably contributed more to the growth than anything else.

Chapter 6 discussed the beginning of the 'Creole Church'. The descendants of the slaves, who joined the church before the abolition, continued in the church. Membership of the church was not always based on discipleship. This challenged the church after the abolition.

Chapter 7 discussed the character, organisation and developments of the church up to the 1930's.

Chapters 8-10 discussed missions among the Maroons, Indians and Javanese. The book concluded with a review and a preview. Besides the indexes, there were two appendices. The first one was a manual on how to study the book. The second one was a missionary atlas. It had 25 maps with all the places where the church worked.

16.4.3.2.3. Jos Fontaine

Jos Fontaine (1985) did a minor revision of the work of Steinberg. He added some new information on the church after the 1930's. His work was published during the celebration of the 250th anniversary of the Moravian Church in Suriname.

16.4.3.3. Monographs

16.4.3.3.1. Cornelis Winst Blijd

In the 1890's the Moravians started a formal programme to train local church leaders. The programme received a boost in 1901 when a missionary came to dedicate his service to this work. A few local workers were trained and they served the church. Due to a lack of students, the institute closed in the 1920's.

Surinamese of the early twentieth century wrote a few popular articles and books about Cornelis Winst Blijd, a student of the theological school and the first ordained Surinamese pastor of the Moravian Church in Suriname[25] (Comvalius [1921], Vrede [1923] and Waaldijk [1931]).

---

25. The online article of the *Christelijke Encyclopedie* (Kampen: Kok 2005), confused

16.4.3.3.2. Dutch theologians

A new initiative to train workers locally started in the 1950's. There were three Dutch theologians who contributed to the development of Surinamese Moravian theologians. These were: Jan Marinus van der Linde, Jan W M Schalwijk and Jan van Raalte. All three scholars published academic monographs that dealt with general theological subjects within the Moravian Church.

16.4.3.3.2.1. Jan Marinus van der Linde

Jan Marinus van der Linde was born on 7 November 1913. He studied theology at the University of Utrecht from 1938-1942. He served as a pastor in the Dutch Reformed Church for eight years before he was seconded to the Moravian Church. He came to Suriname in 1951 to help with the training of leaders in the Moravian Church. He left for the Netherlands in 1954 where he served as the general secretary of the *Zeister Zendingsgenootschap* and rector of the theological seminary in Zeist from 1954-1964. From 1958 to 1976 he was a special professor of the Moravian Church and the church history of the Caribbean at the University of Utrecht. In 1966 he became a regular lecturer at that university, where he lectured for the Reformed Church on the apostolate. In 1973 he assumed a regular professorship in missiology at the same university. He retired in 1980. His first major work was his doctoral dissertation of 1956. His research influenced the early theologians of the Moravians. He was the mentor of the first group of Surinamese academic theologians. Van der Linde died on 6 July 1995.[26]

16.4.3.3.2.2. Jan M W Schalkwijk

Jan Schalkwijk served the Moravian Church in Suriname from 1952 to 1970. From 1974-1978, he served at United Theological College of the West Indies in Jamaica as an ecclesiastical professor. He wrote a major

---

Blijd with R E C Doth. The article stated that Doth was the first Surinamese to be ordained as pastor in 1902. Doth was not the first, it was Blijd. Doth was the first Surinamese to be consecreated as bishop in 1962.
http://www.protestant.nl/encyclopedie/geschiedenis/suriname-kerken.

26. Articles in remembrance of him were written in Suriname by J Kent and H Zamuel (Kerkbode EBGS 16 July 1995) and E C Ritfeld and K Zeefuik (Kerkbode EBGS 30 July 1995). In the Netherlands this was done by J A B Jongeneel (Wereld en Zending. Number 4, 1995) and J M W Schalkwijk (Trouw 7 July 1995).

work on missions among the Indians in the Southern Caribbean. It was published posthumously in 2011 (Schalkwijk 2011).

Schalkwijk started his research for a doctoral dissertation on missions among the (East) Indians of the Southern Caribbean in 1971 and continued after he returned to the Netherlands from Jamaica in 1978. Professor Johannes Verkuyl was his promoter and Dr Jan van der Linde the co-promoter. In 1984, when Verkuyl retired, the Vrije Universiteit of Amsterdam assigned him a new promoter. At that time the dissertation was complete. The new promoter however was of the opinion that the dissertation was too lengthy. He therefore advised Schalkwijk to limit the research to Suriname and to add a few pages on the two other countries in the Southern Caribbean, Trinidad and Guyana. Schalkwijk never completed this task. He passed away in 2004. His son, Prof Marten Schalkwijk, and others prepared the dissertation for publication.

Schalkwijk published a few works that are of importance to the study of Christianity in Suriname (see the bibliography). A full bibliography of his publications appeared in his recently published *Ontwikkeling van de zending in het Zuid-Caribisch gebied 1500-1980 in het bijzonder onder de Hindostanen 1850-1980* (see pp. 696-698).

16.4.3.3.2.3. Jan van Raalte

Jan van Raalte was born in 1926. He studied theology at the University of Kampen. He graduated in 1945. He served the Reformed Church as pastor in Mildam (1951). As an army chaplain he served in Soesterberg (1956), New Guinea (1960-1962), Apeldoorn (1963), Suriname (1965) and Harderwijk (1971-1975). From 1975-1982 he was a lecturer and vice-president of the theological seminary of the Moravians in Suriname. Upon his return to the Netherlands, he served as the secretary of the Werkgroep Pluriforme Samenleving van de Raad van Kerken in Nederland (1982-1988). He died in 1995.[27]

He wrote his doctoral dissertation on secularism and missions in Suriname, of which J M van der Linde was one of the promoters (Van

---

27. Articles in rememberance of him were written by H A M Abrahams-Nelson (Weekkrant Suriname 19 January 1995), J Overduin (Suriname zending. 1 March 1995), J van Butselaar (Vandaar March 1995), M van Reenen (Jaarboek van de Gereformeerde Kerken in Nederland 1996).

Raalte 1973). He was a contributor to the encyclopaedia of Suriname and a work on the cultural mosaic of Suriname (Bruining and Voorhoeve 1977; Helman 1978). He published a few other articles and booklets on Suriname.

16.4.3.3.2.4. Others

F G Schouwenaar (1983) wrote a thesis on the relationship between the Moravian Church in Suriname and the *Zeister Zendingsgenootschap* after the period when the Surinamese church became independent.

Maria Lenders (1996) wrote her doctoral dissertation on the 'Warriors of the Lamb'. Her study was critical and paid a lot of attention to the role of women in the work of the Moravians in Suriname up to 1900.

16.4.3.3.3. Surinamese theologians after 1960

Surinamese theologians contributed monographs as well. Their work was reviewed in Part II of this study. Doth and others gave an overview of the missions work among the Maroons in a work which translated was entitled 'The land will hear' (Doth 1965). The traditional religion in Suriname has not only been the object of study by many Moravian theologians, a Moravian sociologist also contributed (Jap a Joe, 1995). Edwin Marshall (2010) wrote a monograph on church discipline.

A new generation of Moravian theologians, who completed their undergraduate studies at the seminary in Paramaribo, continued their education at the theological university of Kampen, where they completed masters' degrees in theology (MTh). Rosalien Zamuel-Rotgans (Rotgans 2004) wrote about Afro-Surinamese theology. She wrote her undergraduate thesis about some secret societies in Suriname (Rotgans 1993). Roberto Rathling (2005) studied theology and healthcare ethics. Earlier he wrote his undergraduate thesis about poverty and wealth from a Christian ethical perspective (Rathling 1997). Urmie Mingoen studied practical theology (2008).

There is a need for a complete history of the Moravians in Suriname, written by Surinamese Moravian scholars. So far these scholars have written thematic and biographical monographs about the Moravians in Suriname.

16.4.3.4. Moravian missions among ethnic groups

Missionary work in Suriname was conducted along ethnic lines. Articles and monographs were therefore written about each specific group.

16.4.3.4.1. Natives

H Weiss (1921) wrote a series of articles on the mission of the Moravians among the Natives in Berbice and Suriname. Justus Ben Christiaan Wekker (1986) wrote an informative article on the work among the Natives in the eighteenth century. Cornelis N van der Ziel discussed the work among the Carib Natives (1997). His research is not limited to Suriname or the Moravian Church. A monograph published by the Guyanese scholar Benjamin (1991) is also of interest for the work among the Arawak Natives.

16.4.3.4.2. Saramaccans

A lot was written on the work of the Moravians among the Saramaccans. The mission started in 1765, three years after this group signed a peace treaty with the colonial government. Saramaccans have lived as a free people in the interior of Suriname since the seventeenth century, from the time they escaped slavery.

Missionary S Meissner (1848) wrote a detailed account of the work in the village Ganse. H Weiss (1919/20) wrote an article that gave a survey of the work among the Saramaccans.

Izaak Albitrouw (1978; 1979) wrote two important monographs about the Saramaccans. His first monograph is a diary about his work among the Saramaccans in the village of Aurora from 1891-1896. His second monograph was an eye-witness account, although some judged this work to be biased of Paulus Anake, a prophetic figure among the Saramaccans at the end of the nineteenth century. His works were written in Sranantongo and were edited and translated into Dutch by Miriam Sterman.

John Kent (1979) wrote a survey of the missions among the Saramaccans. He also wrote a more detailed monograph on the work of the Moravians in the Saramaccan village Botopasi. This work was based on the diaries of the missionaries in that village and personal interviews. Both works were reviewed in Part II.

Renold Pansa (1993), a Saramaccan theologian, wrote a thesis (BTh equivalent) on contextual mission among the Saramaccans. He studied the development of the Moravian missions on the upper Suriname river from 1765-1992.

Ewald Gregor (2008), a Pentecostal pastor, wrote a bachelor's thesis on one of the early Moravian converts, Christian Grego.

The American anthropologist Richard Price (1990) wrote a detailed monograph on Johannes Alabi, from different sources. His work gave detailed information about this early convert of the Moravians. Theologians may disagree with some of his conclusions, including the reasons for Alabi's conversion.

There is a need for a theological monograph about Johannes Alabi and the work of the Moravians among the Saramaccans, written preferably by a Saramaccan.

16.4.3.4.3. Kwinti

Christofel De Beet and Miriam Sterman published a diary kept by the Surinamese missionary Christiaan Kraag (1980) about his work among the Kwinti between 1894 and 1896.

16.4.3.4.4. Matawai

The Matawai prophet Johannes King wrote about his visions and missionary journeys in the second half of the nineteenth century. His works were published by various editors.

Skrekiboekoe (the book of terror) deals with his dreams and visions and the history of the Maroons (De Beet 1995).

Bekentiboekoe vo den heidenkondre (book of confessions from the heathen lands) was a more detailed work on the Maroons (De Beet 1981).

He wrote a monograph about his village *Maripaston* and his struggle with the traditional religion (De Ziel 1973). He gave details of his missionary journey to various parts of the country (Freytag 1927; Voorhoeve 1964). Zamuel's (1994) doctoral dissertation is an important monograph on the theological significance of Johannes King for his time and for the present Surinamese church. A historical novel on the life of this Surinamese missionary pioneer will be of great encouragement to Surinamese Christians.

16.4.3.4.5. Ndyuka

Except for comments in letters of missionary journeys to the Ndyukas and brief surveys in general works (e.g. Weiss 1911; Steinberg 1933; Fontaine 1985), there has not been an article or a book about the work among them.

Johan George Spalburg's diary, that was published by Hendrik Ulbo Eric Thoden van Velzen and Christofel de Beet, gave inside information of his time among these Maroons from 1896-1900 (Spalburg 1979). There is a need for a critical missiological monograph on the work of the Moravians among the Ndyukas.

16.4.3.4.6. Javanese

A brief survey of the work among the Surinamese Javanese is found in general works (e.g. Weiss 1911; Steinberg 1933; Ismael 1949; Fontaine 1985). Hermann Moritz Bielke (1926) wrote a short biography of Niti Pawiro, the first Javanese evangelist in Suriname. N M Erné (1952) wrote a brief work on the Javanese mission in Suriname. Sylvia M Gooswit (2002a, b) wrote two articles commemorating a quarter-century of missions among the Surinamese Javanese.

Jenny Wongsodikromo-Flier wrote a short overview of the boarding school *Siswa Tama* (1993). See also her theological paper (2002) and a brochure on the Javanese missions of the Moravians (2009).

There is a need for a critical missiological monograph on the work of the Moravians among the Javanese.

16.4.3.4.7. Indians

A brief survey of the work among the Indians is found in the general works of the Moravians (e.g. Weiss 1911; Steinberg 1933; Fontaine 1985; See also the critical monographs by de Klerk, 1951; 1953). Ashruf (1986) gave a brief survey of Christianity among the Surinamese Indians. Schalkwijk (2001) gave a good overview of missions among the Surinamese Indians. He wrote a doctoral dissertation on the Indians of Suriname and the Caribbean (Schalkwijk 2011). This dissertation, even though it was accepted, was not finalised before the writer passed away. It was prepared for publication by his son. It is the most detailed monograph on missions among the Indians in the Southern Caribbean (Guyana, Suriname and Trinidad) up to 1980.

The Danish missionary Magda Martinsen (2003) wrote about her work and experiences at the boarding school Sukh Dhaam in Alkmaar from 1956-1990.

16.4.4. Lutheran Church

The Lutheran Church settled in Suriname in 1741. Prior to that period, the Lutherans in the colony attended the Dutch Reformed Church.

16.4.4.1. C M Moes

Rev C M Moes (1858) published two articles in which he gave a good survey of the history of the Lutheran Church. This was the first survey on the church in Suriname.

16.4.4.2. D A Hoekstra

Rev D A Hoekstra (1941) published a brochure to commemorate the 200th anniversary of the church in Suriname. This work gave an update on Moes, but it lacked the depth of Moes.

16.4.4.3. Leo King

Rev Leo King (1986), the first Surinamese clergyman of the Lutheran Church in Suriname, wrote a brochure to commemorate the 245th anniversary of the church in Suriname. An updated version was co-authored by the Revds. L H King and T R Petzoldt (1991) to commemorate the 250th anniversary.

16.4.4.4. Hanna Hirsch

Rev Hanna Hirsch (1995) wrote a thesis on the history of the Lutheran Church in Suriname. Her focus was more on the 'people of colour' in the church.

16.4.4.5. Pearl Gerding

The Rev Pearl Gerding (2002) wrote a new thematic history of the church. Her work is the first bilingual history of the Lutheran in Suriname. It was based on the works of the previous scholars.

16.4.5. The Roman Catholic Church

16.4.5.1. Introduction

The early history of the Roman Catholic Church in Suriname can be found in the well-documented archives of the church, both in Suriname and in the Netherlands. When the church was established in Suriname at the beginning of the nineteenth century, its clergy published information about the work in the magazines *Godsdienstvriend: tijdschrift voor Roomsch-catholijken*[28] and *Catholieke Nederlandse Stemmen.*[29]

16.4.5.2. Historians

16.4.5.2.1. A C Schalken

Frater A C Schalken, better known as Tranquilinus, published two works that are indispensable for research on Catholic missions in Suriname. The first one is a collection of historical pictures (Schalken 1983). The second one he called a historical guide (Schalken 1985). It is a chronological guide to all the events that took place in the Roman Catholic Church in Suriname, including books and articles that were published between 1683 and 1983. The work is divided into four parts. The first part is a chronological list of all the events that took place within the Roman Catholic Church. The compiler wondered whether his work was complete. The second part included the names of the workers, divided into the various branches of

---

28. This magazine first appeared in 1789. According to one researcher it first appeared in 1818. The third edition of the magazine started in 1818, under the editorship of Joachim George le Sage ten Broek, a Protestant who became a Catholic. The magazine appeared earlier as De Godsdienstvriend (1789-1795) and De Vrije Godsdienstvriend (1796-1798).

The man who inspired Catholic periodical literature with life and vigour and brought it to comparative perfection was Joachim George le Sage ten Broek (died 1847), a convert from Protestantism (1806) and known in Holland as the 'Father of the Roman Catholic Press'. In 1818 he founded De Godsdienstvriend (102 vols., 1818-1869), containing articles of local interest, recent ecclesiastical intelligence, and especially moderate polemics against Protestant and liberal pretensions, by which he united the efforts of the Catholics in their struggle for emancipation. Assisted by his adopted son, Josué Witz, Le Sage displayed a great and wonderful energy, not only in his books, but also in several serials, edited by him or at least with his collaboration http://www.newadvent.org/cathen/11680a.htm (May 2011).

29. The magazine first appeared in 1835, under the editorship of Josué Witz, an adopted son of Le Sage Ten Broek.

the religious orders in the colony. Part three is called 'miscellanea' and part four is a comprehensive index. This work is an important starting point for research on the Roman Catholic Church in Suriname.

16.4.5.2.2. Adrianus Bossers

The first systematic church historian of the Roman Catholic Church in Suriname was Adrianus Bossers. He was born in 1825 and arrived in Suriname on 12 May 1867. He wrote his history *Chronica missionis Surinamensis* which was a detailed history of the Roman Catholic Church in Suriname (Bossers 1884). It was published in an abridged version in 1884 (364 pages!) under the title *Short history of the Catholic Mission in Suriname*. This work gave insights, not only to the work of the Roman Catholics in Suriname, but also to the church's relationship with the Protestants. The history is studied chronologically. The first chapter gave background information about Suriname and its population. In chapter two, it discussed the first settlement of the church in Suriname (1683-1686) and in the third chapter the second attempt (1786-1793). Chapter four studied the activities that took place between 1793 and 1817. Chapter five studied the arrival and mission of the two founding fathers of the Roman Catholic mission in Suriname. Almost a hundred pages are devoted to this chapter. Chapter six studied the church from 1825-1843, when the church was considered an *Apostolic Prefecture*. The chapter discussed the work (1) in the city and plantations, (2) Batavia, a leprosarium and (3) Coronie and Nickerie, in the western part of Suriname. Chapter seven discussed the mission as a *Provicariate Apostolic* from 1843-1852. In chapter eight, the mission was a *Vicariate Apostolic*. This chapter studied the period up to 1865, before the arrival of the *Fathers Redemptorists*. Chapter nine continued with the Vicariate Apostolic under the care of the Fathers Redemptorists (1866-1883). It is not a surprise that Bossers, himself a Redemptorist, gave lots of attention to the work of this order (about 80 pages!). He discussed the staff, their work in the city, including the schools and work among orphans, their work in the plantations and among the Natives, their work in Coronie and Batavia. He concluded this chapter with the possessions of the church. Bossers gave detailed statistical information about the church in his book. The book had a few appendices, which included among others a list of the missionaries. This work was not only ground-breaking; it also was one of the first major church historical works in Suriname.

16.4.5.2.3. Fulgentius (Richard) Abbenhuis

Richard Abbenhuis, better known as Fulgentius, was born in 1897. He came to Suriname in 1923. He died in 1982. Among his many publications[30], Abbenhuis published a number of historical works about the Catholic Church in Suriname.

In 1966, Abbenhuis published a book (1942) and an article (1956) about the church in Suriname, with lots of statistical information. A detailed history that he wrote was published in 1983 (Abbenhuis 1983). This was a reprint of articles that he wrote between 1933 and 1939.

16.4.5.2.4. Joop Vernooij

Johannes Gerardus (Joop) Vernooij was born in Houten in Utrecht in the Netherlands in 1940. He joined the Redemptorists in 1960 and was ordained as priest in 1967. Vernooij studied missiology at the Catholic University of Nijmegen in the Netherlands. He worked as a priest in the diocese of Paramaribo, Suriname from 1969-2001. After he returned to the Netherlands he lectured missiology at the Radboud University of Nijmegen (2001-2005), and served as a parish priest in the same town (2001-2011).

16.4.5.2.4.1. Introduction

Much more than all his predecessors, Dr Joop Vernooij published not only about the history of the church, but about many aspects of the Roman Catholic mission in Suriname. This section will include a more detailed summary of some of his works. It will be impossible to do justice to all his works in this introduction. A doctoral dissertation on the ministry and theology of Dr Vernooij is a better option. A theology student should take up that challenge.

16.4.5.2.4.2. History of the Catholic Church in Suriname

His first major historical work was his doctoral dissertation on the Roman Catholic Church in Suriname from 1866, with the arrival of the

---

30. These include his historical overview (*Historisch overzicht* 1941), geographical overview (*Geografisch overzicht* 1941) and stories and sketches from the history of Suriname (*Verhalen en schetsen uit de Surinaamse geschiedenis* 1943-1946).

Redemptorists, up to 1974 (Vernooij 1985c). This is a thematic study of the Roman Catholic Church in Suriname. He published an update in 1985 that dealt with the church between 1975 and 1985 (Vernooij 1985d).

In 1998 Vernooij published a new handbook on the Roman Catholic Church in Suriname (Vernooij 1998d). This is a thematic study of five periods within the history of the Catholic Church in Suriname. The periods are: I. A modest beginning (1683-1825); II. Confrontation and Consolidation (1825-1945). This period is divided into two parts (the New Beginning 1825-1866 and after the arrival of the Redemptorists 1866-1945); III. Transformation (1945-1975); IV. A New Agenda (1975-present); V. Summary. The work includes a number of appendices. The themes for each part are selected inductively, based on events that took place within that particular period of time. Besides these historical works he published widely on issues related to Christianity and religion in Suriname. There is probably no area in the history of Christianity in Suriname in which he did not contribute a book or an article.

16.4.5.2.4.3. Natives

Vernooij published a few books and articles about the Natives (1989b; 1991a; 1991b; 1992a; 1992b; 1993b; 1994b).

I will give a brief overview of the first work, which was a detailed monograph (Vernooij 1989b). After a short introduction, the first chapter discussed various aspects of the Natives in Suriname. Up to now there has not been a thorough study of the Natives in Suriname. Resources that are available need to be studied. These resources include archaeological material, earthenware objects and art, maps and books. Suriname was successfully colonised by Lord Willoughby. In 1667 it was taken over by the Dutch. The early period saw a guerrilla war fought by the Natives against the Dutch. The early European descriptions about the Natives gave a wrong view about them. A brief survey discussed the relations between Christianity and the Native organisations among the various Native groups and with the government. The chapter concluded with statistical data on the population.

The second chapter studied the Moravian Church. It discussed the beginning and the progress of the Moravian missions among the Natives.

Attention is also given to the missionary methods used. The Moravian mission among the Natives was not successful.

Chapter three studied the work of the Roman Catholic Church. The initial contacts between the Roman Catholic Church and the Natives were sporadic. The first person who started to visit the Natives in a systematic way was Petrus Donders. Other priests followed in the footsteps of Donders. C van Coll studied the culture and language of the Natives. He published catechisms in the Arawak and the Carib languages. The need was felt to have clergymen living among the people and working with them, since it was very difficult for the priests to make weekly visits to all the villages. In 1874, a schoolmaster served in Tibiti. According to Donders, what he did in seven to eight months was more successful than what the clergymen did in the previous three years since many more children and adults were baptised.

Father Mols suggested that the mission should consider the 'reduction' system, in which the Natives would live in one place. This, however, never got started as was planned.

The church built schools among the Natives and provided education. Social work was done by the foundation PAS. Local workers, catechists, became responsible for the church in their own village. The so-called 'waka-kerki' (walking church), with a priest visiting the village from time to time, did not function well. The catechists were to serve their own community on a permanent basis.

Chapter four studied the work among the Natives in the southern part of the country. Work among these Natives was done by the 'Door to Life' and the 'West Indian Mission'. They targeted the Wayana and Trio. Besides church planting, the organisations were involved in medical and school work. In later years, the two organisations joined the local Baptist Church. They started the *Unie van Baptisten Gemeenten* (Union of Baptist Churches).

Chapter five, discussed issues related to 500 years of contact between the Natives and people from outside the continent.

16.4.5.2.4.4. Maroons

In 1996, Vernooij (1996d) published a monograph on the Maroons and the Roman Catholic Church. The subtitle of the work, 'From confrontation to dialogue' showed the church's changing approach to missions among the Maroons.

Chapter 1 gave a description of the research method and the sources for the research. The sources included archive materials, missionary periodicals and interviews. The work is divided into three parts. The first part studied the relationship up to the period after World War II. The second part started around 1948 and continued up to Vatican II. The third phase is the modern period.

Chapter 2 conceptualised research on the Roman Catholic Church and the Maroons in the Surinamese context. The Maroons included all the different groups that ran away from slavery.

Chapter 3 discussed the era of confrontation. It started with a description of the beginning of work among the Maroons. In 1871, the Roman Catholic priest, Petrus Donders, mentioned the desire expressed by a Ndyuka to have a priest in his village. But this was not the way the Roman Catholics worked in Suriname. In 1895, however, a station was built at Albina from where Father F Lemmens visited some Ndyuka villages. In 1898, the Ndyuka paramount Chief Oseyse visited the mission station at Albina. According to Vernooij this visit sanctioned the presence of the Roman Catholics in the Ndyuka area. Father L Luykx, who stayed two months in Albina, followed Lemmens in 1906. Luykx introduced what he called 'an apologetic approach' to the missions; the priests should not baptise the Ndyukas too quickly but should talk to them and ensure they give evidence for the Christian faith. Many of his colleagues disagreed with him. He also introduced what he called a 'Constantine method', in which the priests had to befriend the village leaders and paramount chief. Luykx also emphasised that the missionaries had to keep the fact in mind that the Ndyukas did not trust White people, because of the history of violence done to them by the White folk.

This is followed by the work at the station in Tamarin. A new approach in the work among the Ndyukas was the experiment of Father Wortelboer with what is called 'a reduction'. Tamarin, a former centre of idolatry, was chosen for this experiment. In 1915, a school and a boarding school started there, with a teacher and boarding school superintendent living there. In 1917, a church building was erected. In 1923, Wortelboer moved to

Tamarin. This approach, according to him, was much better. The Ndyukas, who responded to the message of the church, were isolated from the others. They could live together in one village. Wortelboer felt that more of such 'reductions' had to be built. Tamarin was not only a place for a church, school and boarding school but also a sawmill. The experiment with the reduction system was not followed up at other places.

The chapter continued with the work of Morssink and Afaka. In 1910, Father F Morssink went to Albina to work among the Ndyukas. He worked there until 1934. He visited the Saramaccans and other Bush Negro groups as well. During his work among the Ndyukas, he met with Afaka who had developed a syllable script of 56 signs, by which he could write the Ndyuka language. In the Afakascript Morssink saw a tool to reach out to the Ndyukas. With the help of Afaka and his brother Abena, a catechism was translated into Ndyuka in Afakascript. Morssink developed literacy materials and developed a good relationship with the people by writing in the script for them. But Afaka died within a year after he met Morssink in 1917. This script was not used further in the missions and remained the work of linguistic investigators. Another experiment at Lisieux, under the inspiration of Awensi, was also not successful.

> Afaka and Awensi were excellent introductions to the Gospel into the Ndyuka society. Their actions were a part of the process of conversion or transformation of the Ndyuka society. Both experiments were short and they could not gain the recognition of the upper class, the power-makers, the preservers of the heritage (p. 170).

The work continued with an overview of the work at Upper Suriname. In 1907, two Roman Catholic priests, F Bazelmans and L B Luykx, accompanied by a Saramaccan captain Dirifowru, made a visit to the upper Suriname River. The purpose of this visit was to get to know the area and the Saramaccans. After some visits, Father F P Morssink suggested that the Roman Catholic Missions should set up a mission station in that area where they could build a school and a church. The school was built in 1919 at *Sonté*, near *Kabelstation*, followed by the church in 1921. The school building burned down in 1922, and the school was closed. The challenge came in 1925 when a delegation from Gran Rio, upper Suriname River, came to the capital city requesting priests to come to build a school in their area. In 1927, Morssink made his first trip to the *Gran Rio*. There were no Moravian missionaries, so Morssink accepted the challenge to build a mission station there, which he called *Ligorio*. In that same year, a school was also started there.

The chapter ended with a review of the work among the Paramaccans at *Langatabiki*. The paramount chief was a Moravian. But the Roman Catholics went and settled there as well. 'The evangelisation of the Paramaccans was an example of rivalry between the Moravians and the Roman Catholics' (p. 73).

Chapter 4 discussed the era of changes. It started with the period of accommodation.

> Mission and missionaries had to tune more and more to the culture of the people ... the theory of accommodation broke away from the idea that everything from non-Christian religions was idolatrous (p. 78).

Accommodation had boundaries: 1) the untouchability of faith and customs, 2) the unity of the church and 3) the salvation of the soul. This new approach also included mission stations. The first project was in Nason. The second was in Lombe. The mission started with a school there in 1935. In 1957 Father N Spruyt moved to that area but drowned there in the same year. Father Piet van der Pluym and some sisters of Tilburg who gave attention to the school and medical work, followed him. Van der Pluym also drowned in 1961. Due to the lake that was built in that area the station had to be moved to a place closer to the city, also called *Lombe*. In the new era, the catechists played a more prominent role (see chapter 5).

Chapter 5 is identified as the era of renewal. The church developed a new vision after the current way of being church was evaluated. An organisation was founded to:

> Promote the spiritual, intellectual, physical, social and cultural development of the people living in the interior with the help of modern and suitable means of transportation (p. 104).

The new developments called for a renewed discussion about the theology of the clerical office. The following comments were made:

> Without the requirements for celibacy [teachers and catechists] should be allowed to be ordained as priests to serve in all the tasks of the ministry (p. 106).

In the 1940's the idea came to train local people to serve as catechists. But the first training that started in 1946 was not successful. Within half a year, the training had to be stopped due to the lack of interest by the people. In those days, teachers who were trained to serve in the *Bosland*, also served as catechists in their villages. In the 1970's the training of catechists became more successful. It was no longer necessary for the teacher to serve as catechist (p. 116). The church among the Maroons suffered a serious setback during the civil war that took place in the country.

In a summary given in English Dr Vernooij said the following.

> Both churches [Moravian and Roman Catholic – FSJ] despised the culture of the people. The churches came in with substitutions for the most important religious acts and ideas... The people had to live in two cultural sets with a lot of contradictions. The substitution was so deep that till now a lot of people of the interior are despising their own culture and heritage (p. 177).

According to Vernooij the second phase was one of changing the approach. Missionaries listened to the cultures and gave more room to expressions from the culture. According to Vernooij, there is more room within the Roman Catholic Church for special meetings in which the church members can use their own music. There is also an attitude of patience around certain practices such as polygamy and sexual relations without marriage.

16.4.5.3. Other works

A few works were written on the life and work of Father Donders. He worked for many years among the lepers (Dankelman 1982; Groves 1946). Different orders of priests, lay brothers and sisters worked in Suriname. Works were published to commemorate their anniversaries.

Various Catholic missionaries contributed to a commemorative work about half a century of work of the Redemptorists in Suriname (*Halve eeuw*). Abbenhuis published a centennial commemorative work, with statistics and tables about the Redemptorists in Suriname (1966). Another work celebrating their centennial mission work was edited by C F G Getrouw, A J Morpurgo and A Sampers (1966).

16.4.6. Baptist Churches

16.4.6.1. The Vrije Evangelisatie

The Baptist Church started in Suriname in the 1880's. It was the first church started by a Surinamese. A few works were published about the church. However, they were limited to the beginning of the twentieth century. The first survey of the church was written by Bartel de Jong (1911), the first headmaster of the school started by the church. His book covered the first twenty-three years. J M Blufpand (1928) wrote a biography of Meyer Salomon Bromet, the founder of the church. In 1988 Carlo Schuster published a brief overview of the first century of the church, with much attention to the early years. Anderson (1990) has a brief section on the work of the Baptists in Suriname. He referred to the 'small Baptist work' (*pequeña obra bautista*) that started under the leadership of Bromet. Most of his one-page reference focused on the work of the Southern Baptists.

The Baptist Church experienced a split within a few years after its inception. The new group, *Surinaamse Baptisten Kerk*, was founded by Carel Paulus Rier. The Rev N C J Neus (1924) published a biography of Rier. Rier was the first black independent minister. He published a few works. An academic monograph on his life, ministry and theology is outstanding. One key issue that requires further research is his understanding of the emancipation of people of the Black race.

16.4.6.2. Worldteam

In the second half of the twentieth century, other Baptist churches were established in Suriname. Judy Neff (nd) and Alice Nichols (1979) wrote missionary stories about the work of Worldteam in Suriname. However, nothing is written about the period after the 1980's. The civil war in Suriname that took place from 1986-1992 had an impact on the work of Worldteam. Worldteam and *Vrije Evangelisatie* joined together in forming the *Unie van Baptisten in Suriname*.

16.4.6.3. Southern Baptists

The Southern Baptists published a brief survey of their work in the Caribbean and the northern part of South America (*Zendingswerk*). The survey has a brief section on Suriname. Missionaries from Trinidad were transferred to Suriname in March 1971. After they completed their language studies, they started the Southern Baptist Church in Suriname. Anderson (1990) has a brief section on the work of the Southern Baptists in Suriname as well.

16.4.6.4. Conclusion

Other Baptists churches are operating in Suriname, such as the *Bijbel Baptist Kerk*. As far as I could see, there is no book published on their history, theology or ministry.

There is need for a monograph that studies the entire history of Baptists in Suriname.

16.4.7. Pentecostal Churches

The Pentecostal Movement in Suriname started in 1959 with the arrival of an Assemblies of God missionary. Pentecostalism in Suriname can be divided into four main streams: 1) The Assemblies of God, 2) Stromen van Kracht (1961), 3) Evangelisch Centrum Suriname (1969) and 4) Independent churches. Many churches came out of the three main streams. Most came out of the Stromen van Kracht.

The history of Pentecostalism in Suriname has not yet been documented. Publications that have appeared so far are devotional in nature.

16.4.7.1. The Pinksterzending

The first work was published by the *Pinksterzending* 'Pentecostal Mission'. Pinksterzending is a breakaway group from the Assemblies of God (Uyleman and Uyleman 1990). The book was published to celebrate the 25th anniversary of the *Pinkster Zending Suriname*.

16.4.7.2. The Stromen van Kracht

In 1991 leaders of the *Stromen van Kracht* wrote the second book to commemorate the 30th anniversary of Stromen van Kracht in Suriname (Manbodh et al 1991). Stromen van Kracht was the second Pentecostal movement in Suriname. It started after a series of crusades that were held by the Dutch evangelist Karel Hoekendijk. A book was published with testimonies of what happened in the three Guyanas during these crusades (Hoekendijk 1962).

16.4.7.3. Gods Bazuin

Pudsey Meye (1997) wrote an autobiography in which he describes the story of the church that he founded, called Gods Bazuin. Meye was one of the leaders of the second Pentecostal movement in Suriname, Stromen van Kracht. He left the Stromen van Kracht movement and started a new ministry (Jabini 2007).

16.4.7.4. Works about Pentecostalism

There are two articles written on Surinamese Pentecostalism by outsiders to the movement.

Harold Jap A Joe wrote an article on 'Afro-Surinamese renaissance and the rise of Pentecostalism' (2005). In that article, written from a sociological perspective, he argued:

> [Pentecostalism] offered a Christianity which accepted the spirit world as 'biblical reality' and could therefore reduce the tension between 'prescribed order' and 'living practice' (p. 147).

Yvon van der Pijl (2010) wrote along the same lines in her 'Pentecostal-Charismatic Christianity: African-Surinamese Perceptions and Experiences'. She argued:

> To wind up, P/C movements, the individualized New Age movement and the community-based esoteric brother- and sisterhoods have in common that they make up arenas in which existing notions, beliefs, traditions and practices that are assumed exclusive to Winti or African-Surinamese cults, regain significance and are translated or reinterpreted time and again (p. 194).

16.4.7.5. Pentecostal writers

Pastor Frank Nahar, pastor of the *Kroon Des Levens* (Crown of Life), must be considered as the most prolific writer among the Pentecostals in Suriname. Franklin Sahied Nahar was born in 1962. He studied art at the *Academie voor Kunst en Cultuur* in Paramaribo. He is a pastor, leading a church within Gods Bazuin Ministries. Nahar became the director of the training programme of Gods Bazuin Ministries in 2000. He published a few books on the Christian life, with an emphasis on prayer and intercession (see the bibliography). A study of his works will reveal contemporary thinking on these topics from a Surinamese Pentecostal perspective.

Lilian Pickering Neede wrote a book on Proverbs 31 (Pickering Neede 2009). It is the first of its kind among Surinamese Christians. The book was published in English. She also maintains a website that includes histories and biographies of key figures in the Pentecostal movement in Suriname.[31]

16.4.7.6. Conclusion

The Pentecostal movement in Suriname is growing. It consists of various branches. Most of them were not included in this list (e.g. *Evangelisch Centrum Suriname, Bribi Ministry, Gemeenten Gods*).[32] To my knowledge,

---

31. See http://www.suriChurch.net/.
32. See the conversion story of Bally Brashuis (1984). There is also a DVD available that presents the conversion of this former Winti priest entitled: *Bally en Irene Brashuis, ex Winti priester: Ik speel niet meer.*

no major work was published about them.[33] There is a need for a major monograph on the work of the Pentecostals in Suriname, written from an insider perspective, preferably by a Pentecostal theologian.

16.4.8. Other Churches

16.4.8.1. Seventh Day Adventists

The first attempt of the Seventh Day Adventists Church to start a work in Suriname was in the 1890's.

> There was a company of SDA adherents at Nickerie in northwestern Surinam [sic] as early as 1894 (Surinam 1976).

In later years, the church started its mission in the capital city. There are no major monographs on the work of the mission in Suriname. There is a small, popular booklet (Durven) and a short article which appeared in the *Seventh-day Adventist Encyclopedia* (Surinam 1976). An unpublished manuscript provided much information for further research (*De Geschiedenis*). It discussed the birth of Adventism in Suriname and the ministry of a colporteur that led to the growth of the church. There are short reports on the church from 1946 and 1966 and the expansion to other districts.

16.4.8.2. Plymouth Brethren

The first Brethren Assembly started in Suriname in the first decade of the twentieth century. It consisted of a few believers who broke away from a small Baptist congregation. The first assembly did not last long. A second attempt which took place in 1983 was more successful. I wrote a missionary history of the Brethren churches in Suriname, to be published shortly.

---

33. Jan Kool [forthcoming] wrote an autobiography, which included references to his work in *Evangelisch Centrum Suriname*.

16.4.8.3. Methodism

The African Methodist Episcopal Church (AMEC) started in Suriname in 1912. The church's target audience were English-speakers. There are no publications about this denomination in Suriname.

16.4.8.4. Salvation Army

A Surinamese, who studied in the Netherlands, started the ministry of the Salvation Army in Suriname in 1924. Salvation Army (*Leger des Heils*) published two brochures about their work in Suriname. The first was to celebrate its 65th anniversary (Suriname and French Guyana Region) and the second its 75th (Leger des Heils).

16.4.8.5. Wesleyan Church

The Church of the Pilgrim Holiness held its first church service in Suriname on 23 December 1945 in Suriname. Earlier activities took place in *Nickerie* under the name of the Pilgrim Holiness Church of Guyana. In 1950, the work expanded to the eastern part of the country, where a mission station was established, *Pilgrimkondre*.

There is no systematic study about the Wesleyan Church in Suriname. There is a short outline and a brief overview available (*Ingibe nd; Programma ter gelegenheid*).

16.4.8.6. Christian and Missionary Alliance

The Christian and Missionary Alliance (CMA) started in Suriname in 1979. Its main area of focus was the Chinese community in Suriname. Currently, the church is involved with missions among other ethnic groups as well. The church published a brief survey to commemorate their fifth anniversary in Suriname (*Stichting Christelijke*). The Rev Johannes Martoredjo (1994) wrote an update about this work. In 2004, I published an article about the CMA celebrating its 25th anniversary (Jabini 2004b).

16.5. New generation of theologians

The Pentecostal churches in Suriname designed several training programmes. The programmes had a practical orientation and not an academic focus. The Hebron Zendelingen School, a three-year residential programme, was the primary training institution. Its goal was to establish churches in every village in Suriname.

The 1990's saw the emergence of two interdenominational theological institutions. The Apollos Training Institute (ATI) offered an intensive pre-tertiary programme with some of the modules being taught at undergraduate level. The Caribbean College of the Bible International (CCBI) offered undergraduate and graduate distance education, with regular contact sessions. Various leaders enrolled for one of these training programmes or did both. Others completed degrees locally or at an institution overseas.

Carl Breeveld studied theology at the Bijbelsinstituut België in Leuven, Belgium. He wrote his bachelor's thesis on the World Council of Churches (Breeveld 1984).

Johannes Martoredjo did his theological study in the Netherlands, at the Evangelische Bijbel Scholen (EBS). In 1993, he completed a diploma in theology. He received his baccalaureate in theology in 1997 (Martoredjo 1997). He completed his master's degree in the field of Biblical studies, based on an empirical research on the views of Surinamese church leaders on receiving gifts from non-believers (Martoredjo 2005).

A group studied at CCBI after they completed their ATI diploma. Robby Aloewel (2001) studied salvation history and traced the person and work of Jesus in the Old and New Testaments. Pastor Ewald Gregor wrote a bachelor's thesis on a Moravian leader of the eighteenth century (Gregor 2008). In 2011, he wrote a master of theology thesis on the role of elders and deacons in the Full Gospel Church (Gregor 2010). Lydia Jannasch-Werners (2001) studied the word of God as a means of grace. Dennis Redmount (2001) wrote an introduction to systematic theology for a Pentecostal Bible school. Joyce Veira (2001) wrote on being single.

A few students studied in the Netherlands after they completed their ATI diploma. Jair Schalkwijk (Schalkwijk 2011) did an explorative study on the spiritual life of the members of a Free Baptist Church in the Netherlands. He wrote a master's thesis on martyrs in early Christianity (Schalkwijk 2012). Reginald Cairo (Cairo 2011) studied Surinamese leadership from a biblical-theological perspective. He raised questions with regards to the development, function and motives of political leadership in Suriname.

Malty Dwarkasing who studied economics at the University of Suriname wrote a bachelor's thesis at CCBI on poverty alleviation (Dwarkasing 2007). In 2011, she completed her master of theology thesis on outreach to Muslim Arab-Palestinians in Palestine (Dwarkasing 2011).

MAPS

Map 1 *Western part of Suriname and Berbice*

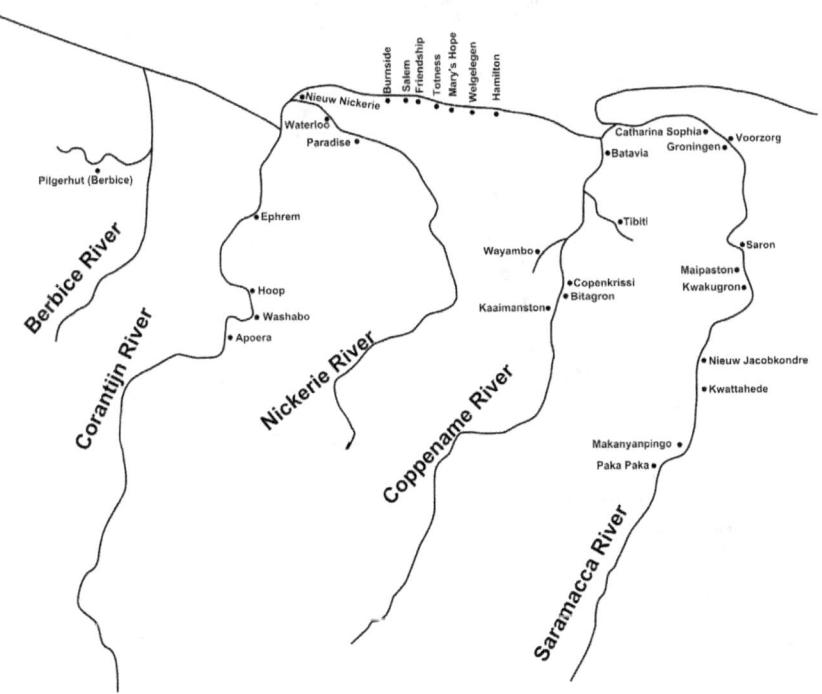

Map not drawn to scale

Map 2 *Eastern part of Suriname*

Map not drawn to scale

Map 3 *Location of Suriname in South America*

Map not drawn to scale

PHOTOS

Picture 1
Interdenominational church service

Picture 2
Interdenominational church service (courtesy U Schalkwijk)

Picture 3
Students of the Evangelical School of Theology with visiting professor

Picture 4
Children's church outing

Picture 5
Interdenominational Saramaccan church service

Picture 6 *Interdenominational celebration of Easter*

Picture 7 *Interdenominational Evangelistic crusade*

Picture 8 *Church and government leaders at the inauguration of a church building*

Picture 9 *Pentecostal Church building (courtesy of S. Djojoseparto)*

Picture 10 *Pentecostal Church building*

Picture 11 *Church outing Christian and Missionary Alliance*

Picture 12 *Church building in Coronie*

Picture 13 *Children's club among Natives in Bigi Poika (courtesy of A. Van Kampen-Elbers)*

Picture 14 *Christian men visiting the interior (courtesy C Breeveld)*

Picture 15 *Javanese traditional dance during evangelistic service (courtesy D Martoredjo)*

Picture 16 *Day of prayer with President DD Bouterse (courtesy Bishop S Meye)*

Picture 17 *Newly baptised Indian Christians (courtesy U Schalkwijk)*

Picture 18 *Ndyuka traditional Gospel Music (courtesy M Dijo)*

Picture 19 *Young men praying (courtesy. C Breeveld)*

Picture 20 *Vacation Bible School (courtesy D Martoredjo)*

Picture 21 *Interdenominational Indian church service (courtesy Mrs U Schalkwijk)*

Picture 22 *Boarding school Stoelmanseiland*

Picture 23 *Moravian theology graduate receives his certificate*

Picture 24 *Men at an interdenominational church service*

Picture 25 *Author's family with visiting Dutch professor Van Bruggen and wife*

Picture 26 *Former President Drs R R Venetiaan with church leaders at a national interdenominational leader's conference*

Picture 27 *Small group discussions at a national and interdenominational leader's conference*

BIBLIOGRAPHY

Note: Particles such as 'de', 'van', 'van der' before Dutch surnames, e.g. 'JM van der Linde' are written after the surname and initial in the bibliography, 'Linde JM van der'.

Abbenhuis MFR 1939. *Arawakken in Suriname*. Enquête-materiaal voor een volkenkundige studie. Paramaribo: Leo Victor.
────── 1942. *De geschiedenis van het Apostolisch Vicariaat*. Paramaribo: Drukkerij Eben Haëzer.
────── 1956. 'De Katholieke Kerk in Suriname'. *Vox Guyanae*. Volume II Number 3. Paramaribo: Radhakishun & Co N.V.
────── 1966. *Honderd jaar missiewerk in Suriname door de Redemptoristen, 1866-1966*. Paramaribo: np.
────── 1983. *Een paapjen omtrent het Fort*. Paramaribo: Uitgeversmaatschappij Vaco.
Adis H 1664. *A letter sent from Syrranam, to His Excellency, the Lord Willoughby of Parham, General of the Western Islands, and of the continent of Guianah, &c. then residing at the Barbados together, with the Lord Willoughby's answer thereunto: with a commendable description of that country*. London: np
Albitrouw I 1978. *Tori foe da bigin foe Anake en moro fara* (Original 1915). Verslag van een messianistische beweging bewerkt door Miriam Sterman. BSB 2. Utrecht: Universiteit van Utrecht.
────── 1979. *Zendingsarbeid in Aurora onder de Saramaka Bosnegers van 1891 tot 1896* (Original 1892-1895). Bewerkt door Miriam Sterman BSB 3. Utrecht: Universiteit van Utrecht.
Albrinck W 1931. *Encyclopaedie der Karaïben, behelzend taal, zeden en gewoonten dezer Indianen*. Amsterdam: Verhandelingen der Koninklijke Akademie van Wetenschappen.
Aloewel R 2001. *Heilshistorie: Jezus Christus zowel in het Oude als in het Nieuwe Testament*. Een scriptie aangeboden aan het Caribbean College of the Bible

ter verkrijging van de titel van Bachelor of Biblical Studies. Paramaribo: Caribbean College of the Bible.

Anderson GH 1999. *Biographical dictionary of Christian missions*. Grand Rapids: Wm B Eerdmans Publishing.

Anderson JM 1848. *The history of the Church of England in the colonies and foreign dependencies of the British Empire*. Volume 2. Second Edition. London: Francis & John Rivingtons and Robert Folthorp.

Anderson J 1990. *Historia de los Bautistas*. Tomo III. Sus comienzos y Desarrollo en Asia, África y América Latina. El Paso Texas: Casa Bautista de Publicaciones.

Arends J and Perl M 1995. *Early Suriname Creole Texts*. A Collection of eighteenth century Sranan and Saramaccan Documents. Frankfurt: Vervuert Verlag.

Ashruf GJ 1986. 'Het Christendom en de Hindostanen in Suriname' *Oso*. Tijdschrift voor Surinaamse Taalkunde, Letterkunde en Geschiedenis. Jaargang 13. Nummer 1. Nijmegen: Stichting IBS.

Bakker E, Dalhuisen L, Donk R, Hassankhan M, Steegh F, and Egger J 1998. *Geschiedenis van Suriname. Van stam tot staat*. Zutphen: Uitgeversmaatschappij Walburg Press.

Beet C de (editor) 1995. Skrekiboekoe - Boek der Verschrikkingen: Visioenen en historische overleveringen van Johannes King. BSA 17. Utrecht.

────── 1981. Johannes Kings Berichten uit het bosland. Bronnen voor de Studie van Bosneger Samenlevingen, deel 7. Utrecht: Rijksuniversiteit Utrecht, Instituut voor Culturele Antropologie.

────── and Sterman M 1981. *People in Between*. The Matawai Maroons of Suriname. Meppel: Krips Repro.

Behn A 1688. *Oroonoko*. First published by William Canning in 1688. London: Penguin Group, reprint 2003.

Benjamin JP 1991. 'The Arawak Language in Guyana and adjacent territories'. *Archaeology and anthropology. Journal of the Walter Roth Museum of Anthropology*. Volume 8. Georgetown: Walter Roth Museum.

Berg WEJ 1845. *De Réfugiés in de Nederlanden, na de herroeping van het edict van Nantes*. Een proeve van onderzoek naar de invloed, welke hunne overkomst gehad heeft op Handel en Nijverheid, Letteren, Beschaving en Zeden. Eerste Deel. Amsterdam: Johannes Müller.

Berggraaf RE 1968. *Vo Singi A de Switi* (Het is heerlijk om te zingen). Een kritische beschouwing over het Singi-boekoe en het lied van Herrnhut in Suriname. Licentiaat Thesis. Brussel: Protestantse Theologische Faculteit.

Berichten van de zendingen der Evangelische Broedergemeente onder Heidenen. Zeist: Societeit der Broeders tot uitbreiding van het Evangelie.

Bielke HM 1926. *Niti Pawiro. De eerste Javaansche Evangelist in Suriname.* Zeist: Zendingsgenootschap der Evangelische broedergemeente.

Bijlsma R 1930. 'De brieven van gouverneur Cornelis van Aerssen van Sommelsdijck aan directeuren der Societeit van Suriname uit het jaar 1684'. *Nieuwe West-Indische Gids.* Volume 11. Nummer 1.

Blufpand JM 1928. *Vier Decenniums.* Biografie van Meyer Salomon Bromet. Uitgegeven ten bate van de Gemeente van Gedoopte Christenen (Baptisten). Paramaribo: De Nieuwe Moderne Stoomdrukkerij.

Boer S 2001. *De Agape-beweging onder de loep.* Een scriptie aangeboden aan het Caribbean College of the Bible ter verkrijging van de titel van Bachelor in biblical studies. Paramaribo: Caribbean College of the Bible.

Bosch D 1984. 'Missionary Theology in Africa'. *Indian Missiological Review* 6, no. 2 (April 1984; reprinted in *Journal of Theology for Southern Africa* 49 (December 1984).

––––––– 1991. *Transforming Mission.* Paradigm Shifts in Theology of Mission. New York: Maryknoll.

Bossers A 1884. *Beknopte Geschiedenis der Katholieke Missie in Suriname* door een Pater Redemptorist. Uitgegeven ten voordele der missie en meer bepaald der R.K. Weeshuizen aldaar. Gulpen: Boekdrukkerij van M. Alberts.

Bowdon J 1850. *The history of the Society of Friends in America.* Volume 1. London: Charles Gilpin.

Brashuis B 1984. *Ik speel niet meer mee.* Paramaribo: np.

Breen LA 2001. *Transgressing the Bounds.* Subversive Enterprises among the Puritan Elite in Massachusetts, 1630–1692. Oxford: University Press.

Breeveld C 1984. *Wereldraad van Kerken: onderzoek naar de politieke koers.* Leuven: Bijbelinstituut België.

Bruijne A de 2006. *Libanezen in Suriname: van Bcharre naar Paramaribo, 1890-2006.* Leiden: KITLV.

Bruining CFA and Voorhoeve J (editors) 1977. *Encyclopedie van Suriname.* Amsterdam: Elsevier.

Bubberman F 1974. 'De Labadisten in Suriname'. *Suralco Magazine.* December 1974. Volume 3/4.

Buddingh H 2000. *Geschiedenis van Suriname*. Een volledig overzicht van de oorspronkelijke, Indiaanse bewoners en de ontdekking door Europese kolonisten, tot de opkomst van de drugsbaronnen. 3^e druk. Utrecht: Het Spectrum.

Buiskool H 1914-1917. 'Hervormde gemeente' in HD Benjamins en JF Snelleman red., *Encyclopaedie van Nederlandsch West-Indië*. Den Haag/ Leiden: Martinus Nijhoff/E.J. Brill.

Byam W 1665. *An exact relation of the most execrable attempts of John Allin committed on the person of His Excellency Francis Lord Willoughby of Parham, Captain General of the continent of Guiana and of all the Caribby-Islands, and our Lord Proprietor*. London : Printed for Richard Lowrdes.

Cairo R 2011. *Het Surinaams Leiderschap in Bijbels, Theologisch perspectief. Een onderzoek naar het ontwikkelen, functioneren en de motieven van het politiek leiderschap in Suriname*. Ede: Christelijke Hogeschool Ede.

Calamy E 1802. *The Nonconformist's memorial; being an account of the lives, sufferings, and printed works, of the two thousand ministers ejected from the Church of England, chiefly by the Act of Uniformity, Aug. 24, 1666*. London: Button and Son.

Carroll KL 1973. 'Early Quakers in Surinam (1658-1659)'. *Quaker History. Vol. 62 Autumn, 1973. No 2*. Baltimore: Friends Historical Association.

Choennie K 1984. *The practice of polygyny among the Saramaka Bush Negroes in Suriname*. An ethical Appraisal. Bachelor thesis University of the West Indies. St. Augustine: University of the West Indies.

────── 1997. Een pastoraaltheologische herwaardering van het Caribisch familiesysteem bij de volkscreolen in Paramaribo. Verhandeling tot verkrijging van de graad van Licentiaat in de Godgeleerdheid, Faculty of Theology. Leuven: Katholieke Universiteit Leuven.

Coll C van 1887. *Sanimee Karetaale Kalienja Kapoewà itooriko-mé*. Gulpen: M Alberts.

Coll C van 1892. *Fidei Catholica Rudimenti Arowaccana lingua exarata*. Paramaribo: J Timmerman.

────── 1886. *Zeden en gewoonten der Indianen in onze Westindische kolonie Suriname*. Gulpen: Alberts & Zonen.

Comvalius TAC 1921. *Ter nagedachtenis van Cornelis Winst Blijd*. Paramaribo: H B Heyde.

Courtz H 2008. *A Carib grammar and dictionary*. Leiden: Universiteit van Leiden.

Dankelman JLF 1982. *Peerke Donders. Schering en Inslag van zijn leven.* Hilversum: Gooi en Sticht.

Darnoud TA 1971. *Afrikaanse mensen en machten.* Een overzicht en een beoordeling van de ontmoeting Afrikaanse religie en Christelijk geloof. Skriptie Missiologie. Utrecht/Zeist.

Dayfoot A and Pierson R (eds) 2004. *Bibliography of West Indian Church History.* A list of printed materials relating to the history of the churches in the English-speaking Caribbean (and Bermuda) with annotations and notes on locations. Introduction by Rev Canon Noel Titus. London: Hansib Publications Limited.

De Geschiedenis en het verloop van het Adventisme in Suriname. Np/Nd.

De Vestiging van de Nederlandsche Kolonisten in Suriname herdacht: 1845-20 juni-1920. 1921. Uitgegeven door de groep 'Suriname' van het Algemeen Nederlandsch verbond.

Deiros PA 2000. 'Suriname'. In A Scott Moreau, General editor. *Evangelical Dictionary of World Missions.* Grand Rapids: Baker Books.

Dissel S van 1877. *Eenige bijzonderheden betreffende de Christelijke Hervormde Gemeente te Paramaribo.* 'S Gravenhage: JK De Liefde.

Donicie A and Voorhoeve J 1963. *De Saramakaanse woordenschat.* Amsterdam: Bureau voor Taalonderzoek in Suriname van de Universiteit van Amsterdam.

Doth REC editor 1965. *Kondre sa jere.* 200 jaar zending onder de bosnegers in Suriname. Zeist: Seminarie der Evangelische Broedergemeente.

Duke BE 2000. *A History of the Anglican Church in Guyana.* Know your Diocese. Georgetown: Red Thread Women's Press.

Durven Dromen ... durven doen. Nd/np.

Dwarkasing M 2007. *Poverty alleviation within missionary programs: The case of the Boven-Suriname River area in Suriname.* Port of Spain: Caribbean College of the Bible International.

———— 2011. *Reaching Muslim Arab-Palestinians in Palestine: An Exploration.* Johannesburg: South Africa Theological Seminary.

Erne NM 1952. *Zending onder de Javanen in Suriname (Post Combé).* Paramaribo: np.

Esajas L 2001. *Bikasi ibriwan jeri dem taki hem kondre tongo.* De functie van taal in de missionering van Surinaamse Creoolse Vrouwen in de Evangelische Broeder Gemeente Suriname. Doctoraal Scriptie religie studies ter voltooiïng van de studie aan de faculteit der theologie. Nijmegen: Katholieke Universiteit Nijmegen.

Evans W and Evans TH editors. 1854. *Piety Promoted in a collection of dying sayings of many of the people called Quakers: with a brief account of some of their labours in the Gospel, and sufferings for the same*. A new and complete edition. Comprising the eleven parts heretofore separately published. Philiadelphia: Friends' Book Store.

Fermin Ph 1770. *Nieuwe algemeene beschryving van de colonie van Suriname. Behelzende al het merkwaardige van dezelve, met betrekkinge tot de historie, aardryks- en natuurkunde*. Harlingen: V van der Plaats junior.

Fontaine J 1985 compiler. *Onderweg. Van afhankelijkheid naar zelfstandigheid*. 250 jaren Hernhutterzending in Suriname 1735-1985. Paramaribo: Evangelische Broedergemeente in Suriname.

Freston P 2004. 'Latin America' in H J Hillerbrand (ed.) *Encyclopedia of Protestantism*. 4 Volumes. New York: Routledge.

Freytag GA 1927. *Johannes King der Buschland-Prophet*. Ein Lebensbild aus der Brüdergemeine in Suriname. Nach seinen eigenen Aufzeichnungen dargestellt. Hernhutt: Missionsbuchhandlung.

Garr AK, Cannon DQ, Cowan RO, and Holzapfel RN editors 2000. *Encyclopedia of Latter-day Saint History*. Salt Lake City: Deseret Book Co.

Gerding P 2002. *Op weg naar grotere hoogten*. Een geschiedenis van een kerk. 260 jaar Evangelisch Lutherse Kerk in Suriname 1741-2001. Paramaribo: Evangelisch Lutherse Kerk in Suriname.

Getrouw CFG, Morpurgo AJ and Sampers A 1966. *Honderd jaar woord en daad: gedenkboek bij het eeuwfeest der Redemptoristen in Suriname, 26 maart 1866-1966*. Paramaribo: Redemptoristen.

Gobardhan-Rambocus L 2001. *Onderwijs als sleutel tot maatschappelijke vooruitgang. Een taal- en onderwijsgeschiedenis van Suriname*, 1651-1975. Zutphen: Walburg Press.

Gooswit SM 2002a. 'Geen bos gerooid, maar een boom geveld: Een kwart eeuw EBG-zending onder Javanen in Suriname, 1909-1935' *OSO*. Tijdschrift voor Surinaamse Taalkunde, Letterkunde en Geschiedenis. Jaargang 21. Nummer 1.

―――― 2002b. 'Geen bos gerooid, maar een boom geveld: Een kwart eeuw EBG-zending onder Javanen in Suriname, 1909-1935', deel 2. *OSO*. Tijdschrift voor Surinaamse Taalkunde, Letterkunde en Geschiedenis. Jaargang 21. Nummer 2.

Governmentsbladen van de Kolonie Suriname 1816-1855. Rotterdam: H Nijgh.

Gregor EFF 2008. *Christiaan Grego*. Bewerkte editie, ongepubliceerde Bachelor's scriptie (origineel 2001). Paramaribo: Caribbean College of the Bible.

―――― 2010. *The Biblical role of elders and deacon within the Full Gospel Church 'The Open Door' in Suriname*: a case study. MTh minithesis. Johannesburg: South African Theological Seminary.

Groot A de 1977. *Woordregister Nederlands- Saramakaans met context en idioom*. Paramaribo: Artix.

――――1981. *Woordregister Saramakaans-Nederlands*. Paramaribo: Artix.

―――― 1984. *Tweedelig woordregister Auka-Nederlands Nederlands-Auka*. Paramaribo: Artix.

Groves N 1946. *Vijf en veertig jaren onder de tropen*. Het leven van den Eerbiedwaardigen Petrus Donders CssR, apostel der Indianen en melaatsen in Suriname. Heerlen: Roosenboom.

Halve eeuw 1916. *Halve eeuw in Suriname, 1866-1916*. Ter dankbare herinnering aan het gouden jubilé van de aankomst der eerste redemptoristen in de missie van Suriname door eenige missionarissen derzelfde missie. 's Hertogenbosch: CN Teuling.

Hartsinck JJ 1770. *Beschrijving van Guiana, of de Wilde Kust, in Zuid Amerika*. Amsterdam: Gerrit Tielenburg.

Helman A editor 1978. *Cultureel Mozaïek van Suriname. Bijdrage tot onderling begrip*. Zutphen: De Walburg Pers.

Herlein JD 1718. *Beschryvinge van de Volk-plantinge Zuriname*. Leeuwarden: Meindert Injema.

Hira S 1982. *Van Priary tot en met De Kom*. De geschiedenis van het verzet in Suriname 1630-1940. Rotterdam: Futile.

Hirsch H 1995. *En de zwarte was een schoon blank man*. Enkele aspecten van de geschiedenis van de Lutherse Kerk in Suriname met het oog op de samenwerking van de kerken in De Nieuwe Stad als multi-etnische gemeenschap. Doctoraalscriptie. Oecumenica/Theologische Encyclopedie. Amsterdam: Universiteit van Amsterdam.

Hoekendijk B 1962. *Gods werk in de 3 Guyana's*. Putten: Stichting Ben Hoekendijk's Evangelisatie Campagnes.

Hoekstra C 1903. 'De Hollandsche Boeren in Suriname'. *Neerlandia*. Volume 7. Nos. 9 en 10. September en October.

Hoekstra DA 1941. *Gedenkboekje van de Evangelisch Lutherse Gemeente te Paramaribo*. Uitgegeven ter gelegenheid van het 200 jarig bestaan der Evangelisch Lutherse Gemeente. 15 november 1741-15 november 1941. Np.

Hofmeyr JW, Millard JA and Froneman CJJ 1991. *History of the Church in South Africa*. Pretoria: University of South Africa.

Holland CL 2006. 'Suriname'. In Thomas Riggs, General editor. *Worldmark Encyclopedia of Religious Practices*. 3 Volumes. Michigan: Thomson Gale.

Holmes A 1805. *American Annals;* or A chronological history of America. From its discovery in MCCCCXCII to MDCCCVI. In two volumes. Cambridge: W. Hilliard.

Hoogbergen W 1993. 'De geschiedenis van de Kwinti'. *SWI Forum*. Jaargang 10, nummer 1. Juni 1993. Paramaribo: Stichting Wetenschappelijke Informatie.

Hooplot F and Sjak-Shie P 1982. *Bijbel negenweekse*. Panda Cahiers. Paramaribo: Katechetisch Centrum.

——— 1983. *Wie zegt gij dat ik ben?* Panda Cahiers. Paramaribo: Katechetisch Centrum.

——— 1985. *Een sprekende wereld: Gods sacrament*. Panda Cahiers. Paramaribo: Katechetisch Centrum.

———. *Adam, wie ben je?* Panda Cahiers. Paramaribo: Katechetisch Centrum.

Ingibe LH nd. *De Wesleyaanse Gemeente*. De Kerk van de Bijbel, z.j.

Ismael J 1949. *De Immigratie van Indonesiërs in Suriname*. Proefschrift. Leiden: Drukkerij 'Luctor Et Emergo'.

Jabini FS [forthcoming I] *Het verhaal van de Broeders in Suriname*.

——— [forthcoming II] *Het Kruis voor een Kankantri II*

——— 2000. *Het Kruis voor een Kankantri*. Overzicht van de Surinaamse Kerkgeschiedenis. Paramaribo: De Christen.

——— 2004a. *Translation and Missions in Suriname*. Unpublished Doctor of Theology Dissertation. KwaZulu Natal: University of Zululand.

——— 2004b. *25 jaren CAMA*. Februari 2004. Paramaribo: De Ware Tijd/ Times of Suriname.

——— 2007. 'In gesprek met Bisschop dr. Steve Meye'. *Nyunsu+* Informatieblad van de Evangelical School of Theology. Nummer 5-2007. Paramaribo: Evangelical School of Theology.

Jannasch-Werners LM 2001. *Het Woord als genademiddel*. Een scriptie aangeboden aan het Caribbean College of the Bible. Ter verkrijging van de titel van Bachelor of Biblical Studies. Paramaribo: Caribbean College of the Bible.

Jap A Joe H 1995. *Tussen kruis en kalebas*. Publicatie van het Theologisch Seminarie der EBGS. Nr 1. Paramaribo: Theologisch Seminarie der EBGS.

────── 2005. 'Afro-Surinamese renaissance and the rise of Pentecostalism'. *Exchange* 34. Volume 2:134-148. Leiden: Koninklijke Brill XV.

────── 2000-2008. 'Suriname' in E Fahlbusch and GW Bromiley eds. 2000-2008 *The Encyclopedia of Christianity*. Five volumes. Translation of the third revised edition of Evangelisches Kirchenlexikon. Grand Rapids; Leiden: Wm. B. Eerdmans; Brill.

──────, Sjak-Shie P and Vernooij J 2001. 'The Quest for Respect: Religion and Emancipation in Twentieth-Century Suriname'. In *Twentieth-Century Suriname: Continuities and Discontinuities in a New World Society*, ed. Rosemarijn Hoefte and Peter Meel. Leiden: KITLV.

Jones JF nd. *Schijnwerper. Gedachten over Nationale Bewustwording*. Paramaribo: Studie en Vormingscentrum der Evangelische Broedergemeente Suriname.

────── 1966. *De Ontmoeting van het christelijk geloof en de West-Afrikaanse Religie in Suriname*. Licentiaats Thesis. Brussel: Protestantse Theologische Faculteit.

────── 1976. 'Christus en Kwakoe in Suriname'. *Wereld en zending*. Tijdschrift voor missiologie. Volume 5.

────── 1981. *Kwakoe en Christus*. Een beschouwing over de ontmoeting van de Afro-Amerikaanse cultuur en religie met de Hernhutter zending in Suriname. Brussel: Protestantse Theologische Faculteit.

────── 1984. *Jezus Christus, bonuman*. Panda Cahiers. Paramaribo: Katechetisch Centrum.

────── 1997. 'Bijbelvertaling en Bijbelgebruik in de Evangelische Broedergemeente' in FS Jabini red. *Kerken en Talen in Suriname*. Opstellen over het taalgebruik binnen de Surinaamse Kerken aangeboden aan het Instituut voor Taalwetenschap. Paramaribo: De Christen.

────── 2000 *Contextuele Surinaamse Theologie, een inleiding*. Publicatie van het Theologisch Seminarie der EBGS. Nr 7. Paramaribo: Theologisch Seminarie der EBGS.

────── 2003. *Het verschijnsel religie in de multi-religieuze samenleving van Suriname. De 'Surinaamse vroomheid'*. Paramaribo: np.

────── 2004. 'Laten we Hem volgen!' In U Mingoen, F Vollprecht, W van Raalte red. *Het visioen van Herrnhut de wereld in: overwegingen bij de viering in Suriname van Zinzendorfs 300e geboortedag*. Paramaribo: Theologische Seminarie der EBGS.

Jong B de. 1911. *De Vrije Evangelisatie te Paramaribo. 1888-1911*. Paramaribo: Vrije Evangelisatie.

Jong C de 1976. 'The Dutch Peasants in Surinam'. *Case studies on human rights and fundamental freedom. A world survey.* Den Haag: Martinus Nijhoff;

Jonge C de 1996. *De Nederlandse Boeren in Suriname 1845-1995.* Eigen uitgave ter herdenking van de vestiging der Nederlandse boeren 150 jaren geleden. Pretoria: np.

Jongeneel JAB 1990. *Protestantse zendingsperiodieken uit de negentiende en twintigste eeuw in Nederland, Nederlands-Indië, Suriname en de Nederlandse antilen: Een bibliographische catalogus met inleiding.* IIMO research publication 30. Leiden: IIMO.

─── 2012. *Utrecht University: 375 years mission studies, mission activities, and overseas ministries (1636-2011).* IC - Studies in the Intercultural History of Christianity. Vol. 154. Pieterlen: Peter Lang - International Academic Publishers

Kalff S 1929. 'Westindische predikanten I'. *West Indische Gids.* Volume 10. Nummer 1.

─── 1929. 'Westindische predikanten II (Slot)'. *West Indische Gids.* Volume 10. Nummer 1.

Katholik-dharm 1924. *Katholik-dharm ka prasnontar Surinam vicariat ke Hindostanon ke liye pasand kiya gaya.* Paramaribo: G Randag

Kempen M van and Enser H 2001. 'Surinaamse kranten en hun vindplaatsen, 1774-2000' in Oso.Tijdschrift voor Surinaamse taalkunde, letterkunde, cultuur en geschiedenis. Volume 20. Number 2.

Kempen M van 2002. *Een geschiedenis van de Surinaamse literatuur.* Vijf delen. Paramaribo: Uitgeverij Okopipi.

Kent J 1978. *The Saramaka Church.* A research on the historical development of the Moravian Church and its influence in the Saramaka Community in Suriname (1765-1950). Unpublished paper, Kingston: United Theological College of the West-Indies.

─── 1979. *Botopasi en de ontwikkeling.* Botopasi: np.

─── 1984. *Heiligenverering en vooroudercultus.* Panda Cahier. Paramaribo: Katechetisch Centrum Bisdom.

─── 1986. *Forms of Reconciliation in family counselling.* A thesis submitted to the faculty of Moravian Theological Seminary in candidacy for the degree of Master of Asters in Pastoral Counselling. Pennsylvania: Moravian Theological Seminary, 1986.

─── 1988. 'Het Winti-verschijnsel in het binnenland tegenover het Christendom en evangelie'. In J Kent en S Loswijk *Winti: de ontmoeting van de Afro-Surinaamse Godsdienst en het Christendom*. Panda Cahier. Paramaribo: Katechetisch Centrum Bisdom.

King L 1986. *Gedenkboekje ter gelegenheid van 240 jaar Evangelisch Lutherse kerk in Suriname*. Paramaribo: Evangelische Lutherse Kerk in Suriname.

King LH and Petzoldt TR 1991. *Gedenkboekje ter gelegenheid van 250 jaar Evangelisch Lutherse kerk in Suriname*. Paramaribo: Evangelische Lutherse Kern in Suriname.

Klerk C J M de 1951. *Cultus en Ritueel van het Orthodoxe Hindoeisme in Suriname*. Amsterdam: Urbi et Orbi and.

────── 1953. *De immigratie der Hindostanen in Suriname*. Amsterdam: Urbi et Orbi.

Klinkhamer K 1952. *Sanimjing kareta kalinja auranda*. Kleine catechismus in de Caraibische taal. Paramaribo: H van den Boomen.

────── 1955. *De Caraïbische Spraakkunst*. Paramaribo: np.

────── 1957 *Sjoko-tikan Katechismus burre-teun-wa Arrowak djan lokono*. Kleine catechismus in de taal van de Arrowak-Indianen. Paramaribo: H van den Boomen.

Knappert L 1927. 'De Labadisten in Suriname'. *West Indische Gids*. Volume 8. Number 1.

────── 1928. 'Schets van eene geschiedenis onzer handelskerken' *Nederlands Archief voor de Kerkgeschiedenis*. Volume XXI. Leiden: Brill.

Koenen HJ 1846. *Geschiedenis van de vestiging en den invloed der Fransche vluchtelingen in Nederland*. Leiden: S en J Luchtmans.

Kool J [forth-coming] *Jan Kool. Autobiografie*.

Koschorke K, Ludwig F, Delgado M and Spliesgart R 2007. *A history of Christianity in Asia, Africa, and Latin America, 1450-1990: a documentary sourcebook*. Grand Rapids: Wm B Eerdmans Publishing.

Kpobi DNA 1993. *Mission in chains. The life, theology and ministry of the ex-slave Jacobus E.J. Capitein [1717-1747] with a translation of his major publications*. Zoetermeer: Boekencentrum.

Kraag C 1980. *Aantekeningen over de geschiedenis van de Kwinti en het dagboek van Kraag (1894-1896)* (Original 1984-1896). Bewerkt door Christofel de Beet en Miriam Sterman. BSS 6. Utrecht: Universiteit van Utrecht.

Kramp AA 1983. *Early creole lexicography*. A study of C. L. Schumann's manuscript dictionary of Sranan. Ph.D. Dissertation. Leiden: Rijksuniversiteit.

Kross E 1987. *The symbolism of light and darkness at Divali*. A Christian theological appraisal. Bachelor of Arts Thesis, St John Vianney and the Uganda Martyrs. Mt. St. Benedict. Trinidad: University of the West Indies.

———— 1990. *Nakedness in 2 Kor. 5:3: Four decades of exegetical interpretation*. A thesis presented in partial fulfilment of the requirements for the Licentiate in Sacred Theology. Leuven: Katholieke Universiteit Leuven.

———— and Sjak-Shie P 1997. *Een vruchtbaar leven*. Panda Cahiers. Paramaribo: Katechetisch Centrum.

Leger des Heils Regio Suriname & Frans Guyana. 75 jarig Jubileum van 3 tot en met 10 oktober 1999.

Lenders M 1996. *Strijders voor het Lam*. Leven en werk van Herrnhutter broeders en zusters in Suriname, 1735-1900. Leiden: KITLV Uitgeverij.

LeNoir JD 1973. *The Paramacca Maroons: a study in religious acculturation*. Ph.D. dissertation. New York: New School for Social Research.

———— 1975. 'Surinam national development and maroon cultural autonomy'. *Social and Economic Studies*, Vol. 24, No. 3 (SEPTEMBER 1975), pp. 308-319. Sir Arthur Lewis Institute of Social and Economic Studies, University of the West Indies.

Lier RAJ van 1971. *Frontier society: A social analysis of the history of Surinam*. Volume 14 of Koninklijk Instituut voor Taal-, Land- en Volkenkunde Translation series. 's Gravenhage: Martinus Nijhoff.

———— 1977. *Samenleving in een grensgebied*. Derde herziene uitgave. Amsterdam: S. Emmering.

———— 1952. 'Hernhutters in Suriname'. *Sticusa Jaarboek*. Amsterdam, 1952.

———— 1953. 'De emancipatie der Negerslaven in Suriname en de zendingsarbeid der Moravische Broeders'. *De West Indische Gids*. Volume 34. Nummer 1.

———— 1954a. 'Nils Otto Tank 1800-1864'. *Gemeenschap II*.

———— 1954b. 'Enige opmerkingen over de zelfstandigheid der Surinaamse Broederkerk en de arbeid der Moravische Broeders'. *Heerbaan VI*.

———— 1956. *Het Visioen van Herrnhut en het Apostolaat der Moravische Broeders in Suriname 1735-1863*. Paramaribo: C Kersten en Co.

———— 1958. *Unitas Fratrum en Caribisch gebied*. Nijkerk: Callenbach.

———— 1966. *Surinaamse Suikerheren en Hun Kerk. Plantagekolonie en handelskerk ten tijde van Johannes Basseliers, predikant en planter in Suriname 1667-1689*. Wageningen: H. Veenman en Zonen.

―――― 1974. 'De taak van de zending in de hudige sociale en politieke situatie van Suriname'. *Vox Theologica*. Volume XLIV.

―――― 1976. 'De Surinaamse kerk in een nieuwe tijd'. *Wereld en Zending* V. 1976:1-5.

―――― 1978. 'Johannes Guiljelmus Kals'. *Biografisch Lexicon voor de geschiedenis van het Nederlandse Protestantisme*. Deel 1. Kampen: J H Kok.

―――― 1980a. *De wereld heeft toekomst: Jan Amos Comenius over de hervorming van school, kerk en staat*. Kampen: JH Kok BV.

―――― 1980b. *Gods wereldhuis. Voordrachten en opstellen over de geschiedenis van zending en oecumene*. Amsterdam: Bolland.

―――― 1981. 'J. Kals'. *Mededelingen*. Augustus 1981. Number 34. Paramaribo: Stichting Surinaams Museum.

―――― 1987. *Jan Willem Kals 1700-1781. Leraar der her-vormde advocaat van indiaan en negers*. Kampen: J.H. Kok.

―――― 1993. *Over Noach met zijn zonen: de Cham-ideologie en de leugens tegen Cham tot vandaag*. Utrecht: Interuniversitair Instituut voor Missiologie en Oecumenica.

Loor A 1993. *1668-1 mei-1993. De Hervormde Kerk van Suriname 325 jaar*. Paramaribo: np..

―――― 1995. 'Nederlandse Boeroes gingen boeren in Suriname'. *Nieuwe Rotterdamse Courant en Algemeen Handelsblad*. Jaargang 25, No 245. 18 juli 1995.

―――― 2003. *1668-1 mei-2003. De Hervormde Kerk van Suriname 335 jaar*. Paramaribo: np.

Loswijk EJA 1979. *Nationalisme en evangelie in de moderne Surinaamse literatuur*. Doctoraalscriptie. Utrecht: Theologische Faculteit Universiteit Utrecht.

―――― 1988. 'Ontmoeting Winti en Christelijk geloof'. In J Kent and E Loswijk *Winti: de ontmoeting van de Afro-Surinaamse Godsdienst en het Christendom*. Panda Cahier. Paramaribo: Katechetisch Centrum.

MAF-Suriname: Wat is dat eigenlijk? 1978. Paramaribo: Stichting MAF Suriname.

Manbodh R, Claver I and Sjiem Fat P 1991. *30 jaar Stromen van Kracht Suriname. 16-10-1961 tot 16-10-1991*. Paramaribo: Stichting Volle Evangelie Gemeente Stromen van Kracht Suriname.

Marcus AW 1935. *De Geschiedenis van de Nederlands Hervormde Gemeente in Suriname*. Paramaribo: De Tijd OC Marcus.

Marshall EK 2003. *Ontstaan en ontwikkeling van het Surinaams nationalisme natievorming.* Academisch proefschrift. Amsterdam: Universiteit van Amsterdam.

Marshall E 2010. *Theologie, kerktucht en samenleving.* Publicatie van het Theologisch Seminarie der EBGS. Nr 11. Paramaribo: Theologisch Seminarie der EBGS.

Martinsen M 2003. *Uit het dagboek van zuster Magda: belevenissen van een Deense zendelinge in Suriname.* Iris: Iris Oirschot.

Martoredjo JP 1997. *Het Verbond.* Bacclaureus scriptie. Veenendal: Evangelische Bijbel School.

——— 2005. *Kunnen christelijke gemeenten elke gift aannemen?* Masters' thesis. Port of Spain: Caribbean College of the Bible International.

——— 1994. *Cma zending.* Ongepubliceerde aantekeningen. Paramaribo: np.

Meissner S 1848. *Verhaal van den zendingspost der Evangelische Broedergemeente in het boschnegerland van Suriname.* Door de zendelingszuster Meissner, eerder weduwe van den zendeling R Smith. Uit het Hoogduitsch. Amsterdam: H. Höveker.

Melton JG and Baumann M 2002. *Religions of the World. A comprehensive encyclopedia of beliefs and practices.* Statistical tables prepared by David B Barrett. California: ABC-CLIO Inc.

Melton JG 2005. *Encyclopedia of Protestantism.* Facts On File Library of Religion and Mythology/Encyclopedia of World Religions. New York: Facts on File Inc.

Meye P 1997. *Mijn Heer en ik.* Levensbeschrijving van Pudsey Meye. Paramaribo: np.

Mingoen UHS 2008. *Over God en mens gesproken: een praktisch-theologisch onderzoek rond de correlatie van godsbeeld en mensbeeld in preken.* Masterscriptie Praktische Theologie Kampen: Theologische Universiteit Kampen.

Misidjang G 2010. *A Case Study of Inculturation: The influence of the Aucaans' Culture on the Roman Catholic Liturgy in Surinam.* Saint Augustine: University of the West Indies.

Missions-Blatt aus der Brüdergemeine. Hamburg: Brüdergemeine

Moes CM 1858. 'Geschiedenis der Evangelisch-Luthersche Gemeente in Suriname' (I). *West-Indië II.* Bijdragen tot de bevordering van de kennis der Nederlandsch West-Indische Koloniën. Haarlem: A C Kruseman.

―――― 1858. 'Geschiedenis der Evangelisch-Luthersche Gemeente in Suriname' (II). *West-Indië II*. Bijdragen tot de bevordering van de kennis der Nederlandsch West-Indische Koloniën. Haarlem: A C Kruseman.

Mulder D and Paap CA 1943. *De hervormde Gemeente te Paramaribo bij haar 275-jarig bestaan*. Paramaribo: Hervormde Gemeente.

Muller JE and Hoekstra C 1895. *Het vijftigjarig jubile der Boeren in Suriname*. Suriname: B. Heijde.

Murray EJ 1998. *Religions of Trinidad and Tobago*. Port of Spain: Murray Publications.

Nahar F 1996. *God maakt een weg*. Paramaribo: np.

―――― 2000. *De kracht van het gebed*. Paramaribo: np.

―――― 2002. *Gebedsuitwerking in de geestelijke wereld*. Paramaribo: np.

―――― 2003. *Profiel van een voorbidder*. Paramaribo: np.

―――― 2004. *Een schreeuw om hulp*. Paramaribo: np.

―――― 2006. *De sleutel voor een geopende hemel...gemeenschap met God*. Paramaribo: np.

―――― 2007a. *Hoe een wonder van God te ontvangen*. Paramaribo: np.

―――― 2007b. *Leven in overwinning*. Paramaribo: np.

―――― 2008. *Om Hem te kennen*. Paramaribo: np.

―――― 2009. *Even Persoonlijk*. Paramaribo: np.

―――― 2010. *Denken als een kampioen*. Paramaribo: np.

―――― 2011. *Gods eindtijdleger*. Paramaribo: np.

Nassy D 1791. *Geschiedenis der kolonie van Suriname*. Geheel op nieuw samengesteld door een gezelschap van geleerde Joodsche mannen aldaar (Dutch Translation of *Essai historique sur la colonie de Surinam*, cowritten with S H Brandon, MP de Leon, J de la Parra and SJV de la Parra published in 1788). Amsterdam: Allart Van der Plaats.

Ndegwah DJ 2007. *Biblical Hermeneutics as a Tool for Inculturation in Africa: A case Study of the Pökot People in Kenya*. Nairobi: Creations Enterprises.

Neff J nd. *The Work of Worldteam in Suriname*. Florida: Worldteam.

Neus NCJ 1924. *25 jarige herdenking. Lezing biografie van wijlen Revd. C.P. Rier, stichter en pastoor van de Surinaamsche Baptist Gemeente*. Paramaribo: Erven H van Ommeren.

Nichols A 1979. *I will build my Church*. Paramaribo: np.

Norwood Jr DP 2002. 'Suriname'. In Burgess SM, Maas EM van der and Maas E van der editors. *The New International Dictionary of Pentecostal and Charismatic Movements*. Revised edition. Grand Rapids: Zondervan.

Oldmixon M 1741. *The British Empire in America: containing the history of the discovery, settlement, progress and state of the British colonies on the continent and islands of America.* Vol. ii. London: J Brotherton J Clarke.

Ort JWC 1963. *Vestiging van de Hervormde Kerk in Suriname. 1667-1800.* Amsterdam: De Sticusa.

—— 2000. *Surinaams Verhaal: Vestiging van de Hervormde Kerk in Suriname. 1667-1800.* Zuthphen: Uitgeversmaatschappij Walburg Press.

Oudschans Dentz F 1916. *De Anglikaansche Kerk in Suriname.* Nederlandsch Archief voor Kerkgeschiedenis, dl. XIII, afl. 2. 's Gravenhage: Martinus Nijhoff

—— 1938. *Cornelis van Aerssen van Sommelsdijck.* Een belangwekkende figuur uit de geschiedenis van Suriname. Amsterdam: P N van Kampen & zoon.

—— 1946. 'Cornelis Winst Blijd. Van Slaaf tot Predikant'. *Nieuw Suriname.* 28 September 1946.

—— 1949. 'De Hervormde Kerk in Suriname in haar begintijd', *De West-Indische Gids.* Volume 30. Number 1.

Oxenbridge J 1661. *A double watch-word, or, The duty of watching: and watching to duty, both echoed ... by one that hath desired to be found faithful in the work of a watchman.* London: J Rothwell.

—— 1671. *A seasonable proposition of propagating the gospel by Christian colonies in the continent of Guaiana: being some gleanings of a larger discourse drawn, but not published.* London: np.

—— 1670. *A quickening word for the hastening a sluggish soul to a seasonable answer to the divine call.* Published by a poor sinner that found it such to him. Being the last sermon preached in the First Church of Boston upon Isaiah 55. 6. By the pastor there, on the 24th of the fifth moneth. Massachusetts: Samuel Green and Marmaduke Johnson.

Paasman A N 1984. *Reinhart: Nederlandse literatuur en slavernij ten tijde van de Verlichting.* Leiden: Nijhoff.

Pakosie A 1999. *Gazon Matodja.* Surinaams stamhoofd aan het einde van een tijdperk. Utrecht: Stichting Sabanapeti.

Palmer S 1802. *The Nonconformist's memorial;* being an account of the lives, sufferings, and printed works, of the two thousand ministers ejected from the Church of England, chiefly by the Act of Uniformity, Aug. 24, 1666. Originally written by Edmund Calamy. London: Button and Son.

Pansa RD 1993. *De ontwikkeling van de Hernhutters Zending aan de Boven-Suriname 1765-1992.* Een Scriptie ter verkrijging van het diploma van de hogere predikantsopleiding aan de Theologische Seminarie der Evangelische Broeder Gemeente in Suriname. Paramaribo: Theologische Seminarie der EBGS.

Periodical Accounts relating to the missions of the Church of the United Brethren established among the Heathen. London: Brethen's Society for the Furtherance of the Gospel.

Pet WJA 1987. *Lokono Dian.* The Arawak language of Suriname. A Sketch of its grammatical structure and lexicon. Unpublished Ph.D. Dissertation. New York: Cornell University.

Petzoldt TR 1991. *Gedenkboek van de Evangelisch Lutherse Kerk in Suriname.* Uitgegeven ter gelegenheid van het 250 jarig bestaan der Evangelisch Lutherse Gemeente. Paramaribo: Evangelisch Lutherse Kerk in Suriname.

Picardt J 1660. *Korte beschryvinge van eenige vergetene en verborgene antiquiteten der provintien en landen gelegen tusschen de Noord-Zee, de Yssel, Emse en Lippe.* [...]. Amsterdam: Gerrit van Goedesbergh.

Pickering-Neede L 2009. *God's woman unveiled: Proverbs 31 Footprints In The New Millennium.* Florida: Xulon Press.

Pijl Y van der 2010. 'Pentecostal-Charismatic Christianity: African-Surinamese Perceptions and Experiences'. *Exchange* Volume 39.

Pistorius Th 1763. *Korte en zakelijke beschrijvinge van de Colonie van Zuriname.* Amsterdam: Theodorus Crajenschot.

Poyer J 1808. *The history of Barbados: from the first discovery of the island, in the year 1605 till the accession of Lord Seaforth, 1801.* London: J. Mawman.

Price R 1990. *Alabi's World.* Baltimore: The John Hopkins University Press.

Programma ter gelegenheid van het 40-jarig jubileum van de Wesleyaanse gemeente en het 40-jarig ambtsjubileum van haar district-superintendent Reverend Leo van der Kuyp z.j.

Raad G de 1665. *Bedenckingen over den Guineeschen slaefhandel der Gereformeerde met de Papisten.* Synde een tractaetje noodigh om in dese dagen van alle gereformeerde coop-lieden wel overwogen te werden tot voorcominge van Nederlandts gedreighde oordeelen. [...]. Opgedragen aen de gereformeerde coop-lieden van Nederland. Vlissinge: Abraham van Laren.

Raalte van J 1973. *Secularisatie en zending in Suriname.* Proefschrift. Wageningen: H. Veenman en Zonen B.V.

Rambaran FM 1981. *Het Gemeenschapsoffer in het Oude Testament.* Verhandeling aangeboden aan de Universitaire Protestantse Theologische Faculteit te

Brussel om de graad van Licentiaat in de Godgeleerdheid te verkrijgen. Brussel: Universitaire Protestantse Theologische Faculteit.

Rambaran J 1980. *De heilswegen in het Ramayana van Tulsidās*. Doctorale scriptie. Den Haag: Universiteit van Utrecht.

Rathling R 1997. *Armoede en Rijkdom vanuit een christelijk ethisch perspectief. Op zoek naar een mogelijke relatie tussen armoede en rijkdom en het menselijke handelen.* Een Scriptie ter verkrijging van het diploma van de hogere predikantsopleiding aan de Theologische Seminarie der Evangelische Broeder Gemeente in Suriname. Paramaribo: Theologische Seminarie der EBGS.

────── 2005. *Liefde ... bouwsteen voor een meer humane zorg: een onderzoek naar de relevantie van de zorgethische visie van Annelies van Heijst in relatie tot de kwaliteit van zorg voor de chronisch ziekemens in Nederland.* Masterthesis Ethiek. Kampen: Theologische Universiteit Kampen.

Redmount D 2001. *Theologie in vuur: een systematische theologie voor leiderschapsvorming aan het Hebron Training Centrum.* Een scriptie aangeboden aan het Caribbean College of the Bible. Ter verkrijging van de titel van Bachelor of Biblical Studies. Paramaribo: Caribbean College of the Bible.

Rens LLE 1953. *The historical and social background of Surinam's negro-english.* Academisch proefschrift Universiteit van Amsterdam. Amsterdam: North-Holland Publishing Company.

Riemer JA 1779. 'Wörterbuch zur Erlernung der Saramakka-Neger-Sprache'. Reprinted in Arends J (ed.) 1995. *The Early Stages of Creolization.* Amsterdam/Philadelphia: John Benjamins Publishing Company.

Ritfeld A 2008. *1956-2006. Jubileumfotoboek predikanten 50 jaar geleden in dienst getreden.* Paramaribo: np.

Roest B 1992a. *Van Krisis naar Kairos voor het eeuwfeest van de RK gemeente Nickerie.* Panda Cahier. Paramaribo: Katechetisch Centrum.

Roest B. 1992b. *Kupido. RK in Marataka.* Nickerie: np.

Rotgans RM 1993. *Enkele Geheime Orden in Suriname. Een korte beschrijving van de ontstaansgeschiedenis en de betekenis van de geheime orden in Suriname.* Een Scriptie ter verkrijging van het diploma van de hogere predikantsopleiding aan de Theologische Seminarie der Evangelische Broeder Gemeente in Suriname. Paramaribo: Theologische Seminarie der EBGS.

────── 2004. *Op weg naar een Afro-Surinaamse Theologie: Christelijk geloof in de context van de Winti Religie.* Masterscriptie Cross Culturele Theologie. Kampen: Theologische Universiteit Kampen.

Schaick C van 1855. 'Bijdrage tot de Geschiedenis vooral van de Hervormde Kerk in Suriname'. Tijdschrift West-Indië. Haarlem: A.C. Kruseman.

Schalken AC 1983. *Historische Foto's van de R.K. Gemeente in Suriname.* Paramaribo: Leo Victor.

────── 1985. *300 jaar R.K. Gemeente in Suriname. 1683-1983.* Historische Gids bestaande uit chronologische lijst naamlijsten varia register. Paramaribo: np.

Schalkwijk J 2011. *Een kijkje achter de schermen: Een exploratief onderzoek naar de beleving en het geloofsleven van gemeenteleden in de Vrije Baptistengemeente Bethel.* Ede: Christelijke Hogeschool Ede.

────── 2012. *Martyrs in Early Christianity: Self-serving or Other-oriented Motivations.* Amsterdam: VU University Amsterdam.

Schalkwijk JMW 1957. 'Caribisch Overleg'. De Heerbaan 6.

────── 1958. *Dictaat Doop- en Belijdeniscatechisatie.* Paramaribo: np.

────── 1961. *Dictaat Sarnami- Hindostani.* Paramaribo: np.

────── 1963. 'Indigenisation and integration in the southern Caribbean'. In: *Great things he hath done.* Ecomics / CCC. Bridgetown: Cedar Press

────── 1966. 'Oecumenische samenwerking in het Caribisch gebied'. *De Heerbaan 3.*

────── 1968. 'Zendings in Suriname 1945-1965'. In Enklaar IH and Verkuyl J eds. *Onze blijvende opdracht.* Kampen: Kok.

────── 1970. 'God voor ons Parmeshwar hamare lieje'. *Kroes kie Rooshnie.* Paramaribo: np.

────── 1971a 'God for us'. Translation of 'God voor ons' by Rev N. Smith.

────── 1971b. 'Mission in the micro-world of the southern Caribbean'. *International review of Mission.* Volume LX. April 1971.

────── 1975. 'Suriname in Caribisch Perspectief'. *Wereld en Zending.* Tijdschrift voor missiologie. Volume 5

────── 1977. 'De Evangelische Broedergemeente in Suriname'. In Bruining CFA and Voorhoeve J (editors) 1977. *Encyclopedie van Suriname.* Amsterdam: Elsevier.

────── 1980. 'Training for Chinese Christian work. In Memoriam for Rev Paul Chan To Kuen and Rev Motilall'. Reflections on the Caribbean Chinese Christian Consultation. *Chinese in the Caribbean for Christ.* Ecomics / CCC. Bridgetown: Cedar Press.

────── 2001. *Hindoestaanse zending. 1901-2001.* Paramaribo: Theologisch Seminary der EBGS.

—— 2011. *Ontwikkeling van de zending in het Zuid-Caribisch gebied 1500-1980 in het bijzonder onder de Hindostanen 1850-1980.* Den Haag: Amrit.

—— nd. 'God met Ons. Parmeshwar hemare saath'

—— nd. *Zendingszaken en zendingsvrienden. 200 jaar C.K.C. en 175 jaar ZZG.*

Schalkwijk M 1994. *Colonial State-formation in Caribbean Plantation Societies.* Structural Analysis and changing elite networks in Suriname, 1650-1920. Ph.D. dissertation. New York: Cornell University.

Schelven AA van 1922-1923. 'Suriname in de 18e eeuw. Ervaringen en idealen van Ds. JOA. GUIL. KALS'. *West-Indische Gids.*

Scherer JA 1969. *Justinian Welz. Essays by an Early Prophet of Missions.* Grand Rapids: Wm B Eerdmans Publishing.

Schiltkamp JA and Smidt JTh de (editors) 1973. *West Indisch Plakaatboek.* Plakaten, ordonnatiën en andere wetten, uitgevaardigd in Suriname. Deel I 1667-1761; Deel II 1761-1816. Amsterdam: Emmering.

Scholtens B 1986. *Opkomende arbeidersbeweging in Suriname. Doedel, Liesdek, De Sanders, De Kom en de werkiozenonrust 1931-1933.* Nijmegen: Transculturele Uitgeverij Masusa.

—— 1987. *Louis Doedel, Surinaams vakbondsleider van het eerste uur: een bronnenpublikatie.* Paramaribo: Universiteit van Suriname

Schomburgk RH 1848. *History of Barbados; Comprising a geographical and statistical description of the island; A sketch of the historical events since the settlement; and an account of its geology and natural productions.* London: Longman, brown, green and Longmans.

Schouwenaar FG 1983. *Zelfstandig en toch ....* Over de relatie tussen de Evangelische Broedergemeente in Suriname en het Zeister Zendingsgenootschap in de periode na de zelfstandig wording van de E.B.G.S. Doctoraalskriptie voor het hoofdvak 'Missiologie'. Amsterdam: Theologische Fakulteit van de Vrije Universiteit.

Schumann CL 1778. *Saramaccanisch Deutsches Worter-Buch.* Reprinted in Schuchardt H (1914) *Die Sprache der Saramakkaneger in Suriname.* Verhandeling der Koninklijke Akademie van Wetenschap. Amsterdam: Johannes Muller.

Schumann T 1755 [?]. *Arawakisch-Deutsches Wörterbuch.* Reprinted in (1882) *Bibliothèque Linguistique Americaine*, Tom. VIII:69—165. Paris: Maisonneuve Et Cie, Libraires –Editeurs. (Available online: see http://www.archive.org/details/bibliothquelin08adamuoft).

―――― 1760 [?]. *Grammatik der Arawakischen Sprache*. Reprinted in (1882) *Bibliothèque Linguistique Americaine*, Tom. VIII:166—240.Paris: Maisonneuve Et Cie, Libraires –Editeurs. (Available online: see http://www.archive.org/details/bibliothquelin08adamuoft).

Schuster C 1988. *Historisch overzicht van de 'Vrije Evangelisatie' en haar arbeid. 1888-11 maart-1988*. Paramaribo: np.

Sijpesteijn CA 1854. *Suriname, historisch, geographisch, en statistisch overzigt, uit officiële bronnen bijeengebragt*. 's Gravenhage: De Gebroeders van Cleef.

Sjak-Shie P (editor) 1988. *Amen; overpeinzingen bij het Christelijk geloven in Suriname*. Panda Cahiers. Paramaribo: Katechetisch Centrum.

―――― (editor) 1989. *Christelijk geloven en politiek handelen*. Panda Cahier. Paramaribo: Katechetisch Centrum.

―――― 1984. *De Geest des Heren rust op mij*. Panda Cahiers. Paramaribo: Katechetisch Centrum.

―――― 1985. *Het blijde bericht van Gods genade*. Panda Cahiers. Paramaribo: Katechetisch Centrum.

―――― 1988a. *Maakt allen tot mijn leerlingen*. Panda Cahiers. Paramaribo: Katechetisch Centrum.

―――― 1988b. *Op zoek naar eigen woorden*. Panda Cahiers. Paramaribo: Katechetisch Centrum.

―――― 1990a. *Een gesprek tussen mènsen: over de dialoog tussen de godsdiensten*. Panda Cahiers. Paramaribo: Katechetisch Centrum.

―――― 1990b. *Jood met de Joden, Griek met de Grieken*. Panda Cahiers. Paramaribo: Katechetisch Centrum.

―――― 1990c. *Scheppingsgeloof en evolutietheorie*. Panda Cahiers. Paramaribo: Katechetisch Centrum.

―――― 1991. *Om zo goed als God te zijn*. Panda Cahiers. Paramaribo: Katechetisch Centrum.

―――― 1995. *Kerk en samenleving*. Panda Cahiers. Paramaribo: Katechetisch Centrum.

―――― 1996a. *Kiezen wat van waarde is*. Panda Cahiers. Paramaribo: Katechetisch Centrum.

―――― 1996b. *Therapeute*. Panda Cahiers. Paramaribo: Katechetisch Centrum.

―――― 1996c. *Waar het visioen ontbreekt verwildert het volk*. Panda Cahiers. Paramaribo: Katechetisch Centrum.

―――― 1997a. *Be watchfull: The Apocalyptic Discourse of Matthew*. Panda Cahiers. Paramaribo: Katechetisch Centrum.

―――― 1997b. *Christenen en andersgelovigen: Katholieken en andere mensen.* Panda Cahiers. Paramaribo: Katechetisch Centrum.

―――― 1997c. *De voorgeschreven orde en de geleefde praktijk.* Panda Cahiers. Paramaribo: Katechetisch Centrum.

―――― 1997d. *Jonas, of: een groot dilemma.* Panda Cahiers. Paramaribo: Katechetisch Centrum.

―――― 1997e. *Waarden-vol.* Panda Cahiers. Paramaribo: Katechetisch Centrum.

Spalburg JG 1979. *De Tapanahoni Djuka rond de eeuwwisseling: het dagboek van Spalburg 1896-1900* (original 1900). Reprinted with an introduction by HUE Thoden van Velzen HUE and C de Beet. BSB 5. Utrecht: Universiteit van Utrecht.

Sprague WB 1854. *Annals of the American Pulpit; or the commemorative notices of distinguished American Clergyman of Various Denominations.* From the early settlement of the country to the close of the year eighteen hundred and fifty. New York: Robert Carter and Brother.

Staëhelin F 1913-1918. *Die Mission der Brudergemeine in Suriname und Berbice im achtzehnten Jahrhundert. Eine Missionsgeschichte hauptsachlich Auszügen aus Briefen und Originalberichten.* Paramaribo: C Kersten & Co.

Steinberg H 1933. *Ons Suriname.* 's Gravenhage: N.V. Algemeene Boekhandel voor Inwendige en Uitwendige Zending.

Stewart SM 1993. *The Influence of Christianity on the Bush Negroes in Suriname.* Mona: University of the West Indies.

―――― 2006. *The Journey to marriage: An essential teaching opportunity for the church.* A Doctor of Ministry Project Report Submitted to the faculty of Columbia Theological Seminary in partial fulfilment of the requirements of the degree of Doctor of Ministry. Georgia: Columbia Theological Seminary.

Stichting Christelijke Alliance Gemeenschap van Suriname 1979-1984. Paramaribo: np.

'Surinam' 1976. In the *Seventh-day Adventist Encyclopedia. Commentary Reference Series. Volume 10.* Neufeld: Review and Herald Publishing Association.

Suriname and French Guyana Region, 1924-1989. Brochure uitgegeven i.v.m. 65 jaar Leger des Heils in Suriname.

Tjon Sie Fat PB 2009. *Chinese New Migrants in Suriname. The Inevitability Of Ethnic Performing.* Amsterdam: Vossiuspers UvA – Amsterdam University Press.

Uyleman H and Uyleman E 1990. *Pinkster Zending Suriname,* 25 jaar. Lelystad: np.

Veira J 2001. *Is alleen minder?* Een scriptie aangeboden aan het Caribbean College of the Bible. Ter verkrijging van de titel van Bachelor of Biblical Studies. Paramaribo: Caribbean College of the Bible.

Veltman H 2001. *Discipelen maken in de 21e eeuw.* Een scriptie aangeboden aan het Caribbean College of the Bible. Ter verkrijging van de titel van Bachelor of Biblical Studies. Paramaribo: Caribbean College of the Bible.

Vernooij J 1969. *De rooms-katholieke missie in Suriname ten tijde van mgr. Grooff* (1826-1852). Nijmegen: np.

────── 1971. 'Werkelijkheid en toekomstvisie in de pastorale Verzorging van de mens in Suriname'. *Het Missiewerk. Nederlands Tijdschrift voor Missiewetenschap* 50.

────── 1973. 'Evangelische Bevrijding in het Caribisch gebied'. *Wereld en Zending.* Volume 2.

────── 1976a. 'Christelijke gemeenten en nationbuilding in Suriname'. *Wereld en zending.* Tijdschrift voor missiologie. Volume 5.

────── 1976b. 'Katholieke Surinamers in Nederland'. *De Bazuin* 59.

────── 1978a. 'De Tweede Assemblee van de Caribische Kerken Konferentie'. *Wereld en Zending* Volume 7. Number 3 (1978).

────── 1978b. *Een nieuwe Tent* (Stencil). Paramaribo: np.

────── 1979. *Kerk voor de Keus. N.a.v. de Celamvergadering Puebla' 79.* Paramaribo: np.

────── 1980. *Caribische Theologie.* Paramaribo: np.

────── 1981a. 'The Christian Churches in Suriname'. *Exchange.* Volume 10. No 29 (Sept 1981).

────── 1981b. 'De sociale leer van de Kerk'. *Sociaal Economisch Tijdschrift Suriname.* Volume 3.

────── 1982. 'De Derde algemene Vergadering van de Caribische Conferentie van Kerken'. *Wereld en Zending.* Volume 11. Number 3.

────── 1983. 'Kerk en revolutie in Suriname'. *Wereld en Zending.* Volume 12. Number 3.

────── 1984. 'De Islam in Suriname'. *Begrip* 70.

────── 1985a. 'Het Vikariaat tijdens de Tweede wereldoorlog'. *De Ware Tijd* 7, 8, en 10 mei 1985. Paramaribo: DWT.

────── 1985b. 'Suriname in de Rui'. *De Bazuin* 68.

────── 1985c. *De Rooms-Katholieke Kerk in Suriname vanaf 1866.* Dissertatie. Paramaribo: Westfort.

────── 1985d. *Lomsu 1975-1985.* De afgelopen tien jaren. Paramaribo: np.

────── 1986a. 'Hindostaanse Islam in Suriname en Nederland'. *Religieuze Bewegingen in Nederland* Volume 12.

────── 1986b. 'Nieuwe religieuze bewegingen'. *SWI Forum*. Volume 3. Number 2 (Dec 1986-Jan 1987).

────── 1987. 'Crisis in de Pastoraal van Suriname'. *De Bazuin* 70.

────── 1988a. 'Afschaffing van de slavernij in Suriname'. *De Bazuin* 71.

────── 1988b. 'Winti Pastoraal'. *De Ware Tijd*, 26 September 1988. Paramaribo: DWT.

────── 1988c. 'Winti-religie'. *De Ware Tijd*, 26 September 1988. Paramaribo: DWT.

────── 1988d. *Aktie grondrechten binnenland*. Paramaribo: Stichting Wetenschappelijke Informatie.

────── 1989a. 'De Nabije Toekomst van Suriname'. *De Bazuin* 72 (1989).

────── 1989b. *Indianen en Kerken in Suriname*. Identiteit en autonomie in het binnenland. Paramaribo: Stichting Wetenschappelijke Informatie.

────── 1990a. 'De historische betekenis van 1492-1992: herdenking, viering, eerherstel, nieuw begin'. *Wereld en Zending* Volume 19. Number 1.

────── 1990b. 'Vernieuwing Surinaamse kerkmuziek'. *De Ware Tijd* 10 November 1990. Paramaribo: DWT.

────── 1990c. 'Woto: een Indiaanse visserijcoöperatie (1974-1985)'. *SWI Forum*. Volume 7. Number 2.

────── 1990d. *Brokken uit de Surinaamse kerkgeschiedenis*. With J Wekker Panda Cahiers. Nummer 26. Paramaribo: Katechetisch Centrum.

────── 1990e. *Jacobus Grooff (1900-1852): apostolisch missionaris, prefekt, vikaris en visitator in de West, de Oost, de West*. Paramaribo: Leo Victor.

────── 1990f. *Kerk in het kort*. Panda Cahiers. Nummer 22. Paramaribo: Katechetisch Centrum.

────── 1991a. 'Indianen en Kerk in Suriname'. In: *De Kracht van ons Erfgoed* (with Lampe AR, Vocking B, Bruggen K van der, Creemers W, Bruggen JJG). Mensen met een Missie. Oestgeest: Week voor de Nederlandse Missionaris.

────── 1991b. 'Injiwinti horen erbij'. *De Ware Tijd*, 20 maart 1991. Paramaribo: DWT.

────── 1991c. 'Naar een Surinaamser Suriname'. *De Bazuin* 74.

────── 1992a. 'De Injiwinti zijn hier thuis'. *De Ware Tijd*, 28 februari 1992. Paramaribo: DWT.

―――― 1992b. *Powaka: woonplaats van Lokonon*. Paramaribo: St. Wilhelmusschool.
―――― 1993a. 'Hindoeïsme in Suriname'. *De Ware Tijd*, 18 juni 1993 e.v. Paramaribo: DWT.
―――― 1993b. *De Pyjai. Religie van Inheemsen van Suriname*. Paramaribo: Leo Victor.
―――― 1994a. 'Indianen en Kerken'. *Oso*. Stichting Instituut ter Bevordering van de Surinamistiek. Volume 13. Number 2.
―――― 1994b. 'Vergeven en Vergeven worden in Suriname'. *Werkmap Liturgie*. 28/4. Baarn: Gooi en Sticht.
―――― 1994c. *Barmhartigheid een levensprogram*: Zusters van Liefde van Tilburg 100 jaar in Suriname. Paramaribo: np.
―――― 1995a. 'Historia social de las Iglesias Surinam'. *Historia General de las Iglesias en America Latina*. IV Caribe. Cehila (ed). Ediciones Sigueme/ Universidad de Quintata Roo, Salamanca-Chetumal.
―――― 1995b. 'Over gender gesproken (in de liturgische gezangen)'. *De Ware Tijd*, 10 april 1995. Paramaribo: DWT.
―――― 1995c. 'Verscheidenheid Surinaams geloof'. 25 jarig bisschopsambt van mgr. A. Zichem. *De Bazuin* 78 (1995).
―――― 1995d. *Recht voor een recht voor allen: grondenrechten in Suriname*. Paramaribo: Stichting Wetenschappelijke Informatie.
―――― 1996a. 'De Nieuwe Scheidslijn in Suriname loopt tussen rijk en arm'. *De Bazuin* 79.
―――― 1996b. 'Moraal in de Surinaamse Politiek en Sameleving'. In: *Special: Politiek in Suriname*. SWIForum. Paramaribo: Stichting Wetenschappelijke Informatie.
―――― 1996c. 'Sociale Rechtvaardigheid en de Katholieke Kerk in Suriname'. In: *Liber Amicorum: 50 Jaar Priesterschap Dr. Amado E.J. Römer*. Willemstad: Universiteit van de Nederlandse Antillen.
―――― 1996d. *Bosnegers en Katholieke Kerk*. Paramaribo: Stichting Wetenschappelijke Informatie.
―――― 1996e. *Chinezen en hun religie* [to be published].
―――― 1997a. 'Bij het afscheid nemen van de Redemptoristen'. Seven articles. *De Ware Tijd*, november/december 1997. Paramaribo: DWT.
―――― 1997b. 'Ecumenical Relations in Suriname'. *Exchange. Journal of Missiological and Ecumenical Research*. Volume 26. Number 1.

―――― 1997c. 'Evangelie en Cultuur in Suriname'. *Ter Informatie* no 71. Mei 1997.

―――― 1997d. 'Taalgebruik in de Katholieke Kerk'. In: Jabini F *De Surinaamse Talen en de Kerken*. Paramaribo: SIL.

―――― 1997e. *Een sociaal-economisch vrouwenproject: een stuk kerkgeschiedenis*. Paramaribo: np.

―――― 1997f. *Kerk in de Maak*. Paramaribo: np.

―――― 1997g. *Redemptoristen in Suriname 1866-1997*. Paramaribo: np.

―――― 1998a. 'Hindostanen en Christendom'. *Van Gya en Boodheea tot Lachman en Djawalapersad*. Grepen uit 125 jaar maatschappelijke ontwikkeling van Hindostanen. Paramaribo/Den Haag: IMWO/Nauyuga.

―――― 1998b. 'Hindostanen en het Christendom'. *Hindostanen. Van Contract arbeiders tot Surinamers*. Paramaribo: Stichting Hindostaanse Immigratie.

―――― 1998c. 'Hindostanen en Katholieke Kerk in Suriname'. *Ter Informatie* no 75.

―――― 1998d. *De Rooms-Katholieke Gemeente in Suriname*. Handboek van de geschiedenis van de Rooms-Katholieke kerk in Suriname. Paramaribo: Leo Victor.

―――― 1998e. *Oecumene weer thuis. Het Surinaams Model*. Voor de herdenking van 50 jaar St. Willibrordvereniging in Nederland. Den Bosch: np.

―――― 1999. *Jopie Vriese 85 jaar*. Paramaribo: np.

―――― 2000a. 'Volksreligie in Suriname'. *Wereld en Zending*. Volume 29. Number 4.

―――― 2000b. *Documentatie. Afschaffing van de slavernij in Suriname*. With H. Helstone. Paramaribo: np.

―――― 2002a. 'Er zijn meer huizen dan kerken: winti en katholicisme in Suriname'. *De verleiding van het vreemde: katholieke eigenzinnigheid in de twintigste eeuw*. Raat J de, Ackermans G and Nissen P editors. Hilversum: Uitgeverij Verloren.

―――― 2002b. 'Javanisme in Suriname'. *OSO: Tijdschrift voor Surinamistiek*. Volume 21. Number 2 (2002).

―――― 2002c. 'Kaart van christelijk Suriname'. *Oso: Tijdschrift voor Surinamistiek*. Volume 21 Number 1.

―――― 2002d. *Libi Nanga Bribi: enkele aanzetten tot Surinaamse theologie*. Feestbundel ter ere van Hein Eersel. Nijmegen: Nijmeegs Instituut voor Missiologie.

——— 2003a. 'Een opvallende relatie: de rooms-katholieke kerk en lepra in Suriname'. *Oso: Tijdschrift Voor Surinamistiek* Volume 22. Number 1.

——— 2003b. '*Winti* in Suriname'. *Mission Studies*. Volume XX-1, 39.

——— 2006a. 'Christendom en multicultiraliteit in Suriname'. *Oso: Tijdschrift Voor Surinamistiek* Volume 25.

——— 2006b. 'God weet waarom Hij de kikker geen staart heeft gegeven. Religie in het Caribisch gebied'. *Wereld en Zending* Volume 35. Number 1.

——— 2006c. *Volwaardig en zelfstandig. 50 jaren Bisdom Paramaribo*. Nijmegen: np.

——— 2007. *Slavernij en Kerken in Suriname*. Artikel nummer 6. www.glocality.net. (Accessed December 2007).

——— and Sjak-Shie P 1990. *Een Kerk die leert*. Gedenkboek bij gelegenheid van het 25-jarig bestaan van het Katechetisch Centrum. Paramaribo: Katechetisch Centrum.

Vigelandzoon KAC 1997. *Roman Catholic Principles Governing Interreligious Dialogue: The Case of Winti Religion in Suriname*. Bachelor of Arts Thesis. Trinidad: University of the West Indies.

Vink MPM 2003. 'A work of compassion? Dutch slavery and slave trade in the Indian Ocean in the seventeenth century'. Paper presented at Seascapes, Littoral Cultures, and Trans-Oceanic Exchanges, Library of Congress, Washington D.C., February 12-15, 2003. http://www.historycooperative.org/proceedings/seascapes/vink.html (Accessed June 2010).

Vollprecht A (1998-2000). *EBGS-Geschiedenis*. 65 afleveringen in de Kerkbode (Feb 1998-Jan 2000). Paramaribo: Stadszending.

——— 2010. *Op zoek naar eerstelingen voor het Lam*. Het begin van de Broedergemeente in Suriname en Berbice (1735-1818) naverteld door Anneli Vollprecht, geredigeerd door Hesdie Zamuel. Publicatie van het Theologisch Seminarie der EBGS. Nr 10. Paramaribo: Theologisch Seminarie der EBGS.

Voorhoeve J and Donicie A 1965. *Bibliographic du négro-anglais du Surinam*. Den Haag: Martinus Nijhoff.

Voorhoeve J 1964. 'Johannes King 1830-1899: een mens met grote overtuiging'. In: *Emancipatie 1863 - 1963: biografieën*. Paramaribo: Historische Kring.

Vrede AP 1923. 'Cornelis Winst Blijd: the first negro presbyter in Surinam'. *Journal of Negro History*. Volume 8. No 4 (October 1923).

Waaldijk AL 1931. *Cornelis Winst Blijd*. Jaarverslag der Evangelische Broedergemeente in Suriname. Paramaribo: np.

Warren G 1667. *An Impartial description of Surinam upon the continent of Guiana in America.* London: Nathaniel Brooke.

Weiss H 1911. *Ons Suriname.* Handboek voor zendingsstudie. Utrecht: Nederlandschen Studenten Zendingsbond

—————— 1919/1920. 'Het Zendingswerk der Herrnhutters in de oerwouden van de Boven-Suriname'. *West Indische Gids* 1919/1920.

—————— 1921. 'De Zending der Herrnhutters onder de Indianen in Berbice en Suriname 1738-1816'. *De West Indische Gids.* Tweede jaargang 1921.

Wekker JB 1986. 'Historische fragmenten rond 18e eeuwse zendingsposten in Suriname'. *Oso.* Tijdschrift voor Surinaamse Taalkunde, Letterkunde en Geschiedenis. Jaargang 5. Nummer 5.

Wielzen DR 1997. *Inculturatie van de Liturgie: een kritische analyse van het gebruik van het Sranan in het proces van surinamisering van de liturgie.* MA thesis. Nijmegen: Katholieke Universiteit Nijmegen.

—————— 2009. Popular Religiosity and Roman Liturgy: Toward a Contemporary Theology of Liturgical Inculturation in the Caribbean. Köln: LAP Lambert Academic Publishing.

Williams E 1944. *Capitalism and Slavery* Richmond, Virginia: University of North Carolina Press.

Williamson J 1926/27. 'Suriname van 1651 tot 1668'. Een hoofdstuk uit James A. Williamson 'English colonies in Guiana and on the Amazon (1604-1668). Vertaald door Nelly van Eyck-Benjamins. *West Indische Gids.*

Williamson JA 1923. *English colonies in Guiana and on the Amazon 1604-1668.* Oxford: Clarendon Press

Wilner S (compiler) 2001. *Bibliography of the Summer Institute of Linguistics in Suriname 2001.* Paramaribo: Instituut voor Taalwetenschap.

Wolbers J 1861. *Geschiedenis van Suriname.* Amsterdam: S. Emmerling.

Wongsodikromo TR 1964. *De herkomst van het woord* amṛta *in de Oud-Javaanse letterkunde.* Scriptie doctoraal examen theologie. Rijksuniversiteit Utrecht.

Wongsodikromo-Flier J 1993. *Humor en ernst in 50 jaar 'SISWA TAMA' der Evangelische Broedergemeente in Suriname.* Paramaribo: Siswa Tama.

—————— 2002. *Indonesische Zending in 90 jaren van zendingsgemeenten tot zelfstandige gemeenten.* Scriptie ter afsluiting van haar Middelbaar Theologische Opleiding aan het Theologisch Seminarie der Evangelische Broedergemeente in Suriname.

—————— 2009. *Javaanse Zending der Evangelische Broedergemeente in Suriname.* Paramaribo: J. Wongsodikromo-Flier.

Wullschlägel HR 1856. *Deutsch-Negerenglisches Wörterbuch.* Löbau: TU Duroldt. Republished 1965. Amsterdam: Emmering.

Zamuel H 1984. *Hosea.* Np.

―――― 1985a. *Profeti tori foe Joel nanga Obadja.* Np.

―――― 1985b. *Profetie taki foe Amos nanga Micha.* Np.

―――― 1986. *Profeti taki foe Sefanja, Nahum nanga Habakuk.* Np.

―――― 1993. 'Dit land stimuleert je niet om naar de kerk te gaan'. *Wereld en Zending* Volume 22. Number 2.

―――― 1994. *Johannes King.* Profeet en Apostel van het Surinaamse Bosland. Proefschrift. Zoetermeer: Boekencentrum.

―――― 1995. 'Popular Religions and Ecumenism'. *At the Crossroads: African Caribbean Religions and Christianity.* B. Sankeralli, ed. St. James: Caribbean Conference of Churches.

―――― 1996a. *Profeti taki foe Hagai, Sacharia nanga Maleaki.* Np.

―――― 1996b. 'Theologische opleidingen binnen EBGS'. *Kerkbode der evangelische broedergemeente in Suriname.* 51e jaargang, no's. 41/42. oktober 1996.

―――― 1996c. 'Theologisch Seminarie'. *Kerkbode der evangelische broedergemeente in Suriname.* 51e jaargang, no's. 45. 17 november 1996.

―――― 1997a. *De Zending der Kerk.* Paramaribo:Theologisch Seminarie der EBGS.

―――― 1997b. *De Missionaire gemeente.* Publicatie van het Theologisch Seminarie der EBGS. Nr 3. Paramaribo: Theologisch Seminarie der EBGS.

―――― 1998. *Inleiding op de Bijbel.* Publicatie van het Theologisch Seminarie der EBGS. Nr 4. Paramaribo: Theologisch Seminarie der EBGS.

―――― 1999. 'Winti en christelijke kerk in Suriname'. *Wereld en Zending.* Volume 28. Number 2 (1999).

―――― 2010. *Caretakers of God's Creation. A short introduction to a Holistic understanding of Christ' commission to the church.* Np.

Zeefuik KA 1963. *De winti en het daarmede samenhangende complex van magische en religieuze handelingen en verschijnselen in Suriname.* Scriptie voor het doctoraal-examen in de Theologie aan de Rijksuniversiteit te Utrecht. Utrecht: Rijksuniversiteit.

―――― 1973. *Hernhutter Zending en Haagsche Maatschappij 1828-1867.* Een hoofdstuk uit de geschiedenis van zending en emancipatie in Suriname. Proefschrift. Utrecht: Rijksuniversiteit.

―― 1976. 'Kerk en politieke constellatie in Suriname'. *Wereld en zending.* Tijdschrift voor missiologie. Volume 5.

Zendingswerk van de SBC in het Caraibisch gebied en het bovenste deel van Zuid Amerika g.d.

Zichem A 1965. *De obligatione testis in processu iuris canonici.* Doctoral dissertation on the Canon Law. Np.

―― 2005. *De Beminde kinderen van een Vader Zijn wij.* Vastenbrieven van Monsigneur Aloysius Zichem. Paramaribo: Dienst voor Geloof, Cultuur en Communicatie.

Ziel CN van der 1997. *Hoe Kwam het Woord dichtbij.* Evangelieverkondiging, Kerkplanting en Bijbelvertaling onder de Karaiben in Suriname, Frans Guyana en Venezuela. Doctoraalscriptie Kerkgeschiedenis: Missiologie. Utrecht: Rijksuniversiteit.

Ziel HF de (editor) 1973. *Life at Maripaston.* The Hague: Martinus Nijhoff.

Zijlmans GC and Enser HA 2002. *De Chinezen in Suriname.* Een geschiedenis van immigratie en aanpassing. 1853-2000. Tweede druk Barendrecht: Batavia Publishing.

Index

Abini, Jan 64, 73, 74
Adis, Henry 27, 28, 29, 305
African Methodist Episcopal Church (AMEC) 16, 17, 122, 123, 181, 335
Afro-Surinamese 14, 39, 48, 55, 56, 57, 62, 63, 64, 76, 77, 78, 80, 81, 87, 88, 90, 91, 93, 94, 95, 96, 99, 100, 103, 105, 106, 107, 110, 114, 117, 118, 119, 121, 123, 125, 144, 145, 146, 147, 148, 182, 202, 203, 204, 205, 206, 208, 209, 210, 214, 216, 218, 228, 229, 230, 232, 233, 234, 235, 244, 249, 253, 266, 268, 316, 332
Agape-beweging 190, 193, 296
Ahlbrinck, Gerardus Wilhelmus Maria 132
Akale Kondre 140
Akuriyo 13
Alabi, Johannes 73, 74, 75, 76, 109, 135, 136, 297, 312, 318
Alkmaar 127, 220, 320
Allen, John 25, 28, 29, 41, 305
Aloewel, Robby 336
Altona 65, 70
Alvares, Henriette 123
Anake, Paulus 136, 138, 205, 237, 317
Angley, Ernest 189

Anglican Church, see also Church of England xxi, 5, 6, 16, 17, 86, 91, 103, 294, 304
Anijs, Conrad 172, 173
Apollos Training Institute 336
Arawak 13, 66, 67, 167, 295, 298, 317, 325
Arya Samaj 126
Asodanoe, Jajo 170
Assemblies of God 3, 16, 17, 155, 156, 163, 165, 302, 331, 332
Austin, Richard 86
Awana Bambai 74, 75
Backer, Adrianus 40, 42, 49, 92
Baptist, Baptist Church 16, 17, 27, 28, 119, 120, 121, 140, 145, 163, 168, 174, 181, 189, 191, 200, 305, 325, 330, 331, 334, 337
Basseliers, Johannes 29, 39, 40, 41, 43, 47, 48, 56, 92, 306
Bekker, Wilhelmus Adrianus Josephus Maria de 185
Berenos, Andre 150
Berggraaf, Ronald 198, 213, 229
Bergh, Johannes van den 156, 157
Bernhard 69
Berwig, Georg 64, 65
Betting, Jan Hendrik 107
Beyman, Fabi Labi 139
Bielke, Hermann Moritz 131, 319

Bijbel Baptist Kerk 174, 191, 331
Binnendijk, Henk 190
Blackson, Purcy 163
Blijd, Cornelis Winst 146, 297, 313
Blom, Glenn 182
Boers, A E 143, 144
Bosch, Albertine Laura 171
Bovetius, Julius 40
Bowron, John 30, 31
Brandhoff, Arend van de 107
Brazilian 270
Breeveld, Carl 182, 184, 336
Bribi Ministries 141, 162
Bromet, Meyer Salomon 120, 121, 297, 330
Brul, Flora 172
Byam, William 22, 24, 28, 29, 30, 31, 37, 305
C Kersten & Co 77
Cairo, Reginald 337
Carbiere, Milton 162
Carib 13, 22, 68, 167, 171, 295, 317, 325
Caribbean College of the Bible International 336
CCK (Comite Christelijke Kerken, Committee of Christian Churches) 149, 179, 180, 188, 189, 193, 207, 299
Cerullo, Morris 189
Chaillou, Francois 40, 41
Child Evangelism Fellowship 296
child, children xix, 32, 39, 44, 46, 47, 49, 54, 55, 62, 69, 83, 94, 96, 97, 105, 115, 117, 118, 120, 127, 129, 137, 156, 157, 159, 160, 161, 190, 204, 221, 232, 243, 266, 267, 268, 269, 283, 284, 287, 325

Chinese 14, 15, 18, 100, 125, 126, 190, 206, 295, 335
Choennie, Karel 185, 265, 266, 269, 271, 273, 274, 297
Christengemeente Dian 132, 133
Christiaan Cupido 77
Christian and Missionary Alliance 16, 17, 132, 190, 335, 345
Christian-based decrees 53
Church of England, see also Anglican Church 21, 23, 24, 25, 26, 27, 32, 91, 93, 304, 305
Church of Jesus Christ of Latter-day Saints 194
Church of the Nazarenes 191
classis of Amsterdam 52, 53, 57
Cock, John de 156
Colin, Tata 110, 200, 205
Combé, Nicolaas 40
Comite Begi nanga Wroko 296
Comité van Christelijke Godsdiensten 149
Committee of Christian Churches 5, 148, 149, 179, 188, 207
Comvalius, Theodorus Adriaan Charles 146, 148
Conformists 23, 24, 25
Conventus Deputatorum 52, 310
Cooper, James 3, 138, 163, 164
Copijn, Dirk 107
Courtz, Henk 172, 295
Crijnssen, Abraham 13, 37, 39, 306
Croll, Petrus 45
Dalfour, Marcia 162
Darnoud, Alexander 197, 198, 199, 200
Day of prayer 347
De Evangelisatie Ebenhaezer 122
De Rank Ministries 162

Dehne, Lodewijk Christoffel 65, 66, 73
Deira, Erle 169, 183, 184
Dielingen, Leonel 198, 199
Dissels, Stanley and Celeste 164
Djamin, Ramin 131
Doedel, Louis 144
Donders, Petrus 108, 151, 297, 325, 326, 330
Donk, Lucien 172, 173
Doornik, Albertus van 81, 82
Dorsthorst, Toon te 185, 193
Doth, Paul and Coby 169, 182
Doth, Rudolf Eduard Constantijn 150, 297, 314, 316
Dutch peasants 107, 293, 311
Dwarkasing, Malty 337
Eenheid in Christus 162, 165
Elbers, Gerard and Roeli 191, 302
Engel, Guno van 182
Ephrem 68, 70, 71
Erb, Barbara 129
Evangelical Methodist Church 16, 17
Evangelisch Centrum Suriname 3, 138, 141, 155, 163, 164, 165, 331, 333, 334
Fell, Henry 31
Ferrier, Johan 147
Fischer, Johann Jakob Gottlieb 69
Fleurentin, Dèjean 158
Fuller, Thomas 45
Gado Genade 162, 165
Ganimet 38, 44
Gemeente Petra 162
Gemeente van Gedoopte Christenen 120
Gemeente van Jezus Christus 159, 160, 162, 163, 165
Geoctrooieerde Sociëteit van Suriname 43

Gerding, Pearl 186, 320
Gimith-Woerdings, Irma 161
Ginge Bambai 75, 135
Glock, Naomi 170
Gods Bazuin 141, 159, 160, 161, 162, 165, 301, 332, 333
Goede, Betty 189
Gottlieb 69, 76, 136
Govaars, Jos 123
Graafstad, Wilhelmina Christina van 64
Graefdorf, Johannes 45
Graven, Diana de 186
Gregor, Ewald 318, 336
Grimes, Joseph 170
Guyanese 15, 18, 121, 122, 123, 164, 169, 177, 189, 191, 304, 317
Gwafu Bambai 74, 75
Haabo, Asoinda 170
Haagse Maatschappij 94, 104, 219
Haitian 158, 191
Handelingen, Stichting Evangelisatie Gemeente Handelingen 162, 165
Hanna 66, 283, 320
Hanneman, Johan Hendrik 185
Hartenberg, Lucky 157
Helferkonferenz 67, 70
Helpers 67, 71
Hessen, Heinrich 198, 199
Hessen, Humbert 199
Hewitt-Guda, Bernadette 159, 163, 169, 297
Hilst, Eddy van der 173, 174
Hindostani Nawyuak Sabha 148
Hindu, Hinduism 2, 6, 15, 126, 129, 158, 180, 181, 197, 206, 211, 221, 222, 223, 226, 264, 275, 276, 277
Hinn, Benny 189

Hoekendijk, Elizabeth 'Bep' 158
Hoekendijk, Johannes Franciscus 158, 159
Hoekendijk, Karel 3, 158, 159, 160, 161, 163, 332
Hofstadt, Frederikus van der 45, 82
Hofwijks, Stanley 163
Hoop 68, 69, 70, 71, 77, 201, 213, 257
Huguenots 45, 48, 294, 306
Huiskamp, Anna Bernada 171
Hulten, Philippus van 45
Huttar, George and Mary 171
In De Ruimte 160
Independent Faith Mission 191
Indian xvii, 2, 15, 43, 95, 98, 101, 126, 127, 128, 131, 147, 152, 160, 171, 177, 206, 220, 224, 225, 226, 230, 233, 325, 348, 350
Isabella of Perica 55
Islam, Islamic, see also Muslim 3, 11, 15, 130, 211
Jabini, Izaak 162
Jan Jacob van Paramaribo 63
Jannasch-Werners, Lydia 336
Jantje 66
Javanese 4, 14, 15, 18, 100, 126, 130, 131, 132, 133, 167, 173, 190, 206, 224, 225, 226, 295, 313, 319, 347
Jehovah's Witness 124
Jephta 66, 67, 109
Jesus Students 183, 184, 193
Jews, Jewish 13, 14, 22, 23, 34, 35, 44, 49, 52, 60, 63, 71, 72, 88, 96, 104, 105, 106, 114, 120, 143, 211, 308
Jodensavanne 44

Jones, Johan Frits 197, 198, 201, 202, 203, 204, 205, 206, 209, 210, 211, 212
Jones, Thomas 73
Juglall, William Emanuël 147
Kaaikusi 38
Kals, Joannes Guiljelmus 55, 56, 92, 93, 306, 307
Kanten, Ludwig and Ilse van 159, 162, 163, 164
Katholieke Charismatische Vernieuwing 183
Kent, John 197, 199, 235, 236, 237, 238, 239, 240, 242, 244, 314, 317
Kerstens, Adrianus 81
Ketelaer, Antonius xvii, 53
Kinderhuis Samuel 157
King, Johannes 4, 133, 134, 139, 200, 202, 215, 246, 247, 248, 249, 312, 318
King, Leo 185, 320
Koanting, Evert 171
Kom, Anton de 144, 228, 229, 282
Kool, Jan 3, 140, 163, 164, 334
Koole, Patrick 185
Kraag, Christiaan 134, 318
Kranenburg, Glenn 158
Krol, Lammy 157
Kross, Esteban 185, 197, 275, 276, 277, 278, 280, 296
Kuypers, Stephanus Joseph Maria Magdalena 150, 151
Kwinti 14, 133, 134, 247, 318
Labadie, Ilse 189
Labadist 47, 48
Lachman, Freddy 128
Lachman, Soecila Prabhoede 160
Lachman, Theodoor Gangapersad 127, 160, 297

Index

Lachman, Wenzel and Wies 159, 160
Landvreugd, Constance 182
Lebanese 15, 18, 125
Legêne, Peter Martin 127
Leliendaal 131
Lemmers, Joannes Gerardus 80, 81
Leverton, Nicholas 26, 32
Lewis, Harold and Martha 191
Lieveld, Max 186
Lim A Po, Rudolf 150
Lincoln, Abraham 127
Linde, Jan Marinus van der xvii, xviii, 198, 199, 213, 305, 306, 310, 314, 315
Linde-Rijksen, Anna van der 198
Linger, Hertog 172
Lob Makandra 160, 165
Logos 163, 165
Loswijk, Edgar 197, 199, 226, 227, 234, 235
Lutheran Church 5, 35, 59, 61, 62, 64, 81, 84, 86, 92, 93, 105, 106, 149, 168, 180, 181, 185, 186, 188, 189, 285, 301, 308, 310, 320
Maasbach, Johan 189
Macnack, Benny and Joan 163, 164
Madanfo 74
Maleko, Charles 172
Manbodh, Ramon 160
Maroon 43, 44, 64, 68, 94, 126, 134, 135, 141, 162, 192, 207, 208, 236, 244, 247, 248
Marshall, Captain 12, 71
Martoredjo, Johannes and Dorothea 132, 190, 296, 335, 336
Mastenbroek, Frits 172
Matawai 14, 133, 134, 139, 247, 248, 249, 318
Merian, Maria Sybilla 48

Meye, Pudsey 159, 161, 297, 332
Meye, Stephanus 'Steve' 161
Mingoen, Soekoer 131, 198, 199
Misidjang, Gerda 197, 282, 283, 284
Mission Aviation Fellowship 296
Missionary Fund 109
Moesai, Harry 151
Mohabir, Philip 164
Monk, Egno 185
Moravian, Moravian Church xv, xvii, xxi, 1, 2, 3, 4, 8, 16, 17, 61, 64, 65, 66, 69, 73, 77, 78, 85, 86, 93, 94, 103, 105, 106, 109, 112, 115, 116, 117, 123, 127, 128, 129, 131, 133, 135, 138, 139, 147, 148, 149, 152, 157, 159, 164, 167, 168, 169, 180, 181, 182, 183, 184, 185, 186, 189, 193, 197, 198, 199, 200, 201, 202, 203, 204, 205, 206, 207, 208, 209, 210, 212, 213, 217, 218, 219, 220, 221, 227, 234, 235, 236, 237, 242, 245, 248, 249, 253, 254, 256, 257, 264, 285, 294, 295, 296, 300, 311, 312, 313, 314, 316, 317, 318, 324, 325, 328, 329, 336, 350
Morsen, Armand and Bianca 190
Morssink, Franciscus Petrus 137, 327, 328
Mulder, 'Bas' 189
Muslim, see also Islam 2, 110, 131, 132, 180, 181, 206, 224, 337
Native 14, 15, 31, 34, 39, 43, 44, 47, 54, 65, 66, 67, 69, 71, 78, 83, 96, 119, 126, 200, 268, 324
Ndyuka 14, 63, 72, 133, 138, 139, 140, 141, 162, 167, 171, 192, 207, 247, 283, 295, 319, 326, 327, 348

Neslo-Claver, Naomi 186
Nickel, John and Marilyn 172
Nimwegen, Herman van 183
Nonconformists 24, 27, 32
Noordermeer, Martinus 188
Odenhoven, Engelbertus 128
Olensky, Aron 134
Oliver, Chester 164
Ommeren, Lucretia van 185
Organisatie voor Gerechtigheid en Vrede 189
Oseyse 140, 326
Oxenbridge, John 32, 33, 36, 305
Paap, Christoffel Alexander 147, 159, 308
Pane, Lienke 172
Pansa, Francis 170
Paramaccan 14, 133, 135, 247
Park, James and Joyce 171
Pater Albrinck Stichting 152
Patton, Robert 174, 191
Pawiro, Niti 131, 297, 319
Peasgood, Ed and Joyce 171
Pelgrim Kondre 140
Pengel, Johan 147, 159, 177, 200
Petrusi, Dawsen 170
Pfaff, Johannes 62
Piesch, Georg 64
Pilgerhut 66, 67, 68, 70, 71
Pinas, Johannes 162
Pinksterzending 3, 132, 156, 157, 158, 165, 173, 301, 332
Plymouth Brethren 16, 17, 120, 122, 141, 191, 302, 334
Polanen, Rudy 189, 199
Pope John Paul II 101
Puritans 21, 23, 24, 25, 32, 36, 304
Quakers 21, 23, 24, 27, 30, 31, 32, 36, 304
Raatgever, Magaretha Elisabeth 109

Radio Shalom 296
Radjiman 131
Raillard, Johannes 198
Rambaran, Frederik 128, 197, 199, 256, 257, 258, 260, 261, 262, 263, 296
Rambaran, Johannes 128, 199, 220, 221
Redmount, Dennis 336
Reformed Church xvii, xviii, xxi, 5, 6, 16, 17, 39, 40, 41, 43, 45, 46, 48, 49, 51, 52, 54, 55, 56, 57, 59, 61, 62, 63, 64, 84, 85, 87, 92, 93, 101, 103, 105, 106, 107, 120, 147, 149, 159, 168, 180, 181, 186, 188, 198, 202, 286, 294, 300, 301, 303, 306, 307, 308, 309, 310, 311, 314, 315, 320
Rennert, Norbert 172
Rickets, Achmed 158
Rier, Carel Paulus 99, 121, 122, 144, 145, 146, 147, 148, 205, 297, 330
Rijts, Rudolf and Johan 144, 146, 205
Rikken, Henri Francois 146
Ritfeld, Emile 198
Roest, Gijsbertus 173, 174, 294, 296
Roman Catholic, Roman Catholic Church xv, xxi, 4, 5, 8, 11, 12, 16, 17, 23, 44, 45, 79, 80, 82, 83, 84, 85, 88, 91, 94, 101, 105, 106, 108, 116, 117, 119, 123, 125, 129, 132, 134, 135, 137, 142, 143, 146, 147, 148, 149, 150, 152, 161, 169, 173, 174, 180, 181, 182, 183, 184, 188, 193, 197, 202, 210, 229, 232, 233, 240, 264, 265, 281, 283,

295, 296, 298, 299, 300, 301,
321, 322, 323, 324, 325, 326,
327, 329
Ronde, Ronald 162
Rountree, Sara 170
Saling, Naifa 162
Salvation Army 16, 17, 123, 149,
168, 181, 335
Samson, Elisabeth 61, 100, 267
Sanatan Dharm 6, 126
Saramaccan 14, 64, 71, 72, 73, 74,
78, 82, 135, 136, 137, 138, 167,
207, 236, 247, 265, 266, 295,
298, 299, 317, 318, 327, 343
Saron 67, 68, 69, 70, 71, 115, 116,
157, 236, 242
Schalkwijk, Jair 336
Schalkwijk, Leo and Maarten 182
Schalkwijk-Doerga, Usha 129
Schambach, Robert W 189
Schinck, Jacobus 81, 82, 83
Schöning, Christian 64
Schotsborg, Eveline 182
Schumann, Theophilus Salomo 66,
67
Senthea Creek 73, 75
Sephestine, Franklyn 138
Seventh-day Adventists, Adventist 16,
17, 119, 122, 141 , 334
Shanks, Louis and Lisa 171
Shekinah 129, 160, 165
SIL International 169, 170, 171,
172, 212, 295
Singh, Cedric 169
Sint Petrus en Paulus 117, 119
Sisal, Antoon 132, 173
Sjak-Shie, Peter 264, 265, 296, 298
Slagtand, Marjorie 186

Sommelsdijck, Cornelis van Aerssen
van 37, 43, 44, 45, 46, 48, 49,
50, 53, 96, 100, 306, 310
Southern Baptists 16, 17, 77, 141,
330, 331
Speyers, Edward and Linda 173
Stadszending 116, 127, 182
Stem fu prijs 162
Stewart, Steve 186, 285, 286, 287
Stromen van Kracht 17, 155, 158,
159, 160, 161, 163, 165, 301,
302, 331, 332
Sukh Dhaam 127, 320
Sumter, Wilfred 193
Surinaams Bijbelgenootschap 169, 172
Surinaamse Baptistenkerk 121, 122
Sussenbach, Rob and Els 140
Tabernacle of Faith and Love 162,
301
Tank, Otto Nelis 93, 94, 105, 139,
219
Tiendali, H C 172
Tjin Kon Kiem, Eric 162
Trio 13, 167, 295, 325
Tsang, Gabriel 190
Tubbs, John 156
Ulrik, Catharina 109
Uyleman, Kitty 157, 158
Veira, Joyce 336
Velanti, Carlo 171
Veltman, Henk and Tiny 190
Vera, De d 12
Verbarendse, John and Donna 156
*Vereniging tot Verspreiding van Bijbels
en Traktaten in Suriname* 168
Vernon, George 26
Vigelandzoon, Kenneth 185, 197,
281
Vlijter, Max 199
Voorhoeve, Jan 168, 295, 316, 318

Vrije Evangelisatie 120, 121, 122, 123, 140, 181, 188, 330, 331
Waakzaam, Ferdinand 162
Waldrip, Leo 191
Warau 13, 66, 69
Warkentin, Joel 170
Wayana 13, 167, 295, 325
Weid Mijn Lammeren 160
Weidmann, Leonardus Josephus 147
Weltz, Justinianus Ernst von 2, 21, 34, 35, 36, 305
Wennekers, Paulus Antonius 81, 82, 83, 84, 85, 108, 297
Wenzel, Julius Theodoor 127
Wesener, Johannes 47
Wesleyan 16, 17, 140, 181, 335
Wesleyan Church 16, 17, 140, 181, 335
West Indian Company xvii, 43, 95, 98
Wi eygi sani 148, 178
Wielzen, Duncan 281, 282
Willoughby, Francis 21, 22, 24, 27, 28, 29, 30, 32, 33, 37, 324
Wilner, John 172
Wong Swie San, Roy 160
Wongosemito, Willem 132
Wongsodikromo, Toekiman Remanuel 131, 199, 224
World Alliance of Reformed Churches 101
Worldteam 16, 17, 295, 331
Wycliffe Bible Translators, see also SIL International 170
Yvelaar, Daniel 137

ABOUT THE AUTHOR

Franklin Steven Jabini was born on January 17, 1965 in Brokopondo, Republic of Suriname. Following his primary and secondary education, he continued tertiary education in Economics at the Management Opleiding Centrum. After the second year, he switched to pursue Biblical languages at the Moravian Theological Seminary. At the Caribbean College of the Bible International, he received a Bachelor of Arts and Master of Ministry, with a major in Biblical Studies. He did postgraduate studies in Bible Translation at the Free University in the Netherlands. He completed his doctorate in theology with the University of Zululand in South Africa.

He taught at various theological institutions in the Caribbean. He serves the Evangelical School of Theology in Suriname (EST) and the Caribbean College of the Bible International in Trinidad (CCBI) in different capacities. He is now the Head of the Postgraduate School of the South African Theological Seminary (SATS).

In 1987, he married Irene. The couple have three children Samuel, Franklin and Anna. Since 1988, he has been a full-time worker with the Plymouth Brethren. He published various books in Dutch, Sranantongo and English.

Other works by the author on Christianity in Suriname

Jabini FS 1994. *De Geschiedenis van het Bijbelvertaalwerk in Suriname. 1749- 1993*. Moengo: De Christen.

Jabini FS 1996. *Carp, Wie zijn ze? De beweging van Sun Myung Moon*. Moengo: De Christen.

Jabini FS (red) 1997. *Kerken en Talen in Suriname*. Opstellen over het taalgebruik binnen de Surinaamse Kerken aangeboden aan het Instituut voor

Taalwetenschap. Met medewerking van Dr M Schalwijk. Paramaribo: De Christen.

Jabini FS 1998a. 'Een Saramaccaans Christen'. *Kabats: blad van de theologische faculteit der Vrije Universiteit*. April 1998. Amsterdam: Vrije Universiteit.

Jabini FS 1998b. *Bijbelscholen in Suriname. Een overzicht*. Paramaribo: De Christen.

Jabini FS 1999. 'Theologisch Seminarie op weg ...'. *Kerkbode der EBGS*. Paramaribo: Stadszending.

Jabini FS 2000. *Het Kruis voor een Kankantrie*. Overzicht van de Surinaamse Kerkgeschiedenis. Paramaribo: De Christen.

Jabini FS 2001a. *35 jaren SBG*. Paramaribo: DWT.

Jabini FS 2001b. 'Winti en de Theologen van de Evangelische Broedergemeente'. *Kerkbode der EBGS*. Paramaribo: Stadszending.

Jabini FS 2002. *Het Nieuwe Testament in het Sranantongo*. Paramaribo: De Ware Tijd/ Dagblad Suriname oktober.

Jabini FS 2003a. *Een nieuwe Bijbelvertaling in het Sranantongo*. Wereld en Zending. Tijdschrift voor interculturele theologie.

Jabini FS 2003b. *Internationale Dag van de Moedertalen*. Paramaribo: De Ware Tijd/ Dagblad Suriname, februari.

Jabini FS 2003c. *Bisschop John Kent* Interview. Paramaribo: De Ware Tijd/ Dagblad Suriname, februari.

Jabini FS 2004a. *25 jaren CAMA*. Paramaribo: De Ware Tijd/ Times of Suriname, februari.

Jabini FS 2004b. *Translation and Missions in Suriname*. Unpublished Doctor of Theology dissertation. Kwazulu Natal: University of Zululand.

Jabini FS 2004c. *Het Nieuwe Testament in Ndyuka*. Schrift. Universiteit van Tilburg.

Jabini FS 2006a. *Godsdienst en gezondheidszorg in Suriname*. Paramaribo: Eigen uitgave.

Jabini FS 2006b. 'In gesprek met apostel Benny Macnack'. *Nyunsu+* Informatieblad van de Evangelical School of Theology. Nummer 4-2006. Paramaribo: EST.

Jabini FS 2007a. 'In gesprek met ds. dr. Michel Stewart'. *Nyunsu+* Informatieblad van de Evangelical School of Theology. Nummer 5-2007. Paramaribo: EST.

Jabini FS 2007b. 'In gesprek met bisschop dr. Steve Meye'. *Nyunsu+* Informatieblad van de Evangelical School of Theology. Nummer 5-2007. Paramaribo: EST.

Jabini FS 2009. *Uit het leven van een zendingsechtpaar* dominee en Mevrouw Rantwijk. Paramaribo: Uitgave Familie Rantwijk.

www.ingramcontent.com/pod-product-compliance
Lightning Source LLC
Chambersburg PA
CBHW061703300426
44115CB00014B/2549